D1711882

On the Way to Theory

On the Way to Theory

Lawrence Grossberg

Duke University Press   *Durham and London*   2024

© 2024 DUKE UNIVERSITY PRESS. All rights reserved
Printed in the United States of America on acid-free paper ∞
Project Editor: Lisa Lawley
Designed by Courtney Leigh Richardson
Typeset in Warnock Pro by Westchester Publishing Services.

Library of Congress Cataloging-in-Publication Data
Names: Grossberg, Lawrence, author.
Title: On the way to theory / Lawrence Grossberg.
Description: Durham : Duke University Press, 2024. |
Includes bibliographical references and index.
Identifiers: LCCN 2023056164 (print)
LCCN 2023056165 (ebook)
ISBN 9781478030850 (paperback)
ISBN 9781478026631 (hardcover)
ISBN 9781478059837 (ebook)
Subjects: LCSH: Critical theory. | Criticism. | Knowledge,
Sociology of. | Thought and thinking. | Philosophy, Modern.
| Semiotics—History. | BISAC: LITERARY CRITICISM
/ Semiotics & Theory | SOCIAL SCIENCE / Sociology /
Social Theory | LCGFT: Lectures.
Classification: LCC HM480 .G78 2024 (print) | LCC HM480
(ebook) | DDC 306.4/2—dc23/eng/20240430
LC record available at https://lccn.loc.gov/2023056164
LC ebook record available at https://lccn.loc.gov/2023056165

Cover art: *The Heat Came Early*, 2019. Acrylic and charcoal on
canvas, 67 × 51 in. © Rusty Shackleford. Courtesy the artist and
Cindy Rucker Gallery, New York.

publication supported by a grant from
The Community Foundation for Greater New Haven
as part of the URBAN HAVEN PROJECT

The most thought provoking thing in our thought provoking time is that we are still not thinking.
　　　　　—MARTIN HEIDEGGER, *What Is Called Thinking?* (1976)

To believe and to think. You can't do both. Either we're going to believe or we're going to think, and the difference is we project electromagnetic thought energy, when we think. So when we're thinking, energy is flowing, it's going where it goes, it's flowing. When we believe, we've taken that flowing energy and put it into the box that is limited by the definitions of the belief. So here's energy that should be going and finding its way into the universe so that we can create solutions, being put into the box of belief, and then every solution we attempt to come up with is limited by the box of belief.
　　　　　—JOHN TRUDELL, "I'M CRAZY?,"
　　　　　U.S. SOCIAL FORUM (2010)

Never consent to be completely comfortable with your own certainties. . . . Never imagine that one can change them like arbitrary axioms.
　　　　　—MICHEL FOUCAULT, *The Politics of Truth* (1997)

THIS BOOK IS DEDICATED

to those who taught me to think

Contents

Preface

These lectures address a single question: How to think about thinking? Thinking matters because our ability to respond to the urgent and often threatening demands the world keeps throwing at us depends on our ability to examine how we think and the theories different ways of thinking enable. Existing theories seem inadequate for the problems we face. The German philosopher Martin Heidegger may have been right that we are not thinking (enough), and when we do, as the Native American poet John Trudell suggests, we do a poor job of it, simply reaching for the comfort of answers already known rather than reaching for the openness and uncertainties of thinking.

I have been teaching humanities classes for half a century, and it has always disturbed me that people will read challenging texts about the current state of the sciences but avoid the more immediately relevant discussions concerning human lives.[1] Why are so many people distrustful and even afraid of theorizing in the humanities but not in the sciences? Why do people assume it is more esoteric? Perhaps it is because we generally assume that the sciences arrive at a consensus on truth, while the humanities revolve around conversations and arguments. Neither assumption is accurate. Perhaps it is because people think science is always politically neutral, while theorizing in the humanities is somehow intrinsically tied to left-wing politics. Again, neither assumption is true. Different ways of thinking and different theories rarely guarantee their own politics, although too many people today, even in the humanities, act as if they do.

What is true is that ways of thinking—and the particular theories they engender—are engaged in an ongoing conversation, although it can sometimes

---

1 Let me explain myself just a bit. My intellectual/academic career has been defined by three great loves/questions: thinking (theory), power (politics), and popular culture. They have come together for me as cultural studies (see lecture 30). Over five decades, I have studied and been influenced by all the ways of thinking presented here—some more, some less, some directly, some indirectly, some positively, some negatively, but all as angels to be wrestled with. That is the way of thinking.

feel more like a war among many forces on many fronts. It began long before my story starts, and it will continue long after these lectures end. I have had to make choices, leaving aside important contributors, both past and present.

Perhaps we distrust theory and are reluctant to think because there are so many theories—about everything, and so many of them seem strange, but perhaps a bit of the strange is exactly what we need in this moment. It may seem almost impossible to find a way to make sense of the seemingly chaotic field of thinking about thinking—but that is what I try to do here. Theorizing can sound arrogant, but in these lectures I try to read and think theory with the humility of knowing that there are always other ways of thinking, and other ways of reading and using them. That may be the most important lesson: there are many ways of thinking!

We need to be open to them. Our future depends on our ability to go on thinking, publicly and collectively, even with those who think differently than we do. We need to think with them even as we think against them. Again, the point is not to tell you how or what to think but to make possibilities visible. With the French historian of ideas Michel Foucault, I have no illusions that we can change our ways of thinking so easily.

Our ways of thinking (and, hence, of living) and the theories they give birth to may not be conscious, systematic, consistent, or even coherent; they may seem obvious, drawn from personal experience and the wisdom of generations. Or they may seem esoteric, beyond our comprehension. But theories exist everywhere; they describe, prescribe, and proscribe particular relations in and to the world and other people. They define the ways we make and justify choices—from the trivial (how to dress) to the significant (the paths of our collective lives). Thinking begins by questioning the things we take for granted, things that remain just outside of our curiosity. But thinking does not leap to judgment—criticizing and rejecting every thought that differs from our own. It unsettles the different ways people understand the questions, at least for a while. After all, the world is messier than our theories imagine; it is filled with multiple and often complicated possibilities.

Given our present dilemmas, given a certain refusal to think, I have chosen one path to find a way to go on thinking. It is not the only path. Many of our current ways of thinking hold traces of the long history of thinking, the sediments of yesterday's efforts, which have embedded themselves in our minds and bodies, our senses and feelings. Perhaps understanding more about the roots and routes of our thinking, the doors opened and those closed, will provide a better grasp of our dilemmas but also resources for thinking our way out of them.

The story I am telling in these lectures does not follow a straight path; some of the lectures are out of place, out of time; sometimes they reach back for another beginning. The story encourages multiple readings. It is already many stories—about the different ways of thinking of relations, and of how the world is constructed, and of the role and nature of thinking itself.

I'd like to think I am Mr. Miyagi in the original version of *The Karate Kid* (dir. John G. Avildsen, 1984): wax on, wax off; sand the floor; paint the fence. These seemingly meaningless exercises teach Daniel the basic moves of karate, and how to understand karate as a long, hard journey. If it works for karate, it may work for thinking. Each way of thinking is a language embodying specific sounds, resonances, harmonies, timbres, rhythms, and codes. Different languages are better at some tasks than others. I do not expect to make you experts in all the languages or even any one. At most, I hope you might be able to recognize the sounds, parse out the words, maybe understand some sentences. I hope you might be able to distinguish among them: Show me wax on, or show me Spinoza. Show me paint a fence, or show me dialectics. I hope you might reflect on what different "moves" can and cannot accomplish. I am trying to give you tools that will let you think about our common ways of thinking and hear some of the other possibilities.

This will involve discovering unfulfilled capacities for thinking, and accepting the open-endedness of the paths to truth. It will demand that we find ways of making disagreements productive. We will have to be willing to learn from unexpected sources and to hear the very things we did not expect or do not want to hear. Many people, including university administrators and management consultants, tell us that we have to teach students to think outside the box, but what they really mean is to think inside, at most, two or three boxes. But the real question is: Why does thinking have to be organized in boxes? What if we actually learned to think relationally—in any of the ways of thinking I have presented or that one might find elsewhere? What if we embraced different ways of thinking, each offering not only its own ways of answering questions but its own ways of asking them? What if we understood these lectures not as a body of knowledge to be mastered or a search for the right theory but as mapping a path—on ongoing conversation for thinking about culture, politics, and the world around us?

Should you decide to continue reading, there will be moments, possibly many, when you may feel lost and befuddled. I cannot promise it will all make sense in the end, but perhaps you will not feel quite so lost and befuddled when you ask whatever questions have led you to these lectures. What if we just kept on thinking and questioning . . . together? I wish us all good fortune on the journey.

It Takes a Community . . .

Thanks to the friends who have sustained me over the years: John Clarke, Cathy Davidson, Paul Gilroy, Chris Lundberg, Meagan Morris, John Pickles, Ellen Wartella, and Ken Wissoker (as well as those who are absent, James Carey, Stuart Hall, and D. Charles Whitney). Thanks to my graduate students who have allowed me the honor of mentoring them. Thanks to those undergraduates who rekindled my passion for teaching. Thanks to all the students who have taken my "theory" classes and the many who talked to me about it.

Thanks to those who read earlier drafts—including John Clarke, John Pickles, and Bryan Behrenshausen, and especially Ted Striphas and Zachariah Claypole White. Thanks to Will Partin and Katrina Marks (as well as rev .com) for transcribing my lectures. Thanks to Brandon Gillette for his help with the images. Thanks to the anonymous reviewers for their generous and insightful comments.

Over the decades, I have drawn on many sources, unashamedly using whatever I could bend to my pedagogical will. Unfortunately, over decades, obligatory references were lost, leaving traces without an inventory. This situation of my own making was made worse by the University of North Carolina's refusal to take responsibility for the mold damage done to my office library, leading to the destruction of over twelve thousand books (and almost all of the sources for my lectures). Thanks to Nicholas Gerstner and especially Maximillian Spiegel, who helped me find references, even if they were not my original ones. I have done the best I could in these circumstances and I apologize for any errors.

Thanks to Olivia Kirby Hopkins for the difficult work of compiling the index.

I thank Lisa Lawley, my ever-patient project editor, for being willing to accommodate my grumpy old style of work.

Special thanks to Ken Wissoker, my friend and editor for this and three previous books, who has always generously shared his impressive knowledge of theory and gently pushed me wherever I needed to go.

Finally, gratitude is simply not enough for my son, the poet Zachariah Claypole White, and my wife, the novelist Barbara Claypole White, who have always believed I am better than I think I am, and pushed me to become what they imagined me to be.

Introduction

I want to begin by telling you how this book came to be. If you are not interested right now, you can skip ahead to or jump around in the various sections, and maybe come back to this introduction later. But knowing the book's origins may help you understand certain choices I have made, without intending to limit the ways you can understand and use it. The lectures printed here capture classroom lectures that evolved over decades of teaching theory at public universities; the academic location set some possibilities, demands, and limits. At their best, lectures are constant and ongoing conversations with students, colleagues, and a growing list of references; at their worst, they impose artificial limits on thinking (e.g., seventy-five minutes per class, fifteen weeks per semester). Lectures are fragile and precarious: might this be so? Chapters are assertive: here it is! By translating these lectures into a generally less interactive, expressive, and nuanced medium, but continuing to call them lectures, I hope to stimulate and contribute to a larger conversation about thinking that seems increasingly difficult to find.

My academic location was also defined by a particular moment in which, for reasons I shall elaborate shortly, there was an excitement around and a demand and desire for theory. The result was an explosion of theories in the humanities and social sciences, and the appearance of Theory, with a capital *T*. Theory took on a life of its own as a new interdisciplinary and transdisciplinary field drawn from and flourishing within numerous disciplines. Theory was imagined playing a role parallel to that of formalization—that is, mathematical quantifications and logical analyses—in the hard sciences. It became and, to a large extent, remains a lingua franca, a common language enabling scholars and intellectuals to talk to one another, across disciplines and even across theories. From the 1970s to the 1990s, scholars specialized in Theory (I "do" Theory) while everyone had to familiarize themselves with it.

How did the moment of Theory come about? Thinking is always related (as both expression and response) to the contexts from which it emerges and the specific social arrangements and relations of power that partially determine who can speak and be heard, what can be allowed to be present and have influence. I want to talk briefly (maybe not so briefly) about some of the conditions of possibility of the emergence of Theory.

It needed the rapid and continuing expansion of (especially public) higher education that occurred after the Second World War (partly for the benefit of veterans). It depended on universities being the central staging ground for many of the protests of the late 1960s and early 1970s; students of this era became the first academic generation committed to Theory. And it required real investments to translate work into English and to create new outlets—journals, organizations, conferences—for sharing and discussing relevant work.[1] Ironically, this depended on the growing capitalization of universities and publishing.[2] But Theory also was a rebellion against the arrogance of science and the dominance of a particular understanding of science: logical positivism.

THE ARROGANCE OF SCIENCE

In the mid-nineteenth century, Auguste Comte, one of the founders of sociology, proposed separating science and philosophy.[a] This new philosophy was dedicated to the clarification of science and had two assumptions. The first, later called **foundationalism**, asserted that there is a Reality or Truth that exists independently of our knowledge of it, which provides the ground of all claims to knowledge and truth. The second—**positivism**—took science, understood in relatively narrow terms, as the only valid form of knowledge. Anything not following the methods and logics of science was nonsense.

Positivism, or "scientism," took on a life of its own. Its rule was simple: follow the model of science and delegitimate all other claims to knowledge. Its claims have become commonsensical. For science, the world is made up of facts that exist objectively. A fact is not influenced by whether anyone sees it, or who sees it, or whatever assumptions and biases they bring. "Facts" are simply there, but facts are, by themselves, mostly useless. The real objects

---

1 The rise of theory was sustained by the appearance of many new and important journals, such as *New Left Review, Critical Inquiry, boundary 2, Substance, New Literary History, Diacritics, Cultural Studies, Semiotext(e), Social Text, Enclitic, Oxford Literary Review, Angelaki,* and *New Formations*. A number of publishers either emerged or gave such work new attention, including Verso, Routledge, Duke University Press, and the University of Minnesota Press.
2 Over the decades, Theory has become a more international formation, with contributions from and variations in every part of the world; exactly when, how, and how successfully this internationalization came about are questions I will not address here.

of science are the objectively real relations between the facts, their effects on one another. It is these relations that science captures and represents in some language as hypotheses. Science can make no claim about reality that is not embodied in hypotheses, which can be tested and determined to be true or false. But Comte's positivism had no theory of language beyond a common-sensical one and, as a result, no theory of the specificity of scientific language.

This was the case until the early twentieth century, when positivism was institutionalized and formalized by a group of scholars in Vienna, as well as by scholars from many other countries, in a philosophy called logical positivism (and, later, logical empiricism).[3] Logical positivism was a response against what its adherents saw as the increasing power of metaphysics and romanticism. It rejected most of the history of philosophy and the questions that drove it. As the logician Rudolph Carnap put it, "We give no answer to philosophical questions and instead, reject all philosophical questions, whether of Metaphysics, Ethics or Epistemology."[b] (Don't worry, this will all make sense to you soon.) Philosophy was little more than the "handmaiden of science,"[c] meant only to clarify the language of science.[4]

The logical positivists were driven by a faith that science was a truly liberating force that could guarantee both material and social progress, against the conservative and authoritarian implications of other philosophies that served only to obscure truth. Like earlier forms of positivism, logical positivism assumed that facts are the only legitimate starting points for knowledge. They are—at least in principle—available to anyone, neutral insofar as they do not carry any theoretical or political assumptions, and uncontaminated by anything subjective (and, hence, cannot be understood psychologically,

3 The Vienna Circle flourished in the 1920s. Founded by Moritz Schlick (the author of *The General Theory of Knowledge* (*Allgemeinen Erkenntnislehre* [1918]), it involved scientists, mathematicians, and philosophers; its most famous members included Rudolf Carnap in Germany and, later, the United States; Ludwig von Mises in Austria; Carl Hempel in Germany; Bertrand Russell and A. J. Ayer in England; and Ernest Nagel, Willard Van Orman Quine, and Charles W. Morris in the United States. It created its own journal, modestly called *Erkenntnislehre* (Knowledge), in 1930 and also began a highly influential book series, the International Encyclopedia of the Unified Sciences. The Vienna Circle fell apart for a variety of reasons—not least the rise of Nazism and so-called Nazi science.

4 Logical positivism also significantly transformed the professional practice of philosophy, which was now seen as an activity based on careful public formulation, analysis, criticism, and revision. It made the "essay" rather than the treatise into the dominant genre of philosophical work.

as David Hume attempted). Consequently, the logical positivists assumed an absolute distinction between facts and concepts, between observation and theory statements.

But they recognized that ordinary language was insufficient for scientific knowledge. Science replaces ordinary language with the formal, propositional language of logical implication (e.g., in its simplest form, if A then B), although they disagreed about the most appropriate formal logic.[5]

Thus, the most revolutionary aspect of logical positivism was that it was fundamentally a linguistic philosophy, an early instance of what is called the linguistic turn.[d] It explored what can be meaningfully said; it was concerned with what is "communicable" by language, and with what constitutes the ("cognitive") meaningfulness of propositions. The logical positivists asserted that a proposition was meaningful only if it could be traced back to empirical statements of fact; all other statements are either meaningless (metaphysical) or tautological.[6] But its meaningfulness also depended on whether it could be put into the logical form of a nomothetic theory, a lawlike hypothesis stating the relations among facts in logical form.

Since these "laws" would necessarily include theoretical terms, the logical positivists had to consider how theoretical statements were related to or could be translated into observation statements. The answer involved a third kind of statement: correspondence or translation rules, which operationalized the cognitive meaning of a theoretical statement. Such rules defined a series of conditional statements (if you do something, then something will happen). To take a simple example, a theoretical term like *being brittle* (it is not an empirically observable fact) is given meaning by translation rules such as: if you hit it with a hard object, it shatters. Translation rules offered predictions that could be empirically tested. The predictions would either come to pass or not, and the law would be verified or falsified.

Consequently, logical positivism was also a theory of what constitutes a truthful statement. At first, truth depended on whether a hypothesis had been verified or not, effectively equating prediction and explanation: if you understood the causality involved, then you could predict the outcome of

---

5 A proposition is a statement or judgment that is or can be stated in a logical form.
6 In Bertrand Russell's theory of description, what would be a meaningless statement, apparently neither true nor false, such as "The present king of France is bald," could be represented in logical terms as "There exists an x that is king and there can only be one such thing and it is bald." This, Russell argued, is not a statement of existence but a proposition that simply names x, and therefore is meaningful and false. Russell, "On Denoting."

any experimental manipulations. The collection of verified ("proven" or "true") hypotheses defines the sum of scientific knowledge at a given moment. As scientific truths are accumulated, there is an expanding body of scientific knowledge.

However, the members of the Vienna Circle quickly realized not only that it was impossible to verify every condition that might be deduced from a hypothesis but also that there were meaningful and possibly true statements that could not be verified (e.g., at the time, the dark side of the moon). So, they weakened the requirement: a statement had only to be verifiable (i.e., one could imagine its possible verification). But even this posed insurmountable difficulties and led the Austrian philosopher Karl Popper (never a member of the Circle) to suggest that meaningfulness and truth depended only on the possibility of falsification.[7,e]

For most of the twentieth century, positivism ruled. (Some would say it still does.) Science was the gold standard of knowledge production in the academy, and outside, people generally assumed that science improved their lives (although they are thinking of technological advances). Inside the academy, the arrogance of science dismissed every alternative as poetic, soft, subjective, intuitive, superstitious, and speculative.[8] And, most damning, such

---

7 There were many other disputes among the logical positivists, resulting in multiple versions. They argued about whether theoretical terms describe real properties or whether instead they were simply instrumental constructs. Could there ever be a fully exhaustive list of conditions (translation terms) that would completely define a theoretical term? They argued about whether translation terms were operational or dispositional. And they argued about what observation statements described, what language was about, and what was outside language, which brought them dangerously close to metaphysical questions. They proposed a variety of theories (from physicalism, which asserted the reality of objects, to phenomenalism, which asserted that only sensations were real) and argued about how the logical structure of true statements could represent or "mirror" the arrangements of facts in the world. Moritz Schlick declared that the elaboration of meaning "always comes to an end in actual pointings, in exhibiting what is meant, thus in real acts, only these acts are no longer capable of, or in need of, further explanation." And Ludwig Wittgenstein (whose *Tractatus Logico-Philosophicus* was much beloved by the Vienna Circle, although he refused any affiliation with the Vienna Circle, eventually reading mystical poetry when he finally accepted its invitation to speak) turned to more poetic responses.

8 Science remains the final arbiter of truth and the normative model of theorizing, despite the many scandals—financial influence, confirmation bias, contradictory findings, and the inability to replicate what are often taken as agenda-setting studies—that have rocked numerous scientific communities.

work was incomprehensible—but to whom? The irony is that the mathematical reasonings of science are no less esoteric, abstract, and incomprehensible than qualitative work in the humanities. For that matter, the knowledge of any craftsperson—whether a plumber or a potter—has its own conceptual vocabulary, which is incomprehensible to outsiders. The illusion that science is comprehensible to the educated or even "ordinary" reader results from the ways science's very existence *as a cultural activity*—its methods and languages—is denied or misrepresented in the classroom and the media. On the other hand, neither schools nor media even attempt to help people make sense of the languages, arguments, and insights of the humanities or qualitative social sciences.

Logical positivism exerted an almost suffocating pressure on scholarship and pedagogy. Textbooks in the social sciences, and sometimes even in the humanities, from the 1950s at least through the 1970s began with a chapter on "deductive-nomothetic theory," in which only the formulations of hypotheses and the verification of predictions defined knowledge. There was palpable institutionalized pressure on most disciplines to seek their proper practice as a science. Research had to be—or at least pretend to be—scientific, despite the apparent lack of opportunities for rigorously controlled experiments and quantification in the fields studying human realities. Some fields (e.g., economics, psychology, sociology, and political science) adopted scientific methods (of experimentation and quantification, statistical analysis, and modeling), although judging from their failures to predict very much, their claim to "scientificity" is suspect. Even as a graduate student in communication and culture in the early 1970s, I felt the demand of "scientism." Fortunately, I pushed back with a little help from my mentors.[9]

BEYOND SCIENTISM

Eventually, logical positivism died; in fact, one might say it has the distinction of being the only philosophy to be proved wrong. When A. J. Ayer, the leading British logical positivist, was asked about its major defects, he responded, "Well, I suppose most of the defect is that at the end of it all, it was false."[f] As this became obvious, it transformed itself into analytic philosophy, which continues to hold on to empiricism, while expanding the possibilities of formalization and logics and blurring the line between fact and concept.

---

9 My task in my first academic position was to teach quantitative research.

While the demise of logical positivism was partly the result of its own internal inconsistencies and inadequacies, it was helped along—especially for those already inclined to question its status and power—by studies in the history and sociology of science. In the American academy, Thomas Kuhn's *The Structure of Scientific Revolutions* (1962) (ironically published in the book series created by the Vienna Circle, which sought a unified understanding of all the sciences) had an immediate and profound impact.[10,g] Kuhn's historical studies undermined the assumptions that there was only one way of doing science, and that science accumulates knowledge, despite changes in its theoretical vocabulary (e.g., Einstein's theory is simply more general than Newton's and encompasses it as a special case).

Kuhn distinguished between normal and revolutionary science. Normal science proceeds on the basis of a shared scientific paradigm, a set of assumptions and practices (embodied in "exemplars" or exemplary experiments) that define the "proper" way of doing science within a particular field. It lays out the important questions, the appropriate methods for investigating them (i.e., how to do research), and the range of possible answers. As long as scientists operate within a paradigm, they do science in basically the same way, and science proceeds "normally," giving the appearance of an accumulation of knowledge.

However, sometimes the paradigm itself is challenged not by addressing its theoretical assumptions or empirical findings but by foregrounding phenomena that the dominant paradigm ignored or marginalized. A new paradigm claims that these phenomena are more fundamental to unlocking the mysteries constituting the field of study. It offers new exemplars of how to do "normal" science and, often, new assumptions about the nature of the reality under investigation. As a result, how facts are identified, the nature of their relations, and the meaning of concepts all change, and the "knowledge" of the old paradigm will not be transferable to or translatable into the new one. What appears to be the same concept or fact in the two paradigms is not the same. For example, Kuhn argued that everything that led Albert Einstein to the theory of relativity was visible in Newtonian physics. It's just that Newtonian physicists didn't think the phenomena were important enough to bother with. Einstein placed them at the center of his research, creating a new paradigm.

10 Kuhn was not the first one to offer an antipositivist view of science, nor was he the most philosophically eloquent; that distinction probably belongs to French philosophers such as Gaston Bachelard and Georges Canguilhem. But the work of various sociologists of science, such as Robert K. Merton, as well as the historical research of, for example, Bruno Latour, also contributed to the criticism of positivism.

As a result, what gravity means in the Newtonian paradigm isn't the same as what it means in the Einsteinian universe (just as the meaning and significance of the "gene" change between Mendelian and biochemical genetics).

Kuhn further argued against the radical separation of observation statements and theory statements. Facts are not theory-free; they cannot be separated from theoretical assumptions. What you "see" depends on what you assume, what you think you already know, and how you go about producing knowledge. Consequently, knowledge cannot be accumulated across paradigms. Instead, science proceeds through a series of shifts between incommensurable paradigms.[11] Whatever Kuhn's intentions, his work turned science into another cultural system, one of multiple ways of seeing and thinking about the world, with no unique claim to authority. The door to other possibilities had been opened, and many lights came shining through the cracks.

A BRIEF NOTE ON POLITICS

Having spent so much time on a rather arcane academic dispute, I would be remiss if I did not acknowledge the turbulent politics of the post–World War II decades, which were marked by many—often interconnected—political struggles nationally, internationally, and globally. The struggles and movements addressed every major dimension of human life, including economic, social, political, and cultural lives. They targeted economic inequalities and greed, governmental corruption and incompetence, war and nuclear armaments, racism and ethnic hatred, gender and sexual discrimination, coloniality and imperialism, overconsumption and commodification, environmental degradation, and even the boredom and stultifying conformity of middle-class life. Anticolonial wars, civil rights, gay rights, feminism, the antiwar movement, the antinuclear campaign, demonstrations against global capitalism, the visibility of socialism, Black Power, hippies, counterculture—all were reshaping the United States, penetrating the interstices of institutional and

---

11 While this was certainly how Kuhn was read, and the reading can be justified from the text, it is important to note that Kuhn eventually criticized such "relativist" readings and moderated his argument, pulling back from the assumption of complete incommensurability, allowing for communication across and transitions between paradigms. Still, his work opened the door as well to more discursive and rhetorical analyses of science, asking how it is that the sciences have constructed and secured—and continue to do so—a unique claim to truth, transparency, and objectivity. Kuhn, "Objectivity, Value Judgment, and Theory Choice," in *Essential Tension*.

everyday life. They undermined the myth of the happy, flourishing nation presented in mainstream culture and media.

But they were not limited to one country or one continent. All over the world, political struggles appeared in the streets as people took on whatever issues mattered. People created broad alliances and often dismantled them just as quickly. And people created and performed their own cultures—in music, film, literature, theater, and the material arts, but also in new forms of community, socialization, spirituality, and learning. Around the world, the taken-for-granted ideas and ways of thinking of modern society were being challenged.

By now, you are probably asking what this has to do with the rise of Theory. Part of the answer is obvious: institutions of higher education were a major site for the organization, expression, and action of many of the struggles and cultures. Not surprisingly, all the "noise" on campuses worldwide reverberated through the entire academy, affecting faculty, students, and even administrators. Often it was resisted or even crushed, but like the music that was its constant soundtrack, it permeated everything. It could not be stopped—in dormitories, classrooms, or even laboratories.

The less obvious part of the relation of these new political movements and Theory was that science was often involved in the very structures that were being attacked. And since the sciences were so visible and accessible in universities, they were immediate targets for their cooperation with and contributions to racism, imperialism and militarism, nuclear weapons and genocide, pollution and the monetization of resources, by dismissing every negative outcome as an unintended consequence, a side effect. Science was called to justify itself, and it mostly failed, which led many to reject the claims of scientific objectivity, political neutrality, and progressiveness that had justified positivism. The door was opened even wider, and even more came rushing through.

NEW TRADITIONS

Some academics and intellectuals in the 1960s began to argue that the uniqueness of human life demanded different concepts and methods from those defining the study of the natural world. They turned to a heterogeneous tradition of theories known as the *Geisteswissenschaften* (literally, the sciences of spirit).[12] The human sciences are built on a distinction between

---

12 It included the seventeenth-century historian Giambattista Vico; neo-Kantians like Wilhelm Dilthey, Ernst Cassirer, and Max Weber; certain Marxist social and cultural

movement (stimulus and response, cause and effect) as the object of the natural sciences, and action, which was unique to humans because it necessarily involved meanings, intentions, goals, and volition. There is a difference between my arm rising and my raising my arm. Human beings make choices about how they behave, and those choices are informed by the understandings, values, emotions, and desires they bring to a situation. Human life cannot be reduced to the status of an object, even a natural (living) one. The study of human life demanded its own ways of thinking, its own sense of the theoretical and the empirical.[13]

The rediscovery of this complex body of work offered new histories of modern thought and set the stage for the emergence of Theory. To a large extent, this revitalization of thinking was built on three fundamental assumptions that were now foregrounded as constitutive of modern thought: First, reality is defined relationally; relationality is the alternative to "facts." Second, reality is constructed rather than given; the world is made to be the way it is. Various versions of constructionism defined the alternative to foundationalist philosophies. And, third, reality is always complex and contingent.

These assumptions posed three founding questions: What are the forms and natures of the relations that constitute human reality? What are the processes and agencies by which relations are themselves constituted? Do such assumptions deny truth and inevitably lead to relativism? Does the denial of a single, universal Truth mean that there are no truths? Do relationality and constructionism mean that the realities we experience are not real? As you shall see, these questions and arguments are woven into many of the lectures here.

Taken together, these assumptions and questions pose thinking as critique, asking, How did the present (or whatever you want to think about) come to be what is? What are its conditions of possibility? After all, if it is all constructed, it could have been otherwise. But this poses further difficulties: To

---

critics like C. Wright Mills and John Berger; pragmatic sociologists like Robert Park, W. I. Thomas, and George Herbert Mead; and phenomenological sociologists like Alfred Schutz and Peter Berger. But it also existed on the fringes of psychology, economics, and political science. These would become visible much later in the twentieth century.

In my professional travels outside the Anglophone academy, I am often greeted as a "scientist," since Wissenschaften presents science as the rigorous excavation and organization of knowledge.

13 The nature of the relations between these two understandings or descriptions of human behavior—e.g., between the neurophysiology or biochemistry of emotions, and more qualitative, experiential, or discursive accounts—remains highly contested.

what extent is humanity an active agent in the processes by which reality is produced? Does this involve matters of language? Subjectivity? Do we need to challenge the hubris of humanity, the assumption of humanity's exceptionalism that makes it into the creator of its own reality, the master of its own fate? Do these processes involve agencies over which humans have little or no control?

Such questions have a long history: Copernicus argued, against common wisdom, that the Earth is not the center of the universe—and, by implication, deprived humanity of its place at the center of creation. Baruch Spinoza seemed to reduce humanity to simply one among the infinite expressions of God. Adam Smith's "invisible hand" and Karl Marx's theory of economic determination suggested that people were not in control of their own lives, that they are driven by forces working behind their backs. Charles Darwin's theory of evolution (and later Gregor Mendel's discovery of genes), as well as Sigmund Freud's theory of the unconscious, further challenged humanity's status and capabilities. And developments in physics (e.g., James Maxwell's theory of thermodynamics and Albert Einstein's theory of relativity) also challenged the special place of humanity in the universe. These are the questions that have haunted and continue to haunt those who try to understand human realities. And these are questions that animate many of the following lectures.

A PEDAGOGY OF THEORY

All this leads me back to my classes and the conditions that defined these lectures. The fact is that students came to my classes with their own agendas. Some were interested in a particular social or political problem; some were interested in particular theories. Some wanted to find the right theories to address specific questions, and some were looking for the theory that would deliver Truth. Some used it to meet requirements, and some found it therapeutic. A few sought new ways of thinking for the times, and some just liked to think, even about thinking itself.

But this was the moment of Theory, and what most of them wanted was a road map to navigate and make sense of the overwhelming number of theories that were rushing through the floodgates, and of the complex relations among them—including agreements and disagreements, appropriations and collaborations. They faced a chaotic hodgepodge of apples and oranges, but also of nuts, vegetables, cereals, and so on. They did not know how to read theories or how to think about them. They were trying to come to grips, responsibly I hoped, with the anarchic and oneiric wonderland of Theory.

There are many ways to teach Theory, each with its own strengths and weaknesses. And each has its own problems. The three most common approaches are the survey, "critical thinking," and what for lack of a better name I will call rhetoric. The survey course does just what its name suggests: it introduces students to a wide array of current theories. The problem is selection; given the constant proliferation of theories, each of which is itself producing its own progeny, how do you decide which theories are important enough to be included? No survey can ever adequately cover the terrain, consider all the possibilities, field all the questions; in the end, the selection criteria usually remain hidden. Inevitably, any survey leaves out what others see as the most important, influential, creative, or original thinker(s). The result is that the many different and often outstanding efforts to introduce people to Theory do not play well together.

Critical thinking attempts to give students the capacity to use theories to criticize specific assumptions and their consequences. The problem is that every theory can be criticized, and there is no way to stop the criticism. The only end points are nihilism, which denies the possibility of going on thinking, or forms of judgment predicated on normative ethical and political values.

The rhetorical approach is a mélange of the first two. It seeks to help students recognize different concepts and their uses, as well as different forms of analysis and argument. It aims to enable them to think about whether this concept, or that analytic practice, is the best or even an appropriate way to engage a particular problem. One has to make choices in thinking about the world, and those choices should never be easy; they should not result from laziness or ignorance, or from personal biases or preconceived certainties. They have to be thought out, fought over. As important as this is, it does not offer a road map of the plenitude of theories.

I looked for another way, which would show how the various theories are related. I wanted my students—you—to see them as participants in different, not always coherent, histories and conversations, responding to and challenging each other's questions. There had to be a way to map the roots and the routes that led to and connect theories, that recognize the range of effective ambiguities, displacements, and disagreements that might circulate around them, and in the modes of argument, commensuration, and equivocation that constitute the conversations of thought. And as if that weren't enough, I needed them (you) to understand the complex relations between thinking and its historical contexts, without giving either too much power. Only then can you understand the continuities and discontinuities through which theories can be appropriated into multiple contexts, with disparate meanings and effects, and with different justifications for whatever power they may have.

I came up with a rather idiosyncratic pedagogy, based around two concepts: deep theory and backstory, both of which I will explain in the first lecture. For the moment, using an uncomfortable metaphor, I offered a representation of the neural net constituting the ground from which Theory emerged. And, much to my amazement, it seemed to work, even after the moment of Theory had passed, in the last years of the millennium.

The concern for theory did not go away with the passing of Theory; if anything it got stronger as it took new forms. Two things happened. First, the multiple reasons why students reach for theory, and the multiple ways they want to use it, became too obvious to ignore or to capture under the sign of Theory. Students increasingly approached theory with a concern for either careers (I have never really understood that one) or social and political activism. The former makes the rhetorical approach reasonable, while the latter tends to put a modifier before theories. Thus, these days, you are more likely to find classes in critical race theory, decolonization theory, communist theory, or trans theory than a class in Theory or some particular school of theory. These students realize there is no direct correlation between theories and political positions, although some theories may be more useful in addressing a particular issue while others may be inadequate to the problem or may even erase it. There are many theories that provide an understanding of a particular issue; there are many ways to theorize a particular struggle, and they may lead you to different conclusions and strategies.

While this change in how theory was taken up was not a surprise—after all, it had always been there—the second development did catch me off guard. There has been a growing if still small interest in a public conversation about theory. A few academics have decided that they need to share the multiplicity and complexity, but also the omnipresence, of theory in order to perhaps create new possibilities for collective thinking. Consider these lectures one such effort! At the same time, there is a growing skepticism about the authority of science (despite the media's continuing scientism), and some people—the numbers do not matter—are looking for other ways of understanding the conditions in which people live and the forces that are determining and changing them. Brought together, they raise a small hope that we might forge common grounds, common languages, and some common trust, for other pathways to knowledge, other ways of theorizing and thinking.

NOTES

a. Comte, *Positive Philosophy of Auguste Comte.*
b. Carnap, *Unity of Science*, 21–22.
c. Ayer, "Logical Positivism," 8:12.
d. Rorty, *Linguistic Turn.*
e. Popper, *Logic of Scientific Discovery.*
f. Ayer, "Logical Positivism," 34:41.
g. Kuhn, *Structure of Scientific Revolutions.*

PART I

On

Thinking

about

Thinking

Thinking and Theorizing

Let's assume that the universe—including our tiny part of it—begins (the Big Bang) and ends (entropy) in chaos. Between the chaos, however, forms of order—relations and organizations—define realities, from the laws of quantum mechanics to the patterns of sensibility, significance, and repetition characteristic of the natural and social worlds we inhabit. We do not have to decide at this moment how the many different orders, each with its own field of influence, came to be. Perhaps there are many origins: perhaps God created them; perhaps they are embedded in the grain of the universe, perhaps they are the result of the behaviors and practices of living beings, or perhaps humans alone are responsible for all of reality.

These lectures begin when it became possible, in particular locations and traditions, to think that humans participate in the processes composing their worlds. There were certainly other traditions, located elsewhere and "elsewhen," asking similar questions. The traditions addressed here—the traditions of Euromodernity—commonly assumed that humans compose and configure order through their ways of thinking, through the theories they bring to bear, and through the meanings and emotions that thinking and theorizing allow, to produce what Martin Heidegger called a way of being in the world (see lecture 18).

COMPOSING REALITIES: CONCEPTS AND THEORIES

There are many ways of thinking, and different ways of thinking enable— manifest themselves as—a limited set of possible theories. Thinking always involves concepts, which define—uncover, impose, produce—relations between individualities (from subatomic particles to social identities), which are themselves already concepts. We cannot think without concepts. They make the world intelligible, perceptible, livable, by making it fundamentally relational. Concepts are always abstractions or generalizations. They cut into the world, offering different ways of structuring—identifying, differentiating, and aggregating—the spectrum of sensory and material encounters.[1]

Consider a concept like "reader," which ignores all the differences among readers to abstract out only one quality. Concepts make visible and hearable the relations (selective qualities) that we take for granted. But they also obscure and even erase other possibilities, defining what can and cannot be seen or said. The fact that the realities into which we are born are constantly changing makes every conceptual order fragile and unstable, confronting us with the need for other, perhaps new, concepts, with the need to go on thinking.

Concepts are the tools of theorizing. Theories gather together and create relations among the concepts, thereby defining how a particular concept functions. Theories are always actively productive and actively produced.[2] In classical Greece, *theoria* described the activity of a representative of one community traveling to another to participate in some "foreign" activity, who then returns to offer an account to his or her own community. The foreign site is not passively given or received but is actively investigated as difference, thus embracing the possibility of otherness, complexity, multiplicity, and change. Theory referred to ways of seeing as active engagements with difference, which could multiply the possibilities of thinking and living without abandoning all the norms or truths of your community. Theories define

---

1 Concepts need not take the forms we are used to. One of my favorite episodes of *Star Trek: The Next Generation* had Picard facing an alien who spoke in specific imagery. It would be as if I said, "Romeo and Juliet on the balcony" when I wanted to speak of desperate love. It's fine as long as you know the reference. But is that any different from our narrative and predicative communication; it's fine as long as you know the language?
2 I am indebted to Christian Lundberg for this insight.

the ways intelligibility is acknowledged, constructed, and expressed. They are built on distinct ways of thinking and offer their own logics and forms of reasoning. Their practice is conversation and convivial argument.

Why are so many people so suspicious of theory? Why are theories in the human sciences either ignored or viewed with hostility? I can offer two reasons. Unfortunately, the most common way of thinking about theories emphasizes its abstractness, sharply distinguishing it from both the empirical world and common sense, as if these were not themselves conceptual. Science is allowed theories, but they are limited to the explanation and prediction of specific events; when they become too general, they become mere speculation.

Thinking about human realities has to start by understanding the theories and languages already producing and disclosing the worlds in which we live. You have to stand back from them, using other concepts, theories, or ways of thinking. You have to make the world strange—defamiliarize it—enough to be able to see what work the concepts are doing. Such thinking often needs vocabularies (and even syntaxes) that seem foreign. Consequently, it is easier to dismiss them as technical, esoteric, even incomprehensible, to condemn them as self-indulgent, intentionally obfuscating, or, more recently, elitist, to assume that they have no relation to or relevance for the empirical world.

Second, we tend to oversimplify the multiplicity and complexity of abstraction. There is no clear and sharp distinction between the particular and the abstract because identifying something as a particular something requires you to have already identified it as an example of an abstract category. Insofar as we are thinking, even commonsensically, there are only abstractions. But not all abstractions are equal, for there are levels of abstraction ranging from the concrete to the universal. The danger is to assume that the former is simple and purely empirical, while the latter is merely speculative with no empirical content. Every level has its own forms of complexity, and its own sense of the empirical. And that empirical reality presents itself to us, at every level, through an already if inadequately organized world of concepts. It may be better to reverse the order of complexity, understanding that the more abstract a concept is (economy, family, gender), the simpler its description of reality. The less abstract concept is the more complicated, for it requires us to take more "variables" or relations into account.

The differences between levels define the differences that matter, the discriminations that can be made, the measurements that can be taken. Consequently, specific concepts and theories will be most appropriate or useful at particular levels of abstraction as they try to make the "truths" of that level intelligible. But levels of abstraction are not objectively discrete, stable, and permanent planes. They are more like the spaces marked by the chalk lines on playing fields or crime scenes, interrupting a continuum.[3]

That leaves us with questions. How do we identify the level of abstraction at which a concept or theory is useful? How do we identify the most appropriate level of abstraction for the questions we are asking? How does thinking move between the different levels? Can we understand the richness of people's lives at the levels on which quantum mechanics or cognitive science operate? If a highly abstract concept cannot provide an adequate description of some particular instance, what sort of work needs to be done in the middle?

DIFFERENTIATING THEORIES

Theory has been around for a long time, although its shape, functions, and effects keep changing. Theory can have different meanings and uses: as everyday problem-solving; as understanding one or more particular activities (e.g., whether science or video games); as exploring the existing conditions of life; and as thinking about the strengths and weaknesses of existing theories and the possibilities of other ways of thinking.

I want to distinguish some of the dominant forms of theory, since they offer different ways of inventing, configuring, and deploying concepts, logics, and measures of rigor. All theories operate and negotiate the relations between different levels of abstraction, which they help to define. Each theory (embodying a way of thinking) asserts its own "proper ratio" between what it constructs as the universal (or general) and particular claims—often misrepresented as the theoretical and the empirical.

Explanatory theories, whether self-conscious (science) or not (everyday life), place almost all the weight on the particular (equated with the empirical). They seek causal relations, but because causality is often hard to identify, they offer generalizations (rules) for behavior that enable you to predict the outcomes of your choices. Such rules are conditions: if A then B. In such theories, including those of science, the major question is how to represent and operationalize the rules.

Speculative theories lean heavily toward the universal; while such theories may be concerned with the particular (empirical?) matters, they often serve

---

3 It may be that concepts produce the very level at which they operate.

primarily as starting points for figurative and meditative logics that sanction leaps (of faith) between distant levels of abstraction. They offer themselves as wisdom rather than knowledge, addressing questions that explanatory theories dare not pose. While speculative theories are common in philosophy and religion, they also exist in, for example, theoretical physics and cosmology.

Discipline-defining theories generally seek a balance between the general (universal?) and the particular. Common in the humanities and social sciences, they conceptualize the objects and methods defining a discipline.[4] More accurately, they produce the object to be studied, by isolating a specific set of relations from the rest of the human world (e.g., the economy, the state, culture). In such theories, theory becomes a tool, a detour, enabling you to make sense of the particular by reconstructing it in all its complexity, so that one can see it in new ways. They claim a different relation and responsibility to the experiential world than either science or speculation and face the challenge of finding forms of rigorous thought capable of dealing with a value-laden reality.

Earlier, I discussed the *Geisteswissenschaften*, or human sciences, which argued that human existence and experience had to be interpreted and understood rather than explained (through experimentation and formalization). It stands as one tradition of such discipline-defining theories, even if it often ended up with interdisciplinarity. Different theories within the *Geisteswissenschaften* defined the "human" in different ways, but most assumed that humanity was different from—more than—other forms of life. Some defined that excess in terms of subjectivity and consciousness, which lean toward questions of meaning, experience, self-consciousness, and so on; others defined it in terms of agency, which leans toward matters of action (and the ability to do otherwise), intention, value, and so on; and still others defined it in terms of capacities, for example, to use language, to make tools, to have a history.

There is another way to differentiate theories, based on the questions they ask. In the contemporary public sphere, many people are concerned with normative matters of values and judgment, including ethics, politics, rhetoric, and aesthetics. Axiology interrogates value. What are the meanings (or criteria?) of value terms like *beauty* or *good*? How do or should people make judgments of value in different domains, and how can they be warranted? While many of the deep theories discussed in these lectures have a great

4 E.g., Max Weber, Émile Durkheim, George Herbert Mead, and Talcott Parsons in sociology; Margaret Mead in anthropology; and Mathew Arnold, I. A. Richards, and F. R. Leavis in literary studies.

deal to say about such normative questions, I do not give much attention to their contributions, partly because such concerns are, in an important sense, dependent on how one investigates and understands the human and nonhuman worlds. I do believe that thinking about our realities must, to whatever extent possible, precede judgment, even as they are bound together.

These lectures focus on three other concerns: First, epistemology addresses questions of knowledge. What does it mean to know? How do you know something? How do you know that you know? What can and can't you know? What is the form or structure of knowledge, and how is it re/presentable? Second, metaphysics (more recently referred to as ontology, although they are not exactly equivalent) addresses questions of reality. What is the nature of reality? What is existence? What does it mean to say something is real or not real, that it exists or does not exist?[5] Third, philosophical anthropology questions the nature of humanity. What kind of beings are human beings such that they experience the world in the ways they do? Are they different and, if so, in what ways, from other sorts of beings?

DEEP THEORIES

Deep theories are a fourth mode of theorizing, not easily compared to explanatory, speculative, or discipline-defining theories.[6] If theories are ways of thinking *about*, deep theories are ways of thinking sui generis. They are also ways of seeing and being seen, listening and speaking. They are not simply sets of concepts and logics, for they are always embodied—sensuous and material, opening to other forms of relations and configurations. Deep theories define what is conceptual and what is empirical, and they create, distribute, and connect the levels of abstraction.

Deep theories often resemble philosophy, and the two might have been the same before philosophy became an academic profession. However difficult it is to differentiate deep theory and philosophy, they are not the same. Many deep theorists may have thought of themselves as philosophers; yet others are rarely included in the pantheon of philosophy. Deep theory is philosophy becoming something else, the ground of the human sciences. It seeks to empower theorizing to reflect on its outcomes, its ability to affect

---

5 Flash forward: the two major schools of epistemology are rationalism and empiricism; the two major schools of metaphysics are idealism and materialism. More to come!

6 As I indicated in the preface, this concept is my own invention.

the world. Deep theory refuses to stay at any single level of abstraction; instead, it offers ways of thinking to foster the ability to move between levels, and for seeing the mediations that both create and connect them. To speak metaphorically again, if theories organize the chaos and multiplicities, deep theories hold back the chaos just enough to enable certain possibilities of thinking, certain kinds of theorizing.

Deep theories are the ground on which theorizing happens, a condition of possibility of theories, and they constitute the capacities and limits of any theory. Deep theories are to specific theories what arithmetic is to mathematics— the necessary starting point, the medium that enables all thought. They are the palettes (changing metaphors) from which theories—including "modern Western thought," with all its accomplishments and barbarisms—are birthed. Deep theories teach us how to think, with what ideas and beliefs, but we are left to consider what they make possible and what they make impossible.

Using an inadequate metaphor (again), think of deep theories as different languages or language families. Some languages are likely to be similar to or different from others, in different ways, and in many cases to be both. Each language has its own sounds, rhythms, compositions, tonalities, and harmonies, its own strengths and weaknesses in terms of what it can or cannot say. Each language identifies those differences that matter. Like languages, there may be deep theories you simply cannot inhabit; deep theories have a voice, and there may be some that you simply cannot speak.

If deep theories are languages, theories are their dialectics. Any deep theory exists only in its multiple variations as dialects, accents, slang, and "minor" languages, some of which are composed from the elements of a single, common language, but many are likely to be hybrids, heterogeneous compositions drawing on several languages and variations.[7] After all, theories appropriate, improvise, and move between deep theories. While there is no one proper way to speak a language (or to escape it), you still have to

---

7 Consider learning how to hear music. I taught popular music for many years, and I was always surprised at how sparsely populated my students' musical universe was. While it was not surprising that there were always styles of music they did not know, it was surprising that there were styles they simply could not hear or appreciate, could not begin to discriminate or judge matters of difference. I found myself at times trying to teach them how to listen to, how to distinguish, the variations of broad musical "master" languages, such as jazz or metal. Unless you have a touchstone, what you hear will sound like noise, or it will all sound the same—which is, by the way, exactly what my father said when my brothers and I brought R&B and rock into our house.

start with some dialect, to begin to recognize the material realities of the language—for example, the sounds, rhythms, and flows—that enable and limit its possible variations. Commonly, you are taught the normative or master dialectic, the one with the most power and status.[8]

The same holds for deep theories. That is why they have to be read in their contexts, and in relation to the questions that have called them into existence. Just as there is no single, true deep theory, there is no proper way of thinking with any particular deep theory. There is never a definitive, unbiased, and agreed-upon reading of any deep theory. It is made up of nothing but the variations, constituted by a whole field of competing and sometimes even contradictory interpretations, emphases, and arguments.

But it may be possible to establish a baseline from which disagreements, tangents, and deviations (including intentional misreadings) can be understood and adjudicated. Such a baseline proposes not the truth of the deep theory but something as close to a neutral (nonpartisan) or middle ground, without simply reproducing the dominant. It describes the point of minimal agreement, minimally viable reading, a common starting point from which we can argue and take off. It also may help to provide some sense of where the often intense disagreements arise, defining sites of divergences and variations. I have no doubt that many theorists will find the very concept of such an ecumenical reading incomprehensible and impossible, and they may be right, but it is worth trying.

Reading deep theory requires a generous and rigorous reading as opposed to a paranoid reading searching out the errors and sins that you already know are there. Every deep theory has been attacked, from both within and without. Often, such criticisms reject a fundamental assumption that the particular deep theory readily admits to holding: Can one criticize humanism for being humanist? Deep theories (most theories, in fact) are rarely abandoned because of such criticisms.

BACKSTORIES

As I searched for a fruitful pedagogical strategy, I realized that deep theories could provide the material for what I call a backstory for contemporary theorizing. What is a backstory? My wife is a novelist; each of her stories starts

8 When I was growing up in Brooklyn, teachers often tried to force us to give up our Brooklyn accents as they supposedly made us sound stupid.

at a particular moment into which we are thrown. But she has to figure out, for herself, how the characters arrived at that moment to know how they will react to whatever she throws at them. This moment and its elaboration provide the prehistory, the conditions of possibility, of what takes place in the story. The backstory sets a story in motion, down the particular paths it follows, to the inevitable end as just what it needed to be. In other words, backstories are written for the purposes of arriving at the events that launch the story she is telling. Different plot? Different characters? They will need different backstories. The backstory, although absent, enables a reader to believe the characters and to believe they would act the way they do. There may be other backstories that would produce the same results or backstories that she is unaware of until she begins writing the novel.

While the end of any backstory is given by the beginning of the novel, it may change as a result of the story. Sometimes, the backstory never ends; sometimes it seems to be frozen in time, imprisoned in the present. And its beginning is always uncertain. Like any story, it starts in the middle. It can always reach back further, or it can follow a different path back. Deciding where to begin a backstory is a judgment of how far back and in which directions she has to go to make the beginning of her actual story sensible.

My backstory is a tool to help organize and navigate the chaos of thinking about thinking. Backstories usually remain invisible, glanced out of the corner of one's eye, but they haunt the stories being told. They are the soil out of which particular problems and challenges emerge; they enable the mobilization of some possibilities rather than others and set particular kinds of stories into play.

Knowing the sources and foundations of our theories does not invalidate them, but it enables them to be subjected to more rigorous forms of scrutiny and criticism. Hopefully, it opens the possibility of thinking differently, of thinking otherwise, and it defines other ways of living and experiencing. My backstory makes visible only some of the forgotten sources of theory, only some of the ways of thinking that enable people to understand their lives and the worlds they live in.

I do not intend to offer a single, linear narrative, suggesting progress toward a better deep theory, in which one theory transcends the limits of previous ones. A linear narrative cannot grasp the contingencies and complexities of all that is going on within the backstory itself. It too easily ignores that each deep theory remains in play even as others enter onto the field, and because every deep theory is always responding to and engaging in conversation with those that preexist and coexist with it, they keep changing. Deep theories (and their subsequent theoretical progeny) operate on contested ground, as ongoing spaces of arguments and struggles, of exclusions and occlusions. Simultaneously, each deep theory is constructing its own backstory.

I hope you will read these lectures as a centrifugal—spiral or helical—story; rather than everything being sewn up in a neat and simple package, my backstory wants to be messy, simultaneously following many strangely intersecting roads. It is built on complexity and logics of "and . . . and . . . but also . . ." What I have actually produced is still too linear; I would ask you to see and hold onto the spiral as much as possible without letting it fly off the handle into chaos. This backstory, like thinking itself, has to hold on to both a sense of purpose (pragmatism) and humility.

I want to introduce you to one story, not the only story, in which you already are located, so that you can find your way to better stories. There are many ways of telling the backstory of contemporary theory. Some are already being told, and more are waiting to be told. Every backstory is constructed with some idea of where it needs to end up, or of the problem space it is trying to open up, excavate, and cultivate.[a] A problem space is a historical context viewed as a space of contested thinking and relations. It poses fundamental questions about the possibilities of thinking. It is the ground out of which deep theories arise, but their conflicts are never resolvable by or reducible to a simple appeal to either "truth" or political righteousness.

The backstory presented here originally responded to the emergence of Theory, but more important, it was responding to a problem space that is not limited to the academy—a problem space of thinking itself, and of the need for theory. My backstory looks back to the European Enlightenment—or, more accurately, enlightenments—as multiple and contested philosophies, which inaugurated the modern appearance of deep theory by opening a space in which questions of relationality and constructionism had to be raised.[9]

Every story is incomplete. It is impossible to display every deep theory, even those within the Euromodern traditions. I have tried to identify and explicate, as much as my capacities allow, some of the main characters—figures or cyphers of ways of thinking—who might be identified, in contemporary terms, as the influencers; for the sake of time (in classes) and space (in print),

---

9 This understanding of (1) the multiplicity of enlightenments as intellectual and social projects, and (2) the complexity of each enlightenment as an assemblage of various bits and pieces, only a few of which are shared, will be elaborated in lecture 4.

I have left out so many important characters. I am sure everyone has their own list that defines the inadequacy of these lectures.[10]

The influence of this particular backstory—through both imposition and seduction—has been felt around the planet, partly through colonialism, imperialism, settlement, enslavement, and trade, and partly through the enhancement of the possibilities of (at least some) people's lives. Thinkers of all sorts, with divergent politics and, often, with their own autonomous traditions, nevertheless found themselves speaking and even defining themselves within, to, and against these deep theories, and the theories to which they gave rise. Some of these deep theories arose out of explicitly political problem spaces; some have been easily adapted to political ends; all of them have opened up spaces in which their own political possibilities have been contested.

Many of the leading scholars of colonialism and postcolonialism, of gender and sexuality, of race and ethnicity, of class inequalities, of bodies and power, as well as intellectuals from other geographic traditions, were educated in these deep theories; their work incorporates, builds on, responds to, and criticizes them. Often, they had no choice since the Western canon defined (and continues to define) "education" and the condition of possibility for entering into the increasingly global conversations. Whether they chose or were co-opted (as "conscripts of modernity") into these spaces, this particular backstory is still worth understanding.[b]

Many found imaginative ways to take Eurocentric stories, to renounce them, to bend them to their needs, to identify their limits, to find the ways in which social assumptions and power relations were always and already coded into their statements. Some struggled to find their "rational core" and their irrational systems of differences.

Others sought to escape their boundaries, to move toward other possibilities, turning to ignored historical or geographically located work, or to other genres of thinking (such as art), or to ways of thinking that exist on the margins or in the subjugated positions of modern thought. It has become urgent to tell these other backstories, to take account of the unacknowledged and prohibited voices, in both the past and the present. After all, these absences

10 Gottfried Wilhelm Leibniz, Arthur Schopenhauer, Henri-Louis Bergson, Theodor Adorno, Mikhail Bakhtin, W. E. B. Du Bois, Frantz Fanon, C. L. R. James, Aimé Césaire, Georges Bataille, Simone de Beauvoir, Roland Barthes, Julia Kristeva, Sylvia Wynter, etc.

are also part of the backstories of where our thinking is now.[11] And we are in desperate need of the wisdom—the deep theories if you will—of other times, places, and relations.

In contemporary classrooms, the bureaucracy demands that teachers lay out their desired or expected outcomes—rarely are they the same, and truth be told, I have never complied. I expect every lecture (both its vocabularies and its logics) to feel strange, even incomprehensible. You may find bits that seem familiar because they have become part of your reservoir of cognitive resources. Let me return to my language metaphor. Imagine a class introducing students to many if not all of the different European languages—English, Spanish, German, Russian, Finnish, Hungarian, Serbian, and so on. In such a class, students would not reasonably expect to become fluent in even one language, but they might be able to recognize what language is being spoken, even if it is only one of its possible variations.

Similarly, my lectures will not make you fluent in all or even any of the deep theories and the languages they speak. At best, you may be able to recognize when someone is talking the talk: they are talking mediation, or dialectics, or intentionality, or diacritics, and so on. Maybe you will be able to see some of the logics, assumptions, and conversations that constitute a particular deep theory, or the particular deep theories that are being used to construct theories in the human sciences.

But if I am being honest, I do hope these lectures give you tools to go on thinking and to join the conversations. I hope they make you more comfortable with theory even as you recognize that theories often seek to discomfort you. I hope they open you to the possibility that human reality might look otherwise viewed through different habits of thought. Perhaps they might enable you to perceive things you had not perceived previously and to no longer perceive things you had. Maybe they will change, ever so slightly, what you can and cannot say, what you will and will not say. And I hope you will realize that each deep theory offers a rich and often bewildering set of ways to go on thinking, to ask questions, and to seek answers.

---

11 Very few women or colonial subjects were able to break the barriers that made philosophy and deep theory almost impossible genres for them to participate in, especially in public; those who were able to theorize in public often appropriated other genres, such as those defined by disciplines or particular historical problems (e.g., Hannah Arendt, Margaret Mead, and Simone de Beauvoir) and often drew on the deep theories I am discussing.

Although I am telling a story, you should feel free to use these lectures in whatever ways work best for you: read the book from beginning to end, skip around, concentrate, skim, reread, whatever you need. Thinking is meant to be useful, but it can also be fun (you will have to trust me on that).

These lectures are addressed to anyone who thinks we need more and better thinking, whether in a classroom, a subway, or a tractor, for the sake of the future worlds we will create. If you are not curious about how this ever-changing quest is unfolding, there is no need to continue reading, but if you are . . .

NOTES
a. Scott, *Conscripts of Modernity*.
b. Scott, *Conscripts of Modernity*.

Modernity, Crisis, Politics
(First Interregnum)

There is another backstory woven into the fabric of deep theory to which, unfortunately, I am not going to pay enough attention. But I do want to bring it to your attention here, and intermittently in other lectures. It may help you get a sense of how this backstory plays out in "historical" time, and, more important, it may enable you to see its connections to the present moment. I start with a simple premise: thinking always takes place in and is related (as both expression and response) to the contexts from which it emerges and the specific social arrangements and relations of power that partly determine who can speak and be heard, what can be allowed to be present and have influence. This lecture provides glimpses into the contexts from and within which a certain history of deep theory was constituted. Yet theories cannot be fully explained by appealing to social realities, or to the positions of those who offer them. The relations between ideas and contexts are rarely that simple or transparent.

THE MODERN

The context lurking behind my backstory is the much larger and more difficult story of the **modern**, both as a claim (of being modern) and as a fantasy (of desiring to be modern).[1] But the concept of the modern is surrounded by numerous and often passionate disagreements. Where is it? When did it begin? What is it? Three common assumptions dominate most of the arguments: First, Europe (in the seventeenth and eighteenth centuries) not only was the birthplace of the modern but was the only place where it could have developed. Second, modernization follows a single—pretty much the same—path of development, which has been described in terms of institutions, processes, and/or cultural logics. And, third, the modern has a relatively stable if developing and consistent identity. That identity consists of an enumerated set of features, many of which you will recognize. Different theories of modernity cherry-pick from among this list to offer their own definitive definition of the modern:

- capitalism, wage labor, new class compositions and the appearance of working and middle classes, the accumulation of profit, new and expanding modes of commodification and marketization
- nation-states, civil society, democratization, the administrative (bureaucratized) state, the identification of nation with ethnicity and vernacular languages
- colonialism and its economy of primitive accumulation and slavery, with its attendant forms of racism, exploitation, and brutalization
- new organizations of gender and sexuality, of the family and domesticity
- radical spatial restructuring (e.g., urbanization), especially in scalar (hierarchical) or concentric modes
- professionalization and industrialization of cultural production, the expansion of education and mass culture, secularism
- emergence of science (and reason as a value), enabling rapid, widespread technological development across all domains
- individualism in both economic and political terms
- acceptance (often unwillingly) of constant change ("all that is solid melts into air"), justified by a linear and progressive temporality.[a]

1 The modern is often elaborated in three terms: *modernization*, referring to the material processes that bring about the modern; *modernism*, referring to the expressions (culture, including theory) of the modern; and *modernity*, referring to the lived reality of the modern. For a more elaborate discussion, see Grossberg, *Cultural Studies in the Future Tense*.

But what if we began instead by pointing out that this list of modern features reproduces the very claim of the modern to prove its uniqueness? The list depends on a prior act in which the modern fractures the unity of social existence into separate domains: economic, political, social, and cultural. And it depends as well on a complex logic of identity and difference, in which, on the one hand, identity is assumed to precede difference ("essentialism" in contemporary theory), and, on the other hand, difference is understood in negative, usually binary, terms. The result is a constant redistribution of identities across a frontier border: modern versus tradition, civilized versus primitive, human versus nonhuman, culture versus nature, public versus private, self versus other, neighbor versus stranger, purity versus hybridity, Black versus white, male versus female, old versus young, and so on.

We might do better if we understand "the modern" to be a site where people struggle over the approbation that has, for so long, been attached to it. Then we can see that the modern is and always has been plural, that there are multiple ways of being modern. There is no completed list of necessary or possible elements, because each appearance of the modern offers itself as its own complex and changing set of *relations* among elements that cannot be specified in advance or from the outside.

Whatever features contribute to the claim of being modern only exist in the larger totality of the society; hence they will appear and operate differently in their respective modern societies. The modern is, then, more than a set of relations; it also is a set of struggles on the already organized ground that the past has bequeathed to a people. Any instance of a modern society is defined by the struggles among multiple overlapping, interacting, augmenting, hijacking, redirecting, competing, completing, limiting, and enabling elements, relations, and configurations. They have involved negotiation and compromise, struggle and wars; they are often forged on top of the blood, sweat, and lives of those who favor or oppose the changes, whether in the name of progress, tradition, freedom, or alternative lived realities. The modern is a contradictory and multidimensional, ongoing production of fragile relations among social institutions, ways of life, structures of experience, ways of thinking, and maps of intelligibility, feeling, and value.[2]

Modern societies can and do look very different because there is no necessary pregiven list of constituent elements, no necessary selection or

2 The social institutions include those of the state (governance), the economy (well-being), and culture (intelligibility, mattering, and belonging).

configuration of whatever enters into the complex unity of a particular instance of the modern, and no way of predicting where and how the struggles over the modern will occur. Each instance builds its own fluid relational structures while seeking to have some control over the struggles and to hold on to whatever stability it can manufacture.

If we accept that there are multiple ways of being modern, then neither modernity's emergence nor its identity can be simply identified with the West. It is unclear exactly when and where the modern begins because we don't know how many ways of being modern there are, or how they have been distributed in time and space. There have always been significant variations among European moderns, and as they were exported and imposed through colonial empires and global trade routes, they were transformed by the encounter with native—sometimes modern—traditions. In some cases, other possible ways of being modern were imagined and possibly even realized, for example, in Arab civilizations, and perhaps these played a crucial role in Europe's struggle to be modern.

DISRUPTIVE CRISES

Let's agree that theorizing goes on all the time, and that the set of deep theories is changing all the time. How can I structure the struggles over being modern so as to help provide greater depth to my backstory? Every society is constantly negotiating the competing and often contradictory needs, demands, and desires of various forces and constituencies. The stability of a society depends on its ability to balance these forces and maintain some equilibrium. I think—and I hope you will go along with me—that there are moments of **crisis** in any society (or civilization) when the existing social order is not only disrupted but comes face-to-face with the threat of chaos. Everything appears to change, and the equilibrium falls apart. The dominant ways of life are no longer viable, and the existing ways of thinking seem inadequate to the current tasks. The society faces challenges to its very identity and coherence, its ways of belonging together, its relations to other realities, its ways of expressing a shared humanity, its ways of knowing and thinking, and so on. The crisis plays out in struggles over how to respond to the changes, take back control of the new forces and arrangements, and find a new equilibrium to create a different social order.

Such crises signal transitional moments that can be experienced in different ways, distributed differentially across the society. They manifest themselves through experiences of social, psychological, and cultural fragmentation. They are experienced as a sense of lost unity and commonality, lost freedoms and subjective coherence, regardless of whether such unities and coherence ever actually existed. They make life "feel" vulnerable and outside of one's control, regardless of whether the agency to shape one's life and social conditions was ever real. They are often translated into a sense of being surrounded by different and strange—even abnormal—others, including peoples, cultures, and languages, regardless of whether the sort of homogeneity implied here ever actually defined society. They often result in a generalized inability to represent oneself, one's experiences, and (one's relation to) the world as truth, whether such truth was ever real. The resulting uncertainty contaminates not only knowledge and values but also the claims of authority, resulting in either irrational expressions of certainty or extreme forms of skepticism and nihilism, regardless of whether such stable authorities of truth and value were ever quite as uncontested and trustworthy as they may appear in retrospect. They are moments when the search for deep theories blossoms and flourishes, and they will serve as the turning points in my backstory.

Such crises can take two forms, depending on their temporality. In an **epochal crisis**, the transitions are generally more gradual and heterogeneous. The forces of change are so profound as to reverberate across every aspect of life, but they usually take time—centuries—to unfold and manifest their effects. These forces—for example, the invention of money, the Protestant Reformation, the creation of colonial empires, the discovery of new forms of power—operate and develop over centuries. I think the transition in Europe from the Middle Ages, through the Renaissance and the Enlightenment, into what was to become the modern world was a response to an epochal crisis, composed of numerous, fundamentally transformative developments. This complicated epochal crisis revolutionized thinking under the sign of reason (and science), as well as the conditions of everyday life. In the next five lectures, I will consider the ways thinking itself was transformed.

Organic crises are both more common and less coherent.[b] A society is overwhelmed by many crises, an accumulation of contradictions and interactions among multiple changes, shocks, problems, confrontations, and disruptions. But the heterogeneous elements are like pieces of a puzzle; they are condensed into a singular but fractured unity. This initiates a struggle that may last for decades, both to define the shape and content of the crisis, and to search for ways to either restore the old equilibrium or produce a new one. There will be passionate struggles among a number of proposed "settlements," or over the very possibility of any settlement, in which case chaos and insanity seem to rule. Organic crises are moments when the modern produces problems it cannot solve. They are often thought to be unique and unprecedented, and while each is different, they seem endemic to the European modern. While each crisis is claimed to pose unbearable sorrows and unbeatable foes, it provides the nourishing ground out of which new deep theories are born.

While epochal crises have continued to disrupt the world, I want to talk about four moments of organic crises, resulting in three versions of the modern and giving rise to three redirections of deep theory. The modern world as we understand it emerged out of the organic crises of the late eighteenth and early nineteenth centuries; these crises also set the stage for modern thought, predicated on the assumption of **relations** as the building blocks of reality, which dominated the nineteenth century.

The second organic crisis, often described as second modernity, resulted from the confluence of the many rapid changes of the late nineteenth century and the first half of the twentieth century and the struggles around them. It involved the Second Industrial Revolution (of electricity, communication, and transportation), the economic dominance of corporations, the growing economic disparities of capitalism in the Gilded Age and the many populist responses (including increased labor unrest and eventually labor unions), waves of migration both domestic and international, rapid urbanization, moments of passionate political polarization, consumer capitalism, and the emergence of a capitalist mass culture. Its contradictions led to the Great Depression and the Second World War, and, eventually, the realization that fascism (and the Holocaust) were not outside of modernity but its consequence. It culminated in what appeared to be a relatively stable settlement of so-called liberal democracy or a weak democratic socialism in the 1940s and 1950s. Predicated on an unprecedented compromise between capital and labor, linking wages to profits (to be overseen by the state), it brought major changes in domestic spaces and life, the interstate highway system, the growth of air travel, the Cold War, the rapid expansion of education, a new relation to youth and youth culture, and a revitalization of the spirit of resistant and bohemian cultures.

The crises of second modernity defined the trajectories of both thinking and creativity for most of the twentieth century. The "high modernists" were aware of living through a prolonged organic crisis.[3] But they were generally

---

3 In the arts, one thinks of the rise of high modernism best symbolized by the Bloomsbury Group and the postimpressionists. One thinks of James Joyce, Gertrude Stein, T. S. Eliot, Marcel Proust, Luigi Pirandello, and William Faulkner; of Pablo Picasso, Joan Miró, Marcel Duchamp, Wassily Kandinsky, Salvador Dalí, Marc Chagall, and Edvard Munch; of Igor Stravinsky and Arnold Schoenberg; and of Ludwig Mies van der Rohe

less optimistic about it than those of the first modernity, who had hoped to bring about a genuinely new, rational, and humane era, a promise that looked quite distant in the twentieth century.

A third crisis, sometimes called third modernity or postmodernity, emerged from the increasingly obvious failures of the liberal settlement and the proliferation of attacks on both the state and society more generally. These attacks, beginning in the immediate postwar years, included labor and political disputes, cultural conflicts, challenges to systems of social difference, and arguments around alienation and conformity. The crisis became widely visible in the 1960s as "the lefts," including the antiwar movement, the New Left and the countercultures, and anticolonial, antiracist, feminist, and gay struggles, as well as in the less visible mobilization of the New Right, an anticommunist conservatism that embraced both religion and capitalism (something that no conservatism had done before) while advocating for a minimalist state. In a sense, every settlement that was offered to the organic crisis proved to be unstable and ineffective. It was a battle between competing visions of how to be modern, of what it meant to be a modern society.

These battles have continued in new ways, constituting a fourth crisis around the turn of the third millennium, involving more polarized and populist appeals to "the people," largely fought out in the "culture wars." It arose out of the increasingly visible failures of the state (and, for some, the capitalist corporation) to live up to its liberal promises. It amplified the attacks on the state and extended them to both the global economy and the values of liberalism itself. It arose out of the growing anger of various minorities who saw little change in the systems of racialization, patriarchy, xenophobia, and so on. But it also arose out of the frustration of other marginalized groups, including rural and lower-middle-class people who resented the entitlements granted other groups and felt ignored by the elite, educated, cosmopolitan meritocracy. It has given rise to increasing cynicism about the possibilities of democratic governance and the political system that supposedly embodied it, increasingly contaminated by corporate elites (although these struggles have a more ambiguous relation to corporations and capitalism).

At times, various constituencies have rejected the authority of reason (and sometimes even science) and defined the struggle in terms of "identity politics":

---

and Frank Lloyd Wright. High modernism marked the end of the Victorian age and the beginning of the Edwardian age, but, as we shall see, it also involved significant turns in deep theory.

on the one hand, the denial that difference matters and that discrimination is real, and on the other hand, the affirmation of the absolute centrality of identity and power. The effects of such challenges were augmented by the growing integration into and saturation of digital technologies into every aspect of people's lives, transforming not only their habits of social life but also their ways of thinking and communicating.

This fourth crisis has ushered in, simultaneously, a sense of perpetual crises and of the banality of crisis, often resulting in exhaustion. It encompasses intellectual and social struggles claiming to reject the structures, processes, and logics not just of liberal modernity but, increasingly, of the value of modernity itself. And the imminent threat of catastrophic climate changes has certainly affected how we think about the relations between the present and the future, local and global, and even human and nonhuman. Hence, this organic crisis is also an epochal crisis, challenging the very desire for modernity. While this is not the first time the legitimacy of the modern has been questioned and alternatives offered, in the past such statements remained on the fringes of both politics and culture. Today, the omnipresence and even mainstreaming of such antimodern appeals results in an increasingly chaotic field of possibilities. While they are sometimes offered alongside appeals for nonmodern or Indigenous ways of life, time itself—especially the future—has become an unstable and contested reality.

Each crisis has elicited many seriously discordant responses and proposed settlements. Often the many differences and contradictions are simplified into a struggle between two homogeneous camps, hiding their heterogeneity. And deep theories are no exception; since the second modernity, there have been multiple deep theories or ways of thinking on offer, and they have rarely given up the ghost. That is to say, deep theories do not die as much as reshape themselves to the demands of later organic crises.

THEORY AND POLITICAL JUDGMENT

European (and Anglophone) modernities have offered profound benefits even as they enacted profound barbarities. For all the advances of these modernities, they have a long history of injustice, violence, and hatred. They have constructed categories—and subcategories within each—of differences among people and then rendered some groups infrahuman or nonhuman. Groups were displaced, made to stand apart from and measured against the also constructed position of "normality" and privilege. These differences provided sustenance and legitimation to the exploitation of resources, including both people and the earth, under the watchful eyes of a fetishized science and technology.

And modern thought has been deeply implicated in both sides of the modern. How do we come to terms with the relationship of thinking and power without reducing thought to a handmaiden of power? Such questions have become very public and urgent, especially when we are faced with authors and texts that proffer unacceptable, even deplorable, social and political positions, even if they were considered reasonable and appropriate in their own contexts. Some characters in my backstory were racist, sexist, misogynist, Eurocentric, and pro-colonialism. Immanuel Kant's racism is quite visible in some texts, but less obvious in others. Martin Heidegger's Nazism can be found in some of his key concepts. What is the impact of Friedrich Nietzsche's misogyny on his philosophy?

We are on dangerous ground here. There are more questions than answers, and these concerns often produce heated and passionate arguments. Many such criticisms have been made, often quite brilliantly, but they have, as a result, become too easy. Should one use contemporary norms to judge those who were thinking in different worlds? Yet, it is too easy to simply claim that they reflected their time (and should therefore be forgiven) or that texts were authored by people who were simply batshit crazy or evil (and should therefore be silenced). Are the politics of ideas, theories, or deep theories guaranteed? Are politics inscribed by origins, for all times, into the heart of an idea or in the words themselves readily available to the reader? Are ideas responsible for the people who hold them or the uses to which they are put?

My answer is no! But these are decisions—and readings—that one has to make as careful, critical readers trying to swim in the currents of thinking. That ideas are always related to their contexts is not the end of the story but the beginning, for the relations are themselves always complex and open to struggle, and sometimes the ideas can be remade to serve different ends. They not only are born from their contexts but also respond to them, representing them in different ways, offering different stories and different forms of agency. And they often prove fecund and productive for a range of intellectual projects in other contexts. Surely, the fact that modern notions of humanity and freedom were formulated out of contexts deeply defined by racisms, colonialisms, patriarchies, and so on cannot close the discussion of the possibilities of such ideas, nor can it assert their necessity.

We need to understand the work well enough to be able to identify where and how deeply it is "contaminated," how it presents itself, what role it plays and with what effects. Are they constitutive elements, that define the very spirit of the work, or are they more incidental features (perhaps crucial to one argument but not another)? Are there other ways of reading a theory that avoid the prejudices of their times? After all, theories do move between contexts, and they are always open to multiple readings. But sometimes you have to ask yourself: Is it worth the effort? Are there other ways to get what you need, from other theorists? That might require you to look beyond the texts and criticism, to see what others have taken from the author's work, how they have engaged with it, criticized it, and transformed it. The question for me is always, Does the author's work enable us to go on thinking, especially toward a more just world? Stuart Hall, the subject of the final lecture, described thinking as "wrestling" with theories, for it is in the struggle—a struggle that refuses simple judgments of celebration or condemnation—that the conversations of thinking continue, and its possibilities are (re)born. How do we find a path between the cynicism of a rush to judgment ("There is nothing save opinion / And opinion be damned") and the anxiety resulting from the realization that the road to better thinking is covered in weeds, each of which is "a singular knife"?[c]

NOTES

    a. For "all that is solid melts into air," see Marx and Engels, *Communist Manifesto*, in *Collected Works*, 6:487.

    b. Gramsci, *Selections from the Prison Notebooks*.

    c. Crane, "Once There Was a Man," in *Works of Stephen Crane*, 28; Crane, "The Wayfarer," in *Works of Stephen Crane*, 52.

PART II

Enlightenment

Routes

Beginnings

Every story you tell, even a backstory, has to have a beginning, however arbitrary it may be—since it could always go back further. Backstories usually remain invisible, glanced out of the corner of one's eye, but they haunt the stories being told. They are the soil out of which particular problems and questions emerge; they enable the mobilization of some traditions rather than others and set particular ways of thinking into play.

I choose to start with the premodern Middle Ages and the Renaissance of the fifteenth and sixteenth centuries and the simultaneous presence of the Islamic world. My historical summaries will be brief and selective, but hopefully they will be enough to set the stage for the last lecture's prefiguration of the modern, and for future lectures. If my account differs from what you have been taught about this period, you do not have to accept my version, but then I would like to think you might do a bit of research on your own. Reading *good* histories is always useful and usually fun.

The Middle Ages—obviously a name given retrospectively—began with the fall of the Western Roman Empire, by deterioration more than conquest, in the fifth century and lasted into the fifteenth century. A thousand years is a long time. (Just think of how much the world has changed in the past century.) It was marked by wars, famines, plagues, intra-church strife, civil conflict, and revolutions. It is usually represented as a barbaric and primitive time of European isolation, a devolution from the high accomplishments of the Greek and Roman Empires (both of which had their own high and low points): hence, the "Dark Ages."

As with all histories, the truth is more complicated, replete with many fluid and fractured realities and contradictions. The Middle Ages were marked politically by both the proliferation of small kingdoms or fiefdoms and the presence of vast empires (Byzantine, Holy Roman), and economically by feudalism/serfdom—with its enormous disparities in wealth—on the one hand, and the expansion of agricultural production, on the other. The church was a powerful political, legal, and economic force, but it was also the central power in the realms of culture and knowledge. While, for the most part, knowledge was subservient to faith (located in the monasteries, which later gave rise to the first European universities), the situation was not entirely bleak. Despite the often stifling power of the Vatican and the poverty of feudalism, the Middle Ages gave rise to great artistic (e.g., Gothic architecture) and philosophical (e.g., by individuals such as Augustine of Hippo, Anselm of Canterbury, Thomas Aquinas, Anicius Manlius Severinus Boethius, John Duns Scotus, Peter Abelard, and William of Ockham) achievements.

Much of the scholarship and thinking was defined by and limited to scriptural problems and a scriptural vision of the world understood as the great chain of being (a hierarchical structure of all forms of being, from God at the top to inert minerals at the bottom). This **scholasticism** is commonly caricatured as posing ridiculous theological dilemmas such as whether God could build something God could not move, or how many angels can dance on the head of a pin. But scholasticism was a rigorous mode of conceptual analysis focused on distinctions and contradictions, often with direct influences from classical Greek philosophy. But even this description underestimates the depth and breadth of the intellectual struggles that spanned centuries and set the stage for a cultural and intellectual revolution. These struggles often involved questions about the relations of the senses, reason, and faith, as well as considerations about the relevant grounds and methods of these different possible sources and orders of understanding, and contrasting claims of fallibility and certainty. They evoked arguments about the possible status of natural law—the principles and precepts guaranteed in advance according to the nature of humanity, the world, and God. Scholasticism was an epistemological project, turning every question into an epistemic query about the nature and possibilities of knowledge and truth, including their relation to faith. Many of these enduring, passionate, and erudite arguments enacted ongoing debates between followers of Saint Augustine's Neoplatonist privilege of the absolute certainty of faith (and religious intuition or revelation) and Saint Thomas Aquinas's neo-Aristotelianism, which foregrounded the possible rational foundations of faith, or at least the harmony of reason and faith.

At the same time, the Islamic world, both Arab and Persian, was flourishing and played a vital role in premodern Europe and the making of modern Europe. Islam was born in Saudi Arabia in the seventh century and rapidly spread across the Middle East, Persia, Northwest Africa (the Maghreb), and part of (Turkic) Asia, and, for over five hundred years, in the Iberian Peninsula, known as Al-Andalus. Its history was marked by numerous wars of conquest, as well as many internal struggles and civil wars, often fought over questions of religious doctrine and the choice of caliph, leader of the religion and inheritor of the mantle of Muhammad. During its history, there were in fact numerous competing dynasties and caliphates, and many competing interpretations of the Quran and Muhammad's teachings. (It was during these struggles that the major division between the Sunni and Shia branches of Islam emerged soon after Muhammad's death in 632.) The Islamic world made substantial advances in philosophy, medicine, astronomy, and mathematics, as well as philosophy. It was a major part of a geo-economic landscape built around water and seas: the Mediterranean, Indian, Red, Adriatic, and so on. It was part of the global Silk Road (second century BCE to 1492), a commercial and cultural trade route that connected Asia (China, India) with the Mediterranean, southeastern European (Balkan), and North African regions.

But the heart of this part of the story lies in Al-Andalus. Prior to the Islamic invasion beginning in 711, the peninsula was ruled by the Visigoths, a Romanized Teutonic tribe. Under Islamic rule, Al-Andalus became a center of financial and administrative innovation. It had a flourishing market but not capitalist economy and played an important role in connecting Europe to the rest of the world. Once established, it was not a particularly militaristic state, fighting mostly defensive wars.

Its strict religious hierarchy privileged Islam, followed by Judaism (both were Abrahamic religions for "people of the book"), followed by the infidels (including Christianity). For a long time, it embraced religious tolerance well beyond anything in Christian Europe, which allowed the practice of other religions but not in public. It also gave Jews (*dhimmis*) a privileged legal status, even welcoming them into state governance. This special relation to Judaism continued for centuries, so that when the Jewish inhabitants of Iberia were forcibly expelled along with Muslims in 1492, they were invited to join the Ottoman Empire (1299–1566).

Under the Caliphate of Córdoba, Al-Andalus became a center of culture and learning, encouraging cultural exchange and advancement. It built great libraries and established schools and universities, although these were configured differently than those that eventually emerged in Europe; it also disseminated its thought across the Islamic world, even as it infiltrated Europe. Its philosophy, mathematics, sciences, and so on were a major source of the knowledge that fueled European "progress." A large part of its scholarly efforts involved keeping alive and engaging with Greek and Roman thought, translating their works—and other (e.g., Hebraic) works—into Arabic and other languages.[1] Al-Andalus was thus a major archive of classical (Greco-Roman) antiquity not only for the Middle Ages—as scholastics within the church (sometimes referred to as schoolmen) often used these traditions to make theology into an epistemic project—but, ultimately, the Renaissance.

Al-Andalus ended around 1492, marking a new path for European development. The year 1492 was not just the year of Columbus's mistaken "discovery" of the "New World"; it also marked the completion of the reconquest of Iberia, which had begun as early as 1085 (as the caliphate began to disintegrate), by the new Catholic Kingdoms of Northern Spain (with assistance from the Holy Roman Empire). The victory of Queen Isabella I of Castille and her husband, King Ferdinand II of Aragon, was figured as the "expulsion of the 'Moors,'" the supposedly barbaric Islamic occupiers, although it also included the large Jewish population. (Both Semitic peoples were considered heretics by the Catholic victors and the Inquisition.) This diasporic moment produced a division within Judaism between the Sephardim (those who migrated south into the Arab and Persian worlds) and the Ashkenazim (those who migrated north, primarily into Eastern and Central Europe, where they were often forced to publicly renounce their religion [the *anusim*, or the coerced]).

The year 1492 (loosely speaking), then, is symbolic of the moment in which European identity began to take shape through the construction of a doubled difference: First, that year saw a revival of the historical "Jewish

---

1 Greek philosophy was itself strongly influenced by North African (e.g., Egyptian) thought.

question," in which Jews were seen as perpetual outsiders. Europe saw the Jew as a problem, a constant threat to the existing social order. It **racialized** Jews in what may have been the first racial difference (created by translating culture into biology). Second, 1492 often marks the *symbolic* beginning of European global exploration (primarily for precious metals) and the colonization and slave trade that bracketed it.[2] Both colonization and slavery required and constructed a further racialized difference between the West (Christian Europe) and the rest, the latter treated as primitive, inferior, or even nonhuman, by translating historical or geographic distance into biology. Finally, since 1492, Southern Europe (the Mediterranean) has often been seen as inferior to and less than Northern and Central Europe. It has always been tainted by its Islamic past, a past visibly inscribed in its art, architecture, and thought.

THE RENAISSANCE

From the fifteenth century to the early seventeenth century, parts of Europe underwent significant changes with which you are more familiar, although I am probably going to challenge some of what you think you know. The self-named *Renaissance* saw itself, and continues to be seen, as a new beginning, a new period of human history, a rebirth of human possibility, emerging out of the ignorance and darkness of the Middle Ages. But if the Dark Ages were not so totally dark, then the rebirth was probably more gradual than suggested, and the constructed difference between what was sometimes called the "modern" and the "traditional" was probably not so sharp.[3] Still, it was a period of profound social transformation and advances.[4]

The Renaissance expanded the capacities, status, and power of monarchically ruled city-states and eventually gave rise to early nation-states as the major sites of social order. The city-states (most famously, e.g., Venice, Florence, and Genoa in Italy and the cities that united within the Hanseatic League as well as the Swiss and Dutch Confederacies) were the first scenes of the emergence of capitalism. Modern forms of finance and debt were invented, which in turn

---

2 Portugal began exploring North Africa in 1414 and created its first colony in 1502 in India. The Middle Passage from Africa to the Americas began in 1619.
3 This partly explains the difficulty of ever confidently identifying the beginning of the modern.
4 There were, however, other—some coterminous, some older—civilizations that were, in many ways, at least as advanced as the Renaissance.

enabled the expansion of markets beyond the various scales of the local. The sciences were radically changing the practices and economies of agriculture. A new class—between serfs and aristocracy, the first middle class—emerged, bringing new political ideologies into the public conversations.

Mercantilism dominated the discussions and policies of economies, until it was eventually replaced by **classical economics** (e.g., Adam Smith) in the enlightenments. Mercantilism saw economies as zero-sum games (not everyone can win) built on a positive balance of trade (maximize exports, minimize imports). This often required active state intervention to protect the economy and to "acquire" the necessary imports (usually through colonization), especially precious metals or bullion, which served as the basis for money. The resulting substantial increase in gold and silver (largely through Spain), along with repeated crop failures and rising prices, resulted in constant economic crises from inflation to struggles over the ownership and use of land. Colonialism also opened the door for new imports, especially the raw materials needed for a slowly emerging manufacturing economy but also goods for the consuming upper classes (e.g., tea, chocolate, and tobacco).

No doubt, you are familiar with the Renaissance as a cultural revolution, made visible in the sciences, arts, and philosophy. These "advances" were partly enabled by the Protestant Reformation in the sixteenth century, which challenged the control of culture by the church, and by the developing technology of the printing press and its attendant distribution systems, which made new forms of knowledge (e.g., news, early novels) more widely available.

The Renaissance is often identified as the birth time of modern science, especially in the fields of astronomy and physics (e.g., the work of Johannes Kepler, Nicolaus Copernicus, and Galileo Galilei). Such work, referred to as **natural philosophy**, brought together two independent ideas: First, it foregrounded Aristotle's concept of **efficient causality**, which describes the world in terms of cause and effect, with a strong commitment to empirical observation. Previously, theology and scholasticism had emphasized the other forms of causality in Aristotle's philosophy.[a] These included **final causality** or **teleology**, which assumes that something is caused by that which it aims to become; and **formal and material causality** (particularly important in Neoplatonic tendencies), which postulates that a common substance is imbued with different forms—for example, everything from horseness to a soul—making it whatever it is. Second, influenced by Islamic culture, Renaissance thinkers took mathematics (including logic) to be the only universal language capable of describing the universe in its entirety.

However, the Renaissance is probably most known for its arts. Across all of Europe, but most famously in Italy and Holland, it invented a wide range of styles; for example, new forms of "realism," which affected even the fantastic and theological, allowed for the artistic consideration of more everyday situations and more mundane subjects. It changed the way people saw the world.[5] It drew attention to the richness of the viewer's experience, emphasizing, for example, meticulous detail, proportion, perspective, and even depth (through depiction of light and shadow through the use of chiaroscuro). This was the age of Hieronymus Bosch, van Eyck, Leonardo da Vinci, Hans Holbein, Albrecht Dürer, Botticelli, Raphael, Donatello, and Michelangelo, and, in literature, of William Shakespeare, Geoffrey Chaucer, Miguel de Cervantes, Dante Alighieri, Giovanni Boccaccio, John Milton, and John Donne.

The Renaissance also ushered in a revolution in philosophy in two ways: it accorded great authority (truth) to classical civilizations, especially their philosophers, and it "invented" a (new) humanism (visible in the works of Francesco Petrarch, Desiderius Erasmus, and so on). The two are related, since humanism was itself, in part, a return to the spirit of Socrates: it is said that when Socrates faced a dilemma or could not advance his own thinking, he turned to the Delphic oracle—a woman—above whose cave were inscribed the words "Know thyself."[6] Renaissance thinkers affirmed the uniqueness and importance of humanity, bringing together three ideas: first, the dignity of human beings, insofar as humanity was a source and measure of value in its own right, beyond being the servants of God, or having been made in the image of God; second, the unique status of human beings meant they were capable of creating knowledge and understanding the world; and, third, as a result, humankind was a worthy object of study.[7]

These cultural changes transformed the very concept of the individual, equating it with **subjectivity** as self-awareness, and **agency** as the capacity of will, implying the freedom to do otherwise. Not surprisingly, this assumption, as well as humanism more generally, was challenged by those who believed that all human life was determined by natural law, whether scientific or theological. It was further challenged by Michel de Montaigne (1533–92),

---

5 Compare the paintings of Jesus by Filiippo Lippi and Leonardo da Vinci.
6 The French philosopher Paul Ricoeur suggested that this command might also be translated as "Philosopher, know thy place in the universe" (personal conversation).
7 Renaissance humanism gave rise to *paideia*—the humanities or liberal arts.

who asked "What do I know?"[b] Montaigne's work, mostly engaged with the classics or the problems of his time, established the essay as a significant intellectual and literary form and began a revitalization of skepticism, an attitude of doubt and uncertainty, which had flourished in classical thought.

The most common story of the Renaissance represents it as a declaration of the independence of thought from the dominance and authority of the church, especially in cultural matters. It separated secular thought (including natural philosophy, rhetoric, and humanism) from theology and church doctrine. This was legitimated and structured, so the story goes, by a return to and revitalization of the authority, ideas, and ideals of classical antiquity.

But this image of the Renaissance as a revolution, as a complete break with the church and the Middle Ages, is neither useful nor accurate. The relation between these two periods was more complicated and prolonged. Many Renaissance thinkers did not reject church doctrine and authority on all matters, perhaps because they were well aware that if they crossed a certain line, the church would exact its revenge. The fate of Galileo Galilei offered a cautionary tale. In 1633, he was tried by the Inquisition in Rome for the heresy of his heliocentric theories; he was sentenced to prison but lived for the rest of his life under house arrest. He was forced to renounce his theories publicly, and several of his books were banned and burned.

Many Renaissance thinkers did not contradict the Christian belief that the universe is an ordered, purposive whole in the service of God and that, as a result, finding one's freedom meant finding one's proper place in it. On the other hand, to a larger extent than is commonly believed, the church went along with the emergence of philosophy and science, albeit grudgingly at times. This precarious balance was possible because Renaissance thinkers often claimed to be only supplementing the knowledge of the church: the classics addressed questions not encompassed by theology and scholasticism, or they allowed fuller and richer answers. After all, the church had already allowed appeals to and recognized the authority of Greek philosophy (Plato and Aristotle) as well as Roman rhetoric (Cicero), leaving the door open to thinkers who wanted to expand their utility, although it probably did not think it was opening the floodgates. Thus, the Renaissance limited—and sometimes even expanded—the authority of the church, while at other times it was able to build walls that separated the spheres of knowledge.

This complex relation between the Middle Ages and the Renaissance was carried out in institutional practices of knowledge preservation and production—especially in the Catholic universities (which were the only ones in the West). There was a struggle between two modes of education: an authoritarianism that demanded indoctrination, and a commitment to logic and rhetoric that valued the art of disputation (the liberal arts). These struggles of thinking—between dogma and empirical evidence, between authority and reason—were as much within the university and the church as between them. After all, many Renaissance intellectuals asserted the absolute authority of classical culture (especially the works of Aristotle), bringing thinking back to a matter of the interpretation of sacred texts. It was these very complications that set the stage, providing the conditions of possibility, for what was to come forth as the enlightenments. Now get ready for the carousel of thought to begin picking up speed.

NOTES
a. Aristotle, *Physica*, in *Works of Aristotle*, vol. 2.
b. Montaigne, "Apology for Raimond de Sebonde," in *Essays of Montaigne*, 263.

Enlightenment(s)

My backstory continues with the European Enlightenment, a heterogeneous intellectual and philosophical movement from the seventeenth century into the early nineteenth century. It was shaped by continuing tumultuous changes that fueled an increasing crisis of faith, calling into question many of the most stable institutions and certainties, liberating and expanding possibilities, and often eliciting a sense of paranoia.

The continuing expansion of colonialism and the slave trade resulted in new markets and commodities, in which Europeans increasingly dominated the global economy. New technologies such as the steam engine, the cotton gin, and the Jacquard loom increased the efficiency of labor and ushered in industrialization and factory production. The new forces of production required, both qualitatively and quantitatively, new workers, bringing peasants who farmed both common and private lands into the cities, where they often lived in squalor.[1]

---

1 In England, peasants living and working on farms (often owned by absentee landlords) were forced off the land by laws aiming to create the necessary labor

A new understanding of economics emerged to support (and sometimes criticize) these developments. "Classical economists" (Adam Smith, David Ricardo, Jean-Baptiste Say, Thomas Robert Malthus, John Stuart Mill) identified the "wealth of nations" not with the private treasure (bullion or land) of a ruler but, instead, with the national income of labor. Capitalism involved the ever-increasing accumulation of wealth (profits) through labor as the source of value. This necessitated an effective division of labor, resulting in increasingly antagonistic class differences. The classical economists argued that markets were self-regulating and that free (unregulated) markets—the heart of liberalism—were the most efficient for the accumulation of economic value (capital).

This growing class consciousness was accompanied by the reconfiguration of many forms of identifications and social relations, including domesticity and gender identities, racial and ethnic distinctions, and new "national" identities. The diminishing power of the anciens régimes—feudalism, monarchy, and the church—enabled the emergence of nation-states, with their new sovereignty guaranteed in the Peace of Westphalia (1648), preventing both the church and empires (operating together in the Holy Roman Empire) from crossing sovereign national borders in the name of protecting their own constituencies and interests. It was a period of enormous political upheaval, from the English Civil Wars (1642–51) to the American and French Revolutions.

These were the first stirrings of demands for the rule of law, the distribution of power (ultimately as democracy), and the rights of citizenship. The Enlightenment reimagined the individual as a subject at the center of political life. Rather than being defined by their subjection to the power of a ruler (with absolute power over death), this new individual was the possessor of inherent civic and political rights (and responsibilities). The struggles over such matters had limited success: although selectively distributed and only partially realized, they set in motion profound changes, especially when linked to Renaissance humanism, which increasingly claimed the autonomy of the individual: self-determination, independence, and freedom, which, for example, provided the justification for the sanctity of private property and contractual relations.[2]

---

force. Read Charles Dickens for a description and indictment of the effects of industrialization.

2 Michel Foucault, discussed in Lecture 29, observes the emergence of a new mode of power: discipline, which imposes a system of norms on individual behavior through surveillance.

Enlightenment thinkers refused any authority other than that of current humanity and its capacity for knowledge, including that of classical antiquity. Enlightenment thought can be defined by four commitments. The most fundamental was that humans have **Reason**, which gives them the capacity to understand the world and attain truth. Reason was a natural and inherent attribute of human beings, of the mind. César Chesneau Dumarsais, one of the French encyclopedists, claimed that "reason is to the philosopher what grace is to the Christian."[a]

The new definition and celebration of reason changed how thought was shared, largely leaving behind commentaries, commentaries on commentaries, guides for living a good life, and the occasional autobiography.[3] The Enlightenment valued treatises of original thinking, presenting "new" ideas and findings. As a result, almost all Enlightenment thinking (and the modern works that followed it) presented itself as starting over, as forging a new way of thinking (and thereby defining the proper use of Reason). Everything that was done before was either wrong or irrelevant.[4] Reason by itself is capable of discovering truth, without granting any authority to tradition, common sense, or anyone else who may have written on the same matters. Reason is in and of itself the only way to discover truth, the only authority.

While there were significant disagreements among Enlightenment thinkers about the exact nature of Reason, most accepted the principle of sufficient reason (Gottfried Leibniz, 1646–1716), which states that there is a reason or cause for everything that exists (and, in some versions, for everything that does not exist as well).[b] The search for truth is the search for such reasons or causes, on the assumption that Reason was capable of discerning or discovering them. But it follows that in addition to studying the world—both nature and humanity—one would have to study Reason itself, to understand its capabilities and limits as precisely as possible, by the use of Reason. (A bit of a paradox?)

3 In the Judaic tradition, for example, the Mishnah collects the commentaries on the Torah; the Gemara collects the commentaries on the Mishnah (together they constitute the Talmud, the rabbinic teachings); and Moses Maimonides compiled the key lessons of the Talmud into the Mishneh Torah.

4 This is a trope, which in the late nineteenth century gave rise to the notion of the avant-garde (writing for the future). It is a celebration of the new. The sense of one's work as a break with the past (and even the present) eventually becomes an almost universal sign of the modernity of modern thought.

In his essay "Addressing the Question: What Is Enlightenment?," published in a popular magazine, Immanuel Kant defined the Enlightenment as an awakening from the long sleep and barbarity of the Middle Ages, as humanity's "release from [its] self-incurred tutelage."[c] He called on people to have the courage to use Reason, to dare to think for themselves. This was the obligation the Enlightenment placed on them: "To renounce [Enlightenment] for posterity is to injure and trample on the rights of mankind."[d]

Enlightenment thinkers were not professional scholars. None had academic careers or taught in universities on a permanent basis until Kant, at the beginning of modernity. René Descartes was a soldier; David Hume was a diplomat. They wrote mostly in the vernacular rather than Latin, the language of the church and the classics, because they thought that such matters were of concern to all humanity and therefore were something in which all humanity, with the proper education, should participate. As Descartes wrote, natural philosophy, which included his own work as well as Galileo's, will "enable us to enjoy without any trouble the fruits of the earth."[e] The search for truth was considered available to anyone who was capable of reason, and everyone (not really, only European white males) had that capacity, even if it was not yet actualized. There is, consequently, a striking mixture of arrogance and humility in many Enlightenment thinkers.

The second commitment, often assumed to be fundamental, was **individualism**. The individual mattered *because* Reason belonged to individuals (as did other capacities and rights). The third commitment identified Reason with **natural philosophy**, that is, the emerging **new science**. While descriptions of science varied widely (many bore little resemblance to the actual practice of science), science defined the proper use of Reason; the methods of natural science would elucidate not only the nature of nature but also the nature of human existence and, ultimately and most urgently, the nature of Reason itself. The success of these mathematically based forms in astronomy and physics was there for all to see, highlighting an account of the world that allowed humanity to intervene in and control its environment, improving its conditions of life. If people were willing to use Reason, they would understand the totality of the world and their place in it. Science's success depended on its refusal to think beyond the capacities of Reason, its refusal to appeal to authority, superstition, the supernatural, faith, or imagination. But it also had to assume that nature was "good" because, otherwise, the very existence of the world might be aimed to deceive us.

The final commitment was to history as **progress**. Enlightenment thinkers affirmed that human reality changed over time, even while they affirmed the fundamental stability of natural existence. Such changes were generally slow, interrupted occasionally by revolutionary moments, such as the Enlightenment itself. Change was understood as a straight line moving in a single direction, almost always forward. Most Enlightenment thinkers had an unshakable faith in progress—if not in its reality, then at least in its likelihood. The use of Reason would make the world a better place, enabling people to enjoy the fruits of their labor, which would make human beings better; humans would then increase their use of Reason, gaining more knowledge and making the world even better, and so on until paradise was achieved. But, as one slightly cynical commentator put it: "Alas, if all humans were wise/ And had more good will / The world would be a Paradise. / Now it is mostly a hell."[5,f] Rather than attempting to recapture a golden past (as the Renaissance did) or await an inevitable apocalyptic future (as in Catholicism), the Enlightenment saw Reason as the agency of change.

These four commitments raised a number of crucial questions for Enlightenment—and subsequently modern—thinkers to address, of which I want to highlight three. The first was fairly straightforward, already expressed by our cynic: If people, by their very nature, possess the capacity for Reason, if Reason is the essence of humanity, why do so few of them actually use it, especially since it promises to make the world (and their lives) better? How is it that the irrational appears to be real to so many people, who hold on to faith, superstition, and the supernatural? Why do people obey authorities other than their own Reason, authorities that are themselves irrational? Why does Reason not dominate society? Why is the world not already much closer to paradise?

Most of the answers offered by the Enlightenment focused on matters of culture and society, on everyday habits and common sense, and on the relations of power that repressed the ability and desire to reason. One can almost predict the responses: the use of Reason is hard work and people are lazy; people are cowards and afraid of where Reason might lead them; people fear the power of existing institutions of authority—for example, the church and the state. But given all these reasons why Reason was not prevailing, how was the Enlightenment itself possible? Perhaps the very possibility of the free use of Reason depended on a system of power that understood or even needed the benefits of Reason, although any such concession would most likely demand

5 These words by Dirck Rafaelsz Camphuysen, a Dutch artist and thinker (1586–1627), are engraved on a table in Baruch Spinoza's house in Rijnsburg.

that people continue to obey the law in practice, even if Reason might question the authority of law or the rationality of a particular law.

The Enlightenment's most common solution was to argue that people had to be educated to use Reason; education would give them the courage to use Reason. But there is something paradoxical about this argument. If the point of Reason is to think for yourself, then you have to be free to choose your own way. So how can you tell people that they have to think for themselves? If people try to think for themselves because they are told this is what they are supposed to do, if they seek education because someone has told them to seek it, are they freely choosing to embrace Reason? How can you teach people to think for themselves?

The second problem was epistemological, a matter of self-consciousness. How can human beings study human being? How can humanity be both the object and the subject of knowledge? How can human beings know themselves? How can Reason know itself? This problem had two faces: solipsism and skepticism. While these problems had some presence in classical and Renaissance philosophy, they had a new urgency in Enlightenment thought, and after.

Solipsism raises the problem of community or sociality (in more contemporary terms, intersubjectivity and communication). It derives primarily from the individuation of Reason: If Reason is the essence of human nature and the locus of truth, and it is entirely invested in the individual, then how are social relations possible? How can I know that someone else is a human being, that they have Reason? How can I know that what I know is what another person knows, that their Reason is at all like mine? If knowledge of the world is individuated, then how do I get outside of my own individual world? If all I have access to is the content of my mind, am I locked into a reality available only to me?[6]

The mirror image of solipsism is **skepticism**, which embraces doubt and uncertainty. If Reason is located in the individual, how do I know that what I know is true, that reason actually captures a reality outside of my individual mind? How can I know the truth of my own knowledge? How can I know that I know anything? How do I know that what I think is reason is actually

6 Gottfried Wilhelm Leibniz (1646–1716) embraced solipsism: the universe is composed of monads—unique, rational, self-enclosed beings, with no relation to anything outside of themselves, whether a world or other monads.

Reason? How can anyone prove the authority of Reason itself? Can you see how you might get caught up in these questions if you begin where the Enlightenment did?

The third problem was both epistemological and political, questioning the nature of the relationship between the particular and the universal. I will call the dominant position of the Enlightenment **synecdochical universalism**, and I apologize for its ugliness and unpronounceability. A synecdoche is a trope that substitutes a part for the whole. Simply put, Enlightenment thinking assumed that its knowledge (as defined by the new science) and concepts—including its definition of humanity—were universal. Humanity is always and everywhere defined by Reason. And since Reason was defined by the European Enlightenment itself, it defined universal human nature by identifying it with the Enlightenment. That is, it generalized from and universalized a particular—highly selective—instance of humanity, living in one small corner of the inhabited world.

There was a frightening circularity at play here: for example, if to be human is to exercise Reason, people who do not exercise Reason (as understood by the Enlightenment) are therefore not human. Problematically, since women and children were assumed not to act according to Reason, they should have been excluded from humanity, but an exception was made for those who were capable of being educated into Reason (even if they were not allowed to be). The result was that those peoples and cultures "discovered" (and usually colonized) by the European powers were, by definition, nonhumans or, at best, inferior humans. This logic "justified" the brutality of colonization and slavery, but it also fueled debates about the civilizing functions of European global expansion.[7]

The logic of synecdochical universalism did not disappear from the modern thought of the nineteenth and twentieth centuries. On the contrary, it continues to plague thought in the twenty-first century. It is still too easy to project the image of a select group—most commonly, that of white, middle-class, educated men—as the proper figure of humanity. But can you imagine a different relation of the particular and the universal?

7 It was not coincidental that the Enlightenment arose in the Christian world, since Christianity is, like capitalism and science, a self-expanding, proselytizing, and universalizing endeavor.

Two major epistemologies—definitions of Reason—dominated the Enlightenment (and continue to dominate even today): rationalism and empiricism. **Rationalism** argues that the mind itself is the true source of knowledge, independently of any sensory inputs (observations) from the world of experience. Knowledge depends only on the innate capacities of the mind. Epistemic authority derives from the forms of reasoning "hardwired" into the mind. Reason grasps, on its own, substantial truths about the world. And true knowledge demands certainty; knowledge can be only certain knowledge. **Empiricism**, on the other hand, claims that knowledge comes from our experience of the world, with only minimal dependence on the cognitive capacities of the mind itself; epistemic authority depends on the use of the senses and what can be discovered through them. Knowledge is only knowledge if it enhances the capacity to engage with the world in repeatable ways.[8]

Enlightenment thinkers usually proposed a metaphysical theory alongside their epistemology, although it was sometimes implicit. Metaphysics inquires into the "nature of reality," but this can be parsed into two related questions, each with two possible responses. First, what is the "substance" of reality? The Enlightenment chose between **materialism**, which claims that reality is composed entirely of matter (although how matter is defined is itself up for grabs), and **idealism**, which claims that reality is composed of some immaterial substance, such as spirit, mind, or ideas. Second, how many **substances** constitute reality? **Monism** argues that there is only one substance, and the problem is how to explain the appearance of the other. **Dualism** argues that two substances (as described earlier) exist, and the problem is the nature of their relation. We might represent the intellectual geography of the Enlightenment as shown in table 4.1.

Having presented something like the standard view of the Enlightenment as a single, stable, and relatively coherent movement and body of thought, even if somewhat heterogeneous, I want to disrupt it with two counterclaims.

FIRST COUNTERCLAIM

There was never a single coherent or consistent movement; there were always and only multiple enlightenments, each shaped by its own geographies,

8 See lectures 5 and 6.

TABLE 4.1 The Dominant Field of Choices of the Enlightenments

	Rationalism	Empiricism
Monism	Spinoza	Hobbes (materialist)
	Leibniz	Berkeley (idealist)
Dualism	Descartes	Locke
		Hume

cultures, and social conditions, each responding to the changes it confronted with whatever intellectual resources it could muster. And there were (and are) other enlightenments in other places, including the colonized worlds. The differences are often as important as the commonalities, if not more so.

Such a view challenges the long-standing assumption that all the enlightenments were (and are) composed of the same necessary elements (my four commitments), stitched together into a seamless, harmonious whole. Instead, each enlightenment was itself a heterogeneous set of elements or ingredients in various relations. I can enumerate some of the "ingredients" that are mixed in different ways and different proportions to produce different enlightenments. And often, what appears to be the same ingredient in different enlightenments may not be; the nature, meaning, and implications of any component will vary according to its place in the totality of a particular enlightenment. And they may further differentiate because many of the ingredients are themselves a composition, a heterogeneous mixture of other ingredients.

Every enlightenment is a way of thinking composed of the many and often difficult relations established among the elements. Consequently, there are so many questions: Are the same concepts substantively or even formally equivalent in different enlightenments? Do they all have the same status? Are they necessarily or contingently connected? How are the relations determined in each one's specific context? The following is the beginning of a list of possible ingredients. Not every enlightenment will include all of these (and many will include others).

1 Reason, which has many forms and sensory registers
2 Humanism, as particular valuations of humanity
   a. Individualism, as the locus of freedom and rights
   b. Subjectivity, as (self-)consciousness

3 Logics of difference—usually binary and negative (dualist) as a formal condition of knowledge and existence[9]

4 Linear, hierarchical, and unidirectional conceptions of time and space, in which time rather than space is the active site of change

5 Universality.

Consider the assumption of humanism, which was central in many of the dominant European enlightenments. In fact, they constructed a "hyperhumanism" by condensing or equating at least five discrete assumptions, implicitly assuming that their relations were necessary and universal: (1) anthropocentrism—the claim that humans are uniquely valued; (2) individualism—the fundamental existence of the human is the individual as a particular mode of embodiment; (3) subjectivity—consciousness is the locus of an individual's own experience; (4) freedom—the autonomy of the subject; and (5) agency—the human being as the site of action and creativity because it is capable of doing otherwise. While some critics might abandon humanism, more often they imagine different configurations.

Some of these concepts (e.g., anthropocentrism, dualism) present simple choices—either you accept or reject it, while others (e.g., universality, difference) can be actualized in different ways. Each concept, and the enlightenment in which it functions, is a geohistorically specific imagined composition that might be directed into any number of ethical and political visions. This makes each enlightenment subject to its own internal struggles even as the various enlightenments struggle with each other. The critique of "enlightenment thinking" is a complicated endeavor, which, if done carefully, can open up creative possibilities for thinking, even as it has closed off other paths of thought.

SECOND COUNTERCLAIM

The traditional view of the Enlightenment reproduces a logic of difference common among most of the enlightenments: a logic that understands difference in binary terms, and the relation between the terms as simple and direct opposition or negation. The multiple enlightenments are condensed into a single self-contained unity that stands outside and against its opposite or, more accurately, two opposites: the past (Dark Ages) and the Counterenlightenment, each assumed to be relatively homogeneous. But what if the

9 This might be traceable to Aristotle's law of noncontradiction (A or not-A).

border between enlightenments and their others was more contingent and porous, recognizing that the supposed opposites interacted with and shaped each other? And what if those others were never as homogeneous as they often are assumed to be?

Grasping the enlightenments requires also grasping the **counter-enlightenments**, which involved a highly disparate collection of thinkers and artists who stood against the fetishism of reason (although individual thinkers may have opposed other elements as well). Unlike the enlightenments, they did not name themselves as a single, unified project.[10] Enlightenment thinkers responded by accusing them of doing just what they said they were doing: propounding versions of **relativism, irrationalism, vitalism,** and **organicism.**

Many counter-enlightenment figures stood alone, uncaptured by any single affiliation, or else captured by too many. Some were aligned with particular movements of thought. Consequently, it is impossible to present a coherent picture of a singular Counter-Enlightenment, and I cannot do justice to the multiplicities and disunities of the counter-enlightenments. While, like the enlightenments, they interrogated human nature and humanity's relation to the world, they followed radically different paths and arrived at strikingly different answers.

Still, for the sake of time and space, I will describe some of the general directions in which the counter-enlightenments set off. In rejecting the status of Reason, many counter-enlightenment figures saw the new science as mere "beekeeping" (keeping everything in its proper compartment). They accused the enlightenments of being mechanistic, atomistic, unfeeling, and dehumanizing. At the very least, they wanted to expand thinking beyond the cognitive or replace it with the realities of emotion, will, feeling, and so on. Rather than looking for the general, the predictable, and the universal, they favored the unique and the particular. They juxtaposed intuition to logic, emphasized the transcendent powers of imagination, and connected theory to the common concerns and possibilities of life.

The counter-enlightenments found the essence of humanity in **poiesis**— creativity, imagination, and spirituality—and privileged language over mind because language was a process of self-realization, self-affirmation, and even self-determination. In the search for true subjectivity, its participants looked

---

10 Although the term has a history stretching back at least to Nietzsche, its current use is often credited to Beck, *Early German Philosophy*, and Berlin, "The Counter-Enlightenment," in *Against the Current*, 1–32.

to expressions of the "irrational" life sentiments. Figures as different as the Marquis de Sade (1740–1814) and Jonathan Swift (1667–1745) emphasized the darker sides of human life, even going so far as to invoke the madness of reason.

Counter-enlightenment thinkers rejected the optimism of inevitable (almost mechanical) progress in favor of an organic, unfolding growth. They proffered visions of decline such as the suggestion, often attributed to Voltaire (born François-Marie Arouet, 1694–1778) by many translators of *Candide*, that the world—and life—is a shipwreck, and the cyclical histories favored, for example, by Giambattista Vico (1668–1744).[11]

Many of its leading figures were deeply concerned with the political upheavals of their time, especially the French Revolution, but their responses varied widely. Some supported the revolution, even helped to provide its intellectual foundations; some supported it until the Terror (1793–94); and some rejected it entirely. Many counter-enlightenment thinkers were liberals, supporting freedom, democracy, justice, and education. Others were deeply conservative and were later (mis?)read and taken up by totalitarian and irrational forces. These often religious (often Catholic) movements defended forms of tribalism, provincialism, and nationalism against the growing cosmopolitanism of the enlightenments. These multiple politics were exemplified by Edmund Burke (1729–97), who was read, even at the time, as both a liberal and a conservative. He supported many of the demands of the American and French Revolutions but did not support the revolutions themselves. He valued reason; but, equally, he valued custom, experience, collective wisdom (tradition), and religion.

Many counter-enlightenment figures emphasized the affective unity of community and a more organic conception of social life over individualism. Rather than simply seeing nature as benevolent, logical, ordered, and comprehensible, they foregrounded its wild, varied, unruly, and spontaneous—and, consequently, creative—side, offering a more vitalist conception, highlighting its beauty and spirit.

The counter-enlightenments existed most visibly in a number of aesthetic movements. I might start, somewhat arbitrarily, with the Baroque style, which flourished in southern Europe during the seventeenth century and the first half of the eighteenth century, especially in the visual arts and music.

11 The origin of this quote from Voltaire is contested. "Life Is a Shipwreck, but We Must Not Forget to Sing in the Lifeboats," April 22, 2018, https://quoteinvestigator.com/2018/04/22/lifeboat/.

Baroque art sought to produce a sense of shock and awe in its audiences as a way toward true subjectivity. It did so, often with the support of the Catholic Church, with overwhelming ornamentation and colors, dense details, and odd juxtapositions. It often portrayed the world as a stage on which everything had gone mad.[12]

Sturm und Drang (meaning "storm and stress") was a German literary movement in the mid-eighteenth century that emphasized extreme emotions as the door to subjectivity. Its leading theorist was Johann Georg Hamann (1730–88), a passionate critic of the enlightenments' secularism.[13] Only spiritual revelation could provide truth and knowledge. Hamann emphasized the joyous possibilities of the emotional and spiritual life, and he, more than anyone, made language rather than knowledge the primary concern of philosophy.[g] Many counter-enlightenment thinkers, including Hamann's student Johann Gottfried Herder (1744–1803) and Friedrich Schiller (1759–1805), continued such arguments, greatly influencing the *Geisteswissenschaften*.

The most influential and well-known counter-enlightenment aesthetic was Romanticism, which, broadly understood, flourished from the late eighteenth century to the mid-nineteenth century in most of Europe. Its influence was felt across all the arts. Consider literature, where its representatives are legion: William Blake, Johann Wolfgang von Goethe, Samuel Taylor Coleridge, Edgar Allen Poe, Percy Bysshe Shelley, Henry David Thoreau, Ralph Waldo Emerson, William Wordsworth, George Gordon Lord Byron, John Keats, Charlotte and Emily Brontë, Emily Dickinson, and so on. The Romantics rejected not only science but also the industrialization of life that it enabled. Consider Blake's poetic rejection of science:

> May God us keep
> From Single vision
> And Newton's sleep![h]

And Wordsworth's even more sweeping rejection of both science and art in favor of the living heart.

> Enough of science and of art
> Close up these barren leaves

12 While the Baroque was not directly linked to any deep theories, Spinoza has been seen as a counter-enlightenment, even a Baroque, theorist. Also, Leibniz and even Francis Bacon have sometimes been linked to it.

13 He is said to have introduced Kant to both Hume and Jean-Jacques Rousseau.

Come forth and bring with you a heart
That watches and receives.[i]

They often celebrated the medieval past and the heroic individual. Their art was based on intuition and emotion, often extreme emotions. They quested after a spontaneous and authentic subjectivity, which went hand in hand with a highly idealized sense of beauty and of the natural world.

Johann Wolfgang von Goethe's (1749–1832) Faust is one of the most powerful archetypes of Romanticism. In earlier versions, Faust proposes to sell his soul to the devil in exchange for knowledge; in Goethe's version, the devil propositions Faust, who has become dissatisfied with the limits of knowledge. Faust seeks the essence or meaning of life, which the devil offers by taking him on a journey through the realms of experience. The height of humanity is to be found in its endless capacity and unquenchable quest for experience. As Goethe writes, "Each one sees [in the world] what he carries in his heart."[j] But like many Romantics, Goethe also saw the darker side of humanity: "Our planet is the mental institution of the universe." And, even darker: "Know thyself? If I knew myself, I'd run away."[14]

But no thinker stands in for the counter-enlightenments more than Jean-Jacques Rousseau, who is worth a closer look. He was born in the Republic of Geneva, part of the Swiss Confederation, on June 28, 1712, into a middle-class, educated, and artisan-based family and died in the Kingdom of France on July 8, 1778. He was a watchmaker who wrote extensively about music and composed numerous musical works. He wrote novels (*Julie, or the New Heloise*, 1761) and what was perhaps the first modern autobiography (*Confessions*, 1782). His most famous intellectual works include *Discourse on the Arts and Sciences* (1750), *Discourse on the Origin and Foundation of Inequality among Men* (1754), *Discourse on Political Economy* (1755), *Emile, or On Education* (1762), and *The Social Contract* (1762). He had a profound influence on the arts, education, political theory, and literature. He is often described as a major inspiration for the French Revolution and was compared to Socrates by Schiller.[k] He was befriended and repudiated by other thinkers, including Denis Diderot, Voltaire, and David Hume.

14 The authenticity of these two quotes is uncertain. The former can be found on the website Goodreads, https://www.goodreads.com/quotes/12884-we-do-not-have-to-visit-a-madhouse-to-find. The latter can be found in Douglas and Strumpf, *Webster's New World Dictionary of Quotations*, 271.

Rousseau spent much of his life moving from one place to another, often economically insecure and living off the generosity of others (including a number of mistresses); he suffered from various mental health problems (apparently including severe hypochondria and paranoia). Yet he repeatedly turned down offers of royal pensions. He was constantly threatened with arrest or deportation (as well as having his books banned), primarily (but not only) because of his "heretical" and often contradictory religious views. He was a theist and a committed Calvinist for most of his life, affirming the vital role of religion in people's lives and the life of society; he defended the spiritual origins and nature of humanity against materialism, even as he decried class inequalities. But he also defended religious tolerance; he even suggested that all religions were equally capable of leading people to salvation—a heresy referred to as *indifferentism*. At the same time, while defending religion, he attacked most of the religions of his day; he emphasized that God was concretely and spiritually present in the beauty of the world, which served as an inherent good against the debilitating influence of society. Moreover, he argued that a truly religious person could not offer themselves as a loyal citizen in the service of existing corrupt states. He advocated for a radical democracy and strongly opposed the Atlantic slave trade but staunchly defended the patriarchal family.

He had a deeply ambivalent—even fraught—relation to the enlightenments. His fundamental concern was universal human nature: What are the possibilities of human existence? He questioned the enlightenments' *absolute* commitment to Reason as well as their assumption of individuality because he could not see how individualism could arrive at community (society) unless Reason belonged to "the General Will."[1] And he rejected the illusion of progress; quite the contrary, Europe was falling ever deeper into inhumanity and barbarity.

By locating the enlightenments in a history of human civilizations, Rousseau became one of their most articulate critics. He agreed on the value of original thought and criticism; he agreed that reason was necessary for the restructuring of social and political institutions. He championed the importance of the free thinker who was not concerned with the rewards of fashion—even though he thought fashion had become a dominant force in the enlightenments and asked, "Why should we build our happiness on the opinions of others, when we can find it in our own hearts?"[m]

Rousseau started with the individual human being, understanding the individual as the whole person in a "state of nature," defined by feeling or sentiments rather than thought.[n] Yet it was humanity as a whole that was divine, not the individual; only humanity itself is perfectible. He constructed something like a developmental history, an imaginary one to be sure, of social life. The "state of nature" was his normative guide, despite it being "a condition which no longer exists, which perhaps did not exist, which probably never will exist, and concerning which it is nevertheless necessary to have some accurate notions in order to assess properly our present state."[o] Unlike Thomas Hobbes's state of nature, in which humans are naturally selfish and vicious, in Rousseau's state of nature (which he sometimes described as the state of being of the "savage"), people live with an individual morality built on instincts and emotion, based on compassion and empathy in the face of suffering. In such a world, people are free, independent, and good. Rousseau referred to this as *amour de soi* (love of self).[p] The character of these individuals is transparently available to everyone, and they live on the basis of natural habits. They seek their own virtue as an expression of their inner self, driven by sentiment rather than thought.

Rousseau contrasted this with the barbarity of Europe, which did not end with the Middle Ages; it was the result of the development of civilization—a state of social existence in which particular norms, habits, and relations of difference and power are reified so as to deny the free possibilities of life. Civilization corrupts the state of nature; it introduces "fatal inequality . . . among men [*sic*] by distinctions among their talents and by the degradation of their virtues."[q] It corrupts individuals by making them into mere artifices of their society, transforming "love of self" into amour propre (vain self-love) in the name of morality. It corrupts sociality "by inspiring in [people] the desire to please one another with works worthy of their mutual approbation."[r] In civilization, people seek the approval of others and judge their own value or worth accordingly. And Rousseau viewed the enlightenments as deeply implicated in this fall from grace: "The sciences, letters and the arts . . . spread garlands of flowers over the iron chains which weigh men down, snuffing out in them the feeling of that original liberty for which they appear to have been born and make them love their servitude by turning them into what we call civilized people."[s]

Character becomes opaque and unnatural, and virtue is abandoned. This is the decadence of civil society, "the lethal enlightenment of civil man," the abandonment of morality.[t] This corruption, degradation, and barbarity are the result of progress—both intellectual and material. They have crushed virtue and individual liberty; they are inimical to the well-being of humanity. Thus, against enlightenment, Rousseau argues

It is reason which gives rise to vain self-love, and it is reflection which strengthens it. Reason is what turns man back onto himself; reason is what separates him from everything which upsets and afflicts him. It is philosophy which isolates him. Thanks to philosophy he says in secret at the sight of a man suffering: "Perish if you wish; I am safe." Nothing troubles the calm sleep of the philosopher and drags him from his bed any more, other than dangers to all of society. One can slit the throat of his fellow man under the philosopher's window with impunity; he has only to put his hands over his ears and argue with himself for a little while in order to prevent nature, which rebels within him, from identifying with the one being murdered. Savage man does not have this admirable talent and, for lack of wisdom and reason, is always surrendering to the first feeling of humanity, without thinking about it. In riots and street quarrels, the populace crowds together, while the prudent man moves away. It is the riff-raff and the women of the market who separate the combatants and prevent decent folk from cutting each other.[u]

But Rousseau offered another possibility: only in a different kind of civil society can humanity return to its true moral perfection. Such a civil society would be based on a social contract, built on self-preservation and reason, in which people agree to abandon their natural rights as individuals (and renounce the possibility of returning to the state of nature) in order to create a society of true citizens. Recognizing the benefits of cooperation and the possibility of true democracy, people agree to submit to the authority of the general will (or what is sometimes translated as the common good) and thereby achieve a new freedom. While the term **general will** was well known in Rousseau's time, people often disagree about its meaning in his writings: from those who think it describes the harmonious, democratic agreement and desire of the people as a whole, to those who argue for a more spiritual vision of it as a living entity. In this new civil society, science, philosophy, and art might once again "raise monuments to the glory of the human mind" because they can be pursued by "those who feel in themselves the power to walk alone."[v]

Besides Rousseau, few capture the spirit of the counter-enlightenments more clearly than the Italian intellectual Giambattista Vico, who was born and died in Naples. He was a professor of rhetoric at the University of Naples but was largely unknown and isolated during his life. Yet he strongly influenced the *Geisteswissenschaften* and the philosophy of history. Vico criticized the increasing prestige and presence of the "scientific" method, which claimed that the only path to certain truth is verification through observation. While not rejecting the utility of this method in some fields, he suggested that it was not useful for discovering the truths of practical life (the civil sphere). Moreover, its dominance was responsible for the decline of Renaissance arts and humanism.

In *The New Science*, Vico argued that a science of the human required a new practice of historiography.[w] His **historicism** asserted that something can be understood only by locating it in its historical context, and studying the processes and forces that brought it into existence as precisely what it was. He offered a radically different notion of truth: *Verum esse ipsum factum*—"the truth is made," or "the truth is that which is made."[x] We can only know with any certainty what we ourselves have created. Enlightenment attempts to understand the mind and Reason were doomed to fail, since the mind can perceive only itself; it cannot make itself. Civil life, on the other hand, like pure mathematics, is entirely constructed.[15]

Now that we have discussed individual representatives of the counter-enlightenments, it is only appropriate to examine the contributions of three iconic representatives of different Enlightenment paths: the rationalism of René Descartes, the empiricism of David Hume, and finally the somewhat mystical enlightenment (or rationalist counter-enlightenment?) of Baruch Spinoza.

NOTES

a. Dumarsais, in Diderot and d'Alembert, *Encyclopedia*, para. 4.
b. Leibniz, *Monadology*, in *Philosophical Papers*, 643–53.
c. Kant, "What Is Enlightenment?," in *Foundations*, 85.
d. Kant, "What Is Enlightenment?," 90.
e. Descartes, "Discourse on Method," in *Philosophical Works*, 119.
f. Quoted in Nadler, *Spinoza*, 182.
g. Hamann, "Metacritique of the Purism of Reason," in Hamann, *Writings*.
h. Blake, *Letters*, 46.
i. Wordsworth, "The Tables Turned," in *Complete Poetical Works*, 85.
j. Goethe, *Faust*, 8.
k. J. Schiller, "Rousseau," in *Schiller's Poems and Ballads*, 259.
l. Rousseau, *Social Contract*.
m. Rousseau, *Discourse on the Sciences*, pt. 2, para. 25.
n. Rousseau, *Discourse on the Origin*.
o. Rousseau, *Discourse on the Origin*, "Preface," para. 4.

15 Vico foreshadowed the constructionism of most modern deep theories.

p. Rousseau, *Émile.*

q. Rousseau, *Discourse on the Origin*, pt. 2, para. 18.

r. Rousseau, *Discourse on the Sciences*, pt. 1, para. 2.

s. Rousseau, *Discourse on the Sciences*, pt. 1, para. 3.

t. Rousseau, *Discourse on the Origin*, pt. 2, para. 17.

u. Rousseau, *Discourse on the Sciences*, pt. 1, para. 36.

v. Rousseau, *Discourse on the Sciences*, pt. 2, para. 24.

w. Vico, *New Science.*

x. Vico, *On the Most Ancient Wisdom*, 46.

Rationalism and Descartes

Rationalism claims that knowledge depends only on the innate, and therefore universal, capacities of the mind. This is not as strange as it sounds; you come across its contemporary versions whenever something is said to be hardwired into the brain.[1] Enlightenment rationalists included Baruch Spinoza, Gottfried Leibniz, Christian Wolff, Nicolas Malebranche, and Pierre Bayle. But René Descartes is the most well-known. He was born on March 31, 1596, in La Haye en Touraine in the Kingdom of France, and died on February 11, 1650, in Stockholm in the Swedish Empire. Suffering from poor health in his youth, he first studied mathematics and physics but went on to study law, following his father's wishes, but never practiced it. Instead, he became a soldier of fortune, fighting first in the Protestant Dutch States Army and then in the service of the Catholic Duke Maximilian of Bavaria.

---

1 For example, consider Noam Chomsky's theory of transformational grammar, which argued that the child's brain is already structured to enable language learning. Chomsky, *Aspects of the Theory of Syntax*.

It was during this latter service, at the Battle of the White Mountain near Prague, that Descartes claimed to have had three divinely inspired dreams on the night of November 10, 1619. These dreams revealed not only the fundamentals of what was to become Cartesian geometry but, even more important, the need to seek truth by reason, by applying mathematical logic to the search for knowledge. The dreams told him that this method would reveal that all knowledge was part of a single system of truth. The proper method of rational inquiry would produce the unity of all knowledge, from science to metaphysics.

Descartes traveled widely around Europe, in 1628 returning to the Dutch Republic, where he wrote most of his major works. As his fame grew, he was invited, in 1649, by Queen Christina to organize a new "scientific academy" in Sweden. Yet his ideas remained extremely controversial. When Galileo was condemned by the Italian Inquisition in 1633, Descartes abandoned plans to publish his first major work, *Treatise on the World*, presumably out of fear that it would be declared heretical. Still, his works were placed on the Vatican's Index of Forbidden Books in 1663, and it was prohibited for others to lecture on his philosophy. In some universities, it was even forbidden to utter his name.

During his life, Descartes published a reflection on music theory (1618), *Meditations on First Philosophy* (1641), *Principles of Philosophy* (1644), and *Passions of the Soul* (1649). Other works were published posthumously, including *Rules for the Direction of the Mind*, *Treatise on Man*, *The World*, and *The Description of the Human Body*. In 1637, he published parts of *The World*, including *Geometry* (introducing coordinate—Cartesian—geometry, which organized space along two perpendicular axes) and a preface called "Discourse on the Method of Rightly Conducting the Reason and Seeking for Truth in the Sciences."

In the "Discourse," he argued that the search for a universal Truth demanded a foundation of certainty or **indubitability**, which, by definition, cannot be doubted. The first principle of his method commanded: "to accept nothing as true which I did not clearly recognise to be so; that is to say, carefully to avoid precipitation and prejudice in judgments, and to accept in them nothing more than what was presented *to my mind* so clearly and [vividly] that I could have no occasion to doubt it."[2,a]

2 In most translations, innate ideas are presented as "clear and distinct," but "clear" and "distinct" mean the same thing: that the idea is self-contained and contains nothing that

This statement has been interpreted in different ways, although most scholars agree that the proscription of "precipitation and prejudice" means that you cannot start with what is generally thought to be true, even obvious, such as customs, traditions, generally held opinions, or existing knowledge. Even philosophy as the supposed collective wisdom of the past and present is not indubitable and cannot provide the necessary starting point. In fact, Descartes rejected everything that had ever been said or thought in the history of philosophy. As he wrote, "Philosophy teaches us to speak with an appearance of truth on all things and causes us to be admired by the less learned. . . . No single thing is to be found in [the history of philosophy] which is not a subject of dispute, and in consequence which, is not dubious."[b]

Reason itself is the only valid source of knowledge. And since it belongs to the individual, the search for truth can only be carried out by the individual, relying only on the capacities of their mind. While Descartes did argue that one must put aside all passion and emotion in the search for truth so as not to be agitated or misled by them, in other contexts he strongly affirmed their importance in human life.

This search for certainty as the foundation of all knowledge was, for Descartes, "the most important endeavor in all the world."[c] Philosophy would ground science, which would master nature, allowing humanity to "enjoy without any trouble the fruits of the earth."[d] Remember that these were tumultuous times, full of uncertainty and insecurity; everything that seemed true in previous centuries, including the forms and content of knowledge and authority, could be questioned. Humanity needed some truth to provide a stable ground for any further investigations.

For Descartes, Galileo's new science offered a method by which we could understand and gain some control over all the changes and uncertainties of the world, although Descartes's understanding of Galileo's work was not very accurate. The new science provided a universal, rational method (*mathesis universalis*) that would demonstrate the unity of all knowledge, represented by the image of the Tree of Knowledge.[e] It would describe a new *ordo cognoscendi* (order of knowledge, order of discovery) as opposed to the *ordo essendi* (true order of things). As we shall see, in the former, Descartes's famous *cogito*

---

is not inherent and apparent in its very identity. Therefore, I have used the more recent translation of "clear and vivid," where the latter describes what is intensely present and apparent to the attentive, rational mind.

(I think) precedes the discovery of God, although in the latter, God precedes the *cogito*.

But Galileo's new science could not provide the necessary foundation of certainty. That was the task of philosophy. Philosophy needed a method for moving from a foundation of certainty to further truths, rules for correctly employing the natural capacities of the mind such that "if a man observe them accurately, he shall never assume what is false as true, and will never spend his mental efforts to no purpose, but will always gradually increase his knowledge and so arrive at a true understanding of all that does not surpass his powers."[f] You start with indubitable truths; their truth is guaranteed by the very fact that we think them and cannot think otherwise. Then, following the rules of the method, you will discover every truth that can be discovered and make no mistakes. And every derived truth will carry the certainty with which the method endows it.

Descartes did not deny that there are truths, even certainties, that the mind is not capable of discovering through his method, things that are simply beyond reason and the capacity of the mind itself. This allowed him to acknowledge the truth of church doctrine and theology. While Descartes offered numerous proofs of God's existence, he may also have been protecting himself from accusations of heresy and apostasy by the church, since God more or less disappears in some of his later writings. For the most part, he steered clear of theological questions, remaining content to assert that there was no contradiction or incompatibility between religion and his philosophy.

Let's consider more carefully the notion of indubitable ideas. Descartes distinguished three kinds of ideas.[g] **Adventitious ideas** come from experience: the sun rises in the east every morning; fire causes smoke. **Factitious ideas** are derived from the mind's activity itself: imagination, dreams, hallucinations, creativity, and so on. **Innate ideas** also result from the activity of the mind, but they are necessarily true ideas presupposed by all the other categories of ideas—and all statements of knowledge and truth.

How do we discover innate ideas? The first principle tells us not to accept anything as true that is not clearly and vividly perceived. Any idea that can be doubted cannot be innate; so, start by doubting everything that can be doubted, a practice often referred to as **universal doubt**, and see what is left. Descartes started by doubting all adventitious ideas of the senses, which are often mistaken and deceptive. You think you perceive something, but you don't. You think you see a friend coming toward you, but it's someone else. Things look bigger than they are. You mishear things, or you confuse a factitious idea for an adventitious one. You might only be dreaming—or hallucinating or imagining—that you are reading a lecture on Descartes. So, we can doubt everything our senses tell us, which means that you can doubt the existence of a physical world, and of our own physical bodies, because you know their existence only through the senses.

What about mathematical truths, which cannot be derived from our sensory experience of the world? Mathematics would be true whether or not the physical world exists. The Pythagorean theorem states that the sum of the squares of the sides of a right triangle equals the square of the hypotenuse ($a^2 + b^2 = c^2$). It is not part of the definition of a right triangle, nor is it the result of measuring all (or even a large number) of right triangles. If someone were to discover a right triangle that violated the Pythagorean theorem, the appropriate response would not be to reject the theorem but to question whether the counterexample is actually a right triangle, or to challenge the measurements and calculation. Similarly, π, the mathematical constant giving the ratio of a circle's circumference to its diameter, will be true even if there were no physical circles. Does that mean we cannot doubt mathematics? Descartes's answer is that we can: imagine that there is an evil genius (demon?) sitting on your shoulder, whispering lies into your ear, including the seemingly universal truths of mathematics.[h] While this may not be a very compelling argument, it is possible to imagine, and therefore it is possible to doubt mathematics.

Finally, most controversially, we can doubt the existence of a universal and perfect god. After all, if there were a perfect god, it would not have allowed the evil demon to deceive me about the truth of mathematics in the first place.

What is it, then, that I cannot doubt? I cannot doubt that I am doubting, and since doubting is a form of thinking, I cannot doubt that I'm thinking. I think! In Latin, *cogito*. But if I think, I must exist. *Cogito, ergo sum*. I think, therefore I am.[i] While this is probably Descartes's most famous argument, it is deeply flawed. Descartes could certainly doubt that *he* was doubting. What he could not doubt is that doubting exists. So, "doubting, therefore, doubt." This is not very useful or interesting as a starting point for philosophical certainty.

But let's go along with Descartes's claim that *cogito, ergo sum* is indubitable. The question remains: What am I that exists? If I must exist because I am thinking, what is it that is doing the thinking? Descartes's answer: I am that which knows it exists because it is thinking. Therefore, I am a thinking thing. He assumed that this too was certain because it followed from a logical chain of reasoning. I am a thinking thing, which needs nothing but itself to exist, which is dependent on nothing because I've already dismissed the world, and mathematics, and God. But if I exist because I think, what happens when I'm not thinking? Do I still exist? This is the problem of **conservation**. How do I know that I continue to exist in those moments when the activity that supposedly defines my existence stops or is interrupted?[3] Descartes's answer is that conservation can be explained only if there is a perfect God because a perfect God would not deceive me and would therefore guarantee my continued existence. Therefore, God exists, and its existence is indubitable.

If the existence of a perfect God is a certainty, then the truth of mathematics is guaranteed because a perfect God would not allow an evil demon to deceive me. Nor would it deceive me about the existence of a world out there or the existence of my body. A perfect God would not delude me into thinking I have a body when I'm really, for example, a brain in a glass jar or an immaterial force field. So, from "I think," we can, according to Descartes, logically deduce my own existence as a thinking thing, the existence of God, the truth of mathematics, the existence of the world and of my own body.

In the end, there are three vibrant and clear ideas: God, Thought, and Extension (where *extension* is his term for physical as opposed to ideational reality, the essence of which is that it is describable within Cartesian geometry). These innate ideas are indubitable; they are necessarily intrinsic to and inherent in the mind and reason. Yet they are only discoverable through the method of doubt and reason as stated in Descartes's first principle. These **Substances** will populate and define Descartes's metaphysics, built out of his epistemology.

The rest of Descartes's method describes the two fundamental logical operations of reason. The second rule is a principle of **analysis**: divide any problem into its simplest parts. Descartes described it as the intuition of "simple natures," from which one cannot deduce conclusions from or about existence. It is a purely intellectual vision that makes available concepts such as figure, motion, existence, unity, and duration, as well as various states of consciousness. The status of these ideas remains somewhat ambiguous: they are clear and vibrant ideas, but they do not have the same status as the Substances. The difference is that while the mind produces these "simple natures" out of its own potentialities, it does so only in the presence of experience. Experience provides the occasion on which the mind, by its own

3 The empiricists have a similar but opposite problem of conservation: How do I know that you're still there when I am not seeing you? Do you just disappear and reappear, blip in and blip out of existence like some special effects in a sci-fi movie?

capacities, produces these ideas, but their truth does not depend on experience. But if an idea that is called into existence by and represents what is outside the mind (experience) can be innate and indubitable, then it would seem to follow that all ideas are innate and indubitable.

The third rule, the rule of **synthesis**, uses deductive logic ("reflections in due order") to turn "simple natures" into more complex wholes.[j] One can then deduce from this system of truths further true knowledge about reality.[4] Finally, the fourth rule: be sure that you have omitted nothing, that your answer is complete. One can point out that, as Leibniz, another rationalist philosopher of the times, purportedly said, Descartes's method adds up to saying, "Take what you need, do what you should, and you will get what you want."[k] After all, this method might just as well be describing an auto mechanic taking apart, diagnosing, and rebuilding an engine.

The metaphysical idea of **Substance**, inherited from Scholasticism, is defined as something the existence of which does not depend on anything else (except, as we have seen, for the divine activity of conservation). A Substance is necessary and universal; it can have or exhibit multiple modes or attributes but is not itself a mode or attribute of anything else. While the Scholastics assumed that a Substance is distinguished by its attributes—properties and qualities—Descartes assumed that each Substance has only one inseparable attribute, which in turn dictates all of its other properties.

And lo and behold, Descartes has derived a metaphysics that is absolutely certain because that which is universal and necessary must exist. The fundamental Substance is **God**. But Descartes allows that there are "created substances," whose existence depends on nothing other than God: **Thought** (mental Substance [*res cogitans*]) and **Extension** (corporeal Substance [*res extensa*]).[l] Thought—mind—is the realm of consciousness and ideas, the essence of which is reason. Extension—body or matter—is existence in space defined by the two dimensions of Cartesian geometry. The human individual is the conjugation of two Substances, mind and body.

This is **Cartesian dualism**. (Most people, including Descartes at times, ignore his theism in which both Thought and Extension depend on God as their creator and conserver.) But the simplicity of the dualism of mind and body is somewhat misleading, because Descartes's universe was populated by a plurality of minds and bodies rather than by two singular, independent,

---

4 This might be interpreted as a form of pan-mathematicism, i.e., that reality necessarily exhibits a mathematical order.

omnipresent existents. For example, he identifies material Substance with extension, and extension with space; consequently, space does not exist apart from bodies defined by their relative place in space. There is no empty space. Other properties of matter, such as motion, are secondary modes of bodies and imply no notion of agency or causality. Similarly, time and duration define what one might think of as a tertiary mode of a body, since it is only a measurement of motion.

Cartesian dualism raises two immediate questions: First, how do the two independent Substances relate to one another? Descartes's answer was that the two Substances **interact** with one another at a particular point in the middle of the human brain.[5] Second, how do we study each of these? For Descartes, following the new science, the body was like a machine in space that could be understood scientifically. The mind, however, had to be studied through the philosophical understanding of the forms of reasoning of the new science. Philosophy was to become the new science of the mind; it would reveal the logic of reason and the nature of the mind; as a result, it would provide the foundation for all other knowledge, including the new science of physics. Philosophy would make visible the logic of reason behind Galileo's science, providing the justification and legitimation of its claims to rational knowledge. The certainty of the innate ideas that reason arrives at through the method of universal doubt and the deductive logic of analysis and synthesis grounds all other claims to truth. But Galileo's truths did not have the indubitability of innate ideas. The truth of innate ideas comes from their very nature and their presence to reason itself. The truth of the new science, on the other hand, which dealt with adventitious ideas, was a secondary structure built on the essence of reason.

Cartesian dualism is still the most common metaphysics in the Western world. It offers the popular image of "the ghost in the machine." In the animated movie *Inside Out*, the brain (body) is inhabited by characters representing different emotions.[m] In the 1950s, schools showed movies that pictured the mind as a stereotypical bookkeeper typing out thoughts as commands for the body. The dualism is still assumed, for example, when we distinguish between the brain and the mind, between lust and love, or when we refuse to reduce love to the firing of neurons or the release of hormones.

5 Today the pineal gland, located close to the center of the brain, is thought to play a crucial role in allowing the brain to interact with the rest of the body.

There are many grounds on which to criticize Descartes. His understanding of Galileo and the method of the new physics was insufficient, despite his recognition of the central role of mathematics and deduction. There are many logical flaws in his arguments and errors in his reasoning. He made plenty of highly doubtful statements as if they were certainties. But that's not the point. Descartes, as much as anyone, helped set the enlightenment project in motion. Continuing many of the concerns of the Renaissance, he questioned what it was that set humanity apart from the rest of creation. His answer centered on the nature of human consciousness and subjectivity, which was defined by Reason. The Delphic Oracle had been correct: know thyself. Humanity need only look to itself. This is the **problem space** of the enlightenments, although these questions have continued to preoccupy intellectuals.

NOTES

a. Descartes, "Discourse on Method," in *Philosophical Works*, 146 (emphasis added).

b. Descartes, "Discourse on Method," 84, 86.

c. Descartes, "Discourse on Method," 94.

d. Descartes, "Discourse on Method," 119.

e. Descartes, "Preface to Principles of Philosophy," in *Philosophical Works*.

f. Descartes, "Rules," in *Philosophical Works*, 9.

g. Descartes, "Meditations on First Philosophy," in *Philosophical Works*.

h. Descartes, "Meditations on First Philosophy."

i. Descartes, "Discourse on Method," in *Philosophical Works*, 101; Descartes, "Principles," in *Philosophical Works*, 22.

j. Descartes, "Discourse on Method," 92.

k. Quoted in P. Lodge, "Leibniz, Gottfried Wilhelm," in Nolan, *Cambridge Descartes Lexicon*, 451.

l. On created substances, see Descartes, "Principles of Philosophy," in *Philosophical Works*, 240.

m. Docter and Del Carmen, *Inside Out*.

Empiricism and Hume

The main enlightenment alternative to rationalism was **empiricism**, which argued that knowledge can only be derived from experience. Empiricists, like rationalists, sought to define the possibilities and limits of human knowledge by investigating the nature of the mind and of reason as its essence. They assumed that by applying the scientific method of the natural sciences to the study of the mind, they could create a new science of the mind, reason, and ultimately social life. Consequently, empiricists wrote about a wide range of topics, and despite their epistemological influence, their greatest impact came in the realms of social, political, and even economic theory. The two most famous figures—John Locke and David Hume—are strongly identified with the birth of liberalism, republicanism, and even private property.

While the rationalists understood the scientific method to be defined by formal logic and mathematics, the empiricists viewed it as grounded in people's experiences, their sensory encounter with, manipulations of, and experimentation on a presupposed external reality. The logic of science was inductive (moving from the particular to the general) rather than deductive (moving from the general to the particular), as the rationalists assumed.

Empiricism identified the capacities of the mind by examining the materials with which it is furnished, and the uses the mind can make of them. The empiricists often assumed that the mind is a tabula rasa, an empty slate on which nothing is written prior to one's sensory encounters with the world (although they were not entirely consistent about this).

Rationalism emerged primarily in continental Europe, while empiricism originated largely from the English and Scottish enlightenments, which occurred simultaneously with the rise of the British Empire. Britain not only controlled the seas but also led the development of both capitalism and liberalism. This geographic divergence was partly the result of the different histories of Britain and continental Europe in the seventeenth and eighteenth centuries. In 1534, King Henry VIII removed England from the power of the Vatican following the establishment of the Church of England in 1532, with the monarch as its head. And in 1611, a new translation of the Bible was published—the King James Version—for the Anglican Church. These signaled a very different role for the church and religion in English life.

In 1215, King John signed the Magna Carta (the Great Charter), which began a long struggle for liberty in England, originally between the monarch and the aristocracy, but later between the gentry and the bourgeoisie, and between the monarchy and Parliament. England's political revolutions—the Civil Wars of 1642–51, the Glorious Revolution of 1688, and the subsequent Restoration of the monarchy—happened much earlier than those in the rest of Europe, even though the struggles continued into the eighteenth and nineteenth centuries.

The Industrial Revolution was both earlier and more advanced in England than in the rest of Europe. There were massive transformations in transportation, mining and iron production, agriculture, and the textile industry. These economic changes fueled the early emergence of an urban working class, brought about by so-called enclosures (the Enclosure Act of 1773). But they also gave birth to numerous organizations and practices of resistance earlier in England than elsewhere. A number of catastrophic events also marked the times, including the Great Plague (1665–66) and the Great Fire of London (1666).

A HISTORY OF EMPIRICISM

Before discussing Hume as empiricism's most iconic figure, I want to start by considering its intellectual development in Britain from the sixteenth century. While all empiricists shared a common project and assumption, there were differences among them, often concerning their metaphysical theories. The story might begin, somewhat arbitrarily, with Francis Bacon, the Viscount St Alban (1561–1621) and Lord Chancellor under James I. He defended the absolute power of the monarchy on the basis of reason (natural law) rather than divine right against those who defended the power of Parliament and common law. His defense assumed that such centralized power was necessary for the advancement of science, which he defended for its utility. Bacon called for a new science of philosophy, which would be in touch with reality. As he stated, "Man appl[ies] himself fairly to facts."[a] This defines both an obligation and a limitation: "The understanding must not therefore be supplied with wings, but rather hung with weights, to keep it from leaping and flying."[b] But first, one had to cleanse one's mind of four false notions ("Idols") that stood in the way of science: Idols of the Tribe are generally shared assumptions; Idols of the Cave are the prejudices specific to the individual; Idols of the Marketplace arise from the misuses of language; and Idols of the Theater are the dogmas of philosophy.[c]

Bacon understood science as the attempt to learn the secrets of nature by planned and organized observation of its regularities. Science amassed data, sometimes through observation and sometimes through experimentation (like ants, he suggested metaphorically), and reasoned or interpreted them (like spiders, again, his metaphoric suggestion). But in the end, he compared science to the work of bees that gather data and transform it by their own power. That is, starting from sense-data, science ascends to axioms (as true grounded and grounding generalizations), which can lead to new facts, which can lead to new axioms, and so forth. In this way, ordinary experiences can be corrected and converted into the facts of sense-data and then into knowledge.

Thomas Hobbes (1588–1679) is most remembered for his contributions to political theory, especially *Leviathan* (1651). He understood Galileo's new science to argue that all changes are changes in motion. He set out to construct a philosophical system based on the laws of mechanics, which would offer a single account of all behavior.[d] This would apply to physical bodies as well as to the bodies of the "commonwealth" (composed of the actions and wills of people). Hobbes grounded this system on a **materialist monism** that assumed all reality to be a "plenum" filled with matter (such as bodies), without empty spaces. Every body is only a moving quantity in a specific region of space.

All knowledge is knowledge of the determinate motions of existing bodies, which is derived from the motions bodies cause on our own bodies.

These motions are experienced as either things or "phantasms" (sensations); the latter are the effects of the **primary qualities** of bodies, that is, the spatial and temporal manifestations of extension and motion. Phantasms follow one another according to certain patterns (what later empiricists will call the association of ideas). All that distinguishes humanity is the capacity to give names to the particular states of the body and their patterns, but this capacity also follows the laws of mechanics.

Hobbes distinguished between truths of definitions and deductions, and truths of fact, but he also asserted that "true and false are qualities of names and propositions, not things."[e] Theory bridges the two by bringing a collection of facts together into an intelligible set of relations within a deductive system. Since more than one such system is possible, no definition or theory can be assumed to identify the "true" cause of an effect. It simply defines a cause sufficient to produce the effect. But, ultimately, adjudicating between competing theories is a matter of power. It is the power of the state that commands the acceptance of a particular theory. And that leads to Hobbes's political theory, which I shall not pursue.

Many histories of empiricism start with John Locke, born on August 29, 1631, in Wrington, Somerset, England, into a liberal Puritan (antimonarchist) family. His early interests alternated between rationalist philosophy (especially that of René Descartes), medicine, and the experimental method of science. He became involved in politics on the side of the Parliamentarians and lived in exile in the Netherlands for five years. Upon returning, he published *A Letter concerning Tolerance, Two Treatises of Government* (both in 1689), and *An Essay concerning Human Understanding* (1690). He also published works on economics and money, education, and religion (*The Reasonableness of Christianity*, 1695). He was a leading and highly visible intellectual, described as pious and unaffected, and was popular in political, artistic, and scientific circles.

His influence was widespread across a range of fields and nations. Like Hobbes, he is best known for his political theories. His defense of individualism, which helped define the enlightenment subject, as well as his social contract theory provided strong arguments against authoritarian governments and for liberal democracies—as well as for private property and laissez-faire capitalism. He was involved in the administration of the Carolina Colony (in the Americas) and its slave economy, and he helped to write the constitution of Carolina, which included chattel servitude even as it embodied many fundamental liberal principles. He died on October 28, 1704, in High Laver, Essex, England.

Locke was perhaps the first thinker to offer an explicit and rigorous empiricist epistemology, which he saw as a new start, applying the principles of the new science to matters of social existence. He assumed this would enable humanity to cure all its ills, whether intellectual, moral, or material, by the use of its own natural capacities, but that required an investigation into the capacities of the mind and its limits. He thought the search for certainty was fruitless and rejected as dogma the assumption of innate ideas. Instead, the mind at birth is a tabula rasa; the best people could hope for was knowledge grounded on rational observation and experimentation. Therefore, it was "necessary to examine our own Abilities and see what Objects our Understandings were, or were not fitted to deal with."[f]

For Locke, this meant investigating the origins of ideas in experience, whether produced by **primary qualities** (properties that inhere in objects and do not depend on the observer) or **secondary qualities** (which describe the effects of bodies on the internal states of the mind). The former result in objective "facts" such as number, extension, solidity, motion, and shape, which represent actual bodies; the latter result in sensations such as color, taste, and smell. But we can only know ideas insofar as they are rooted in states of the mind itself.

Locke distinguished between **simple ideas** and **compound ideas**. Simple ideas contain only one uniform and complete experience, which cannot be made or destroyed by the mind. Echoing Descartes, Locke suggested that "nothing can be plainer to a Man [*sic*] than the clear and distinct Perception he has of those simple Ideas."[g] Compound ideas are the products of the mind's active joining of simple ideas. As a result, "knowledge then seems . . . to be nothing but the perception of the connexion and agreement, or disagreement and repugnancy of any of our Ideas. In this alone it consists."[h]

This theory posed the threat of skepticism. Locke asserted that while the existence of objects and selves cannot be demonstrated, "nobody can in earnest be so skeptical as to be uncertain" of their existence.[i] As to whether ideas truly and accurately resemble bodies, he responded that every object has a real internal essence on which all its discernible qualities—both primary and secondary—depend. If we could discover this essence, we could deduce all the properties; unfortunately, humans cannot do so. This is the ultimate limit of the capacities of the mind.

The Irish philosopher George Berkeley (1685–1753), known as Bishop Berkeley, concluded that Locke's empiricism would end in atheism. He blamed the metaphysical dualism that assumed physical objects to be the cause of ideas, as well as the distinction between primary and secondary qualities. Instead, Berkeley propounded an **idealist monism** or **subjective idealism** in which "to be is to be perceived."[j] Only two kinds of things exist: ideas (perceptions) and minds (spirits) that perceive, in which ideas exist. And the spirit that ultimately guarantees the reality and conservation of ideas and spirits is God itself.

DAVID HUME

The Scotsman David Hume authored the most sophisticated expression and the concluding chapter of enlightenment empiricism.[1] Hume was born on May 7, 1711, and died on August 25, 1776, in Edinburgh. He studied law and tried his hand at commerce but lived much of his life in economic precarity and varied states of ill-health. At the age of eighteen, Hume claimed to have discovered "a new Scene of Thought," which demanded that one never claim to know that which the human mind is not capable of knowing and championed the value of clear thinking and education.[k]

Hume anonymously published his first book, *A Treatise of Human Nature, Being an Attempt to Introduce the Experimental Method of Reasoning into Moral Subjects*, in 1739. One thousand copies were printed, and he received fifty pounds and twelve free copies. Although he described the response to this book as having fallen "dead-born from the press," it was actually greeted with hostility.[l] A year later, he anonymously published a pamphlet, "An abstract of a late philosophical performance, entitled A Treatise of Human Nature, etc. Wherein the chief argument and design of that book, which has met with such opposition, and been represented in so terrifying a light, is further illustrated and explained."

Hume published many works during his lifetime, covering a wide range of subjects, including politics, ethics, history, economics, and epistemology. His major works included *Essays, Moral, Political, and Literary* (1741–42, the first work published under his own name), *An Enquiry concerning Human Understanding* (1748),[2] *An Enquiry concerning the Principles of Morals* (1751,

---

1 Until its revival in the twentieth century.
2 One of the enduring debates among Hume scholars involves the relations between the *Treatise of Human Nature* and the later *Enquiry concerning Human Understanding*. Hume himself thought the latter presented more moderate and rigorously argued versions of his arguments than the more "juvenile" *Treatise*. But, in many cases, the differences are less significant than Hume assumed. See Hume, "My Own Life" and "Advertisement" in *Essays Moral, Political, and Literary*.

which Hume thought was his best work), and *Political Discourses* (1752–58), which foreshadowed the work of Adam Smith's political economy and which Hume described as his only immediately successful work.[m]

Hume was never able to secure a university position, presumably because of his supposed atheism and skepticism. In *A Letter from a Gentleman to His Friend in Edinburgh: Containing Some Observations on a Specimen of the Principles concerning Religion and Morality, Said to be Maintain'd in a Book Lately Publish'd, Intituled A Treatise of Human Nature, &c.*, he denied these accusations as well as the claim that he had rejected the principle of sufficient reason.[n] He eventually obtained a position as the librarian at the University of Edinburgh, which gave him the opportunity to begin his most successful work, the six-volume *History of England* (1754–62). This work, still taught in the twentieth century, brought him the literary fame and financial success he sought.

Despite many controversies and attacks—his books were placed on the Roman Catholic Index of Forbidden Books in 1761—Hume's works were widely influential, even during his own lifetime, especially in Europe, and Hume himself became a highly visible and popular figure. When he went to France as secretary to the British ambassador, "he was flattered by princes, worshipped by fine ladies and treated as an oracle by the Philosophes" (members of the French Enlightenment), and often called "Le Bon David."[o] According to popular accounts, Saint David Street in Edinburgh was named after him. After Hume's death, Adam Smith said, "Upon the whole, I have always considered him, both in his lifetime and since his death, as approaching as nearly to the idea of a perfectly wise and virtuous man, as perhaps the nature of human frailty will permit."[p] Hume's work had a profound influence on many thinkers, from Immanuel Kant to A. J. Ayer, the logical positivist who called Hume "the greatest of all British philosophers," to the anti-enlightenment philosopher Gilles Deleuze.[q]

Hume was the clearest and most complete expression of British empiricism, even as he complicated its arguments. While Hume, like most enlightenment intellectuals, believed that reason defined human nature, like Descartes, he acknowledged the necessity of emotion and passion. But Hume further argued that the passions actually governed human behavior and that all ethics had to be based on emotion and sentiment. Judgments of ideas and facts cannot define or judge an action's pleasantness (pleasure) or unpleasantness (pain), or its usefulness or harmfulness. Reason cannot rule life. Thus, in everyday life, "reason is, and ought only to be the slave of the passions."[r] As a result, he argued that "practical reason" was not possible. There must be something more than reason—a moral sentiment or feeling, which at different times he described as either an instinct of benevolence or a psychological mechanism of sympathy.

Hume believed that the primary task of philosophy was to formulate a naturalist (assuming that everything exists in the same natural world) and experimental science of human nature and the powers and limits of the mind. Whether Hume's **naturalism** was metaphysical (the only things that exist are the natural elements of the kind studied by the natural sciences) or simply methodological (it is a useful assumption), his empiricism was explicitly rooted in a naturalist psychology, describing the psychological basis of knowledge and reason. This was Hume's **psychological empiricism**.

His understanding of the new science was based primarily on the work of Isaac Newton, although Hume reduced Newtonian science to "experience and observation."[s] He ignored Newton's appeal to entities and forces that were not experienced, as well as the use of theories and hypotheses, which Newton himself also denied: "I frame [contrive, feign] no hypotheses."[t] Hume sought "a compleat system of the sciences [including natural philosophy] built on a foundation almost entirely new."[u]

Hume's **fork** distinguished two kinds of meaningful statements and knowledge: relations of ideas and **matters of fact**. If a statement did not conform to one of these categories, he wrote, "commit it . . . to the flames: For it can contain nothing but sophistry and illusion."[v] Relations of ideas, like Descartes's factitious ideas, are necessarily true, depending only on the operations and demonstrations of thought without any reference to an existing reality, but they tell us nothing about the world of experience. They cannot be altered without altering the ideas themselves; any attempt to do so would result in a contradiction. Examples include statements that are true by definition, statements that are tautological, and mathematical statements. Matters of fact, similar to Descartes's adventitious ideas, cannot be discovered by appeals to reason alone, and they can be negated without producing contradictions. They are bound up with appeals to (observations of and inferences from) experience and, hence, offer contingent knowledge about the world.

Empiricism is most concerned with matters of fact. To understand these matters, Hume offered a **principle of empiricism**, which suggested that "if a term cannot be shown to evoke an idea that can be analyzed into simple constituents for which impressions can be produced, then it has no meaning."[w] All ideas are derived from impressions (sensations) of either outer sense or inner feeling. This law led to two methodological rules: the first (**the microscope**) demands that one reduce an idea to its simplest parts; the second (**the**

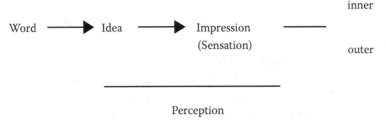

FIGURE 6.1

razor) demands that one trace every simple idea to the impression (sense-data or sensations) from which it arises.[3] This can be illustrated as shown in figure 6.1.

The difference between ideas and impressions, as well as that between inner and outer sensations, is a matter of **vivacity**: "The most lively thought is still inferior to the dullest sensation."[x]

Hume wrestled with a number of questions arising out of this model: What form of existence do perceptions (ideas and impressions) have? Do they exist independently, and is their existence continuous or intermittent? Are impressions dependent on the existence of the mind? What sense does it make to speak of ideas if one does not presuppose the existence of minds (which have ideas) and worlds (which are represented by them)? Is the manner in which impressions occur itself a distinct impression? In the *Treatise*, Hume argued that space and time are nothing but the manner in which impressions occur, but he dropped this argument from the later *Enquiry concerning Human Understanding*.

Hume defined the mind by its ability to make connections among impressions, to combine, transpose, enlarge, or shrink the materials of the senses. (This suggests that the mind is not entirely an empty tablet.) In particular, he identified three kinds of **associations of ideas**. The most basic are **resemblance** and **contiguity** (in both time and space), neither of which leads to any beliefs beyond those that already lie within the domain of the senses or memory. They do not suggest or stand for anything—either observed or inferred—in the object to which they are applied.

The third form of association of ideas, **cause and effect**, does seem to lead to new beliefs and to suggest something about the objects of the relation.

---

3 The actual referents of these terms seem to vary in different texts, and commentators have argued about their meaning.

But it poses serious problems. Hume argued that the idea of causation has no impression from which it derives. Instead, all one finds is contiguity in space, succession in time, and the constant conjunction of like objects (resemblance) in past experience. Experience shows A to always have been followed by B, and moreover, that A has never occurred without B. Additionally, the idea of B is associated with the idea of A in a way that no other idea is. Whenever an impression of A occurs, the mind is determined (by force of habit, he suggested) not only to form an idea of B but to transfer a share of the vivacity of A to B. As a result, there is a transition from an impression of A to the belief in B, that is, to the "necessary" presence of an impression of B.

Hume recognized that most people would not accept this as a sufficient account of the idea of causality. People assume that there is more, that there is a real and necessary connection between A and B, which depends on some nonexperienced power or force—the essence of causality—that is responsible for the connection. But since, Hume argued, there is no impression of such a force (we are only given the repeated contiguity of ideas), the idea of causality is not actually meaningful and, therefore, there is no causality.

Consider a simple example: fire causes smoke. For Hume, there is, first, an association of contiguity in both time and space: whenever I see fire, I see smoke. Second, the vibrancy of smoke is transferred to the memory of the sensation of fire. The power of smoke is transferred to the "experience" of the absent fire. I know that fire exists by virtue of my experience of smoke. But Hume argued that the assumption of causality is more: that there is some special property in the fire that, while invisible, is the capacity to produce smoke. But since there is no impression of this special power or property, the idea of causality has no empirical legitimacy or meaning. We have no reason to believe in causality. The result is what comes to be called Humean skepticism (as opposed to Cartesian doubt).

The problem of causality points to a broader question about induction that, for Hume, is the primary logic of the empirical sciences. How can one ever be justified in making inferences that enable us to move from our past and present impressions, taken as factual evidence, to predictions and judgments? That is, how can reason be utilized? Hume's answer involved "belief," which is something felt by the mind—perhaps akin to the special relation by which vivacity is transferred between impressions in cause-and-effect associations—that distinguishes the ideas of judgment from those of imagination. Actually, Hume seemed to waffle on this matter, sometimes ascribing belief to the vivacity of impressions, and at other times ascribing it to the coherence, constancy, and "involuntary" nature of the general accumulation of impressions.

Consider the ideas of the self and mind, or, more accurately, *my* self and *my* mind, which define who I am. They are not properties of my body, but something about the way minds *work* with the data presented to them. Hume argued that when one looks for the impressions that anchor the idea of a self, or of a mind, all one finds is a bundle of perceptions. There is no additional impression of a unity that binds all the impressions together into a possessive totality. Thus, the mind and self are nothing but the bundle of perceptions (the accumulation of impressions of my experience) related by resemblance, contiguity, succession, and causation, to which one ascribes an identity as a kind of fiction. And, yet, Hume's theory of morality and the passions assumed that one has a genuine idea of oneself. As he wrote, "Memory does not so much *produce* as *discover* a personal identity."[y] Hume recognized this contradiction and struggled in various works to reconcile his epistemological and moral philosophies. Just as important, Hume's skepticism about causality and the self/mind can be extended to many other questions, not least the existence of things, reality, and God.

The common history of empiricism often ends with Hume because he demonstrated, perhaps unintentionally, that empiricism inevitably leads to skepticism. For many thinkers, to say nothing about scientists, skepticism is not a good conclusion. But there is plenty of evidence that Hume himself refused skepticism as the conclusion of his empiricism. Instead, he rejected arguments (of Bishop Berkeley) as "merely sceptical [because] *they admit of no answer and produce no conviction. Their only effect is to cause that momentary amazement and irresolution, which is the result of scepticism.*"[z] Hume repeatedly counseled against skepticism. Consider the following statements:

Nature by an absolute and uncontrolable necessity has determin'ed us to judge as well as to breathe and feel.[aa]

We may well ask: *What causes induce us to believe in the existence of the body?* But 'tis in vain to ask Whether there be body or not? That is a point, which we must take for granted in all our reasonings.[bb]

It seems evident that men are carried, by a natural instinct or pre-possession, to repose faith in their senses; and that without any reasoning, or even almost before the use of reason, we always suppose an external universe which . . . would exist, though we and every sensible creature were absent or annihilated.[cc]

None but a fool or a madman will ever pretend to dispute the authority of experience or to reject that great guide of human life.[dd]

Hume seems to have been arguing for an undogmatic moderation in which inferences are based in common life: in custom and customary associations, in habit and natural instinct. People's common life demands that they assume that the future will resemble the past, that similar causes produce similar effects, that the world and other subjects exist, and that I am myself an individual subject who possesses my own experiences and a mind. Hume's empiricism ends not with skepticism but with common sense and shared habits of thought. But is this really any better than skepticism?

Both rationalism and empiricism were built on a shared admiration for the new science, although different thinkers understood it differently. You may think that both are too abstract and absolute. You may think them naive given their simplistic and often mistaken understandings of science. You may even fault their efforts to unravel the nature of knowledge independently of any social, moral, and political concerns. Still, the "truth" is that we use both of these ways of thinking all the time; they have become common sense for many of us, despite their contradictions. As a rationalist, you might think different ideas or ways of thinking are inherent in some group or, in a weaker version, that people's biases necessarily interfere with the natural working of the mind. As an empiricist, you might remind us to trust our senses, that one can only believe what one sees. These two ways of thinking are, despite their eerie familiarity, the early storms that began to unsettle Europe's thinking.

NOTES

a. Bacon, *New Organon*, 8.
b. Bacon, *New Organon*, 97.
c. Bacon, *New Organon*, 53.
d. Hobbes, *Elements of Philosophy*.
e. Hobbes, *Elements of Philosophy*, 7–8.
f. Locke, *Essay*, 7.
g. Locke, *Essay*, 119.
h. Locke, *Essay*, 525.
i. Locke, *Essay*, 3.
j. Berkeley, *Treatise*, 42n39.
k. Hume, "Letter to Dr George Cheyne," in *Letters*, 13.
l. Hume, "My Own Life," in *Essays*, 21.
m. Hume, "My Own Life," 21.
n. Hume, *Letter from a Gentleman*.

o. Strachey, "Hume," in *Portraits*, 147.

p. Smith, "Letter to William Strahan," in Hume, "My Own Life," in *Essays*, 14.

q. Ayer, *Hume*, 1.

r. Hume, *Treatise*, 2:266.

s. Hume, *Treatise*, I, 4.

t. Newton, "General Scholium," in *Newton's Principia*, 506.

u. Hume, *Treatise*, I, 6.

v. Hume, *Enquiry concerning Human Understanding*, 12.34, 123.

w. D. G. C. MacNabb, "Hume," in Edwards, *Encyclopedia of Philosophy*, 4:77.

x. Hume, *Enquiry*, 2.1, 13.

y. Hume, *Treatise*, I, 171.

z. Hume, *Enquiry*, 12.15, n32, 123.

aa. Hume, *Treatise*, 1.4, 123.

bb. Hume, *Treatise*, 1.4, 125.

cc. Hume, *Enquiry*, 12.7, 113.

dd. Hume, *Enquiry*, 4.20, 31.

Spinoza

Scattered throughout my backstory, you will encounter thinkers who challenge not only your ways of thinking but your very sense of what it means to think. Like a tornado, they tear apart your sense of possibility, verging on the border of incomprehensibility. With that warning, let's talk about Baruch (or Benedictus de) Spinoza. He poses unique problems because almost everything about him is contested. Much of what we know of his life remains cloudy and incomplete. His writings often seem impenetrable, and his ideas can seem ambiguous, obscure, and even bizarre. His work has been interpreted in radically different ways.

Even his significance and influence are debated. Some historians of ideas claim that Spinoza had little influence (except as a proselytizer of René Descartes's rationalism) and offer various explanations: his "hideous hypothesis" of monism;[a] his supposed pantheism, mysticism, and even atheism; his commitment to geometric logic as the method of reason; or his relative isolation and renunciation of the perspective of the outsider as parasitic, which resulted in a self-enclosed system that could only be understood from the inside.[1]

But Spinoza had a profound influence on various counter-enlightenment thinkers (e.g., Johann Wolfgang von Goethe and Samuel Taylor Coleridge). He influenced biblical and literary scholarship by questioning the very nature and practices of reading and interpretation, "link[ing] together . . . the essence of reading and the essence of history in a theory of the difference between the imaginary and the true."[b] Spinoza argued that there were two readings of the Bible.[c] The first reading founded the church's authority and defined most people's sense of religion. Unenlightened people need the Bible's myths, allegories, anthropomorphisms, threats, bribes, and promises to keep them under religious authority, to ensure that they remain law-abiding, and to support them emotionally. Oddly, Spinoza did not treat these as literal readings. The second reading takes scripture to mean just what it says, but this demands serious critical work, locating the texts in their social and historical contexts. This second reading of the Bible underlies Spinoza's unique understanding of religion and God.

Spinoza was also celebrated by a number of modern thinkers. Georg Wilhelm Friedrich Hegel claimed that "you are either a Spinozist or not a philosopher at all."[d] He also argued that Spinoza was the first philosopher to think totality (but, according to Hegel, Spinoza failed because he did not think dialectically). Friedrich Nietzsche identified with Spinoza, claiming that after discovering Spinoza's work late in life, he no longer felt alone.[e] Albert Einstein asserted that Spinoza was "the greatest of modern philosophers."[f] And, in post–World War II France, Gilles Deleuze, offering a radically different interpretation, described Spinoza as "the prince of philosophers."[g] He went so far as to call him "the Christ of philosophers," continuing that "the greatest philosophers are hardly more than apostles who distance themselves from or draw near to this mystery."[h]

Spinoza was born in Amsterdam (in the United Provinces of the Netherlands) on November 24, 1632, and died on February 21, 1677, in The Hague, from lung disease resulting from his illustrious career as a lens grinder, often for early microscopes and telescopes. His family were Marrano Jews— Sephardic Jews in Portugal who were forced to convert to Christianity but

---

1 My undergraduate philosophy adviser would not let me write a thesis on Spinoza because, he said, every question that could be asked was already answered in Spinoza's system itself.

secretly practiced Judaism. Expelled by the Catholics who had defeated the "Moors" in Al-Andalus, they fled to the Netherlands, where they could practice their religion openly. Spinoza grew up there in an established if still vilified Sephardic community.

One of the most passionately debated questions regarding Spinoza concerns his relation to Judaism. We do know that around midlife he renounced all ties to Judaism, but that does not tell us about either his intellectual roots or his continuing faith. He was clearly influenced by the medieval philosopher Moses Maimonides, whose *Guide for the Perplexed* reconciled Aristotelian philosophy with Jewish theology.[i] We do not know whether he was challenged by other medieval works extending back to the Arab and Jewish thought of Al-Andalus and the Maghreb. He is often cited as a predecessor of the Jewish Enlightenment (Haskalah), which began in the second half of the eighteenth century, but that relationship remains cloudy.

Spinoza lived a simple and somewhat solitary life, although he had a network of committed friends, and some commentators have suggested that he lived the "ideal life of the philosopher."[j] He tutored in philosophy but refused university teaching, even a prestigious academic appointment at the University of Heidelberg (a position later occupied by Hegel). He spent most of his life in Amsterdam, until he was exiled when the Portuguese Jewish congregation issued a herem, the highest form of censure in Judaism, in 1656 for "abominable heresies . . . and monstrous deeds."[k] His "heresies" were defined by mistaken accusations of atheism and pantheism, but his "monstrous deeds" remain a mystery. His works were condemned by the Catholic Church and added to the Index of Forbidden Books. Ironically, since he could not be buried in a Jewish cemetery, he was buried in a Protestant cemetery in The Hague.

His work was in dialogue with Descartes, Thomas Hobbes, and Gottfried Wilhelm Leibniz, as well as with Dutch republican intellectuals. He published only two books, both in Latin, while he was alive. The first of these, *Principles of Cartesian Philosophy*, attempted to translate and prove Descartes's rationalist arguments using Euclidean geometry.[l] The second, *Theological-Political Treatise*, was published anonymously and elicited such extremely unfavorable responses that Spinoza stopped publishing (but not writing). His remaining books were published by his friends only after his death, including *Treatise on the Emendation of the Intellect* (written in 1662), *Political Treatise* (unfinished), and *Ethics* (written in 1674).

The many and often extreme differences in Spinoza's interpretation and reception depend partly on the emphases placed on the various elements of his work (rationalism, monism, immanence, geometric method). What are the relations and priorities among his metaphysics, epistemology, and ethics? Which came first in his reasoning? Is his epistemology derived from his metaphysics or vice versa? Was his rationalism merely the expression of Descartes's in geometric terms? What is the significance of this effort? What is the relation between his rationalism and his metaphysics? Was he a rationalist who offered an irrational—mystical, pantheistic—metaphysics based on intuition? Or a Platonist who saw God as the ultimate Reality and Truth? Was Spinoza actually a critic of the enlightenments, a prescient precursor to anti- and postmodern philosophy, as Deleuze argues, whose immanent ontology stood against the various forms of transcendence operating in most enlightenment and modern philosophy?

Clearly, Spinoza cannot be approached in the same way as I have presented previous thinkers. But I assure you, you can grasp at least some of the mystery that is Spinoza.

RATIONALISM

Spinoza has been most commonly located in the history of enlightenment rationalism; his contribution was the geometric logic—the highest form of mathematics at the time—in which he presented his arguments: definitions, axioms, theorems, proofs (QED), and corollaries.[2] (Perhaps you were required to do such work in school?) However, there are serious disagreements about his geometric formalism: Is it the necessary and proper logic of reason and form of truth? Or was it Spinoza's contingent preference of logics? Did geometry as a method of discovery guarantee truth? Or was it a simply a method of presentation?

Most commonly, Spinoza's use of geometry is taken to assert the very nature of Truth itself as a totality, a consequence of his understanding of the principle of sufficient reason. Truth only exists in—or, better, as—a system of logical (geometric) implication, an infinite set of logically interconnected propositions, any one of which is justified only by its place in the deductive order. If there is only one such logical system, then there is only one Reality, and all relations are internal and necessary. If there is no distinction between

---

2 In logic and geometry, the abbreviation QED ends an argument. It stands for *quod erat demonstrandum*, which means literally "what was to be shown," but often is presented as "and so it is proven."

something being deducible and its being real, then anything that is logically true is real and anything that is real is logically true. Everything that exists, exists necessarily, and everything that does not exist is impossible. These are the only two metaphysical states of existence; there is no contingency or possibility.

On this reading, Spinoza's metaphysics follows from his rationalism: if there is only one logical system, then there can only be one Substance in which all relations are internal and necessary. The geometric form of Truth is the very essence of Thought and, therefore, of God and Reality. The claim that the whole, the totality, is more real than and logically precedes any single part is called **holism**. Spinoza's rationalism was itself metaphysical. But these arguments only work if you assume that Spinoza's commitment to geometry provides the best starting point.

FROM METAPHYSICS

I propose following a different path that takes seriously Spinoza's place in the history of Jewish thought, which often combined the rational and the nonrational and assumed a unique relation between reason and religion, as well as between thought, will, and passion. Like Maimonides, Spinoza sought to understand the possibility of an ethical life. Since the path to such a life would start with God, I begin with Spinoza's metaphysics—of monism, immanence, and parallelism—and the geometric rationalism by which he constructed a correspondence or homology between, on the one hand, metaphysics and, on the other, epistemology (the immanent thought of Truth) and ethics (a rational mode of living).[3]

Spinoza presented his metaphysics as an architecture of three levels: Substance, Attributes, and Modes. This same architecture operated in both his epistemology and his ethics (see table 7.1).

Like other rationalists, Spinoza began with the concept of **Substance**. A Substance is defined by its essence—an intrinsic and necessary defining property. If two Substances have the same Attribute, they are the same Substance. A Substance is self-determining; it is "what is in itself and is conceived through itself."[m] It does not depend on the conception or existence of anything else; it cannot have an external cause, and therefore its essence entails its existence. It is always and only defined by the necessity of its own existence.

3 Others offer a similar reading without grounding it in his Judaic heritage.

TABLE 7.1 The Structure of Spinoza's Deep Theory

Metaphysics	Epistemology	Ethics
Substance (God, the One)	Intuition	Actions from one's proper place in the One
Attributes	Rationalism	Actions driven by laws
Modes	Empiricism	Actions driven by external causes

For Spinoza, Substance is "that which stands beneath" everything, as opposed to simply matter.[n] It is infinite, eternal, unique, and indivisible. And therefore, there can only be one Substance. There can be nothing other than the one Substance because that would limit it and make it susceptible to being determined by something else. There can be nothing external to Substance, nor anything it lacks (or desires) because that would mean that it was limited and incomplete. Perhaps influenced by the mystical pantheism of Giordano Bruno, Spinoza identified the one Substance with God; therefore, he concluded that there can only be one God. God cannot be the first cause of something else ("the deistic compromise"), for that too would mean God was incomplete. Similarly, God cannot change, nor does it exist in time, certainly not in a teleological trajectory of becoming something other than what it always and already is. God is everything, the totality of all possibilities of existence. This is Spinoza's **monism**.

When Spinoza famously and controversially equated God and Nature (*Deus, sive Natura* [God, or Nature]), he was not referring to a finite and contingent natural world of common experience, separate from and external to an infinite and necessary divine being.[o] Nature here is the One, what Spinoza calls **natura naturans**, or nature naturing; it is Substance as the active self-production of existence. The One is constantly becoming what it already is. I shall return to this paradox shortly.

Spinoza's monism led him inexorably to **immanence**. In fact, the two are inseparable in his thought. Immanence assumes that everything that exists does so within a single reality (e.g., naturalism assumes the natural world) and that a full account of reality can be offered in the terms of that single reality. Its opposite, **transcendence**, claims that something exists beyond that single reality and is necessary to fully understand it. For Spinoza, that single reality is Substance or God: "Whatever is, is in God, and nothing can be or be conceived without God."[p] All of existence is defined by its being in Substance. Since nothing can exist outside Substance, everything is immanent to God: "God is the immanent, not the transitive cause of all things."[q]

Spinoza was neither a pantheist nor an atheist, despite frequent accusations. He did not believe that God was in everything but that everything was in God. And he certainly did not deny the existence of God. In fact, somewhat perplexingly, he claimed that he was describing the same God as other Judeo-Christian thinkers, with one difference—that what he was saying about it was true. He equated his God with that of Saint Paul and "with that of all the ancient Hebrews."[r] This was despite the fact that he denied God's transcendence of and difference from the world.

The **Attributes**, the second element of Spinoza's metaphysics, refer to what the intellect—not to be equated with or reduced to the human mind—perceives as constituting the essence of Substance. If Substance is infinite, then it has infinite essences, in fact, every possible essence. If not, something could exist with an essence that God did not have; consequently, it would be a second Substance, external to God. Ergo, there can be only one God, and it must have every possible Attribute. Not only are there infinite Attributes, but each Attribute is itself infinite and conceived only through itself, since it is an eternal and infinite essence of God. There can be only one Substance with infinite Attributes.

Attributes are the self-determinations or **expressions** of God. Expression is an important concept for Spinoza, with a unique meaning. Think of the story of Jekyll and Hyde: each is an expression or face of the truth of their existence, but there is not a third term—the real person—behind these two expressions. There are only the expressions; the expressions are the truth, the reality. A Swiss biologist—Adolf Portmann—argued that while evolutionary theory explained much about the natural world, it could not explain its extraordinary multiplicity of shapes, colors, smells, and so on. Instead, he suggested, this diversity is Nature expressing itself, expressing its pure and limitless creativity and beauty.[s]

However, humans do not have access to the infinity of Attributes; only two are knowable: **Extension** (also, somewhat confusingly, called Nature) and **Thought**. Again, these are not properties that belong to God, nor are they "parts" of God. They are expressions of God and, as such, they are one with God. As Spinoza says, "This truth seems to have been glimpsed by some of the Hebrews, who hold that God, God's intellect, and the things understood by God are one and the same."[t] Notice that these two Attributes—Extension and Thought—correspond to Descartes's substantive dualism.

Each of these Attributes exists in or, more accurately, expresses itself in two forms: infinite and eternal, and finite and temporal, although there are serious disagreements about these distinctions. Consider the infinite and eternal expression of Extension. Some commentators have equated it with *natura naturans* (rather than with God itself). In either case, Extension in its infinite expression, in contrast with Descartes, describes the totality of motion and rest, which always exists in a stable and constant proportion. Thought in its infinite expression refers to the infinite intellect of God, the single and wholly adequate idea or Truth (a logical system) that precedes all conscious activity and thoughts.

Each Attribute also has a finite and temporal form, where time, duration, and change exist as the self-differentiation and objectification of the One. In the case of Extension, the finite form is usually identified with ***natura naturata*** as the set of all existents of the past, present, and future. It is the totality of bodies or finite particles moving together and apart, at different velocities, and with different degrees of stability. But every body is itself a compound body, that is, a composition of other bodies, and so on. *Natura naturata* describes the necessary coexistence of everything that is, was, and can be—not as imagined possibility or a stable set of objects but as a topography of differential trajectories and mobilities. Similarly, the finite expression of Thought is the totality of thoughts in relations, in the past, present, and future, always configuring and reconfiguring itself into new logical systems of truths.

Natura naturata points to the third level of Spinoza's architecture: the **Modes** or **modifications** refer to all the bodies—whether things or thoughts—that exist at any moment. If the Attributes are expressions of God, modes are expressions of the Attributes. The Attributes are the immediate (immanent) cause of all their modes. In Extension, the modes are the discrete bodies as they move toward and away from other bodies, apparently propelled by complex chains of causality. In Thought, the modes are the discrete particular thoughts or ideas that appear to have no relation to one another and, often, to be caused by external events rather than the logic of reason itself.

Spinoza offers a **naturalist** (as opposed to a materialist) account of the nature of modes. More precisely, Extension as modes is about movement, and Thought as modes is about the configuring of logical systems, although Spinoza refers to both as bodies. Neither refers to an external body or idea as a static and fixed thing, but to the changes in the state of one body caused by changes in the state of another body. We are dealing with the changes or modifications of bodily states. Spinoza identified a body with its **capacities**:

a body is what a body can do. A body is defined by its capacities to produce changes in (to affect) (the states of) other bodies and to be changed (to be affected) by (the states of) other bodies; these capacities describe how the changing states of one body affect the changing states of another body. Spinoza called them **affects**. A body is its capacities, but since the actualization of a capacity depends on a body's encounters with other bodies, one can never fully know the capacities of any body: "They do not know what the body can do."[u] Or as this is more commonly stated, "Nobody knows what a body can do."

There is one final piece of Spinoza's metaphysics: the rather strange theory of **parallelism**, as opposed to both Descartes's interactionism and reductionisms that treat one Attribute as the ghostly and unreal effect of the other. Thought and Expression, mind and body, neither cause the other nor can either be reduced to the other. Spinoza was not arguing that changes in bodies cause psychic changes, or that psychic changes cause changes in the body; nor was he equating the logical and the psychological. Parallelism asserts that every mode under the Attribute of Extension is also a mode under the Attribute of Thought and vice versa. A mode of Extension *is* a mode of Thought. They are the same thing under the sign of different Attributes: "The order and connection of ideas is the same as the order and connection of things."[v] Whatever happens in one happens in the other. Mind is the idea of body, and insofar as every body is composed of many bodies, the mind is itself a complex whole of ideas. And insofar as every idea is composed of many ideas, the body is itself a complex composite. The logic of reason in Thought and the logic of causality in Extension are the same in the One.

TO EPISTEMOLOGY

Spinoza's epistemology followed the same hierarchical, tripartite architecture. In *Ethics*, he identified three degrees of knowledge, which clearly correspond to the three levels of his metaphysics,[4] describing increasingly "adequate" ideas about the world and one's actions, affections, and thoughts, and ultimately

---

4 In the *Treatise*, there are four: from report (or hearsay); from random (vague or confused) experience; "knowledge that we have when the essence of a thing is inferred from another thing, but not adequately"; and knowledge "we have when a thing is perceived through its essence alone or through knowledge of its proximate cause." The difference seems to be the inclusion of the first as a separate category. Spinoza, *Treatise on the Emendation of the Intellect*, pt. I, 19, 13.

God.[5] While every thought is an expression of the universal and infinite Attribute of Thought, its immanence varies according to its degree of perfection, its capacity to know Truth (God).

The first level of knowledge, called **opinion** or **imagination**, describes knowledge in which ideas are derived from—and are parallel to—immediate bodily sensations and perceptions. Here the mind is passive, simply reflecting changes in the states of the body (affections) produced by other bodies. A simple example is the knowledge that the sun warms the skin. Such knowledge is confused and inadequate, but it is neither false nor useless; it is just that we do not understand the true cause of the sensations we experience because we take the cause to be external. This is where Spinoza located almost all empirical or experiential knowledge (i.e., empiricism).

The second level of knowledge, called **reason**, is defined by concepts or abstract generalities that reflect common properties of bodies. Truth takes the form of both scientific knowledge (laws of nature) and what Spinoza called "common notions," concepts common to all thinking beings, akin to what Descartes called "clear and vivid ideas." This is where rationalism is located. It too is inadequate but is more adequate than imagination.

Finally, there is the knowledge of the essences themselves, which Spinoza called **intuition**. Here the knowledge of all individual modes is thought through their essential relation to God rather than as either isolated phenomena or instances of generalized laws and abstractions; in intuition, every mode is thought in its place in the totality of Truth and its existence in God. You might feel some mystical resonances in this notion of intuition as an immediate knowledge of the whole, an immediate relation to God. But Spinoza did not claim that he had achieved such intuition. (For reasons that I shall elaborate shortly, he could not.) Spinoza wrote from reason, from knowledge of the finite Attributes, while reaching for the knowledge of intuition, a knowledge of God and the infinite Attributes.

AND ETHICS

The final piece of Spinoza's thinking (leaving aside his political philosophy) is his ethics, offered in a work published posthumously because he was afraid of how it would be received. For Spinoza, the question of ethics concerned

---

5 Affections describe the states of bodies—or, if you prefer, the experience of or feelings attached to particular affects.

how to live a rational life in parallel with the achievement of ever more adequate knowledge. Put differently, Spinoza sought an ethics that could free humanity from the bondage of passion (and passive knowledge). He sought a "rational" understanding of "the good" that would eliminate any appeal to contingent circumstances and subjective judgments, or to common principles and generalized laws.

An ethical life was a life lived in freedom, but Spinoza's description was doubly paradoxical: first, because the ability to live an ethical life, to live a life that is free, depended on our ability to embrace determinism and necessity, the freedom to say yes to what happens by understanding that it must happen, that it is already true, already immanent in God; second, because becoming free means becoming what you already are—in God. Spinoza starts with a naturalist account of human life and conduct. Human actions, desires, passions, and thoughts are modes of God, but, more important, they exist simultaneously and in parallel as modes of Extension and Thought. He regarded the study of "human actions and appetites just as if it were an investigation into lines, planes and bodies."ʷ But if all human actions are all modes or affects, there are no clear distinctions among will, action, emotion, and thought. Each expresses a modification; in fact, they all express the same modification. That is to say, when talking about changes in the state of a body, every change and every state is simultaneously bodily, cognitive, and affective. Every thought is an action, and vice versa; and every emotion or affectation is similarly a thought and an action.

Not surprisingly, Spinoza distinguished three kinds of ethics, corresponding to the levels of his architecture. The first is an ethics driven by passion and desire, which connects back to his two readings of scriptures. If most people live epistemologically at the level of imagination, the most we can do is to seduce and frighten them into a more ethical life. The second is an ethics based on generalizable rules and reason—the most common appeal in enlightenment thought. For Spinoza, this knowledge would include not only the new science (natural philosophy) but also an understanding of politics, morals, education, and the material and technological basis of social life.

The third is a truly rational (Intuitive) ethics, defined by the Truth and Knowledge of God. It defines a life of immanence. As our knowledge grows toward a harmony with the totality of knowledge that is God in the Attribute of Thought, we will become the adequate cause of our own behavior. That is to say, the more we understand the holistic being of Thought and Extension, the more we understand the necessity of everything that is and that happens, the more we are fully aware of the real causes/reasons for our conduct, and the more we understand that we exist in and are determined by the immanent totality that is God rather than by any external modes. The freedom of an ethical life depends on the parallelism between Intuition and the increasing perfection of our lives and activities in the Attribute of Extension. We will live a life that is in harmony with our place in God.

Spinoza offered three axioms for this ethics. First, God—and therefore all existence—is determined: everything is what it has to be; nothing could have been otherwise. There is no contingency except that which results from the imperfection or inadequacy of knowledge. Second, God is free but not in the common sense of free will or the capacity to be or do otherwise. Like proponents of Greek Stoicism, Spinoza argued that freedom consists in accepting one's fate, in being aware of the necessity of the natural order and, hence, of what happens. But unlike the Stoics, for Spinoza, perfection is not about embracing what happens as one's fate, but about embracing one's drive to perfection, to become what one is.

The third axiom resolves the contradiction between the first two: "That thing is said to be free which exists solely from the necessity of its nature alone, and is determined to act by itself alone."ˣ Further separating himself from the Stoics, Spinoza argued that freedom requires self-determination. That is, you are free when nothing outside yourself is able to determine your actions or thoughts. Freedom is freedom from the bondage of being controlled by one's sensations and passions, as well as by social forces and convictions; it is the freedom to achieve one's own perfection. One is free only insofar as one finds and lives in one's proper place in God as both Thought and Extension.

How is this possible? Spinoza asserted that every individual mode endeavors to preserve itself, to persist in its own being or essence. But, even more, every mode endeavors to increase its power to act and to determine its own activity, which will enable it to further realize its essence, its self-perfection, as it reaches for its own truth in God. This apparently innate drive is the **conatus**. In a sense, the conatus defines the way of acting that any finite being, including humans, is determined by nature to pursue. Not surprisingly, there are many disagreements about the exact nature of this conatus, but that need not concern us here.

The concept of the conatus speaks against two common mistakes: the first assumes that all our actions are caused by external bodies (as in the knowledge of imagination); the second, the illusion of consciousness, posits that we are the cause of our own actions but only insofar as we understand ourselves as a (transcendent) consciousness existing independently of the body and the world. Against these errors, Spinoza argued that the more rationally we understand our actions and thoughts—here one needs to think of Intuition and not reason per se—as proceeding from ourselves as part of the totality of thought and nature, the more power we have to determine our own actions.

This is why he described actions proceeding from the mind itself, not from consciousness but from the immanence of thought itself. The perfection of the mind increases in proportion to the mind becoming increasingly active, as it moves to reason and then to Intuition. And increasing the power of the mind increases the perfection of the body (i.e., of one's way of living), which increases the power of the mind, and so on. The perfection of the mind and that of the body increase together as they become more active. That is to say, as we increase our power to act and think, we increasingly determine our actions and thought, but only by embracing the drive of the conatus pushing us toward knowing and living our place in God.

Freedom comes, in the first instance, from adequate ideas derived from the mind. Knowing the causes that move us means making the causes internal to ourselves. Just as Intuition seeks to harmonize our mind with the mind of God in the Attribute of Thought, so the freedom of action will harmonize our body with God in the Attribute of Extension. The true good—and the freedom to seek it—comes from understanding and moving toward our place in God. For Spinoza, this is the common goal of humanity.

Generally, our emotions or affections signal the success or failure of the effort to embrace our conatus as it reaches for self-perfection. Spinoza described those affections that strengthen the conatus as **joyous**, and those that diminish it as **sad**. In the beginning, our emotions are passive, and we are dominated by them—our actions seem to be determined by them because we fail to understand their true causes. We become free by understanding the causes of our actions, thus transforming our emotions (affections)—and with them, our choices, thoughts, and actions—from passive to active, from sad to joyous. Sad passions disparage life and diminish power. In this way, good and evil are understood in naturalist terms, not according to some transcendent measure of value but in the functional opposition between joyous and sad, between augmenting and diminishing one's power.

So, what is good is what increases our power and makes us more active. The greater the changes that come from within oneself, the more active one's activities and the greater the power to continue to achieve self-perfection. The conclusion, which some critics find disturbing, is not that we do not strive for the good but, rather, that we strive for whatever makes us more active, more powerful, and more self-determining: "It follows that every natural thing has as much right from Nature as it has power to exist and to act."[y] That is, whatever you do according to the laws of your nature (conatus), you have a natural right to do so, and your right is limited only by your power over Nature.

However, we still have to consider the second paradox. Remember that there is no change in God; insofar as we exist in God, we are already perfect. And yet, to the extent that we do not know that we exist in God, or how we are located in God, insofar as we do not act in harmony with all the bodies of the world, we are imperfect. We are always and already perfect and imperfect. Spinoza's ethics demanded that we become (in the world of finitude and temporality) what we already are (in the perfection of God).

Since one's capacities are actualized only in the engagement with other modes (ideas and bodies), the conatus of every mode is limited by that of every other.[6] Consequently, you cannot achieve perfection by yourself. The will to achieve your own perfection can only be realized when everyone, every mode, seeks and achieves its own self-perfection. No one can arrive at the truly ethical life unless every other mode achieves it as well. Quoting Spinoza, "Men who are governed by reason, that is, men who aim at their own advantage under the guidance of reason, seek nothing for themselves that they would not desire for the rest of mankind."[z] In other words, seeking an ethical life of freedom (and the knowledge of Intuition) is always a social if not universal task. It's a wonderfully collectivist image of the possibility of human history; it is not an apocalyptic image but an incremental image in which we move together to achieve a common perfection. Hence, Spinoza's thinking, even his liberalism, was strongly anti-individualist.

This requirement raises an important question: Can the effort to live in harmony with all existence, what today we might call an ecological way of life, be limited to humans? After all, in his naturalist metaphysics, all modes— including other forms of living beings but also inanimate objects—have a conatus and seek their own perfection. Does humanity's perfection depend on the perfection of everything in the world? How do we accomplish that without conceiving of ourselves as the masters of the universe?

If achieving both Intuition and freedom, which are the same endeavor, is an expansive project involving more than oneself, how do we accomplish this—both personally and collectively? How are we to move people beyond

---

6 In geometric terms, this is a necessary consequence of the theorem that in the Attribute of Extension, the total proportion of motion-and-rest is always constant.

the first levels (of both knowledge and activity)? This challenge led Spinoza to be among the first and strongest advocates of democratizing education as a necessary condition of this task. Perhaps his place in the Jewish diaspora helps to explain his deep commitment to education. Such education would enable people (actualizing their capacities) to move to the level of reason. But how do we collectively scale the mountain of Intuition? How do we empower people to follow their conatus so as to achieve the perfection of their being? Unfortunately, Spinoza did not offer much in the way of guidance.

Perhaps his diasporic history also helps explain other commitments, for example, to Mosaic democracy, implicit in the story of the Exodus. Spinoza advocated for both tolerance and political democracy as further necessary conditions for the effort to realize an ethical life. He also refused the synecdochical universalism of most enlightenment thinkers. He had a more expansive, encompassing, if not quite universal understanding of humanity. Maybe the capacity to think beyond the particular was a result of what today we might call his "double consciousness," being both inside and outside of the dominant European culture.[aa] He was a Jew, a Semite, in white Christian Europe, living within a continuous history of anti-Semitism, never quite equal and never assured of his own humanity; he was a colonized subject inside Europe itself and, often, an ostracized figure within European thought. Yet, he keeps appearing again and again as other thinkers return to him (see lectures 15 and 26) to give him a new life as a deep theorist and an alternative to both major founders of modern thought: Immanuel Kant and Georg Wilhelm Friedrich Hegel.

NOTES

a. Hume, *Treatise*, 1.4, 158.

b. Althusser et al., *Reading Capital*, 16–17.

c. Spinoza, *Theological-Political Treatise*.

d. Hegel, *Lectures on the History of Philosophy*, 3:283.

e. Nietzsche, "Postcard to Overbeck," in *Portable Nietzsche*, 92.

f. Quoted in Viereck, *Glimpses of the Great*, 373.

g. Quoted in Martin Joughin, "Translator's Preface," in Deleuze, *Expressionism in Philosophy*, 11.

h. Deleuze and Guattari, *What Is Philosophy?*, 60.

i. Maimonides, *Guide*.

j. Phelps, "Introductory Note."

k. Kasher and Biderman, "Why Was Baruch de Spinoza Excommunicated?," 98.

l. Spinoza, *Principles of Cartesian Philosophy*.

m. Spinoza, *Ethics*, pt. IV, 217.

n. Durant, *Story of Philosophy*, 188.

o. Spinoza, *Ethics*, pt. IV, 321.

p. Spinoza, *Ethics*, pt. IV, 224.

q. Spinoza, *Ethics*, pt. IV, 229.

r. Spinoza, *Letters*, letter 73, 942.

s. Portmann, *New Paths in Biology*.

t. Spinoza, *Ethics*, pt. II, 247.

u. Spinoza, *Ethics*, pt. III, 280–81.

v. Spinoza, *Ethics*, pt. II, 247.

w. Spinoza, *Ethics*, pt. III, 278.

x. Spinoza, *Ethics*, pt. I, 217.

y. Spinoza, *Political Treatise*, 683.

z. Spinoza, *Ethics*, pt. IV, 331.

aa. On double consciousness, see Du Bois, *Souls of Black Folk*, 6–9

A Brief Coffee Break

Time to take a breath, find a bit of calm, and get your bearings before continuing the backstory into the realms of modern thought. Modern thought did not bring the enlightenments to a sudden end, nor did these enlightenments lose their intellectual and political power; quite the contrary. History never works so neatly and conclusively. The project of the enlightenments, as well as their major ideas and arguments, continued (and still continues) to exert influence, but it faced increasing challenges from both the historical and intellectual developments of the modern. Modern thought did not emerge full-blown from the ruins of enlightenments, but it did alter the project and path, often posing the questions of enlightenment in new forms and frameworks. And it charted new paths, with new questions and assumptions. It is here that deep theory was born.

The next four lectures focus on two founding (and confounding) figures of modern thought: Immanuel Kant and Georg Wilhelm Friedrich Hegel. I present Kant as the first modern thinker, as well as the first deep theorist; he defined the agenda for the dominant trajectories of Euromodern thinking. Hegel offered a different set of modern trajectories, built on commitments of holism and negation. He also was the first to challenge, albeit in very limited ways, Europe's synecdochical universalism.

These two thinkers can also be understood following Michel Foucault's concept of the **founder of a discourse** (see lectures 28 and 29).[1] While Foucault used this concept to describe Karl Marx and Sigmund Freud, I think it offers another, more general view of deep theory. For each deep theory, it suggests that its way of thinking has taken on a life of its own. It has opened up a fertile theoretical field, a way of thinking that can give rise to often radically different theories. Often these differences are played out in arguments over the reading of key, foundational texts. In some cases, the texts take on the status of "sacred" writings. When someone invokes a particular deep

1 Foucault's actual usage is "founder of discursivity."

theory, you have to figure out how they understand it, what exactly they are embracing, and what they are doing with it. This is how a small number of deep theories can produce the multitude of theories that we face.

PART III.

Modern

Routes

Modern

Beginnings

Kant's Copernican Revolution

Immanuel Kant wrote the obituary of the enlightenments by giving them their finest expression. Defining enlightenment as "man's [*sic*] release from his self-incurred tutelage," which demanded that we "dare to know"—and, therefore, to think for ourselves—he set in motion the long history of modern thought.[a] Like his predecessors, he proposed an entirely new science to investigate the nature, boundaries, and contents of reason. But, unlike theirs, his new science was not going to emulate Isaac Newton's physics (as much as Kant admired Newton) but to ground it—in fact, to ground any and all knowledge and judgments.

Acknowledging that his was "a disagreeable task, because the work conflicts with all ordinary concepts, as well as being dry, obscure, and moreover long-winded," he declared that he was, nevertheless, "tired of dogmatism that teaches us nothing [rationalism] and just as tired of skepticism, that promises us nothing [empiricism]."[b] So, Kant changed the questions to fit with modern times. He opened up a radically new scene for thought and transformed the very practice of philosophy—and thinking. All the thinkers and theorists who followed Kant wandered in the space that his revolutionary project inaugurated.

Immanuel Kant was born on April 22, 1724, and died on February 12, 1804, in Königsberg, Prussia (one of the Germanic states).[1] He lived his entire life in this cosmopolitan port city on the Baltic Sea. Kant was raised in a Lutheran Pietist household; Pietists believed that religion is a matter of inner life and moral law, and stressed devotion and humility. Kant remained religious throughout his life and defended the possibility of theological truths from the assault of the new sciences and enlightenment more generally.

He began his education studying natural philosophy, particularly physics and astronomy. In *Universal Natural History and Theory of the Heavens*, published anonymously in 1755, he offered an early formulation of the nebular hypothesis, which argues that the solar system originated from a large gaseous cloud; his version, sometimes referred to as the Kant-Laplace hypothesis, remains a viable account. But not long after that work was published, his interests turned to more traditionally philosophical concerns.

Kant was the first professional academic philosopher in Europe, spending his entire career at the University of Königsberg, where he held the chair of logic and metaphysics but also taught courses on physics, natural law, ethics, rational theology, anthropology, physical geography, and pedagogy—the last being a required class for all students at the time. Kant published over thirty-five books during his lifetime, and his letters, notes, and lectures comprise almost twenty volumes.

Some of Kant's work is deeply troubling. He was among the very first intellectuals to lecture in geography—which was one of his most popular courses—and anthropology.[c] The latter was offered as both a descriptive science (studying human nature as it actually exists) and a normative exploration of the appropriate goals for humanity, becoming a founding text of what was later called philosophical anthropology. But both his geography and his descriptive anthropology classified people into judgmental categories based on temperament and personality. The results were not only Eurocentric but explicitly racist and imperialist. Whether such judgments permeate Kant's major philosophical works and arguments has been the subject of numerous debates, and this question has challenged many later thinkers who followed in his wake. Whether one can look beyond such egregious failures, whether

---

1 Russia renamed the city Kaliningrad, after World War II, and recently Poland has renamed it Królewiec.

one simply chalks them up to the times (or should we expect our greatest thinkers to transcend the sins of their times?), whether one can—or wants to—save the insights, arguments, and efforts that form Kant's "Copernican revolution" from the moments of darkness at the heart of his thought continues to haunt modern thought.

KANT'S CRITICAL PROJECT AND THE THREE CRITIQUES

Kant's greatest work, in fact, one of the most extraordinary achievements in the history of Western thought, was accomplished in a single decade, during which he published three books: *Critique of Pure Reason* ("the first critique," in 1781), *Critique of Practical Reason* ("the second critique," in 1788), and *Critique of Judgment* ("the third critique," in 1790). In these three works, he redirected the ways people thought about epistemology and metaphysics, ethics and politics, and aesthetics and imagination, respectively. He changed how we think about thinking. And, within decades, Kant's philosophy spread, first in Germany, and then throughout much of continental Europe, becoming the new dominant philosophy.

Obviously, given the wording of Kant's titles, critique is a central concept in his philosophical revolution. However, as the term and also the idea of being "critical" have become ubiquitous, it has taken on a variety of meanings: criticizing the structures of power—racism, capitalism, patriarchy—or, more generally, as disapprobation; the analysis of a text to identify its strengths and weaknesses or its deeper meaning; the evaluation of evidence and arguments, as in critical thinking. These are all useful activities, but none comes close to capturing what Kant was proposing.

For Kant, the enlightenments never posed the right question to Reason. Critique investigates the conditions of possibility of whatever is at stake: What are the conditions that enable the different forms of knowledge and experience? What are the conditions of possibility for reason to know the world? To know God? This practice of **critique** both anchors each of Kant's critiques and unifies the three. Beyond this, almost everything in them is the subject of debate. The scope of arguments and disagreements is almost limitless, ranging from the question of the true nature of Kant's project—what it was that he was trying to do—to the minute details of particular positions, some of which I'll discuss as we proceed.

There are at least six different interpretations of Kant's critical project, which are inseparable from how one prioritizes the three critiques and understands their relations. The most common reading starts with the first critique as an epistemological project. Kant was the culmination of the enlightenments, attempting to understand the capacities and limits of reason—by reconciling rationalism and empiricism, accounting for the contributions of both the mind and experience. By escaping the most basic argument defining the enlightenments, Kant provided a new theory of Reason.

A second reading, also emphasizing the first critique, suggests that Kant (the Pietist) was arguing against the enlightenments by defending the possibility of metaphysical and theological knowledge. The empiricists clearly rejected the idea of such knowledge because there were no impressions to which it referred. At least some rationalists seemed willing to accept a belief in God on faith (dressed in logic), without providing an epistemological justification.

A third view foregrounds the second critique as an effort to address the political and ethical paradox of the enlightenments: If the commitment to individualism entails a demand for autonomy or self-legislation, how can human beings define and legitimate *for themselves* their own political and ethical norms and judgments? What is the basis for the assumption of autonomy? How are rational moral and political judgments possible? Where is moral and political authority to be found?

A fourth view privileges the second and third critiques as an effort to protect humanity from the objectification that would result from the application of Newtonian science to humans. These critiques demonstrate why humanity was not subject to the logics and calculations of physics. Newton's universe was a machine (clock) in which all the pieces fit and worked together according to natural laws that allowed for predictability and quantification. Newton was agnostic about the need for or nature of a clockmaker, but a clock can't legislate its own time. People generally don't trust their watch to decide what time it is, on its own, and human beings are not machines describable according to scientifically discoverable laws. Machines cannot think for themselves, cannot make judgments, and cannot imagine. Humans can.

A fifth view uses the third critique to offer an alternative to enlightenment humanism by making imagination and creativity rather than reason and autonomy the true essence of human nature, poeticizing the origins of our most fundamental experiences rather than allowing them to be self-grounded—poiesis rather than Logos. This directly links Kant to the counter-enlightenments, foregrounding the wholeness of human experience and a sense of communion or sympathy among subjects and between subjects and objects. Reality becomes an expression of subjectivity, and subjectivity becomes part of the natural order. Other versions of this reading make either language and expression or feeling the central means by which humanity recognizes itself and achieves its fullest potential.

Finally, a sixth view—on which I will rely—sets the three critiques on an equal footing, with a common project built around transcendental critique. Kant set out to understand the conditions of possibility of all forms of knowledge as well as of their respective truths: mathematics and natural science, metaphysics and religion, ethics and politics, and aesthetics. How is it possible that the mind experiences and knows the world in these different forms? What makes each unique mode of reason possible? But Kant took the project one step further, questioning the very nature and conditions of possibility of experience and reality as they are lived and known. The conjunction of these concerns—epistemological and apparently metaphysical—set the stage for Kant's "Copernican revolution."

KANT'S REVOLUTIONS

The first Copernican revolution was the discovery that the Earth (and, by extension, humanity) is not at the center of the solar system, that the earth moves around the Sun. Copernicus changed the relation, reversing their respective places and roles. Kant did the same. Previously, it was assumed that knowledge must accurately describe or explain a world that exists independently of humanity. Kant reversed the relation: "Hitherto [a delightful but vanished word] it has been assumed that all our knowledge must conform to objects. . . . We must therefore make trial whether we may not have more success in the tasks of metaphysics, if we suppose that objects must conform to our knowledge."[d] Or, again, "Reason has insight only into that which it produces after a plan of its own," suggesting that human beings live in a world that Reason itself has created for them, in some way that Kant is going to uncover (critique), and that this is the only reality they can know.[e]

This claim—called **constructionism** today—is the second (alongside critique) element of Kant's revolution in thought. We must tread carefully here. Insofar as Kant still had one foot in the enlightenments, where reason was individualized, it is easy to read him as claiming that human beings live in a world of their own creation or, perhaps, that humanity creates the conditions for its own experience and knowledge of the world (as culture).[2] Such

2 Today, too many people assume Kant to have been a *social constructionist*, working from a set of theories that assume people construct their own reality, that they create

readings of constructionism opened the door to a number of deep theories; taken far enough, with growing hubris and occasional dissent, such theories made human beings into the masters of the universe, the engineers of reality.[3] But this was not Kant's position, for, as we shall see, the conditions of possibility for the human world (as opposed to an independent Reality) lie not with humans but with realities outside of and incomprehensible within that world. Rather they exist in what Kant described as the **transcendental** realm.[4] In a rather circular argument, *the transcendental* simply refers to the conditions of possibility of the human world.

If both the questions and the practices of thinking had changed, then presumably the objects of thinking changed as well. The third element of Kant's revolution was **relationality** (or at least a new understanding of relations) as the fundamental principle or building blocks of human reality. Obviously, previous philosophers talked about relations among people and things; the enlightenments approached knowledge as a relation between subjects and objects, and politics as the relations among individuals. Their questions concerned the nature of specific relations, as well as judgments about the better relation, whether epistemic or moral.

Kant changed the logic, making thinking itself relational: thinking is always and only about relation not only as the object of thought but as the very medium of construction itself. Relations both construct and are constructed;

---

the world they experience, not as individuals but as members of a shared culture. While animals live entirely by instincts, human beings live in a world of meanings ("culture"). People don't live solely in a world of objects; they live in a world in which objects have meanings that have been composed and attached to them. And people experience those objects and respond to them through the meanings they have been given. Consider an example: You are walking down the street and see someone shaking, maybe even slapping, another person. What do you do? Your first impulse is to stop the violence, but then you have to ask yourself, What is going on? What is the person doing? What is the meaning of the perceived violence? Is it simply brutal violence, in which case you would try to stop it or even call the police? Or is it an attempt to resuscitate someone who has overdosed, in which case you need to lend assistance and call an ambulance?

3 This anthropocentrism has become a central point of contention between modern and postmodern theories; it fuels debates between secular and religious traditions and is a central argument in contemporary environmental and political debates.

4 The term *transcendental* has taken on different meanings by different thinkers. It is often used synonymously with the concept of transcendence. For Kant and many thinkers who followed him, *transcendental* refers to what we might figuratively imagine as what stands below reality, that which is its ground or conditions of possibility.

hence, the processes of construction have to be understood in relational terms. Kant offered a theory of relations, which I call **mediation**, where a relation establishes a space between or encompassing two independent terms. He proposed that human beings live in a "third world," the **phenomenal world**, constructed by the relations that a **Transcendental Subject**— neither the mind as it exists in the phenomenal world nor, I should add, God—imposes on a **Transcendental Reality**, again, not the reality humans live in. Such transcendental concepts exist outside the phenomenal world of human experience and knowledge; therefore, they can be understood only through their effects, that is, the relations they produce that define phenomenal reality. Speaking somewhat figuratively, the former contributes the form of relations while the latter provides the "stuff" on which the relations are inscribed. It is these transcendental realities, which Kant called the **noumenal world**, that construct the phenomenal world of humans. It is the noumenal mind, a universal and transcendent subject, that imposes relations on a noumenal **reality-in-itself**.[5] Kant's three critiques attempt to describe not the truth of the Transcendental Subject but how it constitutes the phenomenal world by identifying the relations it contributes and imposes, making the phenomenal world into exactly what it is and, for Kant, exactly what it must be. This is why Kant's philosophy is sometimes called **transcendental** or **critical idealism**. Our world is constructed for us but not by us.

But relationality is not limited to the construction of the phenomenal world. It is doubled, operating within and defining the interiority of the phenomenal world. The phenomenal world is itself made up of relations, the very sorts of subject-object relations that concerned both rationalists and empiricists, now understood as a construction of mediated relations within that reality (see figure 8.1).

Given the transcendental status of the noumenal realm, Kant asserted that it must be universal, and therefore the phenomenal world it constitutes must also be universal. Consequently, Kant reproduced synecdochical universalism at a deeper—transcendental—level. Since the phenomenal world is transcendentally—universally—constituted, then all humanity must live in the same phenomenal world. In other words, Kant universalized the lived reality that defined a particular version of European society. If you did not experience and know the world in the same way, if your reality was not constituted in

5 Kant referred to the noumenal existence of an object as the *Ding an sich* (the thing in itself).

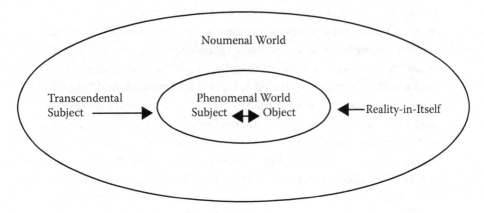

FIGURE 8.1

the same relations, you were not human. In Kant's thinking, the European powers were not colonizing or enslaving humans because those subjected to these horrendous powers did not meet the transcendental conditions of humanity.

Kant was not necessarily wrong to think about the constitution of reality as a universal process of relationality, but he was most certainly wrong to assume that the results of such a process would always be the same, that all people must experience and know the world in the same way. As we shall eventually see, the problem was that he equated the transcendental (the conditions of possibility) and the transcendent (the universal that exists outside of and beyond all experience).

THE SYNTHETIC A PRIORI

Kant introduced the concept of the *synthetic a priori* to describe the nature of the transcendental relationships constituting the phenomenal world, that is, the transcendental conditions of possibility of the phenomenal world being exactly what it is. It is a crucial concept, and I want to take some time to explain it. Remember that both René Descartes and David Hume distinguished two kinds of ideas: for Descartes, these were adventitious and factitious. For Hume, they were ideas of reason and matters of fact.[6]

---

6 I am ignoring Descartes's third category, innate ideas, which in a way served a purpose akin to Kant's synthetic a priori, although they were neither relational nor constitutive.

Kant argued that both philosophers confused two different questions about statements or judgments. The first was whether a statement tells you something, gives you some information, about the world, leading him to distinguish between *analytic statements* and *synthetic statements*. An analytic statement is a tautology; it is necessarily true because its predicate is included in the subject. If you try to negate it, you end up in a contradiction. A common example: all bachelors are unmarried. If a friend walked up to you and said, "I just met a bachelor who's unmarried," you would wonder why this is even worth saying. Predicating bachelorhood to someone necessarily means that he is unmarried. You haven't learned anything new from your friend. Or if your friend said that they knew a married bachelor, you would also question his intelligence. A married bachelor is a contradiction. An analytic statement does not tell you anything new about the world.

On the other hand, a synthetic statement is a statement whose predicate is not contained in the subject. Therefore, it is not necessarily true, and you can negate it without ending up in a contradiction. It does tell you something about the world. For example, that bachelor is a widower. Being a widower is not contained in the meaning of bachelor, so I know something new about that bachelor now. And if I were to negate it, it would just tell me something different about the world.

The second question you can ask of a statement was: From where does its truth derive? Here Kant distinguished between *a priori* and *a posteriori statements*. A posteriori statements are derived from and depend on experience, that is, from the impressions of the senses. Simple enough—basic empiricism. A priori statements are logically independent of all judgments that describe experience or the impressions of the senses; that is, neither the a priori statement nor any statement of experience (nor their contradictions) logically entails the other. For example, consider $a^2 + b^2 = c^2$. Its truth does not depend on any statements of experience. No one examined many right triangles in order to inductively derive the truth of this statement. This doesn't mean that an a priori statement doesn't have relations to experience. The Pythagorean theorem offers a truth that will be confirmed in experience. It may even be formed as a result of or in response to certain experiences, but its truth does not logically depend on them. Notice that empiricism is mostly concerned with synthetic statements, while rationalism is mostly concerned with a priori statements.

Consider the relations between these two sets of distinctions. First, all analytic statements are also a priori. They don't depend on any experience. You don't have to have ever met a bachelor to know that all bachelors are

TABLE 8.1 Locating the Synthetic A Priori in Kant

	Analytic	Synthetic
A priori	Yes	?
A posteriori	No	Yes

unmarried. Second, all a posteriori statements are also synthetic. Any statement derived from experience—such as all swans are white—is going to tell you something about the empirical world. And, as a consequence, such statement can be shown to be false (as when people discovered black swans in the Pacific region). Third, it is impossible to have an analytic a posteriori statement. A statement that is derived from the empirical world cannot be true by definition. Now is a good time to consider table 8.1.

What about the remaining box, the synthetic a priori? No Western intellectual had ever identified this class of statements. (Another new beginning!) A synthetic a priori statement, in which the predicate is not contained in the subject, tells you something about the world, but it cannot be derived from any experience of the world. It precedes rather than arises from experience, although it is constantly confirmed by experience. An example of this would be, once again, the Pythagorean theorem, $a^2 + b^2 = c^2$. It tells you something about the world but is not derived from any set of experiences of the world. It's not an analytic statement because it is not contained in the meaning of a right triangle. It is synthetic—it gives us information about the world that we use, oftentimes when we design or build something. But its truth is a priori. It is not logically dependent on empirical knowledge. It is not proved or disproved by empirical judgments and sensations. If someone were to claim that they had found a right triangle for which $a^2 + b^2$ did not equal c^2, you would appropriately respond that it is impossible, that they have measured incorrectly or misidentified the triangle as a right triangle.

For Kant, the synthetic a priori define the necessary or transcendental conditions of possibility of the various realms of experience and knowledge. They define the relational possibilities of the phenomenal world, which, Kant thought, has and must have the structures or relations that the synthetic a priori constitute. They are the laws or rules that govern both our ways of experiencing and knowing and their objects, as long as these are considered as objects of experience and not as they are "in themselves" (i.e., as noumenal realities).[f] They define both the conditions under which experience is possible and the nature of such experiences. Kant's three critiques sought to identify the synthetic a priori that enable us to experience and know the world in the multiple ways we do.

Kant's synecdochical universalism meant that there could be only one possible set of synthetic a priori or foundational, constitutive relations; consequently, he believed that his inquiries would provide a universal description of the phenomenal world and humanity. Any peoples that do not live in this phenomenal world are, ipso facto, not human. People living in what we today would call a different culture, who experience and know the world differently, are excluded from the class of humanity. This was Kant's—and perhaps modern Europe's—parochialism. And to some extent and with varying degrees of success, this assumption was challenged by many of those who followed Kant, starting with Hegel, who historicized the question of truth, making humanity into a developing project in its own right.

Still, Kant's importance and influence have been profound.[7] His way of thinking and the arguments and ideas (not Ideas) in which they are embodied have, both directly and indirectly, shaped modern thought for more than two centuries. His revolution in thought provided the ground for the emergence of major schools of thought—including phenomenology and structuralism. And it enabled a reframing of thought as deep theory, as ways of thinking the more than human world, and invigorated the *Geisteswissenschaften*. On the other hand, most postmodern and antimodern thinkers start by declaring their opposition to Kant.

7 His immediate influences were on traditions of German idealism (Johann Gottlieb Fichte, Friedrich Wilhelm Joseph Schelling) and especially Georg Wilhelm Friedrich Hegel (the subject of lectures 10 and 11) as well as German materialism, especially Karl Marx, a Kantian who turned Hegel on his head (see lectures 13 and 14). In the second half of the nineteenth century and the early decades of the twentieth century, a number of schools of neo-Kantianism played important and visible roles. While rejecting the noumena, Otto Liebmann (1840–1912) called for a "return to Kant" against other forms of idealism (Liebmann and Baruch, *Kant und die Epigonen*). The Göttingen school (followers of Jakob Friedrich Fries, including Leonard Nelson) offered psychological rather than transcendental interpretations of Kant. The Marburg school (Hermann Cohen, Paul Natorp, Ernst Cassirer) offered a panlogistic transcendental philosophy, which universalized particular constitutive logics (e.g., Cassirer's forms of symbolism), against all psychological and phenomenological interpretations of Kant. Finally, the Heidelberg school (Wilhelm Windelband, Heinrich Rickert, Wilhelm Dilthey) emphasized matters of history, culture, and interpretation, often arguing that epistemology is itself based in normative concerns. But Kant's influence has extended well beyond the neo-Kantians, and even anti-Kantians often started with his arguments and assumptions.

Kant's arguments for constructionism, relationality, and critique remain pivotal moments in the history of thought. His efforts opened fields of questions that future thinkers would have to address or contest. What are the processes by which reality is constructed? Is it only human reality that is constructed? What is the place of humanity in these realities? To what extent do these processes change, and what role do humans play? Can humans create and organize the world in which they live? What is the nature of relations? Are there multiple forms, and do they vary over time and space? How are they constituted, and how do they constitute? What are the nature and practice of critique? Is it the necessary practice of deep theory? What are its limits?

You will, whether explicitly or implicitly, whether positively or negatively, continue to encounter Kant in future lectures. Without coming to some terms with his theories, much of what follows will seem more difficult than it is.

NOTES

a. Kant, "Enlightenment," in *Foundations*, 85.

b. Kant, *Prolegomena*, 4, 13.

c. See Kant, *Physical Geography*, in *Natural Science*, 434–679; Kant, *Anthropology from a Pragmatic Point of View*.

d. Kant, *Critique of Pure Reason*, xvi.

e. Kant, *Critique of Pure Reason*, xiii.

f. Kant, *Prolegomena*, 26.

LECTURE | NO. 9

Kant and Critique

If you are not done with Immanuel Kant, if you want to further understand Kant's significance, it may help to have a better sense of the three Critiques, especially *Critique of Pure Reason*. This is a difficult and dense work, building a complicated series of analyses and arguments, many of which are still debated among Kant scholars. Kant introduced his project by saying that David Hume "interrupted" his "dogmatic slumber," suggesting that Hume's skepticism demanded a response.[1,a] Kant seemed less troubled by Hume's conclusion of skepticism than by his attempts to avoid it. If you recall, Hume asserted that it is common sense, that people have a natural inclination, to believe in the existence of bodies, minds, causality, and so on. Kant thought this was little more than an appeal to "the opinion of the mob," which had no relation to reason.[b]

---

1 *Prolegomena*, published two years after the first edition of the first Critique. This statement is commonly phrased as Hume having "wakened" Kant.

Hume could not find another solution because he was not asking the right questions, and was not looking in the right place for the answer. Hume asked whether reason could think of certain ideas (e.g., cause, mind, body) as real if there were no impressions that grounded their truth. But he understood ground as genesis, which led him to a psychology of impressions. Kant argued that the real question was *how* reason is capable of thinking of such ideas. And the search for their origins required an investigations into their conditions of possibility. How is it that people experience and know the reality of these ideas in precisely the ways they do?

The first Critique sought to identify the synthetic a priori necessary to produce the specific forms of experience and knowledge that define human reality, and then to demonstrate that they are both necessary and sufficient, that is, all that is needed. It has a complicated architectonic structure, starting with the Transcendental Aesthetic (to derive the pure forms of intuition), moving to the Transcendental Logic, which consists of the Transcendental Analytic (to derive a complete list of the categories of understanding and the schemata of imagination), and ending with the Transcendental Dialectic (to demonstrate the necessary existence of the Ideas of Reason).

I will not attempt to rehearse the richness of Kant's arguments and the logic of their order; instead, I will try to provide the "bullet points" to demonstrate the revolutionary nature of his theory and practice. Kant, following the psychology of his day (but without basing his analysis in psychology), identified four **faculties** that are the conduits of humans' relations to and in the phenomenal world. He then seeks the synthetic a priori that enable each faculty to contribute what it must to constitute the phenomenal world. This is his critique of the construction of a human world. I will briefly outline Kant's critique of each faculty, focusing less on the details than on the way of thinking.[2] My exposition is not meant to suggest that the first Critique is correct, but to show how it performs its task.

THE FOUR FACULTIES

The first and most fundamental faculty is **intuition** (no relation to Spinoza's use of the term!), or sometimes sense or sensibility. It is the immediate sensorial encounter with the world. It assumes that our first, completely unmediated

---

2 There is almost no detail, however big or small, that is not the subject of disagreements among Kant's followers and interpreters.

relation to the world is what the pragmatic philosopher William James later described as "one great blooming, buzzing, confusion."ᶜ Perhaps you have seen a pointillist painting, composed of thousands of dots; when you stand close, what you see is chaotic and meaningless. (As you move farther away, you begin to see the shapes that organize the chaos, but we will get to that only with the second faculty—understanding.) This chaotic confusion cannot provide us with any perceptual experience of the world.

The synthetic a priori of intuition, the **pure forms of intuition**, impose specific relations that order the chaos of sensations and make perception itself possible. Kant identified two pure forms: time and space. These forms are not properties of or pregiven relations between particulars; particulars do not yet exist. They are themselves particulars, but particulars that cannot be perceived as such (because we have not yet arrived at the possibility of abstractions or concepts). We do not *discover* space and time in the phenomenal world, and they do not exist in the noumenal world. The mind as intuition constructs and imposes space and time on the chaos of impressions, on reality itself. But "mind" here is not a reference to the phenomenal mind or individual psychology; it is the noumenal Transcendental Subject.

According to Kant, space is the form of outer perception; time is the form of inner perception. He argued that time was the more fundamental because one could think time without space but not space without time. However unfounded this assumption might be, it influenced many later modern thinkers—to be human is to live in time, to live historically—from Georg Wilhelm Friedrich Hegel and Karl Marx all the way to Martin Heidegger.[3]

The pure forms of intuition produce the **manifold of perception**, which refers to the experience of the world as a field organized by space and time. These spatial and temporal relations allow certain kind of judgments— judgments of perception—to be abstracted from and returned to the manifold of perception, and they allow certain kinds of knowledge (particularly mathematics). However, such judgments are "merely" empirical, abstract (they have no content), and subjective, until they can be retroactively reconstituted by the faculty of **understanding**, which produces **concepts** or **categories**.

Let's return to the pointillist painting: up close, it's just chaos. Take a few steps back and you perceive a spatial order (though not a temporal one)

---

3 A theoretical reaction in the 1970s and 1980s foregrounded the necessary spatiality of human existence.

TABLE 9.1 Kant's Categories

Quantity	Quality	Relation	Modality
Unity	Reality	Of inherence and subsistence	Possibility/impossibility
Plurality	Negation	Of causality and dependence	Existence/nonexistence
Totality	Limitation	Of community (reciprocity)	Necessity/contingency

among the dots, but it's still just a lot of dots that are now organized in particular relations to one another. You step back some more, and suddenly you see people and objects. The categories of understanding serve as templates; they serve a unifying or synthesizing function. They divide and organize discrete regions of the manifold of perception by imposing particular relations embedded in the categories. Kant then set out to identify the complete set of necessary concepts that constitute the phenomenal world as exactly what it is. He started with the basic types of judgment that people make of the empirical world, drawing on Aristotle's identification of the logical forms of judgment. These are quantity, quality, relation, and modality. Within each of these, he identified three possibilities. Table 9.1 shows his table of the categories.[d]

Here you can begin to see the logic by which Kant replied to Hume's skepticism. How do we know that bodies exist or that causality is real? Not on the basis of merely empirical (perceptual) experience, not by appealing to the innate structures of the individual mind, and certainly not by appealing to the common sense of the masses. Kant's answer: you cannot *not* experience the world in terms of bodies and causal relations because these are categories of understanding, which the Transcendental Subject imposes on and with which it orders the manifold of perception. Such concepts are the necessary conditions that constitute and organize the phenomenal world, the necessary conditions of all "objective" experience and all empirical knowledge, including the sciences.

Kant famously asserted that "concepts without perceptions are empty, perceptions without concepts are blind."[e] That is, if there were only the empirical field of space and time produced by the pure forms of intuition, without the categories of understanding, we would not know what we were seeing; in fact, we would not see any *thing*. Nothing would be identifiable because there would be no boundaries or relations drawn on the manifold of perception. But on the other hand, if we just had concepts—of an object, a subject, causality—but no perceptual field, the concept would have no particularity; it would remain entirely abstract (but not subjective). It is only the two synthetic a priori—forms and categories—working together that constitute the phenomenal field of experience.

Let's think a bit more about the relations between the two faculties and what they bring to the construction of the phenomenal world. The concepts of understanding organize the manifold of perception, but, Kant asked, how does the mind know how to apply the concepts to the manifold of perception in the "right" way? How does the mind know how to divide and organize the sensations, for example, identifying bodies and causalities where they belong? Why does the mind not constantly create Frankenstein-like bodies or establish absurdist causal relations?[4] How are the categories applied to actual experience in the proper way?

Kant answered this by taking up the third faculty, **imagination**, which brings its own kind of synthetic a priori: the **schemata** somehow direct understanding how to operate on the manifold. They produce the relations—specific synthetic unities—between intuition and understanding. For each kind of category, there is a corresponding kind of schema: the categories of quantity have schemata of number; the categories of quality have schemata of degrees of intensity; the categories of relation have schemata of the order of time (e.g., permanence, succession); and the categories of modality have schemata of Time itself insofar as it pertains to the existence of the object (e.g., possibility at any time, existence at a particular time). Beyond such perplexing claims, there is very little agreement about and numerous interpretations of the schemata: for example, they define uniquely abstract images for the categories; they define the specific conditions under which a specific category is applicable; they are rules—whether referential or procedural—for applying the categories and synthesizing perceptions.

Kant's analysis of the previous faculties attempted to derive the conditions of possibility of the specific nature of the phenomenal world. His arguments assiduously avoided both logical formalism and circularity; that is the point of critique. Yet his analysis of the faculty of imagination is decidedly unsatisfying. It does seem to be a circular argument: if you ask how the mind applies the categories to the perceptual field in the right way, and your answer is that there are synthetic a priori (let's say rules) defining their proper application, one might reasonably object that you haven't really answered the question because you still do not know how they—the schemata—work. In fact, many

---

4 Or does it, e.g., in the form of those we often ridicule as conspiracy theories?

commentators have suggested that this is the weakest moment in Kant's analysis. The question of imagination and schemata lingers through the first (and even the second) Critique, but take heart because Kant returned to the question in the third Critique.

But we are not done with the relation between the manifold perception and the field of experience as constituted through the categories. I might start by noting that there is an additional, unexplained feature of the manifold of perception: it has a unity—bounded, cohesive, coherent, and noncontradictory. Further, that unity is passed along to the field of experience. Elephants are not sitting in our chairs, and aliens are not flying around the room (as far as we know). Actually, Kant argued that the two unities—of perception and understanding—are mutually constitutive, existing as one, necessarily bound together as *my* reality. He called this synthetic unity the **transcendental unity of apperception**.[f]

How does one account for this doubled unity? What is its origin, its condition of possibility? Apperception is conscious perception with full awareness, that is, self-consciousness. Kant argued that the unities are created out of a moment of subjectivity or consciousness. There must be a perceptual consciousness that creates the unity of the manifold of perception, and there must be an experiential consciousness that creates the unity of the field of experience. And the synthesis of the two is not possible except through a unity of consciousness itself. "The *I think* must be *capable* of accompanying all my presentations. . . . Every manifold of perception has a necessary relation to the *I think*, the same subject in which the manifold is found."[g] Hence, the two subjectivities or moments of consciousness must themselves be the same subjectivity, the same consciousness.

Further, this consciousness has to be self-conscious because the subject knows that both the perceptual and the experiential fields belong to it. They are "mine." I am self-conscious about my relationship to the perceptual and experiential fields. Otherwise, I would experience all sorts of dissociative and hallucinatory realities. Consequently, the self-consciousness must also belong to the same subjectivity that is responsible for the unity of each field, and of the two fields together. There must be a subjectivity as self-consciousness that is embodied in every perception, experience, and judgment, and is responsible for the unity of all these relations. But that subject cannot exist in the phenomenal world because it is a condition of the phenomenal world being what it is. It must exist since this sense of unity and coherence exists, but it cannot be the psychological or phenomenal subjectivity that people think themselves to be or have. It is something thinkable but not knowable:

a Transcendental Subject, a form of self-consciousness that exists outside of and constitutive of the phenomenal world. It is responsible not only for the unity of the phenomenal world but also for the very possibility of self-consciousness. Moreover, it must be the same Transcendental Subject, universal and necessary, that is the source of all the synthetic a priori—the forms, the categories, and the schemata. When Kant said that humans can only know the world because reason constructs it, we can now see that it is all on the Transcendental Subject, the unconditional unity of a thinking subject, which cannot be predicated to anything else.

How can humans, living in the phenomenal world, even think the existence of something outside that world, while being incapable of knowing anything about it? What are the conditions of possibility of something that can be thought but never known? Kant turned to the fourth faculty, confusingly called **Reason**, which produces the **Ideas** as another set of synthetic a priori. Reason puts the transcendental in transcendental critique, positing Ideas (of a noumenal reality) that must simply be assumed for the phenomenal world to exist. They are defined only by the fact that they can be thought but cannot be known, rather than by any assertion of their actual existence. They define the boundaries or limits of reason (in the broader sense) itself, or perhaps they too are rules that regulate thought. Kant said, in this context, he had to "abolish knowledge in order to make room for faith."[h] Not surprisingly, this notion of the Ideas of Reason, which expresses the necessity of a noumenal reality, is highly contested.[5]

Kant did think that the Ideas were the legitimate subjects of metaphysical and theological knowledge or, more accurately, the Ideas were their synthetic a priori. Such knowledges do not look like any other kind of knowledge. Metaphysics and theology have mistakenly applied the forms and categories that constitute the phenomenal world to the Ideas, resulting in the **antinomies of reason**. For example: Does God exist in space and time? The very effort necessarily produces paradoxes because the questions themselves are mistaken. Ideas can only be known as Ideas.

The Transcendental Subject is such an Idea. In a wonderful moment of transcendental thinking, the Ideas of Reason are the product of the Transcendental Subject, the very idea of which is itself an Idea of Reason. There

5 As we shall see, modern philosophers after Kant often struggle with the noumena, either transforming it (e.g., Hegel reconstitutes it as the totality of the history of the phenomenal world) or questioning the need for such an assumption.

are others. On what does the Transcendental Subject impose its synthetic a priori? Where do the sense-data that make up the manifold of perception come from? There must be a noumenal reality, a reality-in-itself that precedes the phenomenal world and remains always outside the possibility of knowledge. This idea is necessary because, without it, humans would not experience and know the world in the ways they do. When one experiences a particular thing, an object, for example, one must assume that there is a foundational reality of that object—a thing in itself (*Ding an sich*) because, otherwise, humans would live in a world of appearances and not experience the reality of such things. Take the "fact" that I am seeing a chair. I know that it is part of the perceptual field organized by the forms of intuition, and that it is partly the result of the categories of understanding that create an object. But I also know or, better, I find that I am irresistibly drawn to assume that there is something else, something "real," grounding my experience. I can't ever experience it, or know it, but it has to be there. Without such an Idea, I would experience the world as a subjective hallucination, throwing me into perpetual skepticism and solipsism. Other ideas included the absolute totality of appearances (the world) and the absolute ground of all existences (God). Reason gives us the necessary Idea of God. One cannot know God or prove that God exists, but Kant thought he could demonstrate that the Idea of God is a necessary condition of our phenomenal reality. Kant also added the Ideas of a presupposition that presupposes nothing, and an aggregate that cannot be further aggregated. And in the second and third Critiques, he added even more—including freedom, totality, and God.

A CRITIQUE OF HUMAN LIFE

Kant thought the first Critique answered Hume's skepticism by uncovering the transcendental conditions of both the phenomenal and the noumenal worlds, each in their own way. And by making the transcendental transcendent, he guaranteed its universality. But he understood that Hume's conclusions had implications beyond the questions of experience and knowledge of the first Critique, particularly for matters of morality (and politics).

Critique of Practical Reason sought to realize reason (not Reason) in everyday life by searching for a rational morality, grounded in a **metaphysics of the will** as a self-legislating power of humanity. For Kant, will is not desire but the capacity to decide on a rational course of action.

Reason is the source of moral obligation because it is the ground of the determination of the will. What are the conditions of possibility for a rational morality? What should morality be if reason itself constitutes its conditions of possibility? What is the synthetic a priori of moral reasoning and behavior?[6]

Kant sought the possibility of a will that is good without qualification. Such a will, he asserted, would choose to do something *for the sake of* doing one's duty rather than simply following that duty. That is, rather than doing something because it is the right thing to do, one does it because it is one's duty to do it. Morality does not depend on what one thinks is morally right or wrong. You can think you're doing a morally good thing and be wrong, and you can think you're doing a morally bad thing and also be wrong. Morality does not depend on the intention or purpose. What defines a morally good action, whether it seems moral or not, is only that one does it because it is one's duty.[7]

One's duty—and hence the moral value of an action—lies in the maxim or rule according to which one wills a particular action. As an act of will, a maxim always starts out as a subjective principle, but the key to its moral value lies in whether one can will it to become a universal law, a formal principle that makes no reference to the specifics of the situation in which a choice is made. An action is moral only to the extent that its principle is universalizable, that one is willing to universalize it to all rational creatures, including humans.

Such a principle is a practical synthetic a priori, an instantiation of the **categorical imperative**, which is defined by its purely formal property (of universalizability) and its objective capacity to determine the will. It seeks an end that can, in itself, constitute a rationally determinate law of action. What might such an end in itself be? Kant suggested man [*sic*] himself, as a rational being, might be such an end because its value exists outside of any calculation of means to an end, outside of any causal chains. One expression of the categorical imperative, therefore, would be: treat all human beings as ends in themselves and not as means to be used for other goals.

Consider some rather obvious examples (although many people have disagreed and continue to disagree with Kant's universal theory of morality and its consequences): If you could go back in time and kill baby Adolf Hitler, would it be moral? Would you be willing to universalize the principle—you can kill someone for behavior they have not yet committed? Probably not. Or, again, whether cheating is ever moral depends on whether one can universalize the principle that it's all right to cheat. Hopefully not. Or, finally,

6 This is only one—important—line of argument in the second Critique.
7 This argument is likely tied to Kant's Pietism.

consider something we probably all do—lie to someone so as to not hurt their feelings. Would you be willing to universalize a principle that condones lying, remembering that it must be independent of any empirical content?

According to Kant, any rational being is capable of imposing on itself, if willing, a universal law. This is the condition of human autonomy, which, Kant argued, cannot be explained by any phenomenal knowledge. That is, autonomy is transcendental rather than phenomenal; the transcendental subject constitutes the autonomy (and freedom) presupposed by any claim that we are responsible for governing ourselves individually (morality) and collectively (politics). Furthermore, through a series of intricate arguments, Kant also concluded that the Transcendental Subject, acting through the categorical imperative, posits particular Ideas of Reason (in the narrow sense), including freedom, immortality, and God.

THE PROBLEM OF THE TRANSCENDENTAL SYNTHESIS

The first Critique grounded the truth of "natural necessity"; the second Critique grounded the truth of autonomy and freedom. Both are transcendentally constituted, but since our freedom is realized only in actions located in the natural world (of causality), there seems to be a contradiction between the two experienced realities and their transcendental conditions. Kant attempted to reconcile them, to establish their mutual consistency, in the third Critique, the *Critique of Judgment*, by establishing the relation between the particular and the universal, which remained unresolved in the first Critique. There it was the question of how the schemata of imagination determine the application of the categories of understanding (universals) to the manifold of perception (particulars).[8]

The title of the third Critique is somewhat confusing, since **judgment** is key in both previous Critiques as well. In the first two, Kant was concerned with judgments in which the particular (of intuition) is subsumed by already known universals (of understanding). In the third Critique, Kant turned his attention to judgments in which the universal is absent, neither pregiven nor presented within the experience itself.[9] The third Critique sought the synthetic a priori of the judgments of **imagination** (alongside the schemata), in which the universal is absent from the experience.

8 Again, I am presenting only one, albeit the most central, argument in the third Critique.
9 Kant called the former determinative judgments and the latter reflective judgments.

Aesthetic imaginative judgments concern phenomena that exist as **purposive wholes** without any specific purpose.[i] **Purposiveness** suggests the imposition of an order and unity (totality) on the manifold of perception, enabling us to proceed as if the natural world, for example, were purposively organized. But "purposiveness can be without purpose."[10] Something can be experienced as exhibiting a structured wholeness, thus being purposive, without any appeal to or awareness of its purpose. It may not even have a purpose. Purposiveness or purposive wholeness, then, is the synthetic a priori of aesthetic imagination.

Like the categorical imperative, it is a formal matter predetermining all judgments. It is "the consciousness of the merely formal purposiveness in the interplay of the cognitive faculties of the subject on the occasion of a presentation."[j] That is, it is the imposition of an apparently purposeful structure on an experience, without the necessity of an actual purpose. If our ability to understand the world depends on the schemata, the schemata can now be understood as the construction of wholeness, of purposiveness without purpose, constituting the totalities of perception. In pure reason, the totalities of the imagination work alongside the concepts of understanding to organize the manifold of perception; that is, there is an interplay—even harmony—of imagination and understanding.

There are two instances of purposive wholeness: the purposiveness of art operates as the presentation (or representation) of a limitation; the purposiveness of the **sublime** is totality represented as limitless. If art is a formal totality, the sublime is a formless totality. As a result, the sublime is unrepresentable; it appears to deny the possibility of experience and the harmonious interplay between understanding and imagination. It is the Idea of the absolute limit of human experience, the limit of the constitution of the phenomenal world. Examples include the unenumerable number—a number beyond all count, and the unaccountable encounter with the terrifying power of nature (e.g., the ocean, a tsunami). The sublime is that unity that cannot be accounted for, the limit experience of the possibility of understanding and therefore, of experience itself.[11]

---

10 There are also teleological judgments concerning phenomena that exhibit a purpose or final cause.

11 The third Critique was often taken up by the counter-enlightenments as arguing that aesthetics/imagination provides the fundamental principle of human existence. What enables us to construct reality and to live in the world that we construct is not pure rea-

While a work of art has no purpose in itself, everything in the work has a purpose, which is precisely to create the sense of purposiveness, of wholeness or unity, as a formal quality.[12] Every element has its necessary place in the totality. Imagine changing some small bit of a work of art: changing the *Mona Lisa*'s smile, a line of William Shakespeare ("to be or to die"), a single chord in Gustav Mahler's first symphony, or a single element of my favorite painting, *Guernica*, by Pablo Picasso.[13] Every element belongs exactly where it is, as it is. And you can't change it without the whole thing falling apart.[14]

Such purposiveness doesn't even require an artist. Most likely, you have watched a sunrise or come upon a stunning natural scene (the kind of moments we capture in photographs), and what do you say? "It's beautiful, a work of art." Because it all fits together—an extraordinary moment of unity in which everything is in exactly the right place, just where it needs to be to compose the perfect experience (and selfie). And then something changes, just a little thing, and the experience—the beauty—is gone. But in that first moment, nature becomes an aesthetic experience rather than the meaningful experience described in the first Critique. It's a different kind of experience of the world, one that is constituted by imagination and the synthetic a priori of the unity or totality (of an experience) without purpose.

In many ways, this resembles the commonsense understanding of art. When you have an aesthetic experience, what is important is the particularity of the experience. You cannot simply substitute one poem, one song, one painting for another. Each is defined by its uniqueness, its unique wholeness, the unique harmony among its elements. Your experience does not depend on some concept—of the medium, genre, or style. It is the wholeness of the work in its singularity that produces the aesthetic experience.

In other ways, Kant's theory of art is significantly different from our everyday understandings: his analysis, once again, purports to be transcendental and universal. As such, art is defined neither by a subjective experience nor

---

son but the transcendental imposition of wholes or unities, without any predetermined purpose or concept, on the manifold of perception.

12 This is a highly controversial assumption.

13 I used to visit the Museum of Modern Art in New York almost every week just to sit in front of this large, extraordinarily complicated painting, because it is perfect. Now granted, I thought at the time (and still think) it had a purpose—it's an antiwar painting, but that is not what makes it perfect. Every element belongs exactly where it is, as it is.

14 Some might argue that this is what distinguishes a work of art from the forms of mass and popular culture.

by the objective content of any work. While you feel a necessary pleasure, it is due only to the work of art's formal unity, its purposiveness without purpose. This synthetic a priori of art provides Kant with the means of reconciling causal determination and moral freedom, unifying the three Critiques. And, for our purposes, the sense of holism carried within the work of art provides us with an interesting if somewhat artificial transition into Hegel, one of the first anti-Kantians.

NOTES

   a. Kant, *Prolegomena*, 4.
   b. Kant, *Prolegomena*, 3.
   c. James, *Principles of Psychology*, 488.
   d. Kant, *Critique of Pure Reason*, a80/b106.
   e. Cited in Stählin, *Kant, Lotze, and Ritschl*, 12.
   f. Quoted in Körner, *Kant*, 96.
   g. Quoted in Körner, *Kant*, 61.
   h. Quoted in Körner, *Kant*, 61.
   i. Quoted in Körner, *Kant*, 181.
   j. Quoted in Körner, *Kant*, 185.

Hegel and Dialectics

I am afraid you are in for another difficult—and strange—encounter. Even for German speakers, Georg Wilhelm Friedrich Hegel's work is difficult; his language is dense and obscure, even more so than Immanuel Kant's and Baruch Spinoza's, partly the result of deep knowledge of the history of Western thought. Modern thought for much of the nineteenth and twentieth centuries played out as a battle between the followers of Kant (and the enlightenments) and those of Hegel (and the anti-enlightenment). While previous thinkers saw themselves as offering a new beginning, Hegel claimed a more complicated relation to the history of thought: his was an "overcoming" that both incorporated and surpassed that history. In Hegel's terms, it was a moment in the **dialectical movement** toward a more adequate truth. While Kant located ideas in transcendental relations, Hegel viewed ideas as systematically interconnected. His concepts often operate at the highest levels of abstraction, while simultaneously being inseparable from the details of his readings of history.

Georg Wilhelm Friedrich Hegel was born on August 27, 1770, in Stuttgart, in one of the Germanic dukedoms of the Holy Roman Empire, and died (possibly of cholera) on November 14, 1831, in Berlin, within the Kingdom of Prussia. He was a polyglot (who read at least six languages) and a polymath, with a wide range of interests. He started with a deep interest in theology and critical philosophy, particularly Kant and Johann Gottlieb Fichte (1762–1814), and while his closest friends—the philosopher Friedrich Schelling (1775–1854) and the poet Friedrich Hölderlin (1770–1843)—remained committed Kantians, Hegel expanded his readings to include classical philosophy, Spinoza, and Jean-Jacques Rousseau. He was often involved in heated political and political-economic debates and was an enthusiastic supporter of the French Revolution until the Jacobin Reign of Terror, taking it, along with the Napoleonic Wars that followed, as signs that "a new epoch has arisen in the world."[a] A strong defender of freedom and equality, he advocated for a rational politics, while embracing colonialism and racism. Hegel received his doctorate in 1790, having written a dissertation on problems regarding the relation of astronomy and mathematics, and, in 1793, the more important (theological) certificate. His professors commended his talent in philosophy, although, in one of those flukes of history, their comments were miscopied, and for more than a century it was believed they had said he had no talent in philosophy.

His earliest writings concerned Christianity, including the posthumously published *Life of Jesus* (1793–95), and idealist philosophy (*The Difference between Fichte's and Schelling's Systems of Philosophy*, 1801). Arriving at the University of Jena in 1801, he wrote *Phenomenology of Spirit* (1807), completed just as Napoleon entered the city victorious. After the university was closed, Hegel completed the three volumes of *Science of Logic* (1812–16). In 1818, he was given the most prestigious position in Germanic philosophy, the chair of philosophy at the University of Berlin, having just published, the year before, the three volumes of the *Encyclopedia of the Philosophical Sciences* (*The Logic, The Philosophy of Nature, The Philosophy of Spirit*). In 1821, he published *The Philosophy of Right*. He traveled widely in Europe and was decorated by the king of Prussia with the Order of the Red Eagle 3rd Class for his service to the state. He was, both philosophically and politically, a controversial figure.

I will start by laying out the major terms and assumptions of Hegel's philosophy and then consider selected arguments in more detail. Hegel was a rationalist and an idealist; he agreed with Kant that relations constitute reality but thought that Kant's enlightenment humanism inevitably led to the conclusion that humanity was the agent of history and the engineer of reality.

He offered a nonhumanistic (although perhaps still anthropocentric) theory, which emphasized the whole over the part. Taking his lead from Spinoza, that the Real is the whole, he suggested that "you are either a Spinozist or not a philosopher at all."[b] But the whole does not exist—yet; rather, the Real is the totality of relations bringing itself into existence.

Hegel rejected a number of Kant's central arguments. For Hegel, science is only a moment on the trajectory of Thought; it is not wrong, only incomplete and imperfect. Second, if noumenal Ideas define the limits of the phenomenal world, they must have content; therefore, they have to be knowable. And third, there is no foundational or transcendental reality that grounds the truth of Reason.

For Hegel, the true questions of the enlightenments were metaphysical and moral: What does it mean to be, and how is freedom possible? He argued that those associated with the enlightenments—from René Descartes to Kant—mistakenly assumed that both reason and freedom equated with autonomy, belonged to the individual. Hegel thought freedom belonged to the totality of relations rather than to an individualism that ultimately denies relations. In Spinoza, the totality is the One, God, Nature. In Hegel, it also takes on many names and forms, each realizing its own self-perfection: **Nature, Thought, Spirit, the Idea, the Absolute, Time**, and **the Totality**. Enlightenment thinkers also mistakenly distinguished thought from the natural world, reducing thought to a representation of an independently existing phenomenal reality. Instead, Hegel, again following Spinoza, understood Nature, Thought (Reason), and Spirit (human history) as "emanations" of the Idea, as the way in which Reality produces itself. This is Hegel's constructionism.

However, Hegel criticized Spinoza for following the enlightenment assumption that reality is stable and unchanging, arguing instead that reality is always and only characterizable as change, movement, and development. Time is the essence of Reality, the very definition of the Totality. Consequently, the Subject of freedom and truth, the Real, is the Totality; it is Time itself. But that meant that Time has a history of its own, and that at the end of that history, Time itself will be abolished. As Hegel wrote in *Phenomenology of Spirit*: "Time is the Concept itself which has determinate existence and presents itself to consciousness as empty intuition [think Kant]; thus, Spirit must necessarily appear in time, and it continues to appear in time as long as it does not seize its pure concept, that is, as long as it does not abolish Time."[c] (Don't worry if this seems incomprehensible.)

If Totality and Time were two of the major pillars of Hegel's thinking, the third—the **dialectic**—defined change as proceeding through the **Negative**. Reality itself, as Time, proceeds through negation. One might say that Hegel made the Negative into a theoretical category. Prior to Hegel, its most common use was derived from Aristotle's law of noncontradiction, an assumption that supposedly grounds all judgments of truth and falsity. It says: either A or not A, but never both. A statement is either true or not true. Thinking cannot proceed logically if it embraces contradictions.

Hegel argued that Aristotle's law assumes that reality is a static state of affairs, describable in a propositional or predicative language. But if reality is never stable, the law is simply wrong.[1] Dialectics, the logic of a constantly changing reality, assumes that all relationships are defined by negation. Everything is determined by its negation, by what it is not.[2] Negation (or otherness) does not mean that one term can deny or obliterate the other, but rather that the two terms are co-constitutive in their otherness. They exist as what they are only in their relations of negation; this is how reality produces itself; it is the way thought realizes itself and posits reality.

But, more accurately, the dialectical process proceeds through the negation of the negation of the negation. Reality produces itself, and then negates what it has produced by **positing** its other, which it then can negate to produce a new negation, which it can then negate to produce a new negation.[3] At any moment in this process, the state of Reality (Thought, Nature, History) is inadequate and incomplete until it has fully realized itself in its own perfection.

People often conflate Hegel's dialectic with that of Fichte: thesis (positive), antithesis (negation), and synthesis.[d] While both are triadic rather than binary, they differ in three important ways. First, Fichte's is a purely formal, logical relation while Hegel's is more metaphysical. For Hegel, contradiction can take many forms, depending on whether it is operating in Nature, Thought, or History. Contradiction can manifest as physical causality, the differences within and between concepts, or the clashes that mark human history. Combined with Hegel's constructionism, what is at stake is the determining power of the other, the relational constitution of the Real.

---

1 By rejecting the law of contradiction, Hegel rejects every dualism.
2 This argument had a strong influence on later philosophies, from Marxism to structuralism.
3 The notion of "positing" is a somewhat inadequate translation of Hegel's argument that any state of being conceives *and creates* its other.

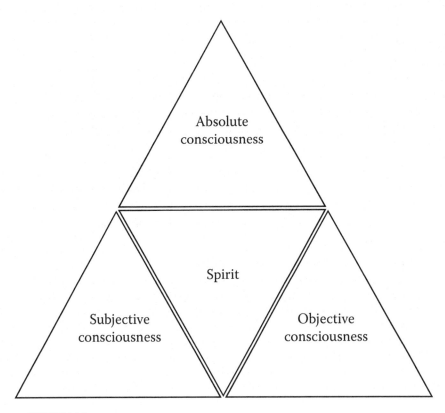

FIGURE 10.1

Second, in Hegel's dialectic, there is no synthesis that overcomes the contradiction in a new, noncontradictory unity. Instead of synthesis, the contradiction is *aufgehoben*, generally translated as **sublated** (admittedly not very helpful). Sublation (*Aufhebung*) is the incorporation of the contradiction *as a contradiction* into a new totality. The contradiction is not erased but incorporated into a new unity, which preserves the contradiction and retains its fruits rather than abolishing it. The contradictory terms coexist in their negation. Hence, the dialectic is represented as an inclusive triangle, which is always expanding and becoming more inclusive. For example, figure 10.1 depicts the philosophy of Spirit, which I will discuss shortly.

Probably the most general example of the dialectic is, in German, *Sein an sich* (being-in-itself) / *Sein für sich* (being-for-itself) / *Sein an-und-für sich* (being-in-and-for-itself). Being-in-itself is pure potentiality, the real meaning or content of which is still hidden; it is unreflective and immediate, separated from all others, devoid of relations. Being-for-itself or, more accurately, being for others is the actuality of existence as defined by relations, which opens the possibility of self-consciousness and subjective freedom. Finally, being-in-and-for-itself is the sublation of the contradiction between potentiality and actuality, between not-being and being, as **becoming**; it is the unity of the difference between that which can be and that which is.

For example: start with a seed, a pure potentiality, and therefore Nothing or a nonexistence. But it comes to be defined by its other: the existence of the tree. A contradiction, and the dialectical resolution is the seed becoming the tree, as the movement from potentiality to actuality (as in figure 10.2).[e]

Third, the dialectic is teleological; it seeks its own perfection in Nature, Thought, and Spirit—and the perfect Totality that ultimately sublates the differences between these realms into the Absolute itself. In each mode, at every moment or state, reality divides itself, posits its other, alienates itself from itself in order to create a more developed unity. The contradiction between A and B (not-A) is sublated into a new whole, C, which is necessarily more complex than either A or B because it includes both as well as their contradiction. C is the negation of the negation. But then C posits and confronts its own

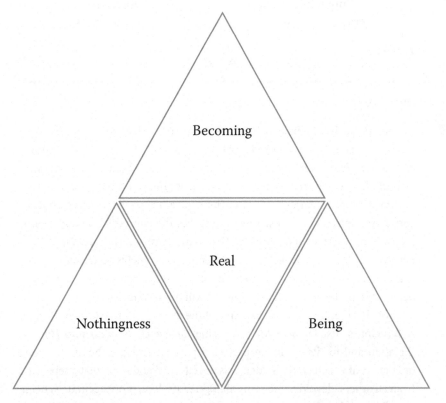

FIGURE 10.2

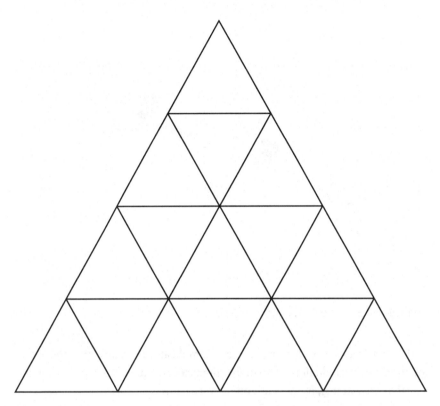

FIGURE 10.3

other, and the process continues, producing ever more complex totalities. In the final analysis, the Subject of this dialectical process (enacted in the various emanations or modes) is the becoming Absolute of reality. Contradiction is the motor force of the becoming perfect of Time, the Idea, and the Real.

The dialectic moves from the simple to ever-increasing complexity. Hegel's philosophy might be thought of as fractal-like insofar as it is dialectics (triads) all the way up and down. That is, every term in any dialectic is itself both the beginning and the end of another dialectic (see figure 10.3).

THE CUNNING OF REASON

Hegel told three dialectical stories, which, taken together, defined his philosophy of **dialectical idealism**: the dialectics of Nature, of the Idea (Thought), and of Spirit (History). The Absolute posits its existence in these three emanations. Each story plots the development of one mode from an empty abstraction to ever more complex totalities and, finally, to the concrete Totality of relations.

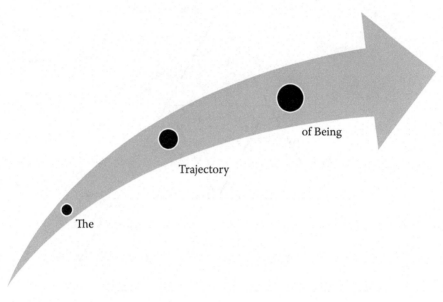

The   Trajectory   of Being

FIGURE 10.4

The totality gets ever larger and more complicated as it incorporates more and more contradictions. The more complex it is, the more concrete, more real, more rational, more true, and more free it is.

Hegel argued that Kant had not grasped the full consequences of thinking relationally. For if everything is defined by its relations, then nothing exists apart from its relations. The nonrelational, the immediate, is not real; it is merely potentiality. Reality, then, is the accumulating sublation of contradictions; consequently, the greater the number of relations that are incorporated or subsumed into ever-larger unities, the more perfect the totality. Each story of the sublation of contradictions is a story of Reality becoming its perfect self, the Absolute (Idea, Time) as Subject. This is what Hegel called the ***cunning of reason***, the process by which Reality brings itself to its own self-completion, its own-self-perfection.[f]

So, each of Hegel's stories narrates a development in which the subsumption of everything that came before defines a dialectical progression (see figure 10.4).

It is a succession of developments that is constantly curving back on itself to sublate that which came before, only to posit a new—its own—contradiction, in order to continue to propel itself forward in the attempt to become the totality as Absolute (per figure 10.5).

It might help to distinguish Hegel's thinking from that of Spinoza and Charles Darwin, both of whom had a concept of development. For Spinoza,

God exists independently of time; God is always and already perfect because it always and already includes everything, and everything that is in God is perfect. Where time is nonexistent, God cannot change; it has no temporality, no history. But humanity lives in the temporal world of modes in which everything, including people, keeps changing. Because the Totality is already given in Spinoza, he could only recognize change as the medium of the project of the ethical life. For Hegel, it is only at the end of Time that the Totality exists. Everything becomes what it must become through the cunning of reason in order to become the Totality that is Spinoza's God and Hegel's Absolute.

FIGURE 10.5

Nor was Hegel an evolutionary—Darwinian—thinker. Not only did he write before Darwin, but there are also significant differences in the two ways of thinking. Darwinian evolution proceeds by accident (random mutation) and without a telos; the only consideration is survival (of the fittest). Hegel's cunning of reason is neither random nor aimless, neither chaotic nor irrational. It is moving toward something, seeking something. Hegel assumed the Absolute to be the necessary realization of a preordained destiny, already implicit in every moment from the very beginning.

FREEDOM

Hegel thought that the fundamental problem of the enlightenments was freedom, but the enlightenments failed to see the connection between freedom and Totality. What does it mean to be free? Freedom for Hegel is self-determination. Determination is the negation of freedom by something external to an individual. The greater the determination, the more limited the freedom. But if the determinations (relations, contradictions) are incorporated into the individual, no longer existing outside its limits, then its freedom increases. The greater and more complex the totality, the greater the freedom. Something that incorporates every other cannot be said to be determined by anything else and is therefore free. Hence, the telos of the cunning of Reason is complete self-determination as freedom.

But the individual is no longer whatever or whoever it was, for it now includes so much more—its others. The subsumption creates a new subject, larger and more internally complex than the isolated, independent individual of the enlightenments.

It might help you to understand this if I use ordinary social life as an analogue. Many contemporary social theories argue that individuals are defined by their social relations. An individual is a product of all the social relationships that have determined them. There is no essence that defines an individual, no authentic self waiting to be discovered or liberated. There may be genetic determinations; there may even be a transcendent soul; but who you are as a social individual depends on the relations that have shaped you.

Every relationship to an other is, in Hegel's terms, a relationship of negation: the other is not you. Whoever they are, they are your others, your negations. They determine who you are. An individual who is not aware of what determines it is not free. Freedom demands that you become conscious of your determinations and subsume them, incorporate them into yourself. The more you know that they have made you, that they are you, and therefore that they are not really outside of your being, the greater your freedom. I am what my parents have made me, what my siblings have made me, what my friends have made me, what my wife and son have made me, what my adversaries have made me, what my teachers and students have made me, and so on, even what all the relations I have refused have made me. I do not exist independently of them; I am them.

But then you are no longer what you were; you expand your boundaries to become something more than what you started out as. You are reaching out to—becoming—the social totality. And then you reach out even further, in time, to subsume the relations that preceded and determined you; and you are becoming the historical totality. And you reach out to the natural world, incorporating its determinations. Freedom belongs to the Totality, and the greater the totality, the greater the freedom, and the closer one is to the self-perfection of Reality.

Consider a simple example. I am a professor, giving a lecture on Hegel. I have prepared an absolutely brilliant lecture, maybe the best lecture I have ever given (at least on Hegel). I have my notes, and I have gone over them repeatedly. Maybe I even practiced the lecture. I am in control and in charge. I am free to give the lecture I want. But not really! The students are determining me at every moment, limiting what I do and defining what I do next. I tell a joke, only to be greeted with silence. So, I try harder. I drop a few pop culture references, seeking to establish a bond, but I look out into blank faces. So, I go back into my notes because I am getting to the really exciting part of the lecture. But when I look to the students for feedback, they seem either dismayed or bored, and many of them appear anxious to get back to whatever they are doing on their phones. So, I conclude that they are not understanding the lecture (because I know how interesting it really is), and I try different words, different examples, different intonations—almost anything to give a successful lecture. I am adjusting myself to them, and they are responding to me.

You might ask, What if I just ignored the students, stuck to my notes, and gave the brilliant lecture I had planned? Then I would be free, right? I would be self-determining, right? Hardly. I could not have given that lecture because it was written without an audience, to be given to an audience. It is, I might say, waiting to be determined. As the audience changes, as the room changes, no matter how hard I try to ignore the consequences of these differences, they determine me, determine the lecture. Besides, the lecture was never mine to begin with; it was already determined by so many things, including previous lectures and students, my professors, my preparations (including the authors I read and the colleagues I consulted), and so on.

So, how do I increase my freedom? I recognize that my students are determining me, and that my lecture is not my lecture; it is not even our lecture but the product of so many relations, even if my others do not understand that. The lecture and my students are a collective production. And when I accept that, when I realize that this is not the work of an individual, working by myself, trying to pass along the wisdom, knowledge, and truth that I have, when I accept that I am determined by the others, that the lecture is becoming as it moves, then I become something more than myself, and the class becomes something more. So, *I* did not screw up the lecture (whew!), nor did the students. The lecture is part of who we are together. It constitutes the class itself as becoming a new unity, a new subject with greater freedom and truth.

My discussion thus far may suggest that the achievement of freedom is something that individuals do and, even more, that it may be something you can choose to do. Not in Hegel's world. Hegel denied that human beings produce reality or achieve freedom; he also denied that a Transcendental Subject—standing both above and below human experience and against a reality-in-itself—produces reality or seeks freedom. Instead, Reality is producing itself by changing itself, by always negating what it is at every moment to become something more. Thus, freedom belongs not to the individual, nor even to the society, but to the Totality of human history. Similarly, truth belongs not to any single idea or system of thought but to the totality of the Idea, of Reason becoming self-conscious of itself. And Nature reaches its own self-perfection, its own freedom, when its apparent otherness—an externality to be represented by science—is sublated into a self-determining system, incorporating all causality into itself. The Subject of the dialectic—of the becoming of Freedom, Truth, and Knowledge—is the whole defined by the growing self-consciousness of an increasingly complex set of relations, a totality making itself through the cunning of reason, the negation of the negation, and the sublation of contradictions. The cunning of reason is the becoming of freedom, which can only be *fully* realized in the Totality of the Absolute.

Are you still with me?

NOTES

    a. Hegel, *Lectures on the History of Philosophy*, 3:551.
    b. Hegel, *Lectures on the History of Philosophy*, 3:283.
    c. Hegel, *Phenomenology of Spirit*, 558.
    d. Fichte, *Science of Knowledge*.
    e. Hegel, *Lectures on the History of Philosophy*, 1:37.
    f. Hegel, *Logic*, 209.

Hegel and Totality

We are not done with Georg Wilhelm Friedrich Hegel, or, rather, Hegel is not done with you. (I can hear you groaning, or perhaps it is an exclamation of excitement.) There is still more to learn about Hegel, more to help you understand his way of thinking. The cunning of Reason posits existence as Idea (Thought), Nature, and Spirit (History). Each further enacts the cunning of Reason to achieve its own completion, self-consciousness, and freedom. And the contradictions among them are sublated to become the totality of the Absolute. Without bringing you to the brink of despair (but perhaps to the brink of comprehension), I want to elaborate some elements of the stories of the cunning of Reason.

THE CUNNING OF REASON

Science of Logic is Hegel's most difficult work, offering his theory of Reason as a metaphysics rather than an epistemology, as the dialectical achievement of Truth. It is a daunting text, and there is no way to make it fully accessible, so bear with me. The Real is rational, and the Rational is real. Reality is Thought, and Reason is self-thinking Thought, governed by its own necessity. Thought, in order to know itself, externalizes itself, continually positing its own contradictions between the abstract, formal being of the immediate (*an sich*), and the particular, objective essence (*für sich*). It then recovers its unity in the **Concept** (*an-und-für sich*) as the concrete universal, becoming ever more self-conscious. Thought is the dialectical sublation of every concept and conceptual contradiction, becoming concrete and complete as the **Idea**. It is the Idea that posits Nature and Spirit. Hence, this is where the story of the Absolute begins: the necessary unfolding of the Idea—in philosophy itself. The history of philosophy is a succession of developments curving back on itself. Each subsequent stage is richer, augmented by determinations, and thus increasingly self-determining. The cunning of Reason seeks what is already implicit in the very notion of a concept: the Totality of Thought or Reason, the self-determining knowledge of the whole by the whole.

Hegel took the Real as Absolute Truth to be the destiny of Thought. In Thought, the Absolute as Idea is the necessary condition of possibility of all reality. But—fasten your seat belts—the becoming of the Idea is Time itself, and the Idea is the totality of Time. Hence, the Idea is the end of Time itself. And Hegel did think there was an end, a moment when Time ceases, when Nature, Thought, and Spirit arrive at their own self-perfection and are themselves sublated into the Absolute in-and-for-itself.

Hegel's particular prediction of the end is not important (and, as we shall see, it did not come to pass). Even the assumption that there is an end when time itself ceases is not important. Rather, Hegel's influence depends on the assumption that the becoming of the Real can only be understood as a temporal trajectory, moving in a certain direction, perhaps even to a particular goal. Later Hegelians often deny there is a final goal or an end of time, but they might agree that there is more freedom—and more rational freedom—now than before. For example, Karl Marx embraced this notion of the trajectory of time toward greater freedom, culminating in communism. History for Marx ends when communism arrives. (We're still waiting.)

Hegel's understanding of the cunning of Reason had profound implications for future deep theories because it challenged the assumption that there was a single definition of humanity, a single way of being human. It was the first major blow against the synecdochical universalism, which had generalized the experience and knowledge of a particular group of people to define humanity, and excluded those who did not experience and understand the world in the same way (which, incidentally, included the majority of peoples in the world and even some in Europe). Hegel acknowledged the reality of different forms of human society, experience, and knowledge. The cunning of Reason explicitly made visible the multiplicity of human existences.

But Hegel did not fully negate the privilege such universalism assigned to Europe. Instead, he transformed it from a substantive and spatial judgment into a temporal movement. The cunning of Reason stretched from a state of infancy and primitiveness to ever more sophisticated and civilized societies, to the ultimately rational and free society that marked the end of History. Earlier human societies are less self-determining and less self-conscious. Each new society moves toward greater freedom by sublating everything that came before: primitive to civilized. But this trajectory was never so neat or linear; a society might take one step forward and two steps backward, or it might occupy a more ambivalent position, as did the Middle Ages. The cunning of Reason sometimes took detours, even going backward, in order to move forward. And as it did, it defined not only the quantitative growth of freedom but also the increasing rationality of the concept of freedom itself. I am sure you can guess where different societies were located.

Hegel identified three moments or civilizations (see figure 11.1). First, the Oriental world represented the childhood or most primitive stage of humanity. Only the ruler was free, and since that freedom was arbitrary, it did not even rise to the level of subjective freedom, the freedom of the individual. Second, classical antiquity represented human adolescence. In Greek civilization, subjective freedom was realized but limited because it was available only to some. Roman civilization more fully realized subjective freedom by defining it as a legal right of all citizens; yet it remained abstract and contradicted by the everyday life of those same citizens. Finally, the adulthood of humanity arrived in Germanic Christian society, where subjective freedom itself is universalized, accorded to all people not as an abstraction but codified within the very practice of the rational state. But true freedom is only possible when the entirety of human existence is subsumed, and the history of humanity becomes self-conscious of that unity. Thus, Freedom exists only in the Totality of History, at its end.

Understanding a society begins with locating it on the trajectory. But historicizing the difference between peoples did not make Hegel or his theories any less racist or colonialist. And Africa—the primary site of enslavement—is completely erased from the scene of "world" history.

Any society had to be treated as a totality in its own right, every aspect of which was an expression of the same, single contradiction (see figure 11.2).

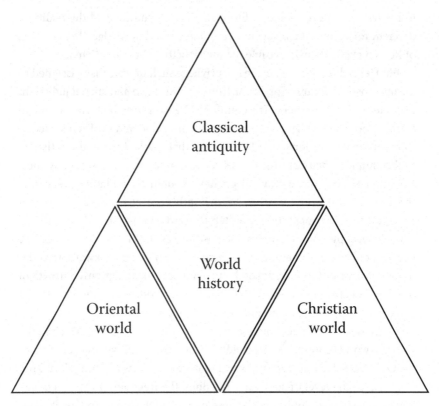

FIGURE 11.1

This theory of **expressive causality** assumed that the contradiction was determined by where it was on the trajectory of the becoming free of humanity: "There is only one spirit, one principle, which leaves its impression on the political situation as well as manifesting itself in religion, art, ethics, sociability, commerce and industry, so that these different forms are only branches of one trunk."[a] Therefore, every relation, value, knowledge claim, and judgment is historically determinate and provisional. It's all about one thing. There is no positivity, no isolatable identity or truth that can exist independently of the particular dialectical totality. That is, at least until the end of Time.

Consider classical Greek society: Hegel thought that traditional ways of interpreting, for example, Greek tragedy were inadequate.[1] Greek tragedy

---

1 There was, at the time, something of an obsession among German intellectuals with classical Greece.

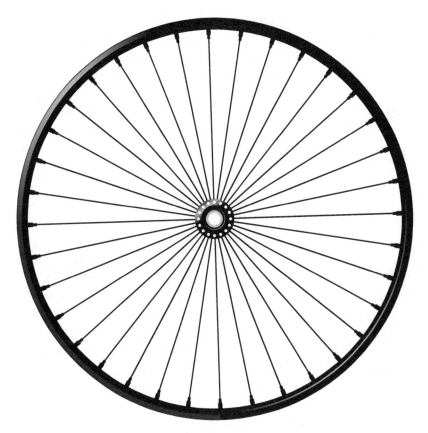

FIGURE 11.2

was often read as cathartic, or as a representation of Greek society, or as a set of meanings, perhaps even an ethics, about a possible way of living. But for Hegel, the tragedies were expressions of a fundamental contradiction that revealed the accomplishments and limits of the society, its degree of freedom and self-consciousness.[b] That contradiction—the difference between the particularity of subjective freedom and the universality of the principles of the state or, in other words, the tension between Greece's invention of democracy and its practice of slavery—was expressed in different emanations of the Idea. Everything in the society—its arts, architecture, domesticity, state, religion, economy, philosophy (and the contradictions between and within them, e.g., rhetoric vs. philosophy), and so forth—expressed this contradiction as the limit of the civilization's ability to move forward.

While it had subsumed previous contradictions, Greek civilization was unable to sublate this contradiction, defining the limit of its self-determination, self-consciousness, and freedom.[c] But there was one exception: Socrates, who was, in both his life and his thought, the beginning of a dialectical resolution. In his life, Socrates reconciled the contradiction of his own subjective freedom with the objective (universal) authority of the law by accepting his own death. In his philosophy, Socrates similarly confronted—even if he could not sublate—the contradiction between the particular and the universal, the finite and the infinite, as essence.[d]

HISTORY

Hegel offered a different story of human history in *Phenomenology of Spirit* [*Geist*]. While it has been widely cited, this is a difficult and highly contested work, with arguments over its status, structure, and project, as well as its specific details. It is sometimes seen as a preface to Hegel's philosophy, and sometimes as an early version, which he later revised in *The Philosophy of Mind* and the posthumously published *Lectures on the Philosophy of World History*. The *Phenomenology* moves between highly dense and technical philosophical arguments and specific examples (although not always "accurate") of people living in various stages of historical consciousness.[2]

My brief discussion follows Jean Hyppolite's (1907–68) and Alexandre Kojève's (1902–68) reading of it as a dialectics of the forms of human consciousness (*Geist*), a story of human history becoming self-conscious, self-determining, and universally free.[e] *Geist* alienates itself through a series of stages, objectifying and externalizing itself into "objective spirit," in order to return to itself at a higher stage. This is the work of the **World-Spirit**— akin to the cunning of Reason—which alienates and objectifies itself, for example, in the material institutions of society (such as the contradiction between the universal claim of the state and the particularity of the family). It acts through the ***Volksgeist***, the experience of particular historical peoples, whose self-understanding is insufficient, as the effect of their determinate history; that is, they could only understand themselves according to their own location in the trajectory of *Geist*.

2 It has been highly influential. Heidegger's *Being and Time*, for example, is often taken as a response to *Phenomenology of Spirit*.

Phenomenology of Spirit presents a series of stages of consciousness, each divided into multiple forms: the "pagan" time of the master or lordship (the time of prehistory); the time of the slave or bondage (defined by the dialectic of the master and the slave); and the dialectical resolution of the contradiction of the master and the slave. I will focus on the beginning, which set consciousness on the path of its own destiny at the beginning of history, and the end, when Hegel proposed the perfection of consciousness at the end of History.

The moment of prehistory is the time of the master, a stage of purely passive consciousness (i.e., no self-consciousness) and the most primitive—abstract and only formally universal—freedom. The master is being *an sich*, a pure potentiality and, as such, pure nothingness. The master's being is ultimately defined by the possibility of their death and hence, of their actual nothingness, not as possibility but as nonexistence (*für sich*). The master cannot accept their own possible death, so the contradiction cannot be sublated; the master can realize their freedom only by risking death.

We might think of the masters as warlords. They enact their existence and power through violence. They have only desire, the desire for recognition. Because they cannot sublate their desire to become something more, they seek to negate, assimilate, and control the other to reaffirm their own being-in-itself. That is, they assert their own being at the expense of the being of the other. The masters seek to have their existence as master acknowledged by the other, without sublating the difference, as the only way to reaffirm their existence against the threat of nonbeing; but only if the other is worthy of granting recognition can the recognition be universalized.

So, the other must be another master, who will also desire recognition. Each demands the other recognize their existence as master. Each one's desire contradicts the possibility of the other's, again without any possibility of sublating the contradiction. Each master must subjugate the other's desire to their own. The result is preordained: a life-and-death fight for recognition. Each risks their own life, but there are only two possible outcomes: one defeats—kills—the other and, thus, is denied the recognition they seek, so that they must start again, endlessly waging a fruitless battle. Or one surrenders, choosing life over death in the face of the terror of their own nothingness, and agrees to be enslaved. But the recognition of one who surrenders is insufficient; it does not fulfill the desire, since the recognition of a coward cannot affirm the being-in-itself of the master. Thus, the master has no way to escape this existential impasse. The master can only continue, outside of history itself, never achieving an understanding of concrete freedom.

Hyppolite and Kojève read "slavery" as domination, as an individual or group being subjected to the arbitrary decisions of another, apparently allowing for varying degrees of freedom. Slavery is the negation of the master as a being *an sich*; it is a being *für sich*, a being whose existence is defined entirely by others, in fact, by its subjugation to others, by its **dependent consciousness**. But while Hegel did not reference chattel slavery—the trade in human flesh as the total absence of freedom—the problem of freedom in Hegel cannot be separated entirely from the colonial and racializing context in which he was writing and which he supported.

The failure of the master has an unintended result: the contradiction between the warlike masters and working slaves, lordship and bondage. By creating the slave and forcing them to work, the master enslaves nature and thus realizes a new freedom in Nature, but this freedom remains abstract and undialectical. The slave, on the other hand, still desiring the recognition that would affirm their existence, negates the world as other, changing the world (and themselves) through work. The slave, then, is the origin of work, which inaugurates Time as History. History will only end when the difference between the master and the slave is finally sublated into a new unity.

The slave, having surrendered to the master, continues to confront the nothingness that defines their contradiction with the master, and the particularity that defines their relation to the world. Moreover, in work, the slave modifies their conditions in the world according to their own desire in the form of an idea or plan, and thus enters into self-consciousness. The slave thinks; the slave invents thought; all thought has its origin in the forced labor of slaves.

By changing the world according to an idea of their own making, the slave becomes something other than what they were, other than just a slave, while the master changes only through their relation to the slave. By changing the world, the slave negates their dependence on nature and removes it as a necessary and universal constraint on their freedom. The more the slave changes the world and themselves, the freer the slave becomes. The slave is creating and expanding the conditions of their own freedom, becoming more self-conscious and more self-determining, by continuously sublating the contradiction between themself and the world in the changing forms of work, as well as the contradiction between themself and the master, whatever form it may take. The slave becomes conscious of their own freedom; the slave is the origin of freedom, but their freedom remains essentially particular and personal. (Only the product of labor appears universal.)

The slave seeks to justify their own existence, to reconcile the emergent idea of freedom with the continuing fact of slavery, by constructing a series of systems of thought (ideologies). For example, in Stoicism, the slave persuades themself that they are free by accepting their fate, by embracing a purely abstract idea of freedom that prevents them from acting. In skepticism and nihilism, both of which Hegel read as forms of solipsism, the slave negates the value and even the reality of everything that is not the self, creating **unhappy consciousness**, a divided consciousness that is aware of its failure to reconcile the contradiction of master and slave.[f]

Mastery does not disappear, and the forms of mastery (the desire for recognition) have their own dialectical history. Despite its apparent renunciation, mastery continues to appear in forms of physical subjugation, violence, and even chattel slavery. But it also embraces (exploits) the ideologies of its slaves, especially in increasingly abstract forms of enslavement, which make the universal immanent in the world. In Christianity, the slave accepts their slavery in this world so that they can be free in the next, but actually, in both worlds, the slave is slave to the divine master (as well as the church), a transcendent, universal God who recognizes and inhabits the particular, first in the being of Jesus and then in the salvation of the believer. In capitalism, the immanent universal is realized in the form of private property and the bourgeoisie (as its owner), on the one hand, and the universal state, on the other. This poses a new contradiction between the worker and the citizen (a legal person) that is sublated in the form of capital as a higher abstraction, which produces and confronts its own contradiction in the form of bourgeois individuality. Hegel recognized that we are all slaves to capital. We live our lives having surrendered to the importance, centrality, and lordship of capital. Under the mastery of capital, the slave works for their own individuality, in the service of an ultimately abstract master, and under the protection of their rights as citizen, so that slavery appears to have been voluntarily chosen once again.

The history of Spirit—the history of History—takes place in this complex dialectical space: the nondialectical existence of the master, the contradictions in the forms of mastery themselves, the contradiction of the master and slave, and the contradiction between the slave and the world. But the real power of negation and sublation lies with the slave. Hegel's *Phenomenology of Spirit* traced the history of and across the many dialectical relations of the changing natures of mastery and slavery in their mutual struggles, through the continuing sublation of the contradictions, as Spirit becomes more self-conscious, more self-determining, and moves closer to freedom. The telos of this history promises the end of History by reconciling the contradiction between the master and the slave, between the particular and the universal.

For Hegel this was (at least almost) the moment of the French Revolution, which, according to Hegel, reenacted, in a higher form, the entire previous history of Spirit. The French Revolution arose out of the bourgeoisie, which recognized that it had enslaved itself to the abstract universality of capital and the immediate particularity of the anciens régimes of the state. Its attempt to free itself demanded that it once again confront the risk of its own death as negation, and this set the conditions of possibility of the Terror. One is human only because one is mortal—one can and will die. It is only as mortal, by embracing death, that humanity can realize its freedom. The dialectical history of Spirit is the sublation of death. But the Terror could not succeed, for it could not overcome its own contradictions, which had to be subsumed into a higher—in fact the final—order of freedom, one that negates the negation of death in a new concrete universal.

Napoleon Bonaparte (1769–1821) was the figure of this final moment. He came from a bourgeois family of modest means (his father was a lawyer), although it was minor Corsican nobility. Having no power, he was a slave who became a master or, better, he sublated the contradiction. He became, in his own person, the human individual in the fullest, proper sense, an individual who is recognized by all, both masters and slaves. Napoleon was a "world-soul" who "reaches out over the world and masters it."[g] But he did more because he made all people citizens of the universal state of the Napoleonic empire. Napoleon conquered in order to create—impose—freedom, to create the universal equality of freedom for all citizens. Hence, the master's abstract concept of freedom is reconciled with the particular freedom of the worker, into the concrete freedom of the universal citizen. Napoleon sublated the contradiction of the bourgeoisie by raising individuality to the level of citizenship as the collective individual of the commune, the Terror, and ultimately the empire. For Hegel, this should have been the end.

But this achievement of freedom in the Spirit still stood in contradiction to the history of the concept of freedom in Thought. That is, Napoleon lacked self-consciousness of the significance of his own actions. Hegel argued that the rise of the bourgeoisie gave birth to a new kind of individual, who neither fought nor worked, who is neither the master nor the slave. This is the bourgeois intellectual, who can conceive (rather than live or enact) the desired synthesis of master and slave. Hence, the final moment must sublate the contradiction between Napoleon's universalization of the concretely free citizen (work) and Hegel's philosophy as the self-consciousness of the dialectic in Thought. Hegel's philosophy is the self-consciousness of Napoleon, and when both are subsumed into the self-consciousness of Spirit or History itself as the achievement of the Idea of Freedom, Time ceases. To quote Kojève: "And since the perfect Man, the Man fully 'satisfied' by what he *is*, can only be a Man who *knows* what he is, who is fully *self-conscious*, it is Napoleon's existence as *revealed* to all men in and by the *Phenomenology* that is the realized idea of human existence."[h]

Hegel conceived this final reconciliation at the moment when, as he was writing the *Phenomenology*, Napoleon's army conquered Jena and Napoleon himself marched into the city. This is the moment when the revolution completes itself, by the movement of what Napoleon had accomplished "in practice" in France, to complete itself "in thought" in Prussia.[i] If only Napoleon had read Hegel, he would have been self-conscious of what he was doing, and all the contradictions would be reconciled. History would end. Unfortunately, Napoleon never read Hegel, and History did not end.

We can agree that Hegel's conclusion was wrong: we have not come to the end of Time or the self-perfection of consciousness; we have not realized absolute freedom, nor are we likely to do so. But that should not stop us from seeing the value, even the importance, of Hegel's argument and his way of thinking dialectically about totalities. Kojève used the failed conclusion to propose that the real question posed by the *Phenomenology* is a transcendental one: "What must man and his historical evolution be so that, at a certain moment in that evolution, a human *individual*, by chance having the name of Hegel, sees that he has an *absolute* Knowledge . . . ?"[j] We need not follow Kojève to recognize Hegel's profound influence, to see his footprints all over deep theory: the dialectic, expressive causality, his theories of difference and negation, as well as his figuring of the dialectic of the master and the slave. I offer Hegel for your contemplation, the second founder of modern thought and the second deep theorist.

NOTES

a. Quoted in Taylor, *Hegel*, 510.

b. Hegel, "Principle of Tragedy, Comedy, and Drama," in *Aesthetics*.

c. Hegel, *Philosophy of History*, 231.

d. Hegel, *Lectures on the Philosophy of World History*.

e. Hyppolite, *Genesis and Structure*; Kojève, *Introduction*.

f. Hegel, *Phenomenology of Spirit*, IV.b.

g. Hegel to Immanuel Niethammer, in Hegel, *Letters*, 114.

h. Kojève, *Introduction*, 70.

i. Pinkard, *Hegel*, 229.

j. Kojeve, *Introduction*, 33.

Second Modernity
(Second Interregnum)

Time to take a breath and prepare for the next twist of deep theory. I have suggested that Immanuel Kant was a crucial transitional figure at a key transitional moment in European history. Kant articulated the fullest expression of the Enlightenment project—in his commitment to humanism, reason, and freedom as autonomy. But Kant also transformed the enlightenments to become the first modern philosopher—offering three innovations: first, humans live in a constructed reality; second, this phenomenal world is both the product of relations and exists only in the form of relations; and, third, thought must become critique. This Copernican Revolution can be seen in part as an expression of and response to the rapid and increasingly established disruptions and crises of the first Industrial Revolution and the emergence of modernity, marked by profound changes across every dimension of people's lives—economics, politics, culture, technology, social relations, and so on. Kant was a child of his time, and just as the uniqueness of a child cannot be simply explained away (nature vs. nurture), so too Kant offered a vision of the world that made sense of, legitimated, and even encouraged the changes that were taking place.

Those who immediately followed continued to embrace some version of constructionism, relationality, and critique. They continued to believe in the necessity of reason, although they imposed greater or at least different limits on its capacities. But they also offered different models of relations, often emphasizing temporality and change over Kant's more static theory, and they slowly began to question and even limit Kant's universalism by allowing for the reality of different societies and different forms of humanity.

In the second half of the nineteenth century, all hell broke loose as a number of deep theorists challenged the assumptions of the enlightenments, interrupting the dominant vectors of modern thought. They reconstituted the practice of critique as an interpretive—hermeneutic—task and rejected transcendence in favor of a deep structure of power that actively hides itself. They distanced themselves in varying ways and to different degrees from what they saw as the illusions of human agency, self-consciousness, and rationality, although some continued to hold onto a faith in reason and science. Taken together with the almost parallel shifts in science, they challenged the hubris of humanism and the assumed capacity of humanity to grasp truth and control its own destiny.

Such thinkers were also children of their time, and the critical ways of thinking they introduced were as much a cause as an expression of the turbulence of the times, not uncommonly expressed in figures of impending doom (in much of early science fiction), a vision that became reality in the US Civil War, the Russian revolutions, and, finally, the First World War, the war to end all wars. This period has been described as "the age of despair," a moment of profound disruption, uncertainty, instability, and fear. It was, as Karl Marx described it, the beginning of a world in which "all that is solid melts into air."[a] It uprooted many established structures, practices, relations, and habits as well as what had been taken as wisdom and common sense.

This turbulent period also established new structures and relations, and opened new possibilities, although people were passionately divided over whether the new world being created was better or worse than that which was being left behind. (Of course, history is never as simple as it is commonly thought to be.) It has often been described as the beginning of a recognizably modern world. That is, if someone from the mid-twentieth century went back in time to the early nineteenth century, they would not find a world they understood or one in which they felt at home, but they would in the late nineteenth century.

This **second modernity** was fueled in large measure by the Second Industrial Revolution, which affected every element of social life, especially the possibilities and experiences of space and time (through communication and transportation technologies including, e.g., the telegraph, typewriters, automobiles, movies, and radio). These in turn enabled the enormous migrations—both domestically and transnationally—and urbanization of the moment. It was a time of major scientific breakthroughs, even paradigm shifts, with explosive advances such as the discovery of thermodynamics, relativity, and quantum mechanics, all of which challenged the Newtonian assumption of a stable, law-driven universe. In the biological sciences, evolution, genetics, and the emergence of molecular biology revolutionized the understanding of life itself.

Economically, this was a period turmoil that saw the rise of the modern corporation, the robber barons, and a new managerial class; the establishment of Fordist mass production and the rationalization of labor processes (and the subsequent need for advertising and public relations to create the equivalent market for mass consumption); the rise and suppression of labor unions; and the reordering and solidification of forms of globalization, imperialism, and colonial empires. The seriousness and complexities of these changes are reflected, especially in the United States, in the fact that this period is marked by the overlapping existence of the Gilded Age and the Progressive Era.

In Europe and the United States, new forms of social relationships and social geographies elicited significant moral debates, often driven by religious and morally conservative attitudes and movements. Every social relation—of the family and childhood, gender, race, and class—became a site of change and struggle. Europe was racked by small wars and the perpetual threat of something more serious, partly the result of both old and new expressions of national and ethnic belonging. The world was being transformed politically, and this transformation was there for all to witness.

The changes in culture—again partly the result of technological advances and economic reimaginings—were equally revolutionary. The human sciences, including functional and behavioral psychology, the development of statistical tools, and the first efforts to define and legitimate the "social sciences" (e.g., the work of such eminent figures as Max Weber and Émile Durkheim) emerged as a viable project. This was also a period of extraordinary and often radical cultural innovation, from the beginnings of expanded popular commercial mass cultures to the rise of the various experimental (and avant-garde) artistic—literary, musical, and material/visual—movements of "high modernism." Many of these cultural changes played a central role in constituting new understandings of the world and new ways of living in it—whether by legitimating or challenging the changes, the losses, and the emerging contours of reality.

Given the turbulence of the changes, and the increasingly visible, consequential, and even catastrophic events around the globe, it is not surprising that the questions of truth became urgent in the late nineteenth century and early twentieth century. People revisited the broad question of the enlightenments: How are human beings capable of finding and knowing truth? How does one ground truth? The growing power and appeal of forms of relativism, skepticism, and even nihilism produced something of a social and cultural storm.

The storm gave rise to at least four intellectual developments. First, there was a major revival (in many forms) of religion and spirituality, which asserted faith as the only possible source and anchor of truth. Second, there was a doubling down on the authority of science, reinforced by the emergence of logical positivism; the latter assumed that relativism was the inevitable result of the idealist and rationalist traditions of Enlightenment thought. Instead, it followed empiricism and assumed that science was the only, the universal, practice of knowledge. Therefore, every possible object of study either was capable of being studied scientifically or else was a metaphysical—and therefore a meaningless—concept with no referent to the world. In a sense, these two emergent traditions opposed each other, although both held an extremely narrow sense of the possibilities of knowledge, and both held onto a sense of the certainty of their positions.

The next four lectures will look to the rise of a number of hermeneutics of suspicion. They will be followed by six lectures that address the two remaining responses: phenomenology, with its attention to experience and subjectivity, and the various deep theories that focused on the nature and role of language. It might even be said that both efforts sought a modern way of thinking that was not predetermined by or condemned to play out in the space of the enlightenments. When you come to the end of these lectures, you will hopefully recognize, retrospectively, how much these various deep theorists prefigured the arguments and positions of more contemporary postmodern and contextualist theories.

NOTES

a. Marx and Engels, *Manifesto*, in *Collected Works*, 6:487.

Power and

the Limits

of Reason

Marx and Dialectical Materialism

At this point, you might feel like you have scaled a mountain; how big a mountain will depend on how well you have attended to the previous lectures. Now you can breathe more easily because the next deep theorists are more commonly referenced both inside and outside the academy. They are probably the first names that come to mind when you talk about "being critical." And they are likely to seem easier—if no less complicated—to understand.

Karl Marx is one of the most widely known, influential, and controversial thinkers, not only in the Western world but globally. While his ideas are often misrepresented and even misinterpreted, they are ever-present in contemporary theorizing. His more abstract work was clearly meant to lay the grounds for questions of empirical social realities.

He was born on May 5, 1818, in Trier, Prussia (part of the German Confederation), and died on March 14, 1883, in London, England. His father was a successful lawyer from a religious Jewish family, who converted in the face of growing anti-Semitism. His mother was a Dutch Jew from a wealthy business family.[1] In 1843, he married a Prussian aristocrat. He studied law at the University of Bonn (at his father's insistence) but followed his passion for philosophy when he moved to Berlin, "where [Hegel's spirit] weighed heavily on the living."[a] He submitted his doctoral dissertation at the more liberal University of Jenna on questions of atomism and contingency in the philosophies of Democritus and Epicurus. In Berlin, he became involved with the "Young Hegelians," a group of radical thinkers gathered around Ludwig Feuerbach (1804–72), who critiqued religion and appropriated Georg Wilhelm Friedrich Hegel's dialectic for social and political ends, while rejecting his idealism and theology.

Marx never held an academic position and lived somewhat precariously with his family, suffering from a variety of chronic health problems. He worked as a journalist and editor at various newspapers and magazines, many of which were eventually suppressed; he was expelled from numerous countries (including the German Confederation, France, and Belgium) and was even tried for sedition. His colleague and friend Friedrich Engels (1820–95) described him as "the best hated and most calumniated man of his time."[b]

He moved to London in 1849, writing for Horace Greeley's *New York Tribune* and researching classical political economy and the English economy in the library of the British Museum. He was economically supported by Engels, the author of *The Condition of the Working Class in England* (1845), who followed Marx to England and managed his family's textile mill in Manchester. They collaborated on a number of books, including *The Holy Family* (1845), *The German Ideology* (1845), and the *Manifesto of the Communist Party* (1848), the last written for the newly formed Communist League.[2] Shortly after its publication, Europe was racked by a series of rebellions, the most successful of which established the Second Republic in France.

Both Marx and Engels wrote many works on their own; Marx's included *Economic and Philosophic Manuscripts of 1844*, *Theses on Feuerbach* (1845), *The Eighteenth Brumaire of Louis Napoleon* (1852), *A Contribution to the*

---

1 The importance of Marx's Judaism has been debated for some time, ranging from those who read him as a "Jewish" thinker to those who assert that he was anti-Semitic (although he was even more critical of Christianity). He did not write about it very much, except for the controversial *On the Jewish Question* (1844). Marx was no doubt affected by the history of the Jews in the Rhineland, who were emancipated when it was captured by the French revolutionaries, only to have their freedom negated when it was reconquered by Prussian forces.

2 The public face of the secretive League of the Just.

Critique of Political Economy (1859), *Das Kapital* (vol. 1, 1867), and *The Civil War in France* (1871, in defense of the Paris Commune). The last two volumes of *Das Kapital* remained unfinished and were edited and published posthumously by Engels.

Marx was regularly involved with various "left" dissident intellectual and political groups. In the early 1860s, he helped found the International Workingmen's Association or the First International (1886–72), which was eventually torn apart by the conflict between Marx's collectivist vision of communism and the anarcho-mutualist politics of Pierre-Joseph Proudhon (1809–65) and Mikhail Bakunin (1814–76). In many ways, Marx was committed to the enlightenment project and to a certain universalism of civic, political, and economic emancipation and freedom. While he agitated for liberal reform against the absolute monarchy, he was committed to the possibilities of more revolutionary struggles.

TOO MANY MARXISMS, TOO MANY MARXES

As is the case for the subjects of previous lectures, there are many disagreements about the details of Marx's project and positions, but these have taken on a life of their own. His work has opened up an entire theoretical and political field, out of which many opposing schools of Marxism have arisen, each with its own movements and identities: for example, political economist, Leninist, Stalinist, Hegelian, Trotskyite, Maoist, Spinozist, humanist, structuralist, syndicalist, anarcho-syndicalist, and postmodernist. Additionally, there are cross-fertilizations among and variations within the schools, creating multiple hybrids.

These differences result not only from competing readings of Marx's texts but also from the selection of which texts to prioritize. Each variant claims that Marx's writings, or particular writings, or particular statements in particular writings legitimate their position. Each claims Marx as its own, but it can feel more like competing prophets and apostles. Actually, the differences are complicated, defined by interrelated questions about the nature of the project, the generational mission, and the political vision.

Consider Marx's project or, actually, his *four* projects. The first was a "philosophical" project that turned Hegel on his head, moving from dialectical idealism to **dialectical materialism**, in order to discover "the rational kernel within the mystical shell."[c] The second, **historical materialism**, offered a historically based social theory for the analysis of the specificity of any society. Hegel had already accepted the plurality of societies, each a totality in its own right. And, like Hegel, Marx also assumed that there is an inevitable progress in history but defined it as a move from primitive or "Asiatic" to feudal to capitalist to socialist to communist societies.[3,d] And, like Hegel, Marx had very little to say about what the end of history—a communist society—would look like.

The third project involved an engagement with the extant traditions of political economy and an analysis of capitalist economies (as a **mode of production**) and of capitalist societies.[4] Marx attempted to identify the fundamental contradictions of capitalism and their relation to the social structures of power and the organization of everyday lives. He offered a very European—but critical—vision of largely European history, although he recognized that capitalism is an expansive economy that necessarily seeks to colonize the world for resources and markets.

His most revolutionary project sought to redefine the relation between the intellectual and the political. As he famously wrote: "The philosophers have only *interpreted* the world, in various ways; the point, however, is to *change* it."[e] (Once again, the modern trope of starting anew!) Consequently, Marx attempted to think through, strategize, and even help organize political revolutions against specific authoritarian regimes and the dominant capitalist mode of production that sustained them.

Unfortunately, Marx's projects rarely correspond to particular books, leaving us with many questions. Did the projects evolve over time? Did Marx's positions on each project and their relations change over time? Since there are significant changes in his language and even in his questions, is it reasonable to seek a single consistent theory in Marx? Are there breaks— minor or major—in his work, and if so, what are they? Many commentators acknowledge the difference between Marx's early—more humanistic, more Hegelian—writings and the later, more analytic and critical works, but these debates and more continue to haunt discussions of Marx.

There is a second dimension of difference that complicates our discussion. At different times and places, different "generations" took up, combined, and pursued different projects in different ways. The first generation, in the late

3 "Asiatic" societies were described as ruled by a centrally located, despotic ruling bloc.
4 Major theories of political economy included mercantilism, which emphasized national economies and precious metals as the source of wealth; Enlightenment liberalism, which emphasized free competitive markets; physiocracy, which emphasized agriculture as the source of wealth; and, most importantly, the classical schools of Adam Smith and David Ricardo, who analyzed capitalism largely in terms of labor.

nineteenth century and early twentieth century, was dominated by Central and Eastern Europeans for whom Marxism was a revolutionary doctrine: for example, it grounded the Russian revolutions—both the failed revolution of 1905 and the successful revolution of 1917. Their work combined analyses of the structural-historical forces of capitalism with a political emphasis on the strategic leadership of a communist vanguard. They faced three issues: the economic laws of the capitalist mode of production; the political machinery of the bourgeois state (including imperialism); and the strategic theory of class struggle.

After the 1917 revolution, this generation sought to explain why the revolution took place in Russia, a possibility Marx had categorically denied. He had argued that a society had to go through capitalism to take advantage of what it makes possible—the working and middle classes, certain fundamental freedoms, certain ideas of individualism, and so on—that are the conditions of possibility of the socialist revolution. But Russia did not possess these conditions: it had not gone through an industrial revolution, leaving it largely a peasant economy without a significant working class; it had not gone through a bourgeois revolution, leaving it without a middle class demanding individual freedoms and limits on the state. At the same time, they sought to define, organize, and control a new revolutionary society. They were deeply involved in real politics as both leaders (Vladimir Lenin, Leon Trotsky, Nikolai Bukharin) and intellectuals (e.g., Georgi Plekhanov, Eduard Bernstein, Rosa Luxemburg).

The second generation, living mostly in Western and Central Europe between the 1920s and 1960s, faced a problem brought on by failure rather than success. Marx had predicted that workers in capitalist countries such as Germany, Belgium, and France would revolt, seeking to establish a socialist society in which they would appropriate the profits of their own labor and the state would act for the benefit of all workers. And there were a series of attempted revolutions in western Europe in the 1840s and 1850s. What Marx didn't predict was that the workers would lose, that capitalism would be able to mobilize resources (besides violence) to defeat such revolutionary efforts. This generation had to explain how capitalism had succeeded in defeating workers' efforts and, later, the rise of fascism within capitalist societies and the devolution of Russia into a totalitarian regime. They were trapped in historical pessimism.

The English Marxist historian Perry Anderson called the fruits of this second generation "Western Marxism."[f] This label applied to a long and diverse list of thinkers such as Georg Lukács, Theodor Adorno, Max Horkheimer,

Karl Korsch, Louis Althusser, Jean-Paul Sartre, Henri Lefebvre, Lucien Gold-mann, Antonio Gramsci, Leszek Kolakowski, Ernst Bloch, and Herbert Mar-cuse. Many of them worked without knowledge of the others. While many were involved with the Communist Party, most were not involved in real politics (with important exceptions like Lukács and Gramsci).

Their efforts took them back to Marx's philosophical project, often put-ting it in conversation with other—non-Marxist—theorists (e.g., Immanuel Kant, Baruch Spinoza, Georg Hegel, Max Weber, Sigmund Freud, Benedetto Croce, and Martin Heidegger). The result was a more abstract and esoteric—often universalizing—version of Marxism. Rather than economics and the state, these theorists focused on the muddier problems of ideology, culture, consciousness, and subjectivity in order to think about power by means other than violence. They attributed revolutionary failure to capitalism's ability to manipulate people's understanding of their experiences and commitments, and to people's susceptibility to such appeals and their willingness to accept their own subordinate positions. They also began to look beyond Europe to "Third World Marxists," both activists and intellectuals (often the same), from Latin America (e.g., Fidel Castro, Che Guevara, Jesús Martín-Barbero, Ivan Illich); the Caribbean (e.g., C. L. R. James, Frantz Fanon); Africa (e.g., Léo-pold Sédar Senghor, Ngũgĩ wa Thiong'o, Kwame Nkrumah); and South and Southeast Asia (e.g., Mao Zedong, Ho Chi Minh, M. N. Roy).

A third generation emerged around events of 1955 (the Bandung Con-ference of nonaligned nations) and 1956 (the Suez Crisis, the Hungarian Revolution) and the global movements of the 1960s, although it was further strengthened and modified in response to the collapse of the Soviet empire in 1989. If the first generation moved between political economy and social theory, and the second generation between philosophy and social theory, the third generation operated between philosophy and a concrete politics of in-surgency and resistance. It includes autonomous Marxists like Mario Tronti, Tony Negri, and Silvia Federici; cultural critics like Fredric Jameson; radical contextualists like Moishe Postone, Étienne Balibar, and Stuart Hall; post-modern Marxists and post-Marxists like Ernesto Laclau and Judith Butler; and postcolonialists like Angela Davis, Gayatri Spivak, and Enrique Dussel.

If you combine the dimensions of difference, you are likely to end up with a not entirely incorrect sense of chaos. So, it is useful to start with some generalized organization of the differences. Most discussions of Marxism start by describing four general takes of Marx. Although I will elaborate on these in the next lecture, it is helpful to at least identify them here. They are economistic, humanist, structuralist, and conjuncturalist Marxisms. **Econo-**

mistic Marxists tend to think in causal, even mechanistic, terms and assume that everything can be explained by the materialist laws of the economy. **Humanist Marxists** see a more interactive relation between the economy and other sectors and assume a more active role for human agency. **Structuralist Marxists** emphasize the formal relations within an organized totality, usually denying the role of individuals in history. And **conjuncturalist Marxists**—with whom my own inclinations lie—emphasize historical specificity as defined by the multiple relations among the elements of a society, as well as the relations of subjectivity and agency.

Now that I have spent all this time telling you why it is so difficult to talk about Marx's contributions, and that there is no middle or neutral ground when discussing Marx, I am going to try to present Marx's philosophical project of dialectical materialism. Be aware that some of my interpretations would be passionately contested by others. In lecture 14, on Marx's historical materialism as a theory of power in societies, I will try to demonstrate how the different interpretations play out and why they matter and will conclude with a few observations about his political economy.

MARX'S DEEP THEORY

Marx's most profound break with the history of European thought was his attempt to theorize power. Previous writers—for example, Niccolò Machiavelli, Thomas Hobbes, and Hegel—understood that power was a key component of human relations and the social order, but they took the concept for granted, often identifying it with a single structure of power, a single locus (the state), and a single figure (such as the prince or the master). Marx claimed that power was a condition of possibility of social existence in general, and of the specific social relations of capitalist societies. No one we have considered thus far attempted to conceptualize power as a constitutive element in the construction of reality.

Like Kant, Marx was a constructionist who situated humanity at the center of his thought. Both argued that the human world was constructed: what Kant called the phenomenal world, Marx called **third nature**. But Marx separated himself from Kant's transcendentalism (and Hegel's idealism) by following Feuerbach's argument that people make the world through the concrete, material social practices by which they produce and reproduce the conditions necessary for their own existence and that of society.

At the same time, he argued that power itself is determined by forces of which people are unaware. His view that historical forces (such as the contradictions of capitalism) driving history forward operate dialectically "behind the backs" of people was his continuing debt to Hegel. This points to a productive contradiction in Marx's theory. On the one hand, his Hegelianism suggested the power of transhuman, historical forces; on the other hand, his Kantianism affirmed a humanism that highlighted the active involvement—in the workers' movement, the class struggle, and revolution— of people. Marx's take on this contradiction asserted the inevitability of such struggles and revolutions. Yet his politics were more sophisticated and more—shall we say—dialectical.

I propose to identify four basic commitments of Marx's dialectical materialism: hermeneutics of suspicion, materialism, dialectics, and contextualism. But let me stress again that while most interpreters of Marx would agree on the centrality of these concepts, there is little consensus about what they mean, nor can I pretend to have found some middle ground. First, Marx was the earliest modern thinker to offer a **hermeneutics of suspicion**. The truth of what one sees is given in not-yet-visible **deep structures**, the **motor forces** of history, operating below the surface of experience. Marx's version of critique relocated the transcendental from the realm of transcendence to within human history itself. In doing so, it deontologized and historicized the cunning of reason.

This hermeneutics of suspicion made Marx a critic of the enlightenment as much as he was its inheritor. If people are determined by forces that are hidden from reason, reason itself is limited. On their own, people are incapable of knowing themselves, and to whatever extent people are capable of intervening in their own history, it is not as individuals but as collectivities (classes). Marx challenged some of the key enlightenment commitments— about reason, individuality, and consciousness. He was, we might say, the first anti-enlightenment thinker living within its broader project.

Second, Marx's deep theory was **materialist**. Marx claimed to turn idealism on its head. Reality cannot be defined in terms of, and it is not constructed by, mind, thought, concept, or idea. Rather, the fundamental nature, the building blocks, of human reality are material relations. There is much disagreement about the nature of this material reality and, hence, about the meaning of Marx's materialism. (I will return to these in the next lecture.) Marx identified two kinds of materialism. **Objective materialism** is about the "stuff" of reality, the brute matter of the world. It's the kind of materialism that often defines both common sense and physics: the world is made of bodies, or atoms, or quanta of matter/energy, or vibrating strings, and so on. It is what both René Descartes and Baruch Spinoza had in mind with the concept of extension, and what Hegel refers to as Nature. Such views have a long history; in his thesis, Marx identified Democritus as the first person to argue that the universe is made up of the materiality of atoms.[g] Some read Marx as offering a version of objective materialism, one that takes the material economy as the fundamental substance of social existence.

Against such views, **subjective materialism** says that third nature or reality is made by and consists of the concrete activities, the sensuous practices, of human beings. By such practices, which are always relational, people produce and reproduce their lives and society or, more accurately, the conditions for the production and reproduction of particular forms of social relations and existences. Subjective materialism makes human practices into—almost—a metaphysics. Thus, Marx argued that social existence—sensuous human practices—determines everything.

In a famous quote from *The Eighteenth Brumaire*, Marx brought together a sense of human agency with his hermeneutics of suspicion:

> Men [*sic*] make their own history, but they do not make it as they please; they do not make it under self-selected circumstances, but under circumstances existing already, given and transmitted from the past. The tradition of all dead generations weighs like a nightmare on the brains of the living. And just as they seem to be occupied with revolutionizing themselves and things, creating something that did not exist before, precisely in such epochs of revolutionary crisis they anxiously conjure up the spirits of the past to their service, borrowing from them names, battle slogans, and costumes in order to present this new scene in world history in time-honored disguise and borrowed language.[h]

That is to say, people make history—reproducing and changing the conditions of social existence—by what they do, but what they can do is determined in part by conditions not of their own making, by what other people have done before them. There are always limits to the practices that you can engage in because you don't have control over the conditions within which you act. Those conditions have been made by history, by human practices, and by the deep structures of power.

Third, Marx's deep theory is **dialectical**, both as a description of the nature of reality and as the appropriate mode of thinking about and changing that reality. His understanding of the dialectic was generally Hegelian: reality is constituted by and as relations; relations are always negative; and the more relations that are dialectically incorporated, the more concrete and real something becomes. Like Hegel's, Marx's dialectic is the negation of the negation, which involves the incorporation of the original negation into a new, more complex reality that does not erase the original contradiction. The negation remains but in a transformed way. And, so, the contradictions of feudalism give rise to capitalism, and the contradictions of capitalism give rise to socialism, and the contradictions of socialism give rise to communism, and no one knows if that is where the story ends.

But Marx's dialectic differed from Hegel's in more ways than turning idealism into materialism. For Marx, the totality is not something at the end of history; the challenge is not to achieve totality but to transform it into a different—better—totality. Marx's dialectic does not transcend human existence to become a universal metaphysics; it operates only in the human/social realm.[5] And while Marx shared with Hegel the faith that there was a telos implicit within the dialectic, Marx conceived it as human and historical rather than absolute. Communism is the moment when humanity is freed from all external relations and demands of power.

Finally, Marx's deep theory demands historical specificity, although it can allow for a wide range of interpretations or measures of specificity.[6] This is perhaps the most controversial commitment because it can problematize the authority (and, some would claim, the generalizability) of Marx's analyses. Yet it was Marx's way out of synecdochical universality. Marx distinguished between the general and the transcendent, the latter inevitably leading back to claims of universality. There is nothing that transcends the specificity of societies. Whenever you take something as universal, natural, essential, or necessary, you create a moment of transcendence. Generalizations, on the other hand, are useful tools for seeing the continuities and discontinuities among societies, but, as I shall elaborate momentarily, the more general a concept or description, the less it can tell you about any society. You can only understand a society by reconstructing the particular relations and contradictions that constitute it as a totality. Like Hegel, Marx argued that everything has to be understood in relation to the social totality in which it exists, including the concepts used to make sense of the totality. Marx wrote, "Even the most abstract categories are . . . in the specific character of this abstrac-

5 There are some Marxists who, drawing on Engels, would dispute this claim.
6 Marx was not the first thinker to emphasize specificity; **nominalism** is a theoretical position that refuses all generalities and abstractions by focusing on individuated events or things.

tion . . . a product of historical relations, and possess their full validity only for and within these relations."[i] That is to say, concepts become true only within specific totalities.

For example, consider the question of human nature, or the essence of humanity. Marx argued that "human essence is not an abstraction inherent in the single individual. In reality, it is the ensemble of social relationships."[j] There is no universal human nature. It is historically specific, a product and expression of the social relations and sensuous practices that constitute a society. As society changes, so does human nature. Human nature in nineteenth-century Germany was different than it is in twenty-first-century America.

Since the enlightenments, Western societies have often universalized the assumption that the individual is the basic unit of social life and the necessary locus of values, rights, and responsibilities. This individuality transcends social differences and the differences between societies. Marx argued that this idea of the individual, as well as its lived reality—after all, people do live it as the truth of their existence—is the product of particular social relations. There is no universal definition of the individual that makes individuality the sacred norm of society. Each society produces its own "individual" whose construction in any society is always the result of complex relations of power.

HOW TO "DO" MARX

The most commonly cited example of Marx's practice is his critique of classical political economy, which claimed to describe, explain, and legitimate capitalism. It assumed that the market was a natural and universal phenomenon and that every economy, in whatever form, was a market economy. The idea and existence of the market are the universal conditions of economies. And since capitalism is the most sophisticated form of market economy, all economies naturally tend toward (and should work to become) capitalism. Marx argued that this idea of the market was abstracted from the concrete social relationships and practices of nineteenth-century European capitalism; that is, it was another example of synecdochical universality. He challenged its universality, without denying that it might be a crucial part of many economies; but he also challenged the assumed singularity of the market, that all instantiations of market economies construct the market in the same way. There is no justification for assuming that markets in eighteenth-century Scotland were necessarily the same as or even closely similar to markets in twenty-first-century America.

This universalization of European capitalisms is itself determined by the specificity of these capitalist societies. Capitalism, as it existed in enlightenment Europe, sought to universalize itself in space in order to increase its profits or, more accurately, to increase its rate of profit. The most direct way of accomplishing that was by expanding the scope of both import (e.g., the supply of raw materials and labor) and export markets. So, these early capitalist societies went off in search of other societies, some of which already had workable economies far older than capitalism, that could be incorporated—by conquest—into their existing capitalist markets. The colonizers told themselves that this was necessary and inevitable because the market was ruled by the impersonal "invisible hand," which was a natural phenomenon, a law of nature.[7,k] They also told themselves that they were bringing "civilization" to primitive and barbaric worlds, whether or not they wanted it.[8] While this expansionary and imperialist logic has continued to determine capitalist societies, Marx's commitment to historical specificity means, at the very least, that the definition of value and profits, the forms of markets and exchange, and the practices of expansion are likely to change in the conditions of new social realities.

Consider a more technical example. Marx is often thought to have argued that everything is determined by something called "production." We shall consider some of the debates around this assertion in the next lecture, but for the moment, suffice it to say that Marx did not have a single, universal concept of production. While he did think that every society has some idea and practices of production, their actual content was only understandable in the social totality. There is no universal concept of production in Marx, and there is no concept of general production. There is a concept of "production-in-general," which only exists within and is central to societies of industrial capitalism.[l] Even then, it exists only as a rational abstraction out of real material relations.

This takes us back to Marx's practice of critique. It is really quite simple: the beginning of any story is always the end of a previous story, often forgotten or erased. Whenever you are confronted with something that is claimed to

---

7 It is worth noting that Smith only mentioned this notion once in *The Wealth of Nations* and offered little explanation for it.

8 It is perhaps not coincidental that European capitalism develops hand in hand with Christianity, and exports Christianity along with capitalism, because Christianity is also a universalizing (proselytizing) religion. Many other religions, including Judaism, do not seek to convert anybody; in fact, it makes conversion very difficult.

be or seems to be obvious, taken for granted, natural, universal, inevitable, or guaranteed, it is time for critique, time for you to demonstrate how this thing was constructed, and constructed in a way that denies its contingency and specificity. Every starting point is the result of previous material and mental efforts, which are often ignored or denied to protect what we assume is certain and normal. All the assumptions people make about "the ways things are and have to be" are where critique begins.

That leads us to Marx's epistemology and the problematic relation of thought and reality. How does dialectical materialism translate into actually thinking about historical realities and political possibilities? What is the process by which one comes to knowledge of the truth of social reality, of the motor forces of history? Unfortunately, Marx did not offer much guidance apart from his actual works, although he did write one (unpublished) essay about his method: the 1857 "Introduction" to the *Grundrisse der Kritik der Politischen Okonomie* (*Foundations of the Critique of Political Economy*), a series of seven unpublished notebooks, written between 1857 and 1861.[9]

If you think thought can ever fully capture reality, in all its material complexity, inside your head as it were, you're an idealist. If you think you can ignore thought and just talk about material reality, you're an empiricist who does not believe that human beings matter as agents of their own reality. Marx offered a dialectical relation between thought and reality, between concepts and sensuous practices, although concepts are themselves material social practices that arise from and act back on other social practices and relations. Social reality produces—provides the conditions for—ideas that exist as abstractions of those conditions, which may appear to exist independently and to both describe and legitimate the social reality. They may even appear to explain it and, consequently, to define the possibilities for either sustaining or changing the existing conditions.

Thus, while thought "occurs in the head," operating by distinctly "mental" practices, thought cannot generate itself. It is mental work that transforms observations into concepts. And from the other side, although thinking has its own logic and practice, its truth rests not in itself but in the social reality that is always its presupposition. This dialectical relation between ideas and materialities leads to a paradox: you can't change the social realities without

9 This is a rich compilation of some of Marx's most rigorous thinking as he prepared to write two of his most important works: *A Contribution to the Critique of Political Economy* (1859) and *Capital* (1867). I am drawing heavily on Hall, "Marx's Notes on Method," in *Selected Writings on Marxism*, 19–61.

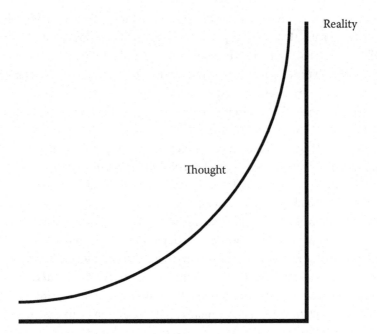

Reality

Thought

FIGURE 13.1

changing the ideas, but you can't change the ideas without changing the social realities. In one of Marx's examples, you must change bourgeois relations before they can be superseded in theory, yet those actual relations cannot be abolished until they are theoretically overcome.

The dialectical nature of the relation means that the contradiction between thought and reality is never entirely overcome; it can only be sublated as the negation of the negation. Thought can never become reality. And reality can never be entirely thought. But the concept is never entirely *in* thought, since thinking is always a practice of appropriating the real, even if thought can never fully and finally appropriate it. Thought tries to capture more and more of the concreteness of reality, to come closer and closer to it, although it can never capture the full concreteness. And reality tries to more completely realize the idea, to embody it in practice, although, again, it can never achieve the idea. The result is an increasingly rich dialectical totality, which can be represented asymptotically, as in figure 13.1.

Marx's critique moves from the simple categories that appear to organize experience (the **phenomenal forms**) to the real complexities that compose them. How is this accomplished? Stuart Hall described Marx's practice as a **detour through theory** (see figure 13.2).[m] As Marx put it, "The abstract deter-

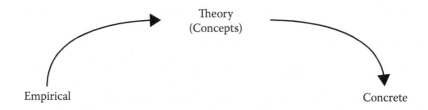

The Detour through Theory

FIGURE 13.2

minations lead towards a reproduction of the concrete by way of thought.["] The analysis begins with empirical reality, the evidence of the senses, which people assume to be the real. But it is not the real or, better, it is not an adequate idea of the real. For that, the analyst needs to "process" the empirical through the conceptual. That is, you need to reorganize the empirical, to make visible relations that are otherwise unavailable, perhaps even hidden. Theory in the form of concepts operates on the empirical "facts," but those concepts do not arise ex nihilo. Quite the contrary, they are abstracted from the overwhelming chaos (and unintelligibility) of the empirical through the work of theorizing. Theory is never completely devoid of reference to the empirical world. The detour through theory is the necessary dialectical movement to produce the **concrete-in-thought**.

Dialectical critique requires you to put aside all the categories you have—since they are likely either commonsensical prejudices or inherited from prior theorizing. Previous thinkers have treated their abstractions as if they existed independently of reality, as the creations of the mind; this is the trap that allows such concepts to be taken as natural and universal truths that are somehow inherent in the empirical realities that confront us. But because such concepts are formulated out of richly complex social relations, they are never merely mental concepts. They are themselves always dialectical, and the more abstract the concept, the larger and less concrete the empirical reality to which it is tethered.

For example, consider the population of the United States. At first glance, it may appear to be a simple, empirically given—even homogeneous—totality. But as you look more closely, you are faced with hundreds of millions of bodies with no way to organize them. There are too many variations, too many relations of identity and difference: shades of skin color and hair color, a broad range of heights and weights and shapes, foot and hand sizes, age, generations, all sorts of styles and presentations of appearance—in fact, a chaos of empirical realities. To put it differently, "the population" is a disorganized totality, the result of too many relations and determinations to be described or even registered, and most certainly an inadequate concept. So, you have to abstract new categories or concepts, in thought, from the empirical population, which can be used to organize the population into a coherent concrete thought-reality. Thus, Marx's concept of **class** is different from previous appearances because it is produced differently, with a different relation to empirical realities. Marx's classes do not exist per se in the empirical world. They are abstractions that construct a difference, bringing some order to the wild distribution of population, even while they do not exist independently of the empirical realities of labor relations.

A further example: Marx argued that labor was dialectically constituted by the social relations of capitalism, which are largely indifferent to the overwhelmingly diverse, empirically specific practices of labor. The result is that labor is usually taken for granted as a (quasi) concept that is assumed to exist outside of the empirical realities of labor. But the concept of labor can also be derived from the empirical practices and used as an abstraction to help organize social relations and reveal their deep structures. This is the dialectic of labor in thought and reality.

Having moved from the empirical, unorganized multiplicities to the abstract concept, the effort to construct the concrete-in-thought is not completed. Theory by itself is incapable of understanding, or offering a critique of, social reality. Rather, the abstraction itself provides a new starting point, from which you can begin to specify the abstraction, systematically and reflectively adding the material social relations and practices—the determinations, the contradictions—that make the historically specific social totality. Constituting the "concrete reality" requires moving through and beyond the abstraction; hence theory is always and only a detour but a necessary one, to get from the empirical chaos (because you have questioned the taken-for-granted categories) to the organized and intelligible rich multiplicity of the concrete.

Again, let's consider some examples. Capitalism is often described as a commodity economy: people make commodities to be sold, purchased, and consumed. But is such a concept sufficient to understand the truth of any particular society? Many societies, for at least five centuries, have had commodity economies. Is the commodity just one thing, always and everywhere the same? Does thought come closer to the truth of the concrete in history by simply repeating the abstraction? Of what use is it to say that any society has a commodity economy when so many different societies have different forms, different actualizations, of the commodity? What you have to do is specify the historical conditions of the commodity—its forms, its practices, its relations. The commodity here will not look like the commodity somewhere else or sometime else, and the economies that are built around them will vary in significant ways. Taking it one step further, Marx argued that industrial capitalism in nineteenth-century Britain was fetishized or mystified in such a way that the social relations of labor responsible for its production were replaced by an apparent relation between things and an objectification of labor itself.

We might return to the concept of class. Marx is often assumed to have offered a description of capitalist societies as a struggle between two classes: the proletariat (whose labor produces value) and the bourgeoisie (who appropriate some of this value as private profit). But, again, this confuses Marx's most abstract theorization of the class structure of capitalism, derived from the empirical study of capitalism, with the results of the detour through theory. It is not sufficient for any historical analysis or political struggle. When Marx looked at a particular historical moment, such as the coup by Louis Napoleon in 1851 in *The Eighteenth Brumaire*, he described multiple classes (some were subdivisions of the two grand abstract classes; others do not appear to be) that entered into an ever-shifting terrain of alliances and struggles.

Finally, consider how this method might apply to other concerns. What does it mean to observe that the United States is a racist society, or that it has always been a racist society? Following Marx's critical practice, Stuart Hall and other antiracist/anticolonial intellectuals have argued against the use of the concepts of race and racism as universal and natural descriptions of reality, which assume that racial identities and structures of racism are always everywhere the same. Instead, these concepts (and their dialectically related material realities) have to be understood as historically specific constructs. There is no single thing as race, no single practice of racism; particular understandings and practices are mutually determining. One might even go so far as to suggest that race only exists because racism exists, and as the forms of racism change, so too do the categories of race.°

Marx's notion of critique was never a matter of simply calling out forms of oppression, or declaring one's opposition to forms of domination, including capitalism. It is not merely the criticism of power. Marx did often talk about capitalism's exploitation of workers, and many Marxist thinkers are driven by such specific political struggles. But critique is not politics, or even politics by other means, and it is not simply the criticism of bad things. Despite his materialism, Marx's critical project is largely a Kantian one, an intellectual project that seeks to discover the conditions of possibility of existing social reality. But, with Hegel, he added a temporal dimension so that the question is not only how these conditions are possible but how they are produced, reproduced, and sometimes changed. Marx's critique sought to make visible the deep structures of history and to understand how they are played out in the thoughts and practices of real social actors. This was, for Marx, the condition of possibility of effective political struggle and social change (even if the result is not knowable in advance).

NOTES

a. Neil McInnes, "Marx," in Edwards, *Encyclopedia of Philosophy*, 5:171–73.

b. Engels, "Karl Marx's Funeral," in Marx and Engels, *Collected Works*, 2:469.

c. Marx, *Capital*, 29.

d. See Marx, "British Rule in India" and "Future Results of British Rule in India," in Marx and Engels, *Collected Works*, 12:125–33 and 12:217–22.

e. Marx, "Theses on Feuerbach," in Marx and Engels, *Collected Works*, 5:5.

f. Anderson, *Considerations on Western Marxism*.

g. See Marx, "Difference between the Democritean and Epicurean Philosophy of Nature," in Marx and Engels, *Collected Works*, 1:25–107.

h. Marx, *Eighteenth Brumaire*, in Marx and Engels, *Collected Works*, 11:5.

i. Marx, *Grundrisse*, 105.

j. Marx, "Theses on Feuerbach," in Marx and Engels, *Collected Works*, 5:4.

k. Smith, *Wealth of Nations*.

l. Marx, "Introduction," in *Grundrisse*, 81–112.

m. Hall, "Marx's Notes on Method," in *Selected Writings on Marxism*, 19–61.

n. Marx, "Introduction," in *Grundrisse*, 100–107.

o. See Hall, *Selected Writings on Race and Difference*.

Marx and Historical Materialism

I would guess that when you think of Karl Marx, you are not contemplating his esoteric deep theory but his critique of existing capitalist societies. But, first, you need to understand **historical materialism**, which begins with an abstract model of society as a totality (as in figure 14.1).

But what is the **base**? The **superstructure**? The relation of **determination**? Unfortunately, Marx offered several answers to each question, creating multiple possible combinations and, thus, multiple historical materialisms.

Let's start with some points of agreement, which, however vague, constitute the common—albeit a passionately contested and contentious—ground of Marxist thought. First, the base refers to the motor forces of history, the deep structures. Often, the base is identified with the **mode of production**, the conditions necessary for a society to reproduce itself. Marx defined it as the contradiction between the forces and relations of production. Generally speaking, the **forces of production** refer to the material processes that produce whatever form those necessary conditions may take (e.g., use value), including human labor, infrastructure, resources, tools, technical knowledge,

$$\text{Society} = \frac{\text{Superstructure}}{\text{Base}} \quad \text{Determination}$$

FIGURE 14.1

and so on. The **relations of production** refer to the social relations of labor (e.g., class relations).

There are two manifestations of the contradiction. First, on the one hand, it exists within the mode of production itself. For example, industrial capitalism is characterized by socialized forces (the cooperation necessary for the factory system) and privatized relations (the bourgeoisie's appropriation of surplus value as profit). On the other hand, the contradiction exists as the class struggle between labor and the owners of the means of production (the bourgeoisie). These two expressions may or may not correspond, depending on the historical conditions. Marx seems to have suggested that the two expressions are, for all practical purposes, the same in industrial capitalism.

Second, the superstructure encompasses everything else: the cultural systems, practices, and institutions of thought, creativity, and expression, of languages and consciousness, including education, media, religion, science, philosophy, and the arts; the political systems, practices, and institutions of the state, law, and civil society; and certain social domains, including family and domesticity and identity formations. The most important and contested element of the superstructure, which I will take up soon, is what Marx (following Napoleon) called **ideology**.

Third, determination is dialectical. More to come.

BACK TO THE BASE, SUPERSTRUCTURE RISING

There are at least three understandings of the base, each of which can be found in Marx's writings. In the first, an **objective materialism**, the mode of production consists of realities that can be empirically—even scientifically—investigated and described. As the true motor force of history, it is defined solely in terms that largely reproduce the modern, taken-for-granted sense of "the economy." Still, people disagree about whether the economy includes only the mode of production or also matters of distribution and exchange (money for goods). Does it include corporate structures, actual companies and corporations, their investors and board members? What is excluded is the work that supports commodity production—domestic work, service industries, retail, public work, education, perhaps even financial services—because it does not directly produce value and profit. These views are most common in **economist Marxisms**, but they can sometimes appear in **structuralist Marxisms** as well.

The second understanding takes a broader, **subjective materialist** view. From this perspective, common in **humanist** and **conjuncturalist Marxisms**, the base refers to the totality of material social practices and relations necessary for a society to produce, sustain, and reproduce itself as a particular way of living. In what is often taken as a softer notion of determination, Marx claimed that "it is not the consciousness of men that determines their existence, but their social existence that determines their consciousness."[a]

The third understanding assumes that the contents of the base are never guaranteed in advance, nor can they be distinguished in some simple and universal way from the rest of the social totality. Rejecting a neat binary division between base and superstructure, it starts with a society as a complex and complexly configured totality, in which the base is always historically specific. Such views are likely to be found in structural and conjunctural Marxisms.[1]

Theories of the superstructure often focus on ideology as its most important element. Marx offered four different theories of ideology. While ideology is commonly limited to systems of political beliefs, Marx started with a broader definition: the system of beliefs through which people understand the world, and the values and logics with which they decide how to live in that world.

The first theory, chiefly associated with economist versions of Marxism, understands ideology as **epiphenomenal**, an illusion or phantom not to be taken seriously. Ideology is like Plato's myth of the cave, where all you can see are the shadows of shadows, imitations of imitations. Ideology is a distraction from the serious business of coming to terms with the base, little more than a tool in the capitalist's arsenal. People's ideology—what people think or how they experience life—is directly determined by their place in the mode of production. The analysis of the base already tells you the illusions that capitalism has created.

When I entered graduate school, I was excited to take a seminar on Marxism and film. At the time, there were almost no classes on popular culture or media culture. I imagined watching films, analyzing them, arguing about them, and having fun. (Popcorn and beer would be optional.) My enthusiasm

---

1 Antonio Gramsci began his conjuncturalist theory by introducing a third term—structure as the realm of the political, between the base and superstructure. See Gramsci, *Selections*.

quickly ended when the professor told us that we were not allowed to watch the films to be discussed. Watching them would distract us from discovering, scientifically, their significance. The content was completely irrelevant.

The second, more common approach to ideology understands it as **false consciousness**. People think the world is one way because those in power (the rich) want them to think that way, but it really isn't. People have been duped into believing the distortions and misrepresentations that those in power tell to keep themselves in power. The **dominant ideology**, the ideology of the dominant group, defines people's experience by convincing them that its "truths" are necessarily true. It **naturalizes** itself by making its presentation of the world seem universal, the unchangeable way things are.[2] Consequently, there are two kinds of experience: the "real" or "**authentic**" experience of reality and the ideologically **distorted** experience of it.

Capitalist ideology tells us that labor is what gives meaning to our lives, and that we freely choose to sell our labor on an open and competitive market. Further, a good person has a job, and the unemployed are failing themselves and society. Communists, socialists, and sometimes labor unions try to lift the veil of false consciousness, to return workers to an authentic experience of their own exploitation and alienation.

Second-wave feminism in the 1970s was all about false consciousness. It suggested that many women had been effectively brainwashed by the dominant patriarchal ideology to believe that their subordination was reasonable and natural. Women are the weaker sex. Women are supposed to stay home, have babies, and take care of their husbands. They have learned this through religion, schools, family life, and more. Consciousness-raising aimed to tear away the veil and reveal the truth and authenticity of women's lives and possibilities.

The third understanding of ideology sees it as a **worldview (Weltan-schauung)**. There is no neutral "Truth" that exists outside of any worldview, no scientific objectivity (or, at least, science is itself a worldview). A worldview defines how people experience and understand the world—but we cannot know the truth of what is behind it. Insofar as people share a worldview, it defines a social **consensus**. You can challenge an ideology, but such challenges always come from another worldview. One worldview might be better than another not because it is truer but because it embodies different values or promises different outcomes.

---

2 It is even possible that those in power come to believe their own ideology.

Like false consciousness, such consensus views of ideology hold that the domination of a particular ideology is secured by naturalizing it, by making its truths (e.g., individualism or private property) expressions of inviolable natural law. In many cases, a worldview works because it presents some truth of our experience—but only a partial truth—as if it were the totality of truth. In that way, it sets limits on our experience and actions; it tells people what they can and can't do, and what they should and should not do. It tells them how to think and what's possible to think. For example, a common observation, often attributed to the Marxist literary theorist Fredric Jameson, is that it's easier for us to imagine the end of the world than it is for us to imagine the end of capitalism.[3] (I leave open whether he was or is right.)

There is a fourth view of ideology, which draws heavily on French structuralism (see lectures 21 and 22). Ideology produces the very possibility of experience. Ideology functions somewhat like Kant's synthetic a priori, but it is historical rather than transcendental. You cannot appeal to anything outside of ideology. There cannot be a world without ideology for that would mean a world without experience. However strange this may sound, please be patient, and I will return to it.

TOTALITIES

Marx began with a concept of a social totality. What is the nature of this totality? If all the elements that constitute a society—economic, political, cultural—fit together to define the whole, both economist and humanist Marxists ask whether it is a harmonious or a fractured unity. If the former, society is a whole way of life that encompasses all the elements into a seamless web of relations, defined by a set of common beliefs, practices, backgrounds, and so on. If the latter, society is understood in terms of conflicts and struggles over the base and superstructure; in this view, society is divided into competing classes, each of which is its own totality, and the sense of a single unified totality merely covers up the differences and contradictions.

On the other hand, both structural and conjunctural Marxists view society as a more seriously fractured unity. The structuralist Marxist Louis Althusser argued that whatever unity characterizes a **social formation** was at

3 See the discussion of the origin of this observation at https://www.reddit.com/r/zizek /comments/wou7ca/comment/iggoyw7/.

best "a sometimes teeth-gritting harmony."[b] Its fractures are not defined by class struggles or by the relation of base and superstructure. Rather, a social formation is organized or structured into three levels of social practices— economic, political, and ideological, each with its own contradictions.[4] Any society is a **structure in dominance**, defined by a specific hierarchically organized relation among the levels—that is, it is defined by the relative force of each level.[c]

But where are the motor forces of history in this view of totality, since you cannot assume that they are necessarily and always located in the same place? Althusser argued that both economist and humanist theories had conflated two distinct relations: **domination** and **determination**. You can ask which of the three levels is dominant in a particular social formation. There is no reason to assume that it is always going to be the economic. For example, in the European Middle Ages, the dominant form of social practice was not the feudal economy but the church, which defined what was both politically and economically possible. An ideological set of practices was the apparent motor force of history. You can also ask what determines the level that is dominant. Althusser's response brought his theory back to more common Marxist ground: it is always the economic, the mode of production, that determines what is dominant. But he avoids reducing the social formation to the economy (as do some economist Marxists who believe that it's always and only about the economy) by claiming that this determination is only "in the last [instance but] the lonely hour of the 'last instance' never comes."[d] That is, you can never actually see where and how the economic is determining. The economic is uniquely powerful, but its power is only visible in the way it structures the society, that is, in the structure in dominance. Consequently, while the economy is ultimately the motor force of history, it can never be empirically confirmed or identified.

Conjunctural Marxism also understands the social totality as a complex and fractured unity, but it sees the totality as constantly changing as a result of its many contradictions and struggles.[5] Consequently, it offers a more processual idea of a social totality, emphasizing the ongoing (re)construction of an at least workable unity. This is the **conjuncture** as the temporary configuration of a totality. Hence, you cannot assume in advance how different practices and relations are organized, or how such organized formations are

4 There is actually a fourth: science, which Althusser equated with Marxism.
5 The concept is usually ascribed to Lenin and, then, Gramsci.

defined. The identification and distribution of practices as, for example, the economy are themselves determined by and within the struggles to construct the conjuncture itself. Concepts of "the economy," "politics," or "ideology," as common and useful as they may be, can only be defined within the fractious unity of the conjuncture. There is no essence or permanence to any of them, nor can you assume how different practices are related to the totality; for example, in Western modern societies, "the economy" and "culture," while deeply embedded in the totality, are often constituted in such a way that they seem to operate independently of the rest of the totality, as if one could speak of them apart from their embeddedness.

DETERMINATIONS

The most difficult question in historical materialism concerns the nature of determination. The first answer, characteristic of economist Marxism, equates it with **mechanical causality**. The relations between the base and superstructure are no different from the behavior of billiard balls; you don't have to know anything about the rest of society because everything is directly caused by, is predictable from, and can be explained by the scientific laws of economic development, just as physics explains the world according to the laws of thermodynamics and quantum mechanics. Marxism is a science with the same claim to objective truth. While critics of this position argue that it is not dialectical, it is a position that Marx (and certainly Engels) sometimes affirmed.

Remember my professor who taught film? His assumption was that films were entirely determined by their mode of production: the economics of the film industry and of the particular film, including the technology of cameras and film, the studio system, the systems of distribution and exhibition, and, often most important and surprising, the people who controlled these various elements. But the actual film—its aesthetics, its narrative, its meanings and representations, and its audiences—was irrelevant.

The second answer emphasizes the interactional nature of determination, the mutual effects that the base and superstructure have on each other. Determination as **mediation** works in both directions.[6] That is to say, the superstructure affects the base even as the base affects the superstructure. While the economy affects everything in society, the other (superstructural) elements affect both society as a whole and the economy. For example, people

6 Not unlike Kant's theory of relations.

having more or fewer babies affects the economy, as does the climate crisis, or the rise of new forms of nationalism. This understanding of determination emphasizes people's agency; people make history or, at least, their choices, experiences, intentions, and practices matter. It is a more voluntaristic vision that recognizes people's capacity to resist, deviate, seek authenticity, and be co-opted. Often the term **praxis** (rather than practice) is used to register the creativity of human practices and their active role in how societies are made and remade.

Not to overwhelm you, but there are at least three variations of this praxis theory of determination. When the base is defined narrowly as the economic, it often ends up with a Hegelian model of **expressive causality**, in which everything in the superstructure manifests the contradiction(s) of the mode of production, even as it acts back on the economy. Alternatively, when the base is understood more broadly as social practices, determination is seen as **conditioning**: "The mode of production of material life conditions the general process of social, political and intellectual life."[e] The base sets limits and exerts pressure on the superstructures, on people's choices and actions, but it does not cause them. The base defines the limits of the possible and pushes people in certain directions, making it more likely people will act this way rather than that, that these relations will endure over others, but it does not compel any particular action or choice. For example, the base may "suggest" that it's easier to be an entrepreneur than it is to be a good person.

A third variation of the praxis theory is a model of **homology**, or structural correspondences, in which different elements have similar structures or logics. These homologies may be ultimately determined by the economy, but they operate across many different spheres. For example, liberal individualism and private property are homologous; the privacy of the home, the privacy afforded by cars, and the location of public media in the private home are all homologous, exhibiting a common structure of **mobile privatization**, which describes a relation in which the uncertain and often threatening outside world is brought into more secure domestic spaces.[f]

The final theory, **overdetermination**, is generally associated with conjunctural and structural Marxism. The complexity of the social formation means that you can never identify a single cause (A is determining B). Every practice is at least potentially if not actually determined by every other practice—albeit with different intensities and across different distances. And since those practices are themselves determined by other practices, it is impossible to identify the full measure of determination. If the social totality is organized into different levels of practices (a structure in dominance), then a practice at any level will be partly determined by practices at the other levels, but it will also be partly determined by practices operating at its own level. Each level, defined as a formation of practices, has a **relative autonomy**; it is, to some extent, self-determining.

Consider the determination of Donald Trump's electoral victory in 2016. The economist Marxist might claim it was all about economic developments: the Great Recession of 2008; the effects of economic globalization and the outsourcing of labor; the rise of finance and tech industries; the power of corporations; the increasing economic disparity between urban and rural economies; and so forth.

The humanist Marxists might suggest that Trump's victory was largely determined in the dialectic of politics (the failure of the liberal state) and ideology (the rise of illiberal and populist—often racist, xenophobic, and misogynist— forces on the right, and the return of identity politics on the left, as well as a growing cynicism about politics in general). Or they might point to homologies, for example, between Trump's modes of communication and engagement, and many common social media practices.

The conjunctural Marxist acknowledges all these determining relations but argues that Trump's election success cannot be reduced to a single one; it was not all about any one thing, whether economic, political, or ideological. It was not all about white working-class men, or race, or immigrants, or the struggle between urban and rural populations, or the gap between education and religion/common sense. It was about all these things and more. But it is even more complicated, for there are determining relations among all these determinations. For example, the Great Recession of 2008 was itself overdetermined: partly determined by other economic developments (e.g., the housing boom, the derivatives market, the collapse of the credit market), as well as by political choices (e.g., deregulation, the failures of the state) and ideological practices (e.g., nationalism, neoliberalism). And this is true of every determining practice and relation; it is overdetermined by all sorts of practices and relations, even as its own particular development clearly impacted those that overdetermined it. Nothing is all about one thing, and not all things are about the same things. In the end, we may never be able to satisfactorily explain the singular event of Trump's victory, but what we can do is locate it within the social totality as a conjuncture—a complex, differentiated unity, composed of a cascade of determinations. It is only by moving to a different level of abstraction that we can identify the most pertinent forces—both long-term (organic) forces and more immediate struggles— that shape the conjuncture.

In the introduction to *Grundrisse*, written in 1857, Marx re-presented deter-mination as dialectics by considering the complexity of the relations within the economy, introducing what might be described as a **circuit of produc-tion** (see figure 14.2) After all, the production of value depends on more than the practices of production; it depends on the relations among a number of economic processes. How are they connected, assuming it is not all merely accidental?

We normally think about this circuit in the simplest terms. You produce a commodity, which requires you to have the necessary machinery, resources,

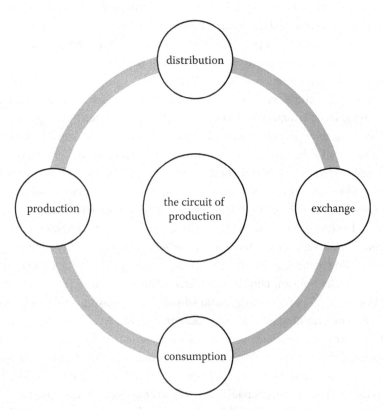

FIGURE 14.2

raw materials, and labor power (whether living labor or the dead labor captured in machines). For some, that is the end of the story. But if all you do is produce things, you're certain to fail. You have to distribute what you produce to retailers (or other producers). Still not enough, because people have to buy them, offering barter or money (whether cash or credit) for the product. But that still isn't enough, because if people never use—and use up—what they have bought, they will never need to buy another similar commodity. Toyota makes millions of cars; if they sit in the warehouse, Toyota goes broke. So, it delivers the cars to its dealers, but if the cars sit in the lots, the dealers (and then Toyota) go broke. People have to buy a car, but if they park it in their garage, or use it as a planter, or drive it around the block once a year, they will never have to buy another car. Again, both dealers and Toyota go broke. The circuit has to be completed. People have to consume the product they've bought once it's been distributed after it's been produced. If the circuit is not completed, the economy collapses in a **crisis of overaccumulation**, which can lead to a recession or worse.[7]

What is the nature of the relations between the moments in the circuit of production? Marx addressed this question by describing three possible forms of identity or correspondence between the terms: **immediate identity** or **direct correspondence, mediated identity** or **mutual dependence**, and **internal connection** or **differentiated unity**. In immediate identity, the moments are essentially equivalent. Production is privileged not only as the inevitable starting point of the circuit but as the essence of the circuit itself. Consequently, there appears to be a direct correspondence in which everything is identified with production. The forms of capitalist distribution, exchange, and consumption are the immediate product of the form of production.

In mediated identity, the moments are independent and only extrinsically related. But they interact with each other in specific ways, and none can complete itself and achieve its defined end without the others. Each element enables the others' completion. Consumption produces production because the product is only finally realized when it is consumed, and as a result of consumption, the need for further production is produced. Similarly, production produces consumption by furnishing consumption with its object. In a sense, consumption is production and production is consumption. Similar relations hold among the other moments as well.

7 There is also a crisis of underaccumulation, where demand is greater than supply, resulting in inflation . . . and possibly recession.

In a differentiated unity, the moments have no independent existence outside the particular unity of the circuit; each moment creates the others by creating itself and creates itself by creating the others. It thus produces itself, its identity, as other. The moments exist only in their relationships to one another. Hence, no moment can be identified with any other. In such inner connections, a practice's identity is produced only as a commodity passes through the distinct processes—"the profane history"—of the circuit itself. The specificity of the circuit, which is only the unity and totality of the moments and their relations, determines a definite form of production, distribution, exchange, and consumption. It preserves the differences among the moments even as those differences exist only within the unity.

We can use this analysis of the circuit of production, along with the earlier discussion of dialectical determination, to return to the question of the relation of thought and reality: How is the concrete-in-thought achieved? You can envision the relation as causal or immediate identity, where thought mirrors or reflects the history of an external reality but is always limited by its own origin. Or you can envision the relation as mediated, in which the two histories—of thought and social reality—exist independently even as they regularly interact and affect one another. Or, finally, you can envision the relation as a **unity-in-difference**, each constituting itself only by constituting the other. Marx seemed to have held each at different times, without offering criteria for choosing among them.

POLITICAL ECONOMY

You may think it strange (and even annoying) that I have said very little about the most frequently referenced, hotly contested, and politically central part of Marx's work: his political economy of capitalism. As with all of Marx's theories, there are serious and particularly passionate arguments between various "schools" around his analysis of capitalism.

To be clear, Marx did not invent political economy, nor was he the first to recognize the importance of the commodity or labor. Marx offered a critique of "classical" political economy (Smith, Ricardo, etc.). He argued that its starting point—its efforts to understand capitalist economies by assuming its essence is given by the circulation of commodities in markets, where price is an expression of the labor of production—hid another (deep structural) story. Understanding what remains hidden, as the condition of possibility of market economies (and the derivation of profit), demanded empirical and theoretical investigations of the mode of production, the nature of commodities, and the relation of labor to value.[g]

Marx's political economy continuously moved between his abstract, theoretical description of capitalist economies and his rich, detailed, technical, empirical, and mathematical analysis of specific concrete instances of capitalism. As he once noted in a letter to Engels, "In elaborating the principles of economics I have been so damnably held up by errors in calculation that in despair I have applied myself to a rapid revision of algebra. . . . By making a detour via algebra, I shall quickly get back into the way of things."[8,h] Since I cannot present a full account of Marx's political economy here, we will have to settle for a brief—hopefully ecumenical—introduction to some of his key concepts and arguments: the commodity as the relation of use value and exchange value, value as labor time, the labor theory of value, surplus value, and so on.

The aim of capitalist economies is the production and accumulation of material wealth as a collection of commodities understood entirely in terms of their **use value**, which refers to their ability to answer our needs. In Marx, those needs are assumed to exist outside of and prior to any economic relations (although subsequent Marxists recognize that capitalism often creates needs that its commodities can then satisfy). The commodity's ability to satisfy a particular need is assumed to depend on the physical qualities of the commodity itself, which are the result of variable, contingent, and heterogeneous forms of labor. But if use value is always specific and attached to the body of the commodity, how are markets possible? How can one compare qualitatively incomparable use values? The answer is **exchange value**, which is initially defined as the amount of one use value that is judged to be the equivalent of a certain amount of another use value. How many shoes would I have to exchange to get a coat? Exchange value is the quantitative expression (in money) of the relations among use values in particular markets; but what determines the exact quantitative equivalence? Smith correctly argued that the commodity bundles together use value and exchange value, with their equivalence depending on the labor that produced the commodity.

But this could not explain the extraction of profit from the market relation. Marx argued that exchange value is the form in which a certain

8 For example, Marx initiated research and debate about the "transformation problem," involving the quantitative relations between value, surplus value, and price.

quantitative content—**value**—is expressed.[9] Ignoring the many different, particular forms of labor involved in the production of use value, value is an expression of the congealed quantity of labor, assumed to be homogeneous, that is, with no regard for its particular labor practices. To establish the possibility of a single, consistent, quantitative equivalence, the measure of such homogeneous labor must be **abstract labor time**. Yet, since labor cannot be entirely divorced from the commodity and its social relations, the value of a commodity depended on the **average socially necessary labor time**—that is, the average amount of time required to produce a certain use value, given specific conditions of production.

Value is therefore a relationship, inside the commodity itself, between the concrete labor of use value and the abstract labor time of socially necessary labor. The relations between commodities in the market are expressed as exchange value (which is not quite the same as price). Consequently, the social relations of labor assume the form of a relation between things—and in this mystification (**commodity fetishism**), the commodity becomes "a social hieroglyphic."[i] The commodity hides itself as a relation of labor in its own objectification: "The determination of the magnitude of value by labour-time is therefore a secret hidden under the apparent movements in the relative values of commodities. . . . By equating their different products to each other in exchange as values, they equate their different kinds of labour as human labour. They do this without being aware of it."[j]

This is why "bourgeois" economic theories emphasized market exchange. They were not wrong but, in fact, were "socially valid" because they do describe the nature of commodity production in capitalism.[k] But in such theories, profit can only be explained as the difference between the cost (made up of both constant and variable capital, i.e., raw material and labor) and the market price. But, once again, the conditions of this relation—presented as the free exchange of commodities in the market—remain hidden. A necessary condition of capitalism is that labor power itself is commodified through the wage market, which conceals the difference between the socially necessary labor time for reproducing labor power (i.e., how much workers need to be paid so that they are able to continue working) and the exchange value of labor (the wages they are paid).

Marx argued that the source of profit is not the commodity market per se but its relation to the labor market. In particular, it is the result of the complex

9 Neither use value nor exchange value!

FIGURE 14.3

relation between the actual value produced by labor within a certain time (which depends on many factors, including technology) and the wages paid to labor based on the calculation of the socially necessary (abstract) labor time. This is surplus or unpaid labor, and it is the appropriation of this **surplus value** by the capitalist that is profit. This can be represented as in figure 14.3, where both M and M' are money (as a representation of value, but that is another story). Money produces commodities, which produce more money, so that M' is always greater than M. This process of value producing value is **capital**, simultaneously a process of the accumulation of value and a social relation of wage labor. Thus, it is a necessary condition of capital that it expand not only in terms of the total amount (accumulation) but also in terms of the rate of accumulation of value.

Capitalism understands itself to be defined by the circulation of commodities in free markets. Marx argued that the "hidden" truth of capitalism is that the processes of production hold mastery over humans. As a result of their exploitation (essentially, they are producing value for the capitalist without remuneration), of which they remain unaware, workers are alienated from their own labor power, from the products of their labor, and from the social relations of production in which they are necessarily involved. Most Marxist politics then understand the class struggle as a struggle against the exploitation of labor and the unequal distribution of wealth. The inauguration of socialism marks their end: "The proletarians have nothing to lose but their chains. They have a world to win. Workingmen of all countries, unite!"[10,l]

There are many arguments about Marx's version of the **labor theory of value**. Does his theory apply to all instantiations of capitalism, or just the industrial capitalism of mid-nineteenth-century England? If it is historically specific, there is no guarantee that it works as a description of other, especially more recent, versions of capitalism. Marx himself, in "Fragment on

10 Commonly said: "Workers of the world unite. You have nothing to lose but your chains."

Machines," seemed to recognize this when he suggested, "As soon as labour in the direct form has ceased to be the great well-spring of wealth, labour-time ceases and must cease to be its measure, and hence exchange value [must cease to be the measure] of use value."[m]

There have been a number of efforts to offer a "new" analysis for contemporary capitalism. For example, **autonomous Marxism** or *operaismo* expands the labor theory of value and argues that labor has moved outside of the traditional spheres of economic production and value, creating a **social factory** in which all human activity has become a source of value.[n] A related alternative suggests that contemporary capitalism has returned to (if it ever left) the primordial practice of **primitive accumulation**, by which what exists outside of commodity markets is commodified.[o] This involved, originally, land, labor power, and money, but more recently human interactions, emotions, and thoughts. **Value form theory** starts with the historical specificity of Marx's analysis.[p] It then suggests that Marx's critique of capitalism was not focused primarily on the production and distribution of value (with its concomitant challenge to the exploitation of labor and the distribution of wealth). Instead, Marx offered a more radical critique, a critique of value itself both as a historically specific definition of wealth and, even more important, as the dominant form of **social mediation**. That is, capitalism—it remains unclear how broad the referent is—is a social reality in which objectified, commodified labor, as defined by abstract labor time, becomes the form in which all relations are understood and experienced. The relations of labor constitute all social relations as objectified. Marx was criticizing the domination of labor itself in (industrial?) capitalist societies. For value form theorists, Marx's political economy is about the nature and imagination of possible human relations and, thus, is inseparable from his philosophical project. He was suggesting a very different kind of political and economic revolution.

Marx's way of thinking has, in many ways, permeated the spaces of contemporary thought and theory. Many theories that would not claim to be Marxist nevertheless operate on the ground of Marx's deep theory as well as his specific analyses. In the next two lectures, I will discuss the work of two other deep theorists who also deployed a hermeneutics of suspicion, arguing that humans were, for very different reasons, incapable of self-understanding because of forces that necessarily hide themselves: Friedrich Nietzsche and Sigmund Freud. If the latter, like Marx, both criticized and supported the enlightenment project, the former consistently worked against it.

NOTES

a. Marx, *Contribution to the Critique of Political Economy*, 21.

b. Althusser, "Ideology," in *Lenin and Philosophy*, 101.

c. Althusser, *For Marx*.

d. Althusser, *For Marx*, 113.

e. Marx, *Contribution to the Critique of Political Economy*, 20–21.

f. Williams, *Television*.

g. Marx, *Contribution to the Critique of Political Economy*.

h. Marx, "Marx to Engels in Manchester, 11 January 1858," in Marx and Engels, *Collected Works*, 40:244.

i. Marx, *Capital*, 167.

j. Marx, *Capital*, 168, 166–67.

k. On social validity, see Marx, *Capital*, 169.

l. Marx and Engels, *Manifesto*, in *Collected Works*, 6:519.

m. Marx, *Grundrisse*, 705.

n. See Tronti, *Workers and Capitalism*.

o. Marx, *Capital*, chap. 26.

p. Postone, *Time, Labor, and Social Domination*.

Nietzsche

Now that you have waded through some of the most difficult deep theories, including a leap into power and politics, it is time to have some fun. No modern thinker has been greeted with such diverse and extreme responses, or read with such great pleasure for so many different reasons, or thought to be as cool as Friedrich Wilhelm Nietzsche.

The Canadian Hegelian communitarian Charles Taylor suggested that all contemporary European philosophy is neo-Nietzschean.[a] The American conservative Spinozist Leo Strauss said that Nietzsche "ushered in the third crisis of modernity . . . the crisis of our times."[b] And the French postmodernist Gilles Deleuze celebrated Nietzsche for having changed both "the theory and the practice of philosophy."[c]

Nietzsche's influence, especially since the mid-twentieth century, has depended partly on the fact that he has been claimed by an extraordinarily wide range of theoretical and political positions, from existentialism to anarchism to Nazism. As an existentialist, Nietzsche described the situation of the solitary individual in a meaningless universe; as an anarchist, he opposed all social power and asserted the necessity of individual freedom; as a Nazi, he celebrated the natural virtues of the heroic individual and of particular peoples. Under the sign of the "new Nietzsche" in twentieth-century France, his ideas were read as an ontology (e.g., Martin Heidegger and Gilles Deleuze), a poststructuralism (e.g., Jacques Derrida), and a postmodern critique (e.g., Michel Foucault).[d] The only agreement is that Nietzsche rejected the enlightenments. Like Spinoza, he was an antihumanist, and in his later works he rejected anthropocentrism: the claim that humanity has a special status and value.

Nietzsche was born on October 15, 1844, in Röcken, Saxony, Prussia, and died on August 25, 1900, in Weimar, in the new German Empire. A generation after Marx, Nietzsche witnessed the rapidly expanding forms and consequences of the Second Industrial Revolution. He grew up in a deeply religious household; generations on his father's side had been Lutheran pastors. After the deaths of his father and brother, he was raised in a household of three generations of five women. He began his studies in theology but moved to classical (Greek and Roman) philology, becoming, in 1869, the youngest ever chair of classical philology at the University of Basel, even before completing his doctorate. He was drawn into philosophy by Arthur Schopenhauer's (1788–1860) book *The World as Will and Representation* (1818) and strongly influenced by his friendship, from 1868 to the mid-1870s, with the German composer Richard Wagner and Wagner's second wife, Cosima.[1]

Nietzsche resigned from Basel after a decade, plagued with a variety of debilitating medical conditions. Even so, he traveled extensively in Europe after having renounced his Prussian citizenship and become stateless (*sans-papiers*). In Turin in 1889, he had a mental breakdown on the street; legend has it that he collapsed after witnessing and attempting to intervene in the flogging of a horse, although exactly when his "mental degeneration"[e] first began is uncertain.[2] After his collapse and a series of strokes, he was cared for by his mother, and then his sister, Elisabeth, until his death, after which she took responsibility for editing his work.

---

1 Wilhelm Richard Wagner (1813–83) is best known as the composer of the opera cycle *Der Ring des Nibelungen.*

2 Some accounts claim that Nietzsche suffered from syphilis. The timeline of his illness affects how some people read the changes in his works.

Nietzsche presents unique challenges to his followers and interpreters. Two accusations have haunted him. The most disturbing claims he was an extreme German nationalist and anti-Semite whose views supposedly later provided succor to Nazism. We now know that the passages in his work that justify this reading were the result of his sister's editing. Elisabeth reworked Nietzsche's manuscripts to fit the ideologies she shared with her husband, Bernard Forster, a leading advocate of German nationalism and anti-Semitism.[3]

Nietzsche himself criticized all nationalisms, especially Germanic. He was so critical of the German culture and society of his time that he sometimes claimed Polish roots (without justification). Further, he repeatedly condemned any expressions of anti-Semitism; in *The Anti-Christ* (1888), he passionately argued against it.

The second accusation—his explicit misogyny—cannot be dismissed so easily. His attitudes toward, comments on, and relations with women were deeply ambivalent, even contradictory. In some writings, he wrote positively about the "perfect" woman as "a higher type of human."[f] Some statements are open to contradictory interpretations, such as when he compared women to "beasts of prey."[g] Or consider, given his negative attitude toward truth, the import of his statement that "from the beginning, nothing has been more alien, repugnant, and hostile to woman than truth—her great art is the lie, her highest concern is mere appearance and beauty."[h] Yet his later works became undisputedly hostile to women, including statements such as "Woman is not yet capable of friendship."[i] Or, perhaps most egregiously: "Woman! One-half of mankind is weak, typically sick, changeable, inconstant. . . . She needs a religion of weakness that glorifies being weak, loving, and being humble as divine: or better, she makes the strong weak—she rules when she succeeds in overcoming the strong. . . . Woman has always conspired with the types of decadence, the priests, against the 'powerful,' the 'strong,' the men."[j]

His views seem to have changed. During his years at Basel, Nietzsche was friends with leading feminists and was a strong supporter of feminist causes. What happened? Was it his emerging dementia? Did it have to do with family and psychosexual histories? Or was it the result of a personal, romantic tragedy—his rejection by the Russian-born psychoanalyst Lou Andreas-Salomé, his one great love? None of these seems sufficient to explain why he went even further than the all too common patriarchy inscribed in the

3 New editions and translations of Nietzsche's work have been published, erasing his sister's deformations.

history of Western European thought. Beyond questions about the extent and focus of his misogyny looms the more troubling question of how deeply it enters his thought, and how much of his thinking was contaminated by it.

But there are other difficulties. While Nietzsche's writing in his early works (e.g., *The Birth of Tragedy*, 1872) was relatively straightforward, even while fundamentally challenging the dominant practices of philology of his times, it became increasingly difficult and, by some standards, increasingly enjoyable. He eschewed the laziness of traditional modes of logical, coherent, and systematic thinking and writing. He rarely made arguments or provided evidence. His writing became poetic, aphoristic, and deeply personal, offering "hieroglyphs" of the truth not as representations of reality but as critiques and possibilities of ways of living.

Nietzsche was perhaps the first self-consciously avant-garde thinker, an avant-gardist before the avant-garde was named.[4] He chose the subtitle *Prelude to a Philosophy of the Future* for his book *Beyond Good and Evil*, and he referred to *Thus Spoke Zarathustra* as "a book for all and none." He broke with the past—not only the enlightenments but also the dominant traditions of Western (Greco-Roman, Judeo-Christian) civilization. He clearly assumed that he could not be heard in the present.

What does it mean to write for the future, and why did he think it necessary? Because, as I will explain shortly, he thought that people living at the time were—and he would probably think that people today continue to be— dehumanized masses, the **herd**, incapable of embracing their condition as humans. Western civilization itself had dehumanized them, trapped them in falsehoods and lies, imprisoned them in a language that was incapable of speaking the truth. Hence people were unable to recognize—to see or hear— the truth, both the painful truths and the affirming truths offered in his writings. He wrote for people yet to come, willing and able to confront the truth, the pain, and the joy. The result: Nietzsche is rarely straightforward.

PERIODIZING NIETZSCHE

One way of dealing with the ambiguities of Nietzsche's work, which opens itself up to so many different interpretations, is to assume that it evolved over

---

4 Until the end of the nineteenth century, the term *avant-garde* referred to left-wing political movements, but it drifted slowly to more aesthetic and intellectual endeavors with the emergence of high modernism in the arts (e.g., Gertrude Stein and James Joyce in literature; impressionism, cubism, and Dadaism in the visual arts).

time, although there are some continuities. His writings are generally divided into four periods. How you understand Nietzsche (or any text) depends on where you start, and which periods you privilege. For example, existential readings valorize the earlier periods, while postmodern readings valorize the later ones. I want to briefly identify the four periods and introduce key concepts, which I will return to later:

1. The earliest works—*The Birth of Tragedy* (1872) and *Untimely Meditations* (1873–76)—are the most widely taught and read, and the most stylistically "traditional." They present a rather romantic, albeit pessimistic, criticism of German culture, especially art. *The Birth of Tragedy*, strongly influenced by Richard Wagner, addresses artistic creativity, particularly musical, using as examples two Greek gods: Apollo, the god of reason, knowledge, order, and morality; and Dionysus, the god of instinctual energy, chaos, and the joyful life. Nietzsche argued that Germanic culture, if not the entire history of the West, had largely repressed the **Dionysian** in favor of the **Apollonian**. Wagner's music was a rebirth of tragedy that sought to reestablish a harmony between these two impulses, although later in his life Nietzsche gave up the ideal of balance, describing himself as "a follower of the philosopher Dionysus," poeticizing that "one must still have chaos in oneself to be able to give birth to a dancing star."ᵏ

2. In works such as *Human, All Too Human* (1878) and *The Gay Science* (1882), Nietzsche adopted his aphoristic style and broke with Wagnerian tragic romanticism. Rejecting all totalizing philosophies, he introduced two central concepts: **eternal recurrence** and the **death of God** (more accurately, humanity's murder of God). Together, they suggested that humans were condemned to live—and repeat—a history without any possible appeal to a transcendent meaning, leaving them alone in a meaningless universe with no way of affirming the significance of their own existence. While this resonates with what would become existentialism, Nietzsche also began to articulate a more affirmative vision of the joyous freedom the acceptance of this condition allows.

3. Works such as *Thus Spoke Zarathustra* (1885), *Beyond Good and Evil* (1886), and *The Genealogy of Morals* (1887) are often considered to be Nietzsche's defining texts. They offer clear statements of his hostility to the Judeo-Christian worldview and its associated moralities. Such moralities, built on the absolute distinction between good and evil, define the good as Christian virtues that celebrate and elevate weakness over

strength and nobility. They are built on **bad conscience** and guilt, and they embrace ascetism and Truth.

His practice of critique as **genealogy** offered a history of **perspectives**, often equated with Marx's ideologies, in which Nietzsche identified different expressions of this morality and linked them with specific sets of social relations. Genealogy addressed not only the distribution but also the origins of different forms and practices of valuation and interpretation. He further introduced many of his most provocative concepts, including the distinction between **slave moralities** and **master moralities**, and between **active and reactive valuations**, as well as the figures of the "prophet" **Zarathustra** and the ***Übermensch*** (literally translated as the "overman").[5] He presented a naturalist view of reality, in which life (if not all reality) is an expression of a natural, creative energy: the **will to power**.

4. In the year before his psychological collapse, Nietzsche wrote *Twilight of the Idols*, *The Anti-Christ*, and (the rather idiosyncratic, intellectual autobiography) *Ecce Homo*. *The Will to Power, or The Transvaluation of All Values* was composed by Nietzsche's sister from his last notebooks. While some dismiss these works as expressions of his dementia, others take them as the fullest statement of his thought.

ORIGINS

Nietzsche was influenced, both positively and negatively, both profoundly and intermittently, by numerous thinkers. He was attracted to the ideas of Heraclitus and to the writings of Voltaire, Ralph Waldo Emerson, and Fyodor Dostoyevsky. He discovered Spinoza after his ideas were already largely formed, but in a postcard to his friend Franz Overbeck, dated July 31, 1881, he wrote:

> I am utterly amazed, utterly enchanted! I have a precursor, and what a precursor! I hardly knew Spinoza: that I should have turned to him just now, was inspired by instinct. Not only is his overtendency like mine—namely to make all knowledge the most powerful affect—but in five main points of his doctrine I recognize myself; this most unusual and loneliest thinker is closest to me precisely in these matters: he denies the

5 Existentialist readings often identify Zarathustra, as a uniquely heroic individual making himself into a new kind of human, with the Übermensch.

freedom of the will, teleology, the moral world-order, the unegoistic, and evil. Even though the divergencies are admittedly tremendous, they are due more to the difference in time, culture, and science. In summa: my lonesomeness, which, as on very high mountains, often made it hard for me to breathe and make my blood rush out, is now at least a twosomeness. Strange![l]

He was extremely critical of Kant's universal transcendentalism and the transcendence of the noumena, but he agreed (a misreading?) that human beings were actively involved in the construction and truth of reality. For Nietzsche, all acts of perceiving and thinking were creative. Truth is a construct, but there is nothing behind the lies.[6]

And despite the fact that he despised Hegel even more than Kant, he agreed that history and time were key to understanding human reality. Like Hegel, he did not see the enlightenments as a break in human history or thought, but just as the latest expressions of the herd morality and mentality that have dominated for thousands of years. But history is not a dialectical progress toward some telos or totality, or an evolutionary process defined by the survival of the fittest. Instead, Nietzsche understood history as a reality without development, comprising a series of moments or periods that have no necessary relation to each other, other than that each is an expression of the power of the herd.

The most important influence on Nietzsche's thinking was Arthur Schopenhauer, a philosophical pessimist influenced by Kant and Buddhism, although a large part of his magnum opus—*The World as Will and Representation* (1818)—presents a critique of Kant.[m] Schopenhauer argued that the true nature of reality was an arational force: **the will** as a vital, cosmic force simply seeking to continue to exist; it is impersonal, blind, meaningless, and purposeless. Consequently, there is no God, and life has no meaning. He is often thought to have compared human life to that of a certain worm, which is born underground, digs its way up to the surface, moves a bit (with no goal or significance), and then burrows its way back into the ground to lay its eggs and then dies. The eggs hatch and eat their "mother" for the energy to burrow to the top, where they move a bit and then burrow down and lay their eggs and die, and so on.

Any attempt to find meaning will lead to disappointment, suffering, and death. In fact, that is what life is! Schopenhauer renounced life and happiness

---

6 We shall see how Nietzsche seems to contradict this assertion in his later work.

and instead embraced reflection and suffering, and a morality based in compassion and ascetism. While Nietzsche rejected the latter as herd morality, he embraced Schopenhauer's pessimism and his notion that reality and life are defined by an arational force. But he refused to see it in negative, malignant terms; instead, it opened the possibility of the affirmation and joy of life.

HISTORY, GENEALOGY

Nietzsche characterized history as a succession of **perspectives** in which truth, subjectivity, and objective reality were constructed. Unlike many contemporary claims of perspectivism—for example, feminist, colonial, or Black—Nietzsche denied that there was truth outside the perspective, not even a metaphysical foundation for the plurality of perspectives, hiding itself from us. All that stands behind a perspective are the desires, passions, interests, and memories of a particular group of people. A perspective is the reality created to defend the interests and power of that group, and if they dominate, it becomes the Truth of the world. People can only live within a perspective. Nietzsche would have nothing to do with ideas of emancipation or authenticity.

His concept of a perspective was more than epistemological and less than metaphysical. A perspective produces its own way of thinking and living, and its own morality, rendering its particular configuration of power unchallengeable. The study of history is the study of perspectives as power, and the history of truth is the history of perspectives. This was Nietzsche's version of critique as **genealogy**, a genetic and interpretive method that sought the origins of people's beliefs/reality not in some metaphysical justification or some epistemological rigor but in a perspective engaged in a struggle for power. There is, at every moment of human history (ignoring the question of geographic variations and limits), a dominant perspective defined by the interest of a particular group.

Every perspective, every truth, every moral value is a lie, because all it does is constantly reinscribe the difference between truth and untruth or, in moral terms, between good and evil. Nietzsche wrote: "What then is truth? A moveable host of metaphors, metonyms, and anthropomorphisms: in short, a sum of human relations. . . . Truths are illusions about which one has forgotten that this is what they are."[11] Thinking produces only errors and lies, but some of them are useful because they preserve the power of a particular perspective or, as we will see shortly, because they preserve life itself. As

Nietzsche said, "Truth is that sort of error without which a particular type of living being could not live."⁰

Lies become truths because they have been repeated so often and have become so embedded in the language people speak that they seem obvious and necessary. Every concept is distorting because it treats unequal things as equal, dissimilar things as equivalent. Nietzsche thought people suffered a kind of inertia, a tendency to persist in using the concepts so deeply imbricated in language. There are psychological—instinctual—sources of people's retreat into and love of concepts, abstractions, and universals. But the more socialized people become, the more powerful the forces reinforcing their desire for stability and conformity; this inertia is in turn further magnified by the rigidity of, and the many traps set for us by, language itself. While Nietzsche's genealogy demonstrated that there is a history of different perspectives, their commonalities and continuities (as the herd mentality) ensured that they continually secure the dominance of the weak.

According to Nietzsche, the enlightenments were only another set of perspectives. While the enlightenments presented themselves as a break from the millennial-long traditions of Western thought, they merely continued, in new clothes, the structures of power, truth, and morality that they claimed to have left behind. The enlightenments did this through two figures of Truth: **consciousness** and knowledge (or the **will to truth**). Nietzsche rejected the privilege assigned to consciousness, describing it as "an evolutionary blind alley."ᵖ The will to truth, as Reason, laid the foundations of equality. The illusion that people are equal because they all have reason, the capacity to seek and recognize truth, was buoyed by the delusion that the purpose of life was to seek truth. Reason and conscience, the epistemic and moral appearances of consciousness, are aberrations in the universe, resulting from the repression of the instincts for life, the vital life-preserving forces, by the claim of Reason. Their subjugation created the illusion of an interiority, an inner psychic world of consciousness, conscience, and thinking, and an outer world of reality. The powerful life instincts continue to exist only insofar as they have been sublimated.

Nietzsche further attacked the privilege accorded to the human since the Socratic appropriation of the Delphic oracle: "Know thyself." He offered the following description in one of his most biting parables:

In some remote corner of the universe, poured out and glittering in innumerable solar systems, there once was a star on which clever animals invented knowledge. That was the haughtiest and most mendacious minute of "world history"—yet only a minute. After nature had drawn a few breaths, the star grew cold and the clever animals died.

One might invent such a fable and still not have illustrated sufficiently how wretched, how shadowy and flighty, how aimless and arbitrary the human intellect appears in nature. There have been eternities when it did not exist, and when it is done for again, nothing will have happened.⁹

The entirety of human history means nothing to the universe. It is a detour leading nowhere, an accident without consequences, leaving no trace of its having existed. While humanity faces a universe without meaning, truth, or order, its own existence is meaninglessness; it simply does not matter. Yet, especially in his later writings, Nietzsche refuses despair and pessimism.

BEYOND PESSIMISM

Despite his claim that truth is a lie, Nietzsche did seem to have a truth of his own. He was, after all, criticizing civilization for denying the life-preserving instincts and championing the life-defeating forces. Some believe that Nietzsche embraced a romantic primitivism that favored the spontaneity of instinctual responses. But this would throw him back into the very logic of good and evil he rejected: a good precivilized human (Rousseau?) versus the evil civilized human. So how did Nietzsche avoid both social relativism and debilitating despair? What is the status of his critical judgments? On what are they grounded?

Nietzsche rewrote Hegel's story of the struggles between the master and the slave, reading Western history as a series of struggles in which weak slaves actively seize power from "noble" masters (persons of greater strength, greater will, greater creative force) by finding strength only in numbers. This ensures the dominance of the slave or herd mentality/morality. That mastery was not a matter of brute force is demonstrated by his examples, which included visionary leaders such as Julius Caesar and Napoleon and creative artists such as Johann Wolfgang von Goethe. He also celebrated both Jesus (not the Christ of Christianity) and Socrates, both of whom claimed the right to declare their own truth, against the truth of the masses and the state. Naturally, both had to die so that their message could be perverted into a perspective of the weak, a statement born out of the humiliation of those who cannot create their own reality and values. Instead, they created saviors to give them values. Jesus was so strong that he could tell the world, "This is what's good, and this is what's evil." The sad result was that people believed him, but they did not understand him. Rather than seeing a master affirming his own capacity to create value and refusing the prescriptions of value from perspectives that were foreign to him, the herd translated his message into a perspective and transformed Jesus into the Son of God, necessarily good, rather than a unique, singular, creative master.

The herd morality turns the tables so that the weak dominate the strong by banding together and equating the good with weakness, equality, charity, piety, humility, sharing—all those values that have been traditionally thought of as "civilized." It celebrates community over the strength of the will and creativity of the life instincts; it asserts an absolute equality against the reality of inequalities. After all, people do not all have the same capacities or the courage to actualize and affirm them in the face of the ostracism of the herd. This unnatural world of the masses is built on ***ressentiment***.[7] This is a condition in which the masses reach for power and self-affirmation by presenting themselves as victims and blaming others (who need not be the masters) for their failures. It is the creation of power out of frustration, weakness, and inferiority, by posing as the loser. It is the victory of jealousy and vengeance, where the very declaration of humiliation becomes the ground for the assertion of power.

This has been happening since the beginnings of Western civilization, over and over in different forms, offering different moralities: Stoicism, ascetism, debauchery and decadence, Christianity, the blessing of labor, the enlightenments, socialism, and, I might add, democracy. This is why he claimed to write for the future. All Western religions, transcendent moralities, and transcendental philosophies claim truth so the masses can avoid the terrible truth of the universe. They make life tolerable by hiding "the black melancholy of the physiologically obstructed," referring to the life instincts rather than physical perfection or strength.[r] Humanity runs from the horror of the abyss: "Man is a rope stretched between the animal and the Superman—a rope over an abyss. . . . A dangerous crossing, a dangerous wayfaring, a dangerous looking-back, a dangerous trembling and halting."[s]

The master is the one who can face the truth that there is no truth, meaning, purpose, or value in the universe except as they make them. There are only the natural drives of life itself, which demand that one create ex nihilo because there is no ground or vision to justify, legitimate, or even help you. Those

7 Although this concept has some similarities to the more common idea of resentment, the two are not equivalent.

who cannot embrace this reality must repress—suppress and sublimate—their own life instincts, their own force, their own will to create, condemning themselves to a life of melancholy, depression, and a politics that turns power on its head in ressentiment.

Consider where the enlightenments brought humanity. The very effort of reason (including science) to find Truth led to the recognition that there is no truth. That is, it undermined and exploded its own myths. There is no cosmic, transcendent order of reality. There is no ultimate transcendental ground for truth and morality. Reason proved that reason itself was its own dead end. The will to truth showed that there is no Truth.

This was the moment of the **death of God**. Humanity murdered God when it realized it could no longer believe in the search for transcendence. Reason told people to affirm their essential rationality, and the result was that they could no longer believe in the possibility of God. The end product of enlightenment rationality was nihilism, which Nietzsche found in both Marx (determination) and Darwin (random mutation).

The enlightenments set out to prove and produce progress but ended up reaffirming **eternal recurrence**: history never progresses but always and only repeats itself. Hatred, war, and suffering all repeat themselves with no point and no hope of escape. Thus, there can be no rationale for human life and struggles until we destroy humanity (and the aliens return to seed the earth with life again, having figured out what they did wrong the first time). The enlightenments led humanity to the realization that the very desire for freedom and autonomy actually expressed a deep fear of independence.

NIHILISM

This is what humanity could never face. This was the terror and the decadence of his age, placing on Nietzsche the burden to tell the horrific, painful truth. Nietzsche thought that people sensed that God was dead, and that humanism and the will to truth ended up in cynicism and **piety** (self-righteousness). As a result, Europe was living through a unique crisis, a crisis of **passive nihilism**, which he also called "Western Buddhism" and a "will to nothingness."[t] Without meaning or purpose, all people were left with was greed, consumer pleasures, and empty spiritualism. Without an ethics or moral compass, there were no limits on behavior. This was the time of the **last man**, who implicitly knew but could not accept that this was a crisis—because they still sought to make sense of their lives, despite living in a world already built on the recognition that there is no sense to be had.

In Nietzsche's most famous parable, Zarathustra comes down from the mountain—a deeply religious image in the Judeo-Christian tradition—to bring the news that God is dead, the news of crisis. Zarathustra, an Iranian/Persian spiritual leader who lived over a thousand years before Jesus, founded the Zoroastrian religion. For Nietzsche, he was a prophet who comes to speak to the last man, who can only think about survival and power and nothing else. The message he brings is that the only way to move beyond the crisis is to transform passive nihilism into **active nihilism**—earlier he called it the **gay science**—that destroys everything that can no longer be believed, even as people continue to live in such beliefs: every perspective, every morality, every truth (and the institutions that support them). It's a war against all existing lies.[8] Zarathustra comes to tell people of their crisis, and that the only way to get beyond it is to tear down all those things that they're still holding on to, even though they no longer believe they matter.

But destruction and negation are not the goals; they clear away the detritus of history to create the conditions of possibility for moving on. Humanity must open the possibility of reconstituting the act of valuing itself: the **transvaluation of value** as a possibility belongs to the one who has yet to arrive, the *Übermensch*. Zarathustra (like John the Baptist) prepares the way, telling individuals they must prepare the ground. But he knows they cannot escape the herd mentality, cannot understand the full nature of the crisis, and will never come out on the other side as a new kind of human, the master who creates their own values, the Übermensch. Perhaps Nietzsche thought of himself as Zarathustra, addressing the masses but knowing they were not ready to hear the message.

But if thinking is only lies, illusions of consciousness, how is Zarathustra (or Nietzsche himself) possible? If consciousness is a dead end, then it cannot be responsible for the thought of active nihilism and the Übermensch. Nietzsche suggested that thought does not come from the subject: "A thought comes when 'it' wants, not when 'I' want; so that it is a *falsification* of the facts to say: the subject 'I' is the condition of the predicate 'think.'"[u] Thought itself is a force, a life force of bodies, wills, and the poiesis of language.

The concept of the Übermensch has often been misunderstood, with some critics going so far as to suggest that it prefigured the Nazi celebration of the superiority of the "Aryan race." The Übermensch is the exceptional individual, the noble master—which is not to say that there is only one—who

8 It is sometimes referred to as *the ideological wars*.

stands apart from the dehumanized masses. These individuals are truly creative and recognize themselves as the only source of truth and value in the universe. They are the enactors of the transvaluation of values, claiming the power to declare for themselves what is true and valued; they are not answerable to anyone else. They accept the sole responsibility for their actions, their choices, their way of living. The Übermensch laughs in the face of the abyss, with the strength and courage to move through pessimism and nihilism to affirmation. These rare individuals have the courage to master themselves, their passions, powers, and weaknesses, claiming the right to control their vital instincts or life forces and assert them in the most productive and creative ways. The Übermensch lives a life of heroic self-mastery, turning the horror and absurdity of the universe into affirmations of life. In the face of eternal recurrence, they live a life of **amor fati**, literally, the love of fate. They embrace the present (without looking to a future or purpose that would give meaning to their life) and accept life as it is given: "That one wants nothing to be different, not forward, not backward, not in all eternity. Not merely bear what is necessary, still less conceal it . . . but *love* it."[v]

The Übermensch is not interested in worldly power and does not seek to control or cause pain to others. It is only the weak, living in ressentiment, who seek to hurt others because they live in negativity, which only finds expression in their frustrated and desperate search for power. The Übermensch is only interested in their own power as creativity, which can be expressed in many ways. Nietzsche seemed particularly drawn to the artist as Übermensch, although his understanding of the instinctual work of art changed over time: from a notion of harmony and balance between order and chaos, between the Apollonian and the Dionysian, to the necessary, ongoing contestation between these competing principles and, finally, to a vision of the destruction of order so as to release the chaos and violence of Dionysus that enable the creativity of the passions.

THE WILL TO POWER

Nietzsche did, however, impose a limit on the transvaluation of value: it must constantly reaffirm, support, and strengthen the life-affirming forces, the life instincts, that are the truth of life and reality. Rejecting the enlightenment science built on the figure of a machine, Nietzsche offered a biological/psychological figure of the life-preserving and life-affirming forces. He finally saw them as expressions of the **will to power**, which defines the only undeniable good in itself, for it is not the expression of any particular position of power. The will to power is the affirmation of life and existence, and of the power of life to assert and control itself, even in its destructive potential and chaos. It is the essence of life (and/or reality) and the affirmation of the creativity of life (and/or reality) as the fundamental being of reality.

The concept of the will to power seems, at least at times, to suggest a new fundamental ontological or cosmological principle, a naturalist ontology of energy and change that explains the totality of life and the material world. As Nietzsche put it,

> The question is in the end whether we really recognize the will as *efficient*, whether we believe in the causality of the will: if we do . . . then we have to make the experiment of positing the causality of the will hypothetically as the only one. . . . One has to risk the hypothesis whether will does not affect will wherever "effects" are recognized. . . . Suppose, finally, we succeeded in explaining our entire instinctive life as the development and ramification of *one* basic form of the will—namely, of the will to power.[w]

It may seem that Nietzsche's defense of an ontology based on a universal force contradicts his own arguments against any kind of transcendental truth. But we can avoid the contradiction by affirming that the will to power is not a singular and universal force; it only exists in the multiplicity of wills that populate the universe.[9] The concept of the will to power presents the world as struggle and competition among the many existing wills, each of which exists as an ongoing drive to confront and overcome obstacles in order to increase its life force, and this in turn entails a never-ending desire for more obstacles to overcome. It figures life and reality as agon, the continuous and necessary battle between forces or wills to power—some active and some reactive, some dominant and some submissive; the active forces are continuously seeking domination against the other forces they encounter, whether equally or less active, and even reactive forces operating out of their submissiveness and ressentiment. It is the joyous affirmation of life as struggle, with the Übermensch as its agent.

9 This is key to understanding the "new Nietzsche" and its rereading of eternal recurrence. See lecture 26.

NOTES

a. Taylor, cited in Pippin, *Modernism*, 82.

b. Strauss, *Natural Right and History*, 25.

c. Deleuze, *Nietzsche and Philosophy*, ix.

d. On the "new Nietzsche," see Allison, *New Nietzsche*.

e. Dr. Baumann (of Turin), cited in Crawford, *To Nietzsche*, 182.

f. Nietzsche, *Human, All Too Human*, 150.

g. Nietzsche, *Beyond Good and Evil*, 359.

h. Nietzsche, *Ecce Homo*, in *Basic Writings of Nietzsche*, 673.

i. Nietzsche, *Thus Spoke Zarathustra*, in *Portable Nietzsche*, 353.

j. Nietzsche, *Will to Power*, 460.

k. Nietzsche, *Ecce Homo*, in *Basic Writings of Nietzsche*, 673; Nietzsche, *Thus Spoke Zarathustra*, in *Portable Nietzsche*, 129.

l. Nietzsche, "Letter to Overbeck," Reddit.com, accessed January 24, 2024, https://www.reddit.com/r/Nietzsche/comments/k2ouke/nietzsche_on_spinoza_in_a_letter_to_franz_overbeck/.

m. Schopenhauer, *World as Will and Representation*.

n. Nietzsche, "On Truth and Lies in a Nonmoral Sense," in Medina and Wood, *Truth*, 17.

o. Nietzsche, "On Truth and Lies in a Nonmoral Sense," in Medina and Wood, *Truth*, 17.

p. Jones, *History of Western Philosophy*, 243.

q. Nietzsche, "On Truth and Lies in a Nonmoral Sense," in Medina and Wood, *Truth*, 14.

r. Nietzsche, *Genealogy of Morals*, in *Basic Writings*, 566.

s. Nietzsche, "Zarathustra's Prologue," in *Thus Spoke Zarathustra*, 43.

t. Nietzsche, *Genealogy of Morals*, 599.

u. Nietzsche, *Beyond Good and Evil*, 47.

v. Nietzsche, *Ecce Homo*, in *Basic Writings of Nietzsche*, 714.

w. Nietzsche, *Beyond Good and Evil*, 238.

Psychoanalysis and Freud

Sigmund Freud's hermeneutics of suspicion addressed questions of individual behavior and development in a social context; many of the concepts and theories of **psychoanalysis** as psychotherapy have entered popular culture and common sense, even as they disturbed the ways human experience was understood. Freud put four questions on the table, raising issues that had yet to be taken seriously or, in some cases, even acknowledged in modern thought: subjectivity and the psyche, sexuality, repression and the Unconscious, and the relation of psychic and social realities.

Freud was born of religious Jewish parents on May 6, 1856, in Freiberg, Moravia, in the Austrian Empire (now part of the Czech Republic). He grew up in Vienna and studied medicine (neurology) at the University of Vienna. After doing neurophysiological research on animal tissue, he began a medical career in Vienna, where he remained until he fled to London to escape Nazism a year before his death on September 23, 1939. Vienna, at the turn of the century, was one of the artistic, musical, and intellectual centers of Europe. Yet, Viennese bourgeois society, from which most of Freud's patients came, was dominated by morally conservative (approximating Victorian) values, making many of his ideas extremely controversial.

In 1886, Freud opened a practice specializing in analysis and therapy for "nervous disorders" or neuroses, which are non–organically based, nonconscious, obsessively repetitive behaviors or thoughts, often accompanied by excessive anxiety.[1] At first, he used hypnosis.[2] But soon he developed his own therapeutic technique—**free association**—in which patients said whatever came into their head, (ideally) without censoring themselves or letting social inhibitions interfere. He placed increasing effort on the analysis of patients' dreams as doorways into the causes of their neurotic symptoms.[3] His appointment as professor in 1902 gave his ideas a more public platform. He devoted much of his life to defining psychoanalysis and orchestrating its professionalization.

The first International Congress of Psychoanalysis was held in 1908 in Salzburg and included Alfred Adler, Otto Rank, Carl Jung, and Ludwig Binswanger. The International Association of Psychoanalysis was founded in Nuremberg in 1910. Its first female member was Margarete Hilferding. However, Adler, Jung, and Rank, followed by Karen Horney and Melanie Klein, quickly resigned over substantial disagreements with Freud, resulting in a number of competing schools of psychoanalysis. The dominant school, **ego psychology**, led by Ernest Jones and Anna Freud (Sigmund Freud's daughter), emphasized the need to strengthen the ego, which manages the conflict between internal and external forces by placing itself between the other two divisions of the psyche: the id (desire) and the superego (social norms). Melanie Klein pioneered child analysis and **object relations theory**, which postulates the importance of preverbal existential anxiety, resulting in the world being split between good and bad idealizations. Carl Jung's **analytical psychology** emphasized individuation and introduced the concepts of archetypes and collective unconscious. After Freud's death, other schools emerged, such as Jacques Lacan's structuralist psychoanalysis and the antipsychiatry of R. D. Laing and Félix Guattari.[4]

1 Freud did not provide treatment for psychoses, such as schizophrenia, in which the patient no longer has a secure grasp of what is real.
2 He had learned hypnosis from Jean-Martin Charcot and Josef Breuer.
3 Many of Freud's ideas and practices emerged partly out of his own efforts at self-analysis, when he developed physiological and psychological symptoms after his father's death in 1902.
4 See lecture 27.

One of the unique difficulties in discussing Freud's work results from the generic diversity of his writings. His most important contributions often were derived directly from his clinical analyses and therapeutic practice, from psychoanalysis as the **talking cure**.[a] Many concepts appeared first in rich case studies (e.g., Anna O., Dora, Little Hans, the Rat Man, Wolfman) and in essays extrapolated from or supplementing them (e.g., *Three Essays on the Theory of Sexuality*, 1905; "Mourning and Melancholia," 1917; and "Instincts and Their Vicissitudes," 1915). These works embodied the changes in his ideas that resulted, over time, from his therapeutic practice. Not surprisingly, the efforts to generalize his concepts (e.g., melancholia, transference) have been contentious.

But Freud also wrote at least four other kinds of texts, directed at different audiences. The first provided insights into and overviews of his method, analytic tools, and diagnostic concepts (e.g., *The Interpretation of Dreams*, 1899; *The Introductory Lectures on Psychoanalysis*, 1917). The second extended his theories and methods beyond the therapeutic encounter into other realms of social behavior (e.g., *The Psychopathology of Everyday Life*, 1904; *Jokes and Their Relation to the Unconscious*, 1905; *Group Psychology and the Analysis of the Ego*, 1921). The third offered more theoretical models of the psyche and psychic forces (e.g., *Beyond the Pleasure Principle*, 1920; *The Ego and the Id*, 1923). Finally, despite earlier admonitions against doing so, Freud projected his ideas beyond the realm of social behavior onto society itself, speculating on anthropological questions of kinship, religion, and culture (e.g., *Totem and Taboo*, 1913; *The Future of an Illusion*, 1927; *Civilization and Its Discontents*, 1930; *Moses and Monotheism*, 1939).

SUBJECTIVITY AND THE DRIVES

The enlightenments generally equated human nature with subjectivity, but they rarely analyzed it as a problem. Instead, they assumed both its existence and its nature—as consciousness, reason, and self-consciousness. Freud made subjectivity into a theoretical problem by locating it within the **psychic life** or "interiority" of individuals. The psyche is intimately bound up with an individual's sense of self, and with how an individual has a sense of self. This required a more complicated psychic system than subjectivity as a simple entity. This psychic system is not ever given in its totality; identity and self-consciousness are not formed once and for all time. Because the psyche is an emerging and ever-changing structure that never quite achieves the unity that the enlightenments took for granted, its development is ongoing as it comes into being through scientifically (psychoanalytically) analyzable processes. So, Freud asked: How does subjectivity come into being? How do consciousness and self-consciousness come into being? What does it mean for an individual to be self-conscious? How does a human being come to have a sense of self, an identity? How is it possible for a subject to be so divided that it can be conscious of itself?

Freud postulated that human existence is characterized by an innate set of foundational drives or instincts, each defining a psychic process or developing structure.[5] Throughout his career, he elaborated on these forces in a number of models and typologies. Drives combine two elements: an **idea** and an **affect**. Every instance of a drive has an object, but that object is "in the mind"; it is an idea of the object. For example, the mother's breast (as the source of milk) is an idea in the child's psychic reality. It does not involve thought, reason, or consciousness. A drive invests or **cathects** the idea with a certain amount of psychic energy or affect. In different instances, involving different individuals (not just children), anything can become an instinctual object (from the penis to six-inch stilettos to a teddy bear), and there are no limits or thresholds to the quantity of affect that can be invested. The psychic economy proceeds from **drives** to **needs** to **demands** and, finally, to **desires**.

Initially, the infant is determined by the **ego drives** (i.e., the instincts for survival) or what Freud later called the **life-preserving drives**. For example, the child has a drive for nutrition enabled through the sucking reflex. The infant develops "needs" and "demands" the mother's breast (an idea invested with affect). But beyond satisfying the infant's hunger, sucking on the breast produces a pleasure on the lips and in the gullet as the warm milk is ingested. A new drive emerges, leaning on the drive for nutrition. The infant now wants to suck on the mother's breast, even when it's not hungry (and, hence, the use of pacifiers). A second set of drives emerges: the sexual or **libidinal** drives.[6] While this complex relation between ego and sexual instincts begins

---

5 Freud most commonly used *Trieb*, which has been translated as both "instinct" and "drive." The former emphasizes its inherent biological origin, the latter its energy and propulsion. Over time, Freud increasingly used *drive* rather than *instinct*. For the most part, I will use *drive* whenever possible although the most widely used translation (by Strachey) uses *instinct*. See Colin Beer, "Instinct," *Britannica*, accessed January 26, 2024, https://www.britannica.com/topic/instinct/Freuds-Trieb.

6 In Freud's earlier texts, all affects were **libidinal**, although he later identified libido with the sexual drives.

with the infant, it certainly does not end in infancy. It is the basic structure of the psychic economy for the entirety of an individual's life.

While some previous thinkers recognized that sexuality was an important part of human life, they either took it for granted or treated it as an ethical problem; they generally identified it with the body as the negation of reason and rational morality, and with women. Freud argued that sexual development—the process by which the infant comes to have a sexual/gendered identity, which Freud assumed to be either male and female—was the most crucial dynamic through which humans achieve identity and self-consciousness.

That was outrageous enough for Vienna's conservative culture, but his particular theories about the role of sexuality in his patients' neuroses were even more damning. Most of Freud's patients were women from Vienna's middle class who suffered from a variety of "hysterical" symptoms (a gender-specific diagnosis) and obsessional neuroses. Freud's first explanation—the **seduction theory**—suggested that these patients had suffered sexual trauma as children, including being sexually abused. The experience, having happened before the child was fully sexualized and gendered, before the child was able to psychically process the trauma, remained only as a memory trace until something triggered the memory, which then had to be repressed. The neuroses were symptoms or distorted re-presentations of the repressed event. They were the manifestations in everyday life of the sexual trauma in an unrecognizable form.

Freud gave up his seduction theory, no doubt partly to protect himself from public outrage. Telling members of the Viennese middle class that they were abusing their children, even at the very youngest ages, was simply beyond the pale. Historians now believe that, beneath the surface of Victorian life, hidden from many and impossible to publicly acknowledge, was a subculture of deeply "deviant" (often violent and abusive) sexual desire and behavior. So it may be that Freud's seduction theory was, in some ways, grounded in actual behaviors.

In its place, Freud offered the theory of **infantile sexuality**. He asserted that infants are always and already sexualized but that their sexuality is not yet gendered or genitally organized (in which only particular regions of the body become the locus of sexual pleasure). The entire body of the infant is sexualized; everywhere is a source of sexual demand and pleasure, independently of the life drives. Freud called this **polymorphous perversity**.[b] He continued to account for neuroses by arguing that the child had a sexual experience, whether an experience of its own body or witnessing a sexual encounter (e.g., sodomy) of its parents, whether an imagined fantasy or a witnessed trauma. The theory then described the same processes as the seduction theory. As you might imagine, the theory of infantile sexuality did little to assuage the Victorian sense of moral self-righteousness, only now Freud was not attacking the behavior of the male adult population but the very deeply held and cherished image of infant and child innocence.

Freud maintained that questions of sexual trauma and fantasy, and of the sexual difference—between masculine and feminine organizations of sexuality, of desire and affect, of behavior and self-presentation—were central in the production of identity and self-consciousness. And since that production is ongoing, the sexual-libidinal economy of drives and desires, ideas and affect, has a profound determining effect on human behavior throughout an individual's life. To a large extent, Freud figured this production as the Oedipal drama, which I will discuss briefly in a moment.

THE RUSE OF REPRESSION

Freud's first attempt at a systematic theory of the mind, which grew out of a long-term dialogue with the German physician Wilhelm Fliess, was never published. In the "Project for a Scientific Psychology," also called "Psychology for Neurologists," he offered what the French phenomenologist Paul Ricoeur (1913–2005) called an "energetics model."[c] Based on an early but accurate anatomical description of the nervous or "neuronic" system, Freud envisioned the psyche as a hydraulic system through which neuronic energies flow, pushed on by instinctual as well as external excitations. There were nodes of heavily cathected neurons where energy was bound and stored, to be used when necessary for the system to defend itself from disruption. These nodes constituted the ego as a self-defense mechanism rather than as subjectivity. They directed the flow of energy, following the principle of (quantitative) constancy: the neuronic system sought to maintain the flow of energy as low and steady as possible. Arousal or excitation increased the flow, producing rising tension that was experienced as unpleasure. Returning the flow to the level of constancy (e.g., when the arousal is satisfied) was experienced as pleasure. But the flow could also be blocked at specific nodes, producing neurotic symptoms. Freud never used this model in clinical practice, and his thinking took a very different direction.

Instead, Freud turned first to hypnosis and then to interpretation, postulating the reality of **repression** and introducing a psychological "deep structure." He argued that something was missing in all previous understandings of psychic life: **the Unconscious.** The human psyche is, metaphorically, divided into at least two parts or, better, two processes: the conscious and the Unconscious. The psychic realm can never achieve the unity it seeks (and that had previously been assumed) because it is always radically divided against itself; it is inherently a conflictual rather than a harmonious whole. Certain cathected ideas cannot be grasped or accepted by the conscious mind; so, the mind actively represses them, resulting in the Unconscious. Freud was not simply saying that there are some things the individual is not aware of or has forgotten—located in the **subconscious.** Repression is an active agency by which something is made unavailable, inaccessible to consciousness, because repression erases the very fact of its existence, as well as the very fact of repression. What is repressed is the affect that has been invested in a particular object/idea, usually involving sexual desires, behaviors, and fantasies.

Repression constitutes a necessary inability to access part of who and what you are. Any attempt to become fully self-conscious is doomed to failure; the subject is always incapable of knowing itself. Every attempt to understand human behavior is doomed to failure because there is always something that cannot be accessed, that has been displaced beyond availability, that has been lost—the Unconscious.

But the Unconscious is always inserting itself into consciousness, without consciousness being able to recognize what is happening. It appears through forms of indirection and misdirection, guaranteeing that there is always only misrecognition. The repressed refuses to be represented, and therefore it cannot be grasped in consciousness. That is the challenge of psychoanalysis: How does one move from forms of misrepresentation (e.g., dreams, jokes, neurotic symptoms) that are the necessary result of repression, to forms of understanding? The practice (and theory) that Freud eventually arrived at was an interpretive one. His hermeneutics of suspicion, laid out most clearly in *The Interpretation of Dreams*, approached the Unconscious through its manifestation in processes of symbolization.

Therapy moves us, through various processes and layers, from **manifest** (visible, surface) to **latent** (deep, hidden) meaning: for example, from the explicit content of a dream to the unconscious desire or trauma that has been repressed; or, more generally, from a neurotic symptom to the latent cause expressing itself in obsessive behavior. The latent meaning, which might still be a distorted representation of the repressed event, always takes the form of a desire to fulfill a particular wish.

Freud argued that this hermeneutic was possible because it was reversible. The **dreamwork**, the construction of dreams within the psychic life of the individual, comprises the process(es) by which the repressed event is both hidden and represented. In the talking cure, the therapist leads the patient through this process in reverse. Instead of moving from the latent to the manifest, analysis moves from the manifest to the latent. For both, the dreamwork involves processes of **symbolic representation**. Uncovering and retracing these processes is especially challenging because repression causes the patient's psyche to actively, if unconsciously, resist the effort. The patient will, both consciously and unconsciously, do everything in their power to undercut and impede the hermeneutic process.

What, then, are these processes of symbolic representation? How is the psyche representing—hiding in plain sight—a repressed cathected idea in conscious behavior? Freud identified four nonrational processes of psychic representation: condensation, displacement, symbolism, and secondary revision. **Condensation** combines or fuses disparate, even contradictory, ideas into a single idea. **Displacement** moves an idea into another idea, which may even seem unrelated. **Symbolism** figures an idea, often in visual or other sensible forms only indirectly related to it. And **secondary revision** unites the disparate results of these processes into a relatively coherent whole (such as the dream).[7] Freud referred to the total effect of these processes as **overdetermination**.[8] This suggests that any manifest content is determined by the sum of, and relations among, these four symbolic processes. Thus, a particular symptom may have numerous causes; it may even be the expression of more than one repressed event. These are the processes or practices by which the psyche translates the repressed into manifest content, and these are the processes that the analyst has to get the patient to work through.

A toddler witnesses its parents having anal sex; it does not understand this, so it tucks it away until the memory is triggered. But then the child's conscious mind refuses the memory and represses it. And in so doing, it transforms the memory, condensing it with other ideas into a figure of, let's say, walking the dog. At the same time, the memory is displaced into another idea, perhaps the zoo, which is further displaced into a snake. And the event

---

7 Structuralists (e.g., the influential Russian linguist Roman Jakobson) argued that condensation and displacement could be understood as metaphors and metonyms, respectively.

8 Remember the discussion of Marx.

is symbolized as a crack in their own bedroom wall. Finally, secondary revision combines the pieces into a dream narrative, which in one sense feels coherent and in another makes no sense to the conscious mind, for example, a narrative in which a dog and a snake crawl through a crack in the wall. Psychoanalytic therapy works to reverse engineer the whole process through the practice of free association.

THE INSIDE AND THE OUTSIDE

Freud posed the question of the relationship between psychic and social realities, between the inside and the outside. Most enlightenment thinkers were content to hold the two domains apart, with some leakage allowed but unexplained. Hegel assumed a formal, guaranteed relation between history and thought but never really dealt with individual consciousness. Marx focused on social reality but paid little attention (beyond the concept of ideology) to psychic life or consciousness. Freud argued that psychic and social life were inseparable, mutually determining. You cannot understand psychic life solely on its own terms; the psyche internalizes (**introjects**) the external world, particularly sociosexual relations and norms, including the dynamics of the nuclear family. Nor can one understand social life solely on its own terms; the psyche **projects** its own psychosexual dynamics (always misrepresented) onto the exterior world of social relations. The inside and the outside, the psychological interiority and the social exteriority, can only be thought together, in their constitutive relationality.

Freud expressed this relation in an evolving series of models. The most famous is the **genetic model**, which tells the story of the psychosexual development of the individual.[d] It starts with infancy, when the body is polymorphously perverse and ungendered; the infant has no consciousness of itself as differentiated from the world, and no sense of its unique self or identity. The model maps out a series of stages of the child's changing relation to "his" own body, to the world, and to "his" family: the oral stage, the anal stage, the phallic stage (commonly referred to as the Oedipal stage), a latent period, and finally the adult genital stage. One can also describe the (male) infant moving from polymorphous perversity to an identification with the image of the primary caregiver (mother) to an identification with the father.[9]

9 The child "destined" to be female enacts the Electra complex, in which the daughter competes with the mother for the father's desire—obviously, not a very satisfying solution. I will discuss this further in lecture 22.

However widely known some elements of this story have become, it is, in many ways, one of the most controversial and criticized of Freud's contributions. Critics have pointed out that its model of development is built on a single, historically and culturally specific model of the relations and dynamics of a "normal" family—largely Jewish and bourgeois. (Perhaps a new version of synecdochical universality?) Feminist scholars have pointed out that while most of Freud's patients were women, the model focuses on the development of the male child. It is the story of how a biologically male infant comes, under the "proper" conditions, to define itself in the normative gendered terms of masculinity.

Freud is often further accused of establishing or at least repeating the common, simple difference between normal and "perverse" sexual desires and behaviors. While it is clear that he sometimes embraced this binary, he also explicitly rejected it on the grounds that whatever leads to such "perversions" is innate in every human, and therefore cannot usefully be described as "perversions."

Freud offered two other models of the psyche. The **topographical model**, often pictured as an iceberg, distinguished three layers: consciousness as awareness is entirely above the water line; the Unconscious, the realm of the drives and repressed ideas, is entirely below the surface and by far the largest layer; and the surface itself is the preconscious or subconscious and includes all the ideas that are just outside of awareness but which can be accessed and made conscious.[e]

The **structural model** described the relations among the id, ego, and superego.[f] The **id**, governed by the **pleasure principle**, encompasses the instinctual forces that constantly operate and assert themselves in the psyche. The **superego** embodies (in the psyche) the values and morals of the external society. The **ego**, governed by the **reality principle**, is harder to pin down because Freud held different, often contested, views at different times.

In Freud's earlier works, the ego was the locus of the sense of self. It is who I am—between the forces of instinctual passions and societal laws, expectations, and constraints. Often, especially in ego psychology, the ego is the home of consciousness, of reason and common sense, of intellection and cognition, of perceptual awareness and decision-making; its function is to protect and defend the self, that is, itself. It always needs to build up its strength and resilience (the function of therapy). When I was young, this was often oversimplified: the ego was an innocent, virginal young girl caught between a sex-starved gorilla (the id) and an old, weak nun, trying to hold off the gorilla with nothing but a ruler (the superego).

But as Freud's theories developed, he suggested that the ego is "that part of the id which has been modified by the direct influence of the external world."[g] It is the thin line where consciousness meets reality, the boundary layer that separates the drives from society. It is, therefore, not actually a part of the psyche as such but the defensive transit line that decides what to let in and out. In either case, in some sense, it mediates or arbitrates between the id and the superego.

SOCIETY CANNOT BE DEFENDED

Although Freud always maintained that psychoanalytic theory was, before all else (and sometimes only), a clinically based practice, he became increasingly interested in extending his theories into more generalized psychological, anthropological, and even speculative concerns. He claimed that the development of society and civilization recapitulated the processes of individual psychosocial development. He saw society as a collective psyche that could be analyzed. In many of his published works, religion plays a crucial role in mediating the competing demands of familial sexuality and social morality. In a series of books—*Totem and Taboo*, *The Future of an Illusion*, *Civilization and Its Discontents*, and *Moses and Monotheism* (his last book)—Freud analyzed the psychosocial roots of monotheism, which he characterized as an illusion based on an originary act of patricide, which becomes a repressed, founding collective memory and the basis of patriarchal monotheism.

In different works, he assigned different values to religion: as a necessary imposition of morality on the dangerous impulses of the masses (like Spinoza); as the establishment of the incest taboo necessary for social peace; as an answer to the fear of nature. In *Civilization and Its Discontents*, however, he suggested that religion is motivated by "a sensation of eternity," by an "oceanic feeing" that he admitted never having experienced.[h] But he still explained such experiences as infantile wish fulfillment. Throughout his work, he held up the virtues of reason and science over religion, although he remained ever pessimistic about the possibility of their eventual victory, largely because of humanity's aggressive impulses.

Like Spinoza, however, Freud found a second, redeeming interpretation of religion, especially in his own Jewishness. On its surface, *Moses and Monotheism* retells the origin of Judaism through the story of Moses and the

Exodus.[10] But Freud found the uniqueness of Judaism in the Second Commandment's prohibition of making or worshipping images of God, thus making God abstract and internalized. As he wrote, "A sensory perception was given second place to what may be called an abstract idea—a triumph of intellectuality over sensuality."[i] Freud argued that this emphasis on the capacity for abstraction had profound consequences. It made possible an "advance in intellectuality" across the fields of art and thought, enabling both more control over nature and the possibility of a more humane social order. Put differently, the renunciation of the pleasures of religious imagery strengthened the capacity for introspection and self-understanding that is the condition of possibility of reason and art.[11] This advance began with Judaism but eventually extended itself to the broader forces of Western culture. In the end, and nearing the close of his life, without giving up his atheism or his psychoanalytic reading of religion, Freud nevertheless saw the promise and poetry of religion.

Finally, Freud offered a highly speculative, metaphysical model of the fundamental forces of life, an effort that may well have been influenced by the emerging paradigm of thermodynamics. He proposed that life was determined by the relations of three transcendental and impersonal drives: Eros, Thanatos, and Ananke. **Eros** is the life force, the will to live and to survive, and the creative power of life itself. It is distinct from both the sexual drives and the pleasure principle, although Freud sometimes wrote as if Eros included them. Freud sometimes even associated Eros with love.

Thanatos, or the death drive, evolved in Freud's thought. In his first references to it, he equated Thanatos with the force of psychic inertia in the earlier "Project for a Scientific Psychology," a principle of the constancy and

---

10 According to Freud's interpretation of then-recent archaeological evidence, Moses was an Egyptian prince, a priest, and eventually the leader of a rebellious monotheistic sect (worshipping Aton) who was killed by his followers (hence the same guilt narrative that he had laid out previously, giving rise to Moses's prophetic status and the myth of the Messiah). This group then joined up with a tribe of Midianites (descendants of Abraham) who worshipped Yahweh. The resulting religion is defined by the need to hold in tension a loving god and an angry god.

11 Two points are worth suggesting. First, this may explain the disproportionate contributions of Jewish culture in the literate humanities, criticism, and sciences rather than in the more visceral and material arts. Second, the prohibition against images may partly explain the long and dispersed history of anti-Semitism because it made it more difficult for Judaism to be articulated to more local and even indigenous forms of religion and sacrality compared with, e.g., Christianity, which used its capacity to be reinflected to aid its use in colonization.

conservation of energy, as opposed to the activity and excitation secured by the pleasure principle (and later Eros). Thanatos is the reduction of tension—and hence of the energy that produces it. But this changed as Thanatos was increasingly presented as a force that eliminates all tension, that eliminates all life energy. Death became the zero state. This change seems to have resulted from Freud's effort to explain the compulsion to repetition so common among neurotic patients, which led him to propose "an urge inherent in organic life to restore an earlier state of things," and which, in turn, produces "a pressure toward death."[j]

Apparently, Eros cannot hold back the power of Thanatos on its own. So there had to be a third force, **Ananke**, which is the most difficult to define. Eros is called to a project "instigated by Ananke—by the exigencies of reality."[k] Ananke is usually linked to the reality principle and, somewhat mysteriously, to both work and fate. It is the principle of necessity, not a logical or even metaphysical necessity but, rather, a material and historical necessity. It is only through Ananke that Eros is assigned and can fulfill the task "of uniting separate individuals into a community bound together by libidinal ties."[l]

The fact that Freud's theories are vulnerable to both misunderstandings and important criticisms (many from feminists and queer theorists), that he sometimes contradicted himself and often changed his position, should not mask the importance and productiveness of this thought. Like other deep theorists, he opened up vital new spaces for thought and new ways of thinking about human realities.

Whatever your take on psychoanalysis, Freud moved modern thought from the individual to the family, from psyche to society (and back again), from drives to desires, from consciousness to the Unconscious, from normality to neuroses, from pleasure to reality, and from life to death. Like Marx, he challenged enlightenment thinking at some of its most sensitive vulnerabilities, even while affirming the enlightenment project of scientific truth-seeking. Like Marx, he shook Western societies to their core and posed questions that we are still trying to answer.

NOTES

a. See Freud and Breuer, *Studies on Hysteria*.

b. See Freud, *Three Essays on the Theory of Sexuality*.

c. Freud, "Project for a Scientific Psychology," in *Origins of Psycho-Analysis*; Ricoeur, *Freud and Philosophy*.

d. This model is offered but not fully developed in Freud, *Three Essays on the Theory of Sexuality*.

e. Freud, *Interpretation of Dreams*.

f. Freud, *The Ego and the Id*, in *Standard Edition*, vol. 19, 1923–1925.

g. Freud, *Ego and the Id*, in *Standard Edition*, 19:363.

h. Freud, *Civilization and Its Discontents*, 11.

i. Freud, *Moses and Monotheism*, in *Standard Edition*, 23:113.

j. Freud, *Beyond the Pleasure Principle*, in *Standard Edition*, 18:316.

k. Freud, *Civilization and Its Discontents*, 104.

l. Freud, *Civilization and Its Discontents*, 104.

Phenomenology

Phenomenology and Husserl

Phenomenology is a broad movement that encompasses numerous projects, schools, and positions. It is commonly said that there are as many phenom-enologies as there are phenomenologists. Versions vary depending on whether they are concerned primarily with questions of epistemology or ontology, human nature, or ethical life; where they focus (science, perception, art, emotion, etc.); where they look for answers (consciousness, the body, modes of existence); and what sort of methods they invoke. One might hear ref-erences to eidetic phenomenology, constitutive phenomenology, existential phenomenology, existentialism, hermeneutic phenomenology, phenomeno-logical psychology, and phenomenological sociology.[1]

---

1 When Theory emerged in the 1960s, with scientism/positivism as its enemy, phenom-enology, or more accurately phenomenological social theory (e.g., Alfred Schütz and Peter Berger), largely rooted in Husserlian phenomenology, was a powerful alternative. This was sometimes synthesized with humanistic Marxism, for example, in the influen-tial work of Peter Berger and Thomas Luckmann.

While Edmund Husserl is generally identified as the founder of the movement (associated with eidetic and constitutive phenomenology), the term *phenomenology* itself has a longer history, including Georg Wilhelm Friedrich Hegel's *Phenomenology of Spirit*. The two other major figures are Husserl's student Martin Heidegger (hermeneutic phenomenology) and Maurice Merleau-Ponty (existential phenomenology).[2] Phenomenology's roots lie in Immanuel Kant's distinction between the phenomenal and the noumenal worlds. However, rather than seeing the transcendental subject as the condition of Truth, or the noumena as the ground of Truth, phenomenology argues that Truth has to be found within the phenomenon itself, within the realm of experience, through careful and concernful analyses. The one thing people can be sure of is their experience. I know I experience the world and that it is *my* experience. But I do not yet know what the truth of my experience is. And I do not yet know how Truth is grounded in my experience. If we cannot appeal to anything outside of experience, thinking must start by investigating experience and the experiencing subject.

Husserl was born on April 8, 1859, of Jewish parents in Prostějov, Moravia, in the Austrian Empire (presently located in the Czech Republic). He studied mathematics and physics in Leipzig and Berlin, but under the mentorship of the philosopher Tomáš Masaryk (1850–1937), later the first president of Czechoslovakia, he turned his attention to psychology and philosophy, a move that led him to attend the lectures of Franz Brentano (1838–1917) in Vienna, the primary influence on his thought. In 1901, Husserl began teaching at the University of Göttingen; in 1912, he founded and edited the *Jahrbuch für Philosophie und Phänomenologishche Forschung* (*Yearbook for Philosophy and Phenomenological Research*), which remains a major outlet for phenomenological scholarship. In 1916, he moved to Albert Ludwig University of Freiburg, where Heidegger served as his assistant from 1920 to 1923. He retired in 1928 and died in Freiburg on April 27, 1938.

Husserl published ten books, some of which comprise multiple volumes, including *Logical Investigations* (1900, 2 volumes), *Ideas* (1913, 3 volumes in English), *Phenomenology of Internal Time-Consciousness* (1928), *Cartesian Meditations* (1931), and *The Crisis of European Sciences and Transcendental Phenomenology* (1936). After his death, with the rise of Nazism, his archives,

---

2 I do not have the space to discuss Merleau-Ponty, whose phenomenology focused on the embodied nature of individuated human existence, nor will I talk about existentialism, which was primarily concerned with individuated ethics.

including over forty thousand manuscript pages of shorthand notes, were smuggled to the Catholic University of Louvain, Belgium.

THE SEARCH FOR CERTAINTY, AGAIN

Husserl was obsessed with the need for certainty. Why? We can use the metaphor of a ship to explain the importance of certainty in the turbulent late nineteenth and early twentieth centuries. If society is a ship sailing on the calm sea, it doesn't worry about the state of the anchor (Truth) or where it will anchor. But when a storm hits, then it has to worry about anchoring. Husserl assumed that modern societies were in the midst of a serious storm, which threatened their very existence.

A large part of the storm was the skepticism and relativism of the various hermeneutics of suspicion. Romanticism and religion were also problematic because they were not rational and were incapable of grounding either themselves or other claims to knowledge. Finally, science and the positivistic philosophies that purported to legitimate it were leading thinking astray. Such "objectivist" or "naturalist" ways of thinking treated everything as an empirical object, with perceptual objects providing the model. Science made consciousness and mind into things in the natural world, which could be observed and analyzed in the same way as all other things. Husserl described such philosophies as dogmas that were also unable to ground their own validity. Against these, Husserl called for a new philosophy, committed to finding a stable ground for human truth and value. It was the sacred duty of philosophers to recapture the capacity of humanity to anchor itself in Truth, to enable people to find and live in the calm waters of Truth.

Philosophy had abandoned the quest for certainty and the ground of Truth that had defined René Descartes's project. But Descartes's effort to ground Truth in consciousness and establish reason as the transcendental condition of the mind failed because it did not go through an analytic of experience, a new kind of empiricism. Phenomenology was considered a "rigorous science."[a] It was a "first" or **presuppositionless philosophy** that could establish its own truth with absolute certainty (*apodeixis*), as well as the truth of all other forms of knowledge. It would be the foundationless foundation of knowledge because its truths were indubitable.

Philosophy had to become more Cartesian than Descartes himself, which meant that it had to start with and stay within the realm of experience. Husserl followed Descartes by proposing to understand experience entirely in terms of consciousness, so that the path to Truth lay in the very nature of consciousness itself.

Husserl described himself as "a perpetual beginner."[b] In book after book, Husserl began again: starting from the same understanding of consciousness (which I will describe momentarily), he tried to derive rational and logical solutions to the problems of epistemology. Each time, he hit a dead end. Most commonly, the problem was intersubjectivity: If the only indubitable truth is my own consciousness of my experiences, how do we avoid falling into so-lipsism? Then he started over, taking a different path but always beginning from consciousness; sometimes he found the solution to the problem that had eluded him only to come up against another brick wall. The result is that each book presents a different phenomenological system. In Husserl's first book, *The Philosophy of Arithmetic*, he explored the psychological processes that grounded mathematics. Kant's appeal to the Transcendental Subject and the pure forms of intuition could not be justified in the terms of consciousness as it is given. Instead, Husserl derived his answer from the psychology of his day, but then, in *Logical Investigations*, he criticized all psychologisms, which grounded reason in psychological processes, if only because you cannot assume that such processes were universal and unchanging.

I will lay out the broad parameters of Husserl's philosophy, and some of the problems and solutions he proposed. Husserl sought a **rationalist philosophy of consciousness**. Husserlian phenomenology set out to understand how consciousness operates in order to find truth there. It places the subject—as consciousness—at the center of the lived world, in order to understand the relations between consciousness and its object, the knower and the known. He claimed that by turning to the subject and their experience, phenomenology would reveal the truth of everyone's experience. That is, you discover universal—objective—Truth, precisely by concentrating exclusively on the object in consciousness to the complete elimination of everything extraneous and subjective. Thus, a new kind of objectivism, an **objectivism of the phenomenon**, was born.

PHENOMENOLOGICAL METHOD

If phenomenology was to be a rigorous science, it needed, like any science, its own method, a cognitive or analytic procedure.[3] This method—**intuition**—

3 The terms used to describe Husserl's method vary with different texts and different interpreters.

had to be empirical, but neither inductive nor experimental; intuition is the intellectual observation of the object. It seeks to "**go back to the 'things themselves,'**"[c] to the phenomenon, as what is directly given to consciousness in intuition. Husserl's "principle of principles," a revision of Descartes's clear and vital ideas, stated that "whatever presents itself to us by 'intuition,' at first hand, in its authentic reality as it were . . . , is to be accepted simply for the thing as which it presents itself, yet merely within the limits within which it presents itself."[4,d] This is the phenomenon; in phenomenological terms, it is that which is itself and truly shows itself to be what lies clearly before us.

Intuition comprises a series of practices designed to move you from the **natural attitude** to the **phenomenological attitude**. It involves a change in the way you perceive and know the world. The world still remains there, exactly as it was, but one's attitude toward it changes, so that it can be viewed with a new clarity. Ordinary people live their lives in the natural attitude. They are absorbed in a world that they take for granted, which is objectively real and which exists whether or not they experience it at the moment. They assume that they can know it, that other people exist in the same world and experience it in fundamentally the same way, and that they are free to move through the world, which can result in different experiences and perspectives. And all this is possible because they constantly suspend any doubts they may have about this world and all they take for granted. When things happen that don't fit our sense of reality, we cope with it, make excuses for it, or dismiss it: it's an aberration of nature, a practical joke, a hallucination. We refuse to give up our certainty. To use an analogy, when a religious believer is confronted with evidence challenging their assumptions about God—for example, how could a loving God have allowed the Holocaust?—they will often refuse the doubt by claiming that God works in mysterious ways. The natural attitude is the world of common sense, and it is, for Husserl, the world of both the natural and social sciences.

The phenomenological method consists of three steps to move the analyst out of the natural attitude and to the phenomenon itself. The first step, the **threefold exclusion**, requires you to put aside everything you think you know or remember about the object of your investigation so that you can focus single-mindedly on the object itself. You exclude all theoretical and scientific knowledge; all traditional knowledge and whatever you have been taught, including folk wisdom, gossip, and so on; and, finally, all personal

---

4 Different phenomenologists have their own "principle of principles."

experiences and feelings you may have. To offer a trivial example of the final exclusion, which is often the most difficult: I know a lot about cats, both biological and cultural, but, more important, I have a lot of strong feelings about them—because I have had cats (as well as dogs). My last cat, Hank, was the cat from hell. Whenever I think about cats, I recall my experience of Hank, and my feelings that cats are dangerous, malevolent, vicious, and antisocial creatures who take over whatever space they can (and maybe ultimately the world). I must put all this aside.

Emulating Cartesian doubt, the threefold exclusion puts aside every possible contaminant of truth—everything that may not be true, warranted, or pertinent to the object; it returns you to something that cannot be doubted, to the phenomenon as it presents itself to your consciousness. Not surprisingly, many thinkers, including later phenomenologists, reject this demand as utterly impossible: one cannot simply forget everything one knows and feels, or even pretend to do so. Without such "contaminations," one would not have any reason to continue the investigation.

The second step is the *epoché*, or the **phenomenological reduction:** you bracket the question of whether the object exists. It doesn't matter if it exists or not, if it is extinct or imaginary. The *epoché* takes you out of the world in which objects really exist and into a world of **irreality**. It's not that the object does not exist, merely that the question of its existence is irrelevant to the investigation (although even Husserl had to return to the question of the experience of the existence of an object).

The final step is the **eidetic reduction**; the word *eidos* means **essence**. Take the result of the first two steps and reduce it to its essential being; eliminate everything that could be otherwise. This is accomplished by **imaginative free variation:** vary the characteristics, both qualitative and quantitative, of the object present in consciousness, asking whether it still is what it is. If the answer is yes, cast that characteristic aside. If the answer is no, it is essential to the phenomenon as what is directly given to consciousness in intuition. I used a rather trivial example a moment ago: cats. What is the truth of "cat"? Eliminate everything you think you know, everything you believe, everything you've heard, everything you feel. Eliminate the question of whether cats are real or not. Eliminate all the contingencies, all the accidents: the color, the length of its hair, the number of legs, and so on; all these things are accidents. What is left is the phenomenon—the essence, the truth, of cat.

What, then, is a phenomenon? It is not a mere appearance as contrasted with something real behind the appearance. The phenomenon is what appears to the phenomenologist in the appearance, all appearances being equal. It is not an empirical experience, something that permits a direct sensual observation, for that would cast us back into the natural attitude. But it is also not the real "substance" of existence, as in **phenomenalism**, where reality is assumed to consist only of appearances. The phenomenon is a new kind of object, an object of and in consciousness itself, which excludes matters of existence and all contingencies, and includes everything that necessarily belongs to the object. Husserl described it as the fundamental **meaning-structure** of the object, but meaning here does not refer to cognitive, propositional, or semantic meaning; rather, it refers to an object as a conceptual totality. And since it is an essence, it is, according to Husserl, necessarily universal. Many of Husserl's critics, as well as some of his followers, argue that he confused linguistic meanings, which can vary over time and space, with universal essences.

INTENTIONALITY

The phenomenological method formed one of the two cornerstones of Husserl's phenomenology. The other, which is common to almost all versions of phenomenology, was a particular model of the fundamental structure of consciousness as relationality: **intentionality**.

Husserl took the concept of intentionality from his teacher Franz Brentano, who wrote:

> Every mental phenomenon is characterized by what the scholastics of the Middle Ages called the intentional (and also mental) inexistence of an object, and what we would call, although in not entirely unambiguous terms, the reference to a content, a direction upon an object (by which we are not to understand a reality . . .), or an immanent objectivity. Each one includes something as object within itself, although not always in the same way. In presentation, something is presented, in judgment something is affirmed or denied, in love [something is] loved, in hate [something] hated, in desire something desired.
>
> This intentional inexistence is exclusively characteristic of mental phenomena. No physical phenomenon manifests anything similar. Consequently, we can define mental phenomena by saying that they are such phenomena as include an object intentionally within themselves.[e]

Husserl disavowed two points here.[f] First, he refused to assume that all mental events were intentional; for example, he denied that feelings were intentional.[5] He simply limited phenomenology to the study of those events of consciousness that were intentional. Second, Husserl rejected Brentano's immanent theory of objects (i.e., that natural objects are completely given within a finite set of experiences) and instead argued that objects always transcend any particular set of experiences.

The concept of intentionality, the phenomenological theory of relations, says that consciousness is always relational, that consciousness is always consciousness of something. This does not describe the natural attitude but, rather, the deep structure of consciousness as the co-constitutive relationship between an act of consciousness and an object of consciousness, between consciousness of and that of which one is conscious. Every act of consciousness directs itself toward something, and therefore it always holds its object within itself. Every act of consciousness—of seeing, hearing, remembering, dreaming, and so on—has its own proper object (of consciousness). And every object of consciousness is an object for a particular act of consciousness. Husserl referred to the act as the **noesis**, or **noetic act**, and the object as the **noema**, or **noematic object**.

There is no abstract, generalized act of seeing—independent of any object—to which an object is accidentally attached after the fact. Each act has its own proper object. Every act of seeing is a seeing of, and every object of seeing is an object as seen. I don't just see; I see something. I don't just smell; I smell something. I don't just hear; I hear something. I don't just imagine; I imagine something. I don't just remember; I remember something. There is always the relation: the seeing of a tree and the tree as seen. Similarly, the tree does not exist for my consciousness except as it is seen. Each object is an object for a particular act of consciousness. I see the tree as seen. I touch the tree as touched. I smell the tree as smelled. I taste the tree as tasted. That people commonly assume that there is a real tree out there, behind all these experiences, is irrelevant. Although he did not deny the existence of the tree, Husserl did not think phenomenology could demonstrate its existence with certainty (see figure 17.1).

For Husserl, intentionality required two kinds of phenomenological investigation. First, noetic phenomenology seeks the essence of any particular act of consciousness, for example, the act of seeing in consciousness. What

5 Brentano solved the problem by allowing for second- and third-order intentional objects (in which intentionality could become its own object). The matter was addressed by Sartre, *Sketch for a Theory of the Emotions*.

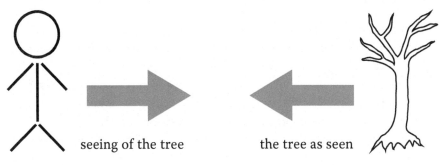

seeing of the tree   the tree as seen

FIGURE 17.1

makes an act of consciousness an act of seeing rather than something else? We might begin by noting that an act of seeing is focused and unidirectional. What about hearing? What distinguishes an act of hearing from one of listening? Second, noematic phenomenology seeks the essence of the particular object of a noetic act; for example, what is the essence of all objects of sight? What makes an object an object of seeing, rather than an object of hearing? We might begin by noting that the noematic object of vision exhibits a very particular structure, marked by the distinction between the focal point and the background. Noemata are also constituted by unique **horizons**, which carry essential elements of the noema that are nevertheless not present to consciousness. For example, visual noemata often carry dimensional horizons so that what is technically a two-dimensional image is actively experienced with a three-dimensional horizon. The noema of dreams, on the other hand, often does not.

Consider this anecdote. There was a significant malaria problem in the Pacific front of the Second World War. To eliminate the mosquitoes that carried malaria, the US Army tried to enlist the aid of Indigenous peoples. But the people would not cooperate, and no reward would change their minds. After the war, the army tried to figure out why its approach didn't work. The Indigenous islanders told them, "You came in and showed us pictures of these giant mosquitoes—six feet tall—and you told us we need to kill these things. Rest assured that if we ever saw one of those, we would help you kill it, but our mosquitoes are tiny little things. They're harmless. Why do you care about killing them?" The two populations—the army researchers and the Indigenous population—were having different experiences involving different noetic acts (perception, representation) and different noematic objects (mosquitoes, pictures), with decidedly different horizons.

CHALLENGES

But Husserl still faced at least three problems that threatened phenomenology's ability to arrive at certainty: origins of phenomena, relations of intentionality, and the possibility of intersubjectivity. First, Husserl had argued that phenomena were immanent to consciousness, that they are dependent on and exist only for consciousness. Yet they cannot be created by the subject, nor can they be reduced to acts of the mind, for if they were, that would inevitably lead to subjective idealism or solipsism. The question of origins arises as well when I have multiple noetic acts (seeing the tree, touching the tree, remembering the tree), each with its unique noema. Yet the noemata are somehow connected because they are all experiences of what I assume, no, what I know, to be the same tree. Further, you and I "know" that we are seeing the same tree. There is a unity to the noemata, which passes on to my assumption of the phenomenon of the tree itself. Where does this totality come from? How can a noema transcend any particular act of consciousness? In the natural attitude, the solution is easy. The tree is real and exists outside of consciousness as the hidden source of the noema. But Husserl could not take the easy path. These questions gave rise to **genetic phenomenology**.

The remaining questions were considered in **constitutive phenomenology**. The second problem involved the relation between the noetic act and the noematic object. To put it simply, why does the relationship always—or at least almost always—work? I see the tree as seen. A noetic act: the seeing of the tree. A noematic object: the tree as seen. My very sense of selfhood depends on the coherence of my experience, such that when I intend—not in the sense of choice or motivation but in the phenomenological sense—to see a tree, I do in fact see a tree. That is, my noetic act is always fulfilled by its proper noematic object. Why do noesis and noema line up, so that the object of consciousness is the proper object of that act of consciousness? Why does consciousness get it wrong so infrequently? Husserl acknowledged the fallibility of intentionality—you think you're seeing Jordan, but you're actually dreaming Jordan, or you think you're seeing Jordan, but you are actually seeing Susan—but failed to explain it or why my experience is not filled with contradictions and inconsistencies. What constitutes and guarantees the relationship between the noesis and the noema?

The third problem involved intersubjectivity. How can I know with certainty that other persons exist as consciousness, which works the same way as mine, as the site and source of its own noetic acts? How do I experience another subject as the author of their own self-consciousness? Can another consciousness become the object of my consciousness? Husserl's answer to the last question was no; your consciousness is never a noematic object for my act of consciousness. Your body may be, your words may be, but I have no access to your consciousness. So how is the unique connection between subjects, intersubjectivity, even possible? In fact, how do I become conscious of my own consciousness?

Husserl's attempts to define an adequate phenomenology kept running into one or more of these problems. His answers were necessarily limited by two assumptions: first, he could not appeal to anything outside of experience; second, because intuition reveals the essential and universal truth of experience, its truths cannot be limited to my reality. Perhaps now we can understand why Husserl was a perpetual beginner. In each version, he offered a different solution, which either failed to provide a way out or led him to yet another problem. So, he tried again and again, offering different ways forward, some of which I will present, in no particular order.

One proposal involved **regional ontologies**, which were phenomenologies of different realms of being—such as nature, the psychic, the spiritual, the social, and so on. One could explain how objects transcend subjectivity, without falling back into noumena, by identifying the different fundamental forms of intentionality that provide the founding acts of constitution—the meaning-structures—of the different realms.[g]

A second take suggested that a Transcendental Consciousness (or subjectivity) guaranteed the constitution of an intentional object as a universal essence, and the correspondence of noesis and noema. Aware that this solution violated his principle that the ground of Truth is in consciousness itself, Husserl went through some elaborate machinations to suggest that one has a consciousness of a Transcendental Subject, but most phenomenologists agree that he failed to demonstrate this possibility.[h]

His third effort, generally thought to be the most interesting and productive, proposed a different phenomenological ontology, which distinguished between two kinds of intentionality: **act-intentionality** as described earlier, and **functioning- intentionality**.[i] The problems of constitutive phenomenology arose because in act-intentionality, consciousness presents itself as a series of discrete, independent noetic acts, each with its own noematic object. But functioning-intentionality operates at a more fundamental level of consciousness as a process of nondiscrete, continuous, and overlapping events. Within it, all acts are interrelated, bound together in the **unity of inner time consciousness**. Husserl reread Kant's privileging of time as the form of inner life, asserting that inner life is the temporality of consciousness itself; consciousness is the continuing flow of intentionality as the pure flow of time itself. (One might think here of stream of consciousness.) Internal time consciousness is the continuous coming to be and passing away of heterogeneous, intentional moments of experience in time, in which their specificity and individuality disappear into the flow of time itself as the ground of experience.

In both the natural attitude and intuition, the subject **thematizes**—turns its attention to, shines a light on—a particular moment, thus pulling it out of the flow of functioning-intentionality.[6] Consequently, it is possible to thematize not only "the present" but also sedimented (retrospective) and projected experiences. One might think of this, analogically, like meditation, where the first step is to let all experiences flow over and past you; the minute you stop and focus on a particular moment, on something happening, you've broken the flow. You've got to get beyond noticing anything so that you can experience the unity or continuity of everything.

Still, Husserl had a problem, because functioning-intentionality cannot belong to individual consciousness, to the individual subject. To solve the problem, Husserl had to describe functioning-intentionality as a dynamic process through which consciousness continuously transcends itself, as **anonymous world-experiencing**. But what is the subject of such experiencing, given that it must also enable the thematization of particular events of consciousness or phenomena? The only solution would seem to take Husserl back to the assumption of a transcendent and Transcendental Subject. Despite this dilemma, this notion of internal time consciousness, sometimes referred to as **duration**, continues to be an important element in later phenomenologically influenced theory.

Finally, Husserl proposed the concept of the **Lebenswelt**, or **lifeworld**.[j] This is a common reality in which all humans live, which grounds all experience and consciousness, and all reflections on and knowledge of the world. It is the pregiven, universal condition of possibility, the fundamental and universal meaning-structures, which guarantee the unity and coherence of reality. And it is, in a serious reversal for Husserl, an immediately intersubjective field of meaning, moving Husserl from his starting point in individual consciousness to the assumption of a foundational, intersubjective realm of experience.[7]

---

6 Husserl has a complex diagram of the forms of subjectivity or ego, which need not concern us here.

7 Later phenomenologists (including Heidegger and Alfred Schütz) use the concept to refer to the everyday world of the natural attitude, a socially and historically specific configuration of meanings, relations, and practices.

But Husserl provided no basis for the assumption that all humans, independently of the social and historical conditions of their experience, live in a pregiven, universal field of meaning. How could the Lebenswelt account for the enormously varied forms of experience and knowledge? Why is the assumption of a transcendental world of essential meaning-structures any less problematic than that of a transcendental consciousness? In fact, doesn't the assumption of the Lebenswelt presuppose the existence of a universal— transcendental if not transcendent—subject?

While some later phenomenologists have followed Husserl's efforts to center phenomenology on consciousness, they usually limit claims of the essential and universal nature of the phenomenon. Others, rejecting the *epoché*, moved from consciousness to existence, whether understood as the structures of human existence, the body, or existence itself. Thus it was that Martin Heidegger, perhaps the most influential phenomenologist, took deep theory to places where it had not gone before.

NOTES

a. Husserl, "Philosophy as Rigorous Science," in *Phenomenology and the Crisis of Philosophy*, 71–147.

b. Carl Schmitt, "Husserl, Edmund," in Edwards, *Encyclopedia of Philosophy*, 4:97.

c. Husserl, *Logical Investigations*, 1:168.

d. Quoted in Spiegelberg, *Phenomenological Movement*, 114.

e. Franz Brentano, "Distinction between Mental and Physical Phenomena," in Chisholm, *Realism*, 50–51.

f. Husserl, *Logical Investigations*, vol. 2, investigation V.

g. Husserl, *Ideas*.

h. Husserl, *Ideas*; Husserl, *Crisis of European Sciences*.

i. Husserl, *Phenomenology of Internal Time-Consciousness*.

j. Husserl, *Crisis of European Sciences*.

Heidegger

Martin Heidegger was Edmund Husserl's most famous, most controversial, and most influential student. He transformed phenomenology by rejecting the first two steps of Husserl's methodology. The threefold exclusion was supposed to lead us to pure experience. Heidegger argued that these prejudices or **pre-understandings**—everyday knowledges, beliefs, and feelings—defined human life and provided the necessary starting point for any investigation into human experience, making phenomenology into an interpretive endeavor: a **hermeneutic phenomenology**. Against the *epoché*, Heidegger argued that the truth of experience can't be reduced to a matter of consciousness and, further, that intentionality as the fundamental structure of relationality is not, in the first instance, an epistemological structure. The truth of experience necessarily raises fundamental ontological questions about the nature of existence: **an ontological phenomenology**.

Heidegger's transformation of phenomenology into a hermeneutic ontology began a revolution as significant as Immanuel Kant's Copernican revolution or Georg Wilhelm Friedrich Hegel's invention of the dialectic, both of which he staunchly opposed (following Friedrich Nietzsche—whom he greatly admired, but who refused to offer a coherent critique and alternative). Along with Nietzsche's and Baruch Spinoza's, Heidegger's thinking proffered a radical antihumanism. Since he thought he was challenging both everyday and theoretical common sense, his writings are uniquely difficult— dense, unfamiliar, and full of neologisms. His thought cannot easily be translated into more accessible language because, like Nietzsche's, it challenges the very assumptions embedded within ordinary language. So be forewarned and be patient with yourself as you struggle to grasp Heidegger's work.

Martin Heidegger was born on September 26, 1889, in Baden-Württemberg, a rural region of the German Empire, to a working-class Roman Catholic family. He studied theology before turning to philosophy at the University of Freiburg. Both his dissertation (on psychologism) and his habilitation (on Duns Scotus, a medieval philosopher and rhetorician) were strongly influenced by Husserl.[1] In 1923, he began teaching at the University of Marburg, lecturing on the topic that dominated his entire career: the **meaning of Being** or, if you prefer, of existence. In 1927, he published his first book, *Sein und Zeit* (*Being and Time*), which, somewhat unusually, became his most influential work. The following year, he succeeded Husserl as professor of philosophy. He was a prolific writer: his collected work—including published works (16 volumes), lectures, unpublished materials, and various other contributions—comprises 102 volumes. His other important early works include *Kant and the Problem of Metaphysics* (1929), *Introduction to Metaphysics* (1935), *Nietzsche* (two volumes, 1936–46), and a number of essays that presage his later, even more radical ontological turn.

In 1933, he was elected rector of the university, but he resigned after one year. In that same year, Heidegger joined the Nazi Party. Although he was never fully embraced as the philosopher of the party, he was deeply committed to it and to both its nationalism and its anti-Semitism. In 1941, he removed the dedication to the Jewish Husserl in *Being and Time*, although it was restored after the war. He delivered numerous speeches and short essays—many of them collected and published as the *Black Notebooks* (2014)— in support of National Socialism. After the war, he was prevented from having any association with universities until 1950, when he returned to Freiburg and continued teaching until 1967. He died on May 26, 1976, in Freiburg, West Germany.

---

1 In Germany, the habilitation is a second degree after a doctorate required to teach at a university.

Heidegger's association with Nazism was well known in Europe, creating a dilemma, especially among postwar French philosophers. Many acknowledged the importance of Heidegger's thought but could not reconcile it with his fascism. His fascism was less well known in the English-speaking world, where it was often presented anecdotally, suggesting that he was not a true believer but used his position in the party to assist a number of Jewish intellectuals. While some of these claims may be true, there is no doubt that he was a true believer. The controversy posed by Heidegger's Nazism has become even more pressing in recent years: To what extent, if any, is his fascism embodied in his philosophy? Can it be directly read off his writings? If there are fascist elements, are they essential to it, thus contaminating the entirety of his system, or can they be subtracted out? Does his Nazism make his work untouchable? Some people simply refuse to give Heidegger a stage, refusing to discuss or use his work. Others argue that ideas are not responsible for the people who create or hold them. (Bad people can have good ideas!) But Heidegger made the question of the politics of thinking unavoidable.

Yet Heidegger's deep theory cannot be ignored, if only because of its influence. His immediate students included Hannah Arendt, Hans-Georg Gadamer, Leo Strauss, Herbert Marcuse, and Emmanuel Levinas, although each used his theories in a very different way. But his influence extends much further, and it is fair to say that his theories helped shape many of the most visible philosophers and deep theorists of the late twentieth and early twenty-first centuries. Heidegger is a crucial chapter for the rest of the narrative of theory's backstory.

THE PHENOMENON

If previous philosophers, including Husserl, felt they had to "prove" the existence of the world, Heidegger found the very effort to be misplaced: the question is not does the world exist—of course it does—but what is existence or Being (with a big *B*), as opposed to the various beings (small *b*) that exist and which Being itself grounds? But because he was operating within the phenomenological realm of human experience, the question of Being was really the question of the meaning—in the phenomenological sense of intentionality—of Being. Or, in other words, what does it mean "to be" or to exist, not as an idea of consciousness but as the truth of experience and, eventually, the world? What are you saying when you add the verb "to be" to something, when you say something exists? How does Being itself provide the ground for or the possibility of beings, and for their specific modes of being? What needs to be reclaimed as the meaning of Being is how Being presents itself, how it enacts itself within experience but also, how Being constitutes experience.

Heidegger opposed his own hermeneutic thinking to the **representational thinking** that dominated both rationalism and empiricism, as well as science and sometimes even art. Representational thinking is dualistic in two ways. First, it divides truth and experience into the subject or consciousness and the object, the knower and the known. The subject stands apart from the object. Representational thinking further assumes that language represents the real, that knowledge is a representation in consciousness of something outside of consciousness. The problem is then to determine how well or accurately reality is represented.

Second, representational thinking is predicative; it separates the subject (not the phenomenological subject but the grammatical or logical subject) from those characteristics or qualities that modify it, from the predicates that are assigned to it. The human being is rational; the ball is blue. (Just to remind you, the question of the nature of the predicative relation is what lay behind enlightenment efforts to distinguish between analytic and synthetic statements.)

Kant not only continued to practice representational thinking but carried it further than anyone else by making the subject the master of reality, the architect or engineer of the world, presumably on top of an independent albeit unknowable reality. Or, seen from another angle, Kant actually made the subject into the totality of existence. Existence becomes the whim of the (transcendental) subject.

If truth is to be found within the field of experience, experience cannot be reduced to consciousness; experience **always and already** (a common phrase in Heidegger) entails existence within itself. But representational thinking is incapable of understanding experience as an existential reality and, consequently, is itself responsible for the contemporary failure to even know how to ask the question of the meaning of Being. The question of truth demands another way of thinking, a hermeneutics, not of suspicion but of Being.

If the phenomenon necessarily involves existence, then it is something that "proximally and for the most part does *not* show itself at all."[a] That is, the truth of experience—the phenomenon—does not show itself; truth is a problem because the phenomenon conceals itself. But it does not—as a hermeneutics of suspicion might assume—distort experience so that experience cannot know itself. The phenomenon hides itself because we are finite beings; we are incapable of experiencing the truth of the phenomenon because of our finitude (think of this as mortality). Heidegger's hermeneutics offered an interpretation of what is given that attempts to **unconceal** or **disclose** the phenomenon. Interpretation is an active act of *"letting [the phenomenon, the truth] be,"* letting it show itself to us as finite beings.

HERMENEUTICS

But what is the truth of the phenomenon that is unconcealed, what Heidegger called *aletheia*? The answer depends on a different understanding of relations. All the theories of relations we've considered thus far define a relationship as the coming together of two entities. Heidegger thought that a relation preexists the terms (relata) of the relation itself; it precedes the distinction between two independent realities. Their separation enacts a kind of violence, which conceals their truth as always and already existing together. Consequently, for Heidegger, there is no problem of mediation, negation, or constitution. The truth of human experience is that of a **being-in-the-world** or, later, the **belonging together**, for example, of Man and World. This hermeneutic essence of experience precedes the existence of either man or world. This relation itself is the **primordial relation** or **connection**, the ontological truth of reality. It is where truth lies, and what is concealed from us.

The relationship of belonging together, however, is not an objective fact. It is a process, a way of existing, an active relating; it can be understood as a performance or a happening. It describes the Being of any being as a way of existing in the world, and thus, there are different modes of being in the world. Consider an analogy: What is baseball? It's the relationships that always and already exist among hitting, fielding, throwing, running, and catching. Baseball is a set of activities or processes, a set of active **involvements**, that exist together. Baseball is the performing or happening (or, to use a neologism, an **eventing**) of these relations. Heidegger's hermeneutics sought to unconceal not a set of facts or a state of being but an active relationality, a way of being together with the world. The question of hermeneutics is not what something is but *how* it is.

What disturbs Western humanism is that this is not something that humans do. It is the very Being of Being: Being (big *B*) is given in the Being (big *B*) of beings (small *b*). (You have to love Heidegger-speak.) This is Heidegger's antihumanism! The question is: How does a being—an existent—give itself to us as existing? What is its mode of appearing, where appearance is not separated from an existence that is unavailable to us? Instead, existence is given only in and as appearance. How does existence as appearing occur? What is unconcealed—truth—is precisely how Being (existence) presents itself in the phenomenon, as a *relationing*.

How does hermeneutics unconceal the presencing of Being to make presencing itself present? Consider another analogy. Think back to your days studying algebra. The least popular assignments were generally those in which the teacher put some long and unbelievably complicated equation on the blackboard (yes, I know this dates me and, yes, I know there are apps for this now) and told the class to reduce it to its simplest expression. Here's a simple example: the equation $(x^2 - y^2)/(x - y)$ can be reduced to $(x+y)$. There were steps you could follow, preferably in the right order: combine like terms, multiply/divide terms where appropriate, remove brackets and distribute properties, cross multiply, isolate variables using inversion. There was a procedure by which complexity could be reduced to its simplest, crucial core, which might be thought of as the essential meaning of the complex statement. To use a second analogy, one that perhaps avoids the danger of cold formalism: think about culinary reductions, where one thickens and intensifies the flavor of a liquid. Heidegger's hermeneutic took the messy complexity of experience and reduced it, simplified it, to reveal the essence at its core, its mode of Being, the how of its existence. This is the unconcealing of ontological truth, the primordial relationality that constitutes the reality of experience itself.

Heidegger interpreted the everyday world of experience—an **ontical** or **existentiell** reality, something akin to the world of the natural attitude—in order to unconceal or let be (like peeling away the layers of an onion) the **ontological** or **existential truth**.[2] Such ontological reduction is not simply a leap between two states but an ongoing movement along a continuum from the ontic to increasingly ontological truths, as illustrated in figure 18.1.

HERMENEUTIC OF DASEIN IN *BEING AND TIME*

Heidegger was trying to understand, to interrogate, Being. This is the *Seinsfrage*—the question of Being. But there was a serious problem: across the millennia of Western thought, from Socrates to Kant, not only has the answer been forgotten but the question itself has been forgotten. We no longer know how to ask the question of Being; we no longer know what we are asking when

2 The "existentialist" philosophers such as Jean-Paul Sartre took the latter term (*existential*) but were, Heidegger later argued, actually describing the former (*existentiell*). See Heidegger, "Letter on Humanism," in *Pathmarks*, 239–76.

Ontical, *existentiell*, experience

Ontological, existential, ways of Being as primordial relations

FIGURE 18.1

we ask about existence. We have to recover the question before we can get to the truth. We want to arrive at the truth, but the path to truth goes through existence. Truth is an ontological question, not an epistemological one.

The question of Being has been buried under the inheritance of two metaphysical questions. The causal question asks why there are beings rather than nothing. It searches for origins or causes. Why do things exist? Because God made the heaven and earth, and everything that exists is the expression of God's will. Or because there was the big bang, which brought reality into existence in the form of quantum particles and the fundamental forces. Or because the transcendental subject called it forth. On the other hand, the theo-metaphysical question searches for the proper hierarchically ordered values of different beings, from the highest (God, or perhaps humans) to the lowest (I will leave that to your imagination). Neither question addresses the Being of Being: What does it mean to say that the quantum universe is real? Or that God exists?

We no longer know what we are looking for; how can we know what an appropriate answer to the question might be if we do not know the question? How do we find or, better, uncover the *Seinsfrage*, unconceal the question of the meaning of Being? Heidegger attempted this task in his influential first book, *Sein und Zeit*, whose title is badly translated as *Being and Time*.[3] His solution is both ingenious and difficult. He knew that there are certain beings (small *b*) who seem, at least at times, to question, worry, and care about their

3 While *Zeit* does mean time, it is not time as an object. And the translation of *Sein* as "being" similarly makes it sound like a noun. But *Sein* is the infinitive form of the verb "to be." Even if one takes the gerund form to signal the continuous present tense of the verb, emphasizing its active nature, this still does not capture the generality of the infinitive.

own Being. These beings often reflect on and examine their own existence, asking themselves: Who am I? Why do I exist? What is the meaning of my life? These are beings whose Being (big *B*) matters to them. Not every being reflects on its own existence. I may be wrong, but I don't think chairs or viruses fret over these matters.

But these beings somehow know that their essence is defined by their existence, by how they exist. They must have some **dim pre-understanding** that their very being is at stake in their own Being and, consequently, of what an answer would look like. And so, they must also have some dim pre-understanding of the *Seinsfrage*. We might think of this as akin to Plato's argument (although Heidegger is no Platonist) that if I pose a question such as What is truth? I must already have some sense of what to look for, some ability to recognize the answer when I find it. But for Heidegger, at this point, it is not about the answer but about the question.

Being and Time offers a hermeneutic of such beings; it was to serve as a preamble to Heidegger's actual project. It was a necessary detour to investigate that being for whom Being is an issue, in hopes of finding his way back to the *Seinsfrage*. Heidegger called this being, or, better, this mode of being, **Dasein**, a **Being-there**. *Sein*—to be; *Da*—there. Dasein is any being that cares about its own Being. Obviously, human beings are Dasein, but there may be others: Dogs? Cats? Doubtful. Dolphins? Aliens? Maybe. Heidegger insisted that his hermeneutic of Dasein was not a philosophy of human existence; it was not equivalent to a philosophical anthropology, despite the fact that he started with the ontic reality of everyday human life.

Dasein is not conscious of its ontological existence as a **being-in-the-world**, not because it is lazy, stupid, or afraid (contra Kant), not because there is some evil power trying to trick or deceive it, and not because some group is exerting its power over it, but because it is a finite creature. Dasein's capacities are limited by its **finitude**, which is an essential ontological feature of its being-there. Dasein's Being is defined by its being **situated** in the world, by its having a place or, better, by being placed in the world, in a set of primordial relationships. When it questions its existence, it is questioning these relations. Dasein is inseparable from the—its—world. Its experience is precisely that of a subject who is always embodied, placed into a material and historical world. This belonging together of Dasein and world precedes the existence of the subjective and the objective worlds.

Heidegger's hermeneutic phenomenology of Dasein moves from the ontic, everyday life of Dasein toward ever more ontological understandings, uncovering the primordial relationalities that constitute the being-in-the-world of Dasein, the how of its existence. I want to present some (and, I emphasize, only some) of Heidegger's major findings—truths. I will inevitably oversimplify Heidegger's arguments and largely ignore his actual method—the interpretive acts by which he moves, through hundreds of pages, from the ontic to the ontological.

Heidegger began by (somewhat artificially) separating the mode of Being of the world in Dasein (the **worldhood of the world**) from the way Dasein exists or is situated in that world (the **being-in**). The former does not refer to an objective or natural reality that exists independently of Dasein. Nor is it a collection of independent things and facts with which Dasein enters into relations. It refers to the world, always and only locatable within the situatedness that is Dasein, always and only in relationship to the "being-in" that completes Dasein's mode of being-in-the-world. It is a region of involvements from which Dasein cannot separate or distinguish itself, a space in which Dasein is inextricably involved with the world.

In Dasein's everyday life, the "worldhood of the world" does appear as a collection of objects that exist independently of their relation to what appears, correlatively, as individual subjects. Here's a coffee cup, and a phone, and a computer, and a notebook, and a T-shirt, and so on. They are available to the subject whenever it wants because they are there whether or not the subject is present. This mode of presencing or appearing of the worldhood of the world is the **present-at-hand**.

But there's a more primordial, more ontological Being of the world—not in and of itself—but within the being-in-the-world that is Dasein, in a necessary relation in which Dasein comports itself to the world **concernfully**. This mode of Being of the world, **the ready-to-hand** or **equipmentality**, is the more ontological precondition of the present-at-hand. The being of equipment is always relational rather than objective. To experience something as equipment is to relate to it as a resource meant to serve whatever purpose or need you may have, but equipment does not exist objectively, apart from Dasein. It is the happening of Dasein's situatedness in the world, an ontological disclosure of the world's primordial relation to Dasein's situatedness.

If the ready-to-hand is the more fundamental Being of the worldhood of the world, how does the present-at-hand come into being? This happens when equipment no longer works or there is no longer a need for it. Something loses its functionality and becomes an object. I have a hammer; for the most part, I don't notice much about it except for those features that shape its utility. Suddenly, it breaks, and I look at it as if for the first time: the quality and grain of wood, the way it is bound together. Cell phones may still work, but without the capacities and status of later phones, they become mere objects. On the other hand, I have an Apple SE computer in my office. I have no idea if it works, but it is no longer a working computer in my life. But it has been refunctioned; it is now useful as a collectible, or even a work of design art. Sometimes the process of relating may actually work in reverse, without changing the ontological truth of the worldhood of the world. Consider what archaeologists do: they do the work of ontology in reverse. An archaeologist comes upon an object, or a fragment of an object. Beyond its being a "relic," it is present-at-hand. The real work of the archaeologist is to return it to its equipmentality. A bouncy blue sphere with a picture of a fantastical horned creature apparently named UNC. A god? A totem? A child's chair?

The major part of *Being and Time* attends to the nature of the being-in, inquiring into the ways Dasein comports itself in its life, in its Being-there. How does Dasein exist in and alongside the worldhood of the world? Heidegger moved through a series of increasingly ontological descriptions, ever deeper levels of the truth, of Dasein as a being-in-the-world. He began by identifying and interpreting a number of key, common ontic sites—experiences and behaviors—that characterize **Dasein in its everydayness**. He finds that Dasein always lives its own life, claiming it as **my life**. That is to say, Dasein is always "mine," not in the sense of a possession (present-at-hand) but as a mode of being or comportment with the world. But, proximally and for the most part (another Heideggerianism), Dasein does not actually live its life as an individual self. Its self is a practical effect of its living in the world with others (*Mitsein*). My self always belongs to others, a **They-self** (*Das Man*, best translated as "the one," as in "one decides to . . ."). In its everydayness, Dasein is nothing but its *Mitsein*, its being with others; its self is defined by, and it understands itself in, the ways others see it. Dasein is what it is seen to be. The answer to the question Who am I? or, better, Who is Dasein? is that Dasein is never itself; it is always other, living outside of and apart from itself. In other words, intersubjectivity does not need to be proved; it is always and already given in every ontic moment of Dasein's situatedness. Everyday life is precisely the existence of intersubjectivity.[4]

4 Similar ideas were widespread and more popular in the 1950s, when sociologists contrasted inner-directedness (describing people whose actions and lives are defined and driven by their own internal sense of identity) and other-directedness. For Heidegger, Dasein lives its everydayness as other-directed. To use another example, in the 1960s and 1970s, young people often had what the psychologist Erik Erikson called an "identity crisis." They knew that most of the time, they were the social roles they played:

Heidegger then turned his attention to two other key ontic features of Dasein's everydayness, allowing them to disclose more ontological structures— or modes of comportment—of Dasein's being-in-the-world: **attunement** (*mood* [*Stimmung*] or *state of mind* [*Befindlichkeit*]) and **interpretation**. Dasein always finds itself in a mood. You wake up in the morning, and you're always and already in a mood, without any thought or reflection, and you experience the entire world through that mood. For example, when you're in a bad mood, your clothes are ugly and don't fit, you're too fat or too skinny. That pimple on your face is enormous. Your friend is a pain in the ass. Your class is the most freakin' boring class you've ever had. Life just sucks.

On the other hand, when you're in a great mood, the weather is beautiful, your significant other is the most amazing partner in the world, and the sex is great. Your friends are wonderful. You can't believe that you have the opportunity to take this class. Can life get any better? There are many other more specific moods, both negative (such as fear, anxiety, and depression) and positive (such as contentment, happiness, and love). Each shapes how one experiences, even if only temporarily, but there is always a mood.

The experience of mood as defining or coloring Dasein's relation to the world discloses two important things. First, it makes clear that Dasein is always attuned to the world in a specific way not of its own choosing. Dasein is not in control of its mood; it does not choose its mood, and it rarely is able to control it.[5] But such attunement is the condition of possibility of Dasein's finding itself as an ongoing concern in the world. It is what orients Dasein in ways that tell it what matters and that often enable it to lose itself in its environment. Second, Dasein always already finds itself in a world not of its own making. It is born into that world. No one ever asked if it wanted the world to be this way or even if it wanted to be in this world. Mood discloses that a constitutive—ontological—structure of Dasein's being-in-the-world is that the world is given to Dasein as **factical**, existing apart from Dasein's intentions. Dasein finds itself always and already engaged with it, entangled within it, as a finite space of involvements. Heidegger called this Dasein's **Thrownness**. Dasein is thrown into the world of facticity, a world that

---

student, roommate, son or daughter, brother or sister, cousin, hockey player, and so on. But what is left when one takes away all the social roles? Is that all there is? Where is my true self? For many at the time, the answer was that there was nothing more, which led to a surprisingly large number of attempted suicides.

5 I have argued for many years that music is the means by which we try to create or change moods.

already exists, in which it is always already in a particular mood or mode of comportment to that world.

Dasein is also constantly **interpreting** the world, "things" in the world, experiences of the world. Interpretation is the—usually linguistic—ground of intelligibility, the act by which Dasein takes account of what is happening by taking something as something else (close to predication). Interpretation is not the production of meaning but the taking up of meaning that is always already given so as to perform the world as intelligible. Interpretation acts on the already meaningfulness of experience, presenting it "as" something. Interpretation has its own structure according to Heidegger. Dasein always brings something—**forestructures of interpretation**—to the task of appropriating the meaningfulness of the world. The result is that interpretation always enacts what later thinkers have called the **hermeneutic circle**—from the forestructure, which partly determines how one moves through the circle, to an interpretation, which can in turn become a new forestructure.

Even in the ontic realm, interpretation discloses to Dasein its own possibilities. Interpretation is the actualization, the self-development, of the more ontological structure of **Understanding (*Verstehen*)**. Dasein understands itself by its capacities, by the possibilities of what it can and cannot do. Dasein understands itself by understanding its possibilities—as involvements rather than deliberations. Dasein, then, is its possibilities. Understanding is not a mental state or process, and its possibilities are neither things present-at-hand nor unrealized and therefore unreal things out there, waiting in the future. If Dasein is its possibilities, then those futures are already present as ready-to-hand; they define what Dasein is and what it is not. Thrownness provides the beginning (the forestructures) of the hermeneutic circle, from which the possibilities of self-understanding are defined. Thus, *Being and Time* is itself an interpretation, the self-understanding of understanding.

Understanding is an active comportment to possibilities as projects; it is the ground of the very possibility of Dasein's possibilities. By taking up or actualizing possibilities that Dasein finds in the world into which it is thrown, Dasein projects itself into them. By not taking up other possibilities, Dasein's own Not-Being becomes a constitutive part of Dasein's Being-in-the-world. This is, one might say, the space of Dasein's freedom. Only Dasein has finding itself in its possibilities as a possibility because Dasein is itself possibility. Dasein's being as the projection of its possibilities of Being is *Existenz*, a being beyond oneself.[b] Dasein lives outside itself, projecting itself into and as possibility. *Existenz* is a mode of Being in the world defined partly by what it is not yet; it is, however, inseparable from facticity: "By way of having a mood,

Dasein 'sees' possibilities, in terms of which it is. In the projective disclosure of such possibilities, it already has a mood in every case."[6]

At this point, still operating in the first moves toward an ontology of Dasein, Heidegger asks how Dasein lives the ontological conditions of Thrownness and *Existenz* in its everydayness, in which it lives alongside and with people (*Mitsein*). In its everydayness, Dasein is **absorbed** into the world of ordinary concerns and activities, largely through **discourse** as the unreflective use of language. Discourse includes idle talk as the unexamined fetish of information without any concern for its relevance, curiosity as the endless search for novelty and entertainment, gossip as the ambiguity of superficial chatter, and so on. The vast majority of the things we say are trivial, trite, and repetitive; very little is original and creative, or contributes to our understanding of our own condition.

Dasein's *Mitsein* also enacts a leveling or averageness—a "Being-lost in the publicness of the 'they.'"[c] Not only is Dasein's own self concealed, but others disappear as well, all becoming indistinguishable and inconspicuous. This is the total domination of the indeterminate They-self (*das Man*)— superficial, trivial, possibly stupid, and completely unself-reflective (Nietzsche's herd?). Dasein in its everydayness is completely absorbed in and fascinated with the ontic world; it is constantly closing off or covering up any real self-understanding. It is not at all concerned with who it is, what it could be, or what it should be. Heidegger called this way of comporting itself **Fallenness**. Dasein is fallen into its everyday world.[7] This completes the first hermeneutic circle of *Being and Time*: having begun with Dasein in its everydayness, Heidegger has produced a new—more ontological—understanding of Dasein, unconcealing Facticity and *Existenz*, and finally returning to Dasein's everydayness as Fallenness. Dasein's mode of Being-in-the-world is its being **thrown** into a world of involvements, **fallen** into a world of everydayness, and **existing** (projecting itself) beyond itself. This might be represented as in figure 18.2.

THE CARE STRUCTURE AND TEMPORALITY

These three moments—Thrownness, Fallenness, *Existenz*—constitute the unity of Dasein's being-in, as its primordial relation to or way of comporting itself in the worldhood-of-the-world. Dasein is ontologically constituted

6 In later works, *ek-sistence*.
7 This term clearly has religious connotations, which Heidegger vehemently denied.

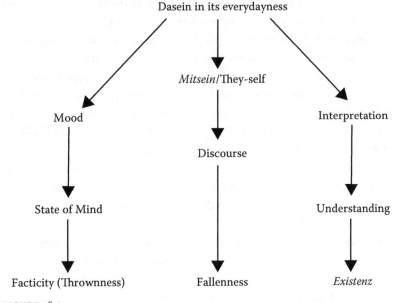

FIGURE 18.2

(thus far) by the unbreakable connections among its being already in the world, being always alongside others, and being ahead of itself. This ontological unity, the **Care structure (Sorge)** is what it means for Dasein to care about its existence. Care is the Being of Dasein!

But this was not the end of Heidegger's ontological quest; he continued his hermeneutic, taking his analysis one step further; he argued that Fallenness, as the way Dasein lives its Being-in in its everydayness, is inauthentic. Dasein's mode of being-in-the-world includes, as one ontological possibility, its own **inauthenticity**. Despite its ethical connotations, Heidegger claimed that inauthenticity was simply an ontological possibility, one modality of Dasein's being-in-the-world. "Dasein has, in the first instance, fallen away from itself as an authentic potentiality for Being its Self, and has fallen into the world."[d] But if inauthenticity is an ontological possibility of Dasein, then so is **authenticity**. But authenticity has no claim to privilege; it is not more fundamental, more ontological, or more moral. Inauthenticity and authenticity describe different modifications of the self's relation to the They and the everyday. Authenticity, at this point in the hermeneutic, refers to the reclamation of one's self from the They-self, a claim that is, at least in part, an existential choice (see figure 18.3).

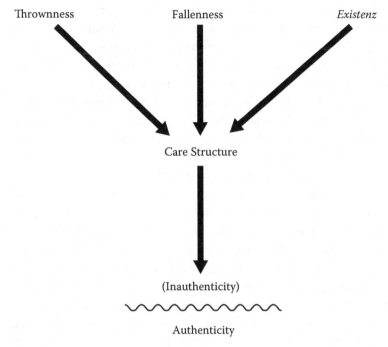

Throwness   Fallenness   *Existenz*

Care Structure

(Inauthenticity)

Authenticity

FIGURE 18.3

But there are at least two more spins of the hermeneutic circle, in which Heidegger deepened the ontology of the Care structure: as ***a being-toward-death*** and as **Temporality**. The Care structure reveals Dasein to be a being-toward-death, to be finite, in at least two ways. First, since Dasein is always understanding and, hence, a being ahead of itself, it is always incomplete. Only death completes Dasein. How does Dasein "understand" death, since one cannot experience it, and the death of another cannot disclose the Being that belongs to me, that is my Being? My death is, in a very special and radical way, mine. *Existenz* discloses that death is the ever-present possibility of my own not-being. But that possibility can never be actualized, for that would mean the end of my *Existenz* as possibility. It would be the possibility that negates possibility itself. Yet, death remains the always present, impossible possibility of my own finitude, and it is that finitude that individuates me, that defines my being as mine, that fixes my Being. In Heidegger's terms, it is the possibility of my "*ownmost possibility*." I am defined by the possibility of my own death, by that not-yet which is always with me and always belongs to me.

The second way that Dasein's finitude as a Being-toward-Death is un-concealed is through the **superlative disclosure**.[8] In Thrownness, **anxiety** (*Angst*) is not directed at a specific object or experience; it is not any of the forms of anxiety disorders that have become increasingly common in the con-temporary world. Anxiety is a particular mode of attunement or mood, which throws me into an unintelligible world because it is a world without me, a world in which I have no place, in which I am not and cannot be situated. It discloses a world in which I cannot belong. And, thus, the possibility of my own not-being is once again unconcealed.

This now explains the source of the difference between inauthenticity and authenticity. This ontological unconcealing of my own finitude can be embraced either inauthentically or authentically. Inauthentically, my death be-comes the ontic reality of my inevitable but unpredictable death. My death becomes a fact out there in an as yet undetermined but necessary and real future, something to be feared. But I can also approach my death authentically, by recognizing that everything I do, every choice I make, matters. If you're im-mortal, if you live forever, what you do or choose doesn't matter because you will always have the time to make another—different—choice. My choices, then, would not define me. But as *Angst* unconceals my finitude, I am called to take responsibility for every choice, for my own life.

The **call of conscience** calls Dasein to authenticity, where conscience is an ontological disclosure rather than an ethical or psychological event. It calls Dasein out of its They-self. But responding to the call of conscience is not a voluntary—*existentiell*—choice; it is not about free will or responsibility. In-stead, **anticipatory resoluteness** is the ontological event that sounds the call of conscience, which leads Dasein to authenticity. But authenticity is not the unconcealing of Being because it is Dasein's Being-toward-Death that defines its temporality as finite. It is another layer of the hermeneutic ontology (see figure 18.4).

There is yet one final turn of the hermeneutic circle, one more ontological reduction. Consider the three moments of the Care structure: Thrownness, Fallenness, and *Existenz*. They constitute Dasein as always already behind, alongside, and ahead of itself. Thrownness says that Dasein is always thrown into a past that was there before Dasein arrived. Fallenness says that Da-sein is always involved—living—in the present. *Existenz* says Dasein always

8 The phrase "*ausgezeichnete Erschlossenheit*" appears in the heading of s.40 of *Being and Time* (228). Macquarrie and Robinson translate it as "The Basic State-of-mind of anxiety as a distinctive Way in which Dasein is Disclosed."

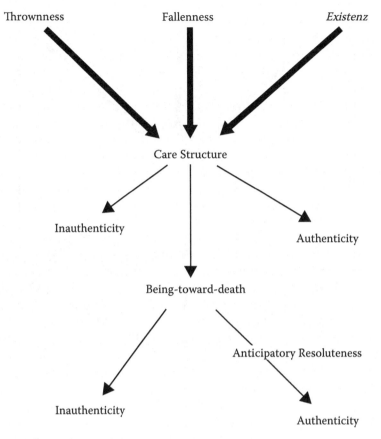

Thrownness   Fallenness   *Existenz*

Care Structure

Inauthenticity

Authenticity

Being-toward-death

Anticipatory Resoluteness

Inauthenticity

Authenticity

FIGURE 18.4

projects itself into—has—a future. But such statements continue to treat time as an objective present-at-hand, as a series of moments of "now" in which the future slides into and becomes present, which then slides into and becomes past. Such "clock time" is ontic. It is better to say that Dasein **is** past, presence, and futurity. Rather than being moments in a linear succession, they exist only within the unity of the **three *ecstases* of time** that is the Care structure. The very meaning of Dasein's Being is the ecstatic unity of time.

Thus, Temporality is the ontological condition of Care; and Dasein's Being-in-the-world is Temporality itself. Dasein is Time, and Time exists only as the ontological Truth of Dasein. Dasein brings time into the universe by its very existence. Dasein is, in one of my favorite Heideggerianisms, "Temporality temporalizing itself" by taking up the past in the present to project its future.[e] This is not Kant's pure form of time (because it is not transcendental), not Husserl's internal time consciousness (because it is not in consciousness),

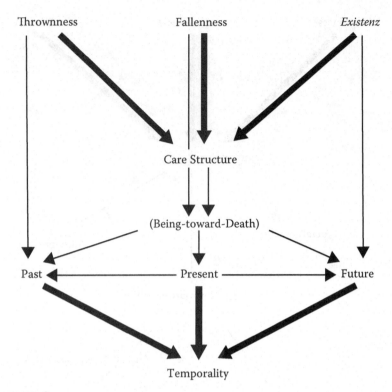

FIGURE 18.5

nor Hegel's Idea as the totality. Time does not exist in the world, even as telos; it cannot be conceived independently of Dasein. Thus we end up with Figure 18.5.

Dasein's temporality is lived as **historicality** or, more accurately, as a historicizing. Dasein is a happening of time, a **stretching along** between birth and death.[f] Just as Dasein's being-toward-death is not defined by a particular moment present-at-hand, its birth is similarly not a particular, objectively given date. Its birth is a receiving of a **heritage** or tradition that discloses the possibilities of its situatedness. Dasein is thrown into a historically specific, culturally determined world of possibilities. Dasein's being-there, then, is a dialogue, a creative retrieval of the past through which the past is enlivened in the present as a set of opportunities for future action. Dasein takes over and projects the possibilities that are already inherited in its very birth. That is, Dasein *ist gewesen*: **Dasein is been.**

Heraclitus observed that you can never step in the same river twice. The river is never the same, and hence, what is true at one moment is not true at another; thus, we are condemned to historical relativism. But Dasein can step in the same river twice since it is time itself and moving at the same speed as the river. Truth is not relative because history and Dasein are always together, ontologically equivalent.

The dialogue that is historicizing takes place in language, but language is neither present-at-hand nor ready-to-hand. Language is the ontological medium in which Dasein's mode of being-in-the-world is constituted. This final move in the hermeneutic of Dasein is the disclosure of Dasein as a mode of **being-open** to its own possibilities; this is Dasein's **intelligibility**, its existence as a sense-making being. Recall my previous discussion of understanding (*verstehen*).

This act of sense-making is not the result of speech and interpretation; rather, it is meaning as "the upon which" of an interpretation. Interpretation is the taking up of that which is already pre-understood, that which is already taken-as.[9] This pre-understanding is a prestructured field of intelligibility, a preinterpretive openness to Being. And it is constituted precisely through the historicizing that is Dasein's temporality of Care: a making present of what is already past, a taking up of what is already understood. This places Dasein into a "there," an opening, a constitutive field of intelligibility; Dasein's existence is always already situated. Language is the very possibility of being-in-the-world; it is the openness in which Dasein cares about its own being and always already has a dim pre-understanding of Being. This is the Truth of Dasein, in which Dasein comes to be itself (authentically) in understanding itself. Dasein is understanding coming to be itself in understanding.

But Heidegger's task remained unfinished in *Being and Time*, since the question that led him to interrogate Dasein in the first place involved the *Seinsfrage*. Does the hermeneutic of Dasein provide the forestructure of an understanding of the *Seinsfrage* itself? Was Heidegger any closer to understanding the Being of Being itself? The exciting conclusion is coming in lecture 24. If you think this discussion of *Being and Time* was difficult, that Heidegger's thinking was strange, and his language impenetrable, you have a real treat coming when we consider his later works. But for the moment, we can take a bit of a respite as we turn to deep theories built around language.

---

9 Heidegger referred to it as the "as-structure."

NOTES

a. Heidegger, *Being and Time*, 59.
b. Heidegger, *Being and Time*, 188.
c. Heidegger, *Being and Time*, 220.
d. Heidegger, *Being and Time*, 220.
e. Heidegger, *Being and Time*, 378.
f. Heidegger, *Being and Time*, 426.

Linguistic

Turns

Pragmatism

The **linguistic turn** responded to the profound changes of second modernity by foregrounding the place of language in the construction of human realities. It included logical positivism and pragmatism, and later, as the processes of change continued apace after the First World War, Ludwig Wittgenstein, and after the Second World War, structuralism. All these deep theories challenged the Enlightenment by refusing to privilege subjectivity and consciousness.

Pragmatism is the only deep theory native to the United States, in which, in the late nineteenth and early twentieth centuries, the changes of second modernity were most visible, most powerful, and consequently most disturbing and challenging. The period between the end of the American Civil War and the First World War and Great Depression was transformative, bringing dispersed regional and cultural identities into a newly emergent national identity, transforming the cultural and economic spheres and, by proxy, the political as well. It was in this period that a peculiarly American faith in science and technology took shape (providing a common bond between the pragmatists and the positivists).

Pragmatism is a movement in which there are "as many pragmatisms as there are pragmatists."[a] There were, however, three founding figures, each of whom defined and elaborated it differently: Charles Saunders Peirce, William James, and John Dewey. Additionally, F. C. S. Schiller (1864–1937), George Santayana (1863–1952), Jane Addams (1860–1935), Mary Parker Follett (1868–1933), and George Herbert Mead (1863–1931) were significant contributors. Pragmatism is generally thought of as a method or **process of inquiry** (i.e., thought), but this has itself been interpreted differently: some link it closely to science and experimentalism, even to logical positivism; others see a shared commitment to instrumentalism or consequentialism; and still others understand it as a broad question of what uses something might serve for solving a problem or making a difference.

Pragmatism as a reflection on the practice of thinking rarely stands on its own; it is commonly supplemented with other theoretical commitments, including but not limited to ontological and ethical theories. Often, these supplementary—but defining—elements are uniquely specific to an author. Often pragmatism is combined with other theories. Both Dewey and James seem to draw on a phenomenological concept of experience, although the pragmatists disavowed any subjective connotations. Karl-Otto Apel and Jürgen Habermas integrated pragmatism with Marxism, Reinhold Niebuhr with Christian realism, W. E. B. Du Bois with a critical theory of race, Charlotte Perkins Gilman with feminist theories, and Kenneth Burke with rhetorical theories; Stephen Toulmin combined it with Wittgenstein; Willard Van Orman Quine and Donald Davidson brought it into (postpositivist) analytic philosophy; and thinkers as different as Gilles Deleuze and Félix Guattari, Michel Foucault, and Stuart Hall incorporated elements of it into their thought.

The nature of these relations is not always clear. Is there an intrinsic, necessary connection between, for example, Dewey's pragmatism and his commitment to a metaphysics of experience, or between James's pragmatism and his radical empiricism? Or are they independent of one another? However one understands it, pragmatism was and continues to be widely influential across geographic boundaries and numerous disciplines, including sociology (e.g., symbolic interactions, urban sociology), education, literary studies, communication, and politics.

Pragmatism is, at its core, an epistemic project. Its fundamental questions are: Under what conditions does a statement have meaning? Under what conditions is a statement "true"? But it differs from the enlightenments in a number of fundamental ways. First, it rejects all rationalisms and any appeal to some nonempirical knowledge based on, for example, intuition; but it also rejects the psychological sensationalism of David Hume's empiricism.

Second, pragmatism rejects universalism, offering a form of **contextualism**. But context is not a matter of historical specificity as in some Marxisms; rather, pragmatism's contextualism assumes that thinking or inquiry always takes place in a **situation** defined by a problem, by the *"irritation of doubt."*[b] Such situational demands require the practical use of words and ideas.[1] But it rejects the universal doubt of René Descartes and the skepticism that is presumed to result from empiricism in favor of the real doubts and challenges that come from the uncertainties of a specific, lived situation. What is true in one situation, responding to one problem, may not be true in another. Meaning, knowledge, and truth change from one situation to another; they have no locus outside of the situation itself. For example, I am lost—and language/thinking gives me the truth of the situation, and the tools to reconstruct the situation so as to enable me to find my way home. Pragmatism analyzes any meaningful statement, any concept, as a collapsed response to a particular situation that poses some problem. Rather than reifying ideas and concepts, pragmatism treats them as specific tools for solving problems.

Although meaning, knowledge, and truth vary, pragmatism rejects relativism. There is truth, but it is never abstract or universal. Truth "happens to an idea."[c] It happens only in an actual, situated act of inquiry, which aims to make the possible stability of meaning and truth prevail over the instability of experience. In this sense, "ideas become true when their 'draft upon existence' is honored by the verifying facts they promise."[d] Truth is defined by what is useful, not by either an imagined correspondence (verification) between word and thing, or an appeal to universal or transcendental conditions (e.g., logic or synthetic a priori). The pragmatists embrace **pluralism** and **fallibilism**.

Third, pragmatism understands meaning and truth to be the processes of inquiry by which we seek and produce knowledge. It assumes that **language** is the crucial agency here, but language is not a description, representation, or mirror of the world. Nor is it simply the medium of thought and inquiry. Rather, thinking is language as the use of **signs** or **symbols**. And since the use of language is both public and social, thinking itself is also both public

---

1 We shall come to other forms of contextualism in future lectures: Wittgenstein's theory of language games and forms of life, Foucault's notion of the epoch, and Hall's conjunctural theory.

and social. Language is the repository of concepts in symbols, each concept itself being a condensed rule for responding to a particular problem. Language embodies the history of the indivisible relation between thinking and problem-solving in human experience. Words or symbols embody ways of doing things, rules for acting. The meaning of a word, symbol, or statement is the difference it makes. The most common "maxim" of pragmatism, usually ascribed to William James, is **a difference that makes no difference is no difference**.

Fourth, pragmatists argued that epistemological questions cannot be separated from metaphysical questions of existence. But they usually equate the metaphysical "real" with the natural reality of everyday life. Their metaphysics is **naturalist**, built on experience. That is, it attempts to explain all that is given in experience—including relations, meaning, thought, and value—only in the terms that experience itself discloses. They reject both the seductive and the reductive fallacies. The **seductive fallacy**, which characterizes every appeal to transcendent or even transcendental conditions (the noumena, the Spirit, etc.), assumes there is more to reality than what experience shows us. The pragmatists reject any appeal to something outside of experience to explain experience itself, including all idealisms. The **reductive fallacy** denies the reality of what experience shows. Such theories reduce experience—to economics, consciousness, language, and so on, rendering it less rich and complex than the actual experience itself. Hence, pragmatism rejects materialisms. The point is to embrace the fullness of the experiential world, while experience itself is understood as a nonsubjective process rather than as the substantive origin of thought.

Finally, like most modern deep theories, pragmatism assumes that the world is always relational or **transactional**. Since mind, experience, and nature are all part of the same immanent reality, the relation between the knower and the known, the observer and the observed, is such that the very act of observing or knowing changes that which is observed and known, and vice versa. Since the world, as the sum of people's situations, is always changing, inquiry—the search for meaning, knowledge, and truth—is open-ended and ongoing. There is never a final meaning or truth. These processes are always mutable, self-correcting, evolving (some early pragmatists were influenced by evolutionary theory). This sense of the openness and processual nature of truth and reality, where nothing is settled once and for all, leads pragmatism to reject enlightenment, especially teleological, conceptions of temporality. Pragmatists think of thinking as a social and public conversation, which has to be kept going. Anything that stops the conversation of truth is bad. One must always go on thinking—together, suggesting an ethics of tolerance and equality, and a politics of democracy.

Pragmatism's origins are usually located in a philosophical "conversation club" in the early 1870s at Harvard University, known as the Metaphysical Club.[e] Its members included Peirce, James, Oliver Wendell Homes Jr., and Chauncey Wright. The club was devoted to finding a middle ground between abstract Continental metaphysics and narrow-minded logicisms (e.g., logical positivism). While both Peirce and James are thought of as pragmatism's progenitors, the two of them understood it very differently. When combined with their competition for public recognition, their close friendship was sometimes tested. At one point, Peirce renamed his theory "pragmaticism" to distinguish it from what he saw as the overly "soft" pragmatism of James, as well as from the ways pragmatism was being represented in other disciplines and the popular press.

PEIRCE

Charles Saunders Peirce, the son of a leading astronomer and mathematician, was born in Cambridge, Massachusetts, on September 10, 1839, and died in Milford, Pennsylvania, on April 19, 1914. He suffered from a painful neurological disorder that seriously impacted his psychological state. He worked as an astronomer (on photometry), a physicist (on the problems of measuring gravity for the US Coast and Geodetic Survey), a mathematician (who made important contributions to statistics), and, above all, a philosopher of language and logic, with a rather expansive understanding of both. Despite having written a series of highly admired and influential essays and achieving a strong reputation as a scientist and mathematician, his only academic appointment was as a lecturer in logic at the newly founded Johns Hopkins University, but he was terminated because of supposed immoral behavior (living with one woman while married to another). He spent the last decades of his life in near poverty. In addition to the many articles and one quite technical book published during his lifetime, he left over 100,000 pages of manuscripts.

Peirce was the first person to offer a pragmatic theory of meaning and truth: "Consider what effects that might conceivably have practical bearings you conceive the objects of your conception to have. Then your conception of those effects is the whole of your conception of the object."[f] Or, as he put it in a different and possibly more generalized context: "There is no distinction of meaning so fine as to consist in anything but a possible difference of practice."[g] Pragmatism was a method for promoting linguistic—conceptual—clarity, for replacing unclear meanings with clear ones, for bringing about successful communication when one faced intellectual problems.

Peirce's pragmatism was relatively narrow given that he defined "intellectual concepts" as "those upon the structure of which arguments concerning objective facts may hinge."[h] These were the "**hard concepts**" of science. The "arguments" were those that depended on experimental techniques such that, "in order to ascertain the meaning of an intellectual conception one should consider what practical consequences might conceivably result by necessity from the truth of that conception; and the sum of these consequences will constitute the entire meaning of the conception."[i]

Peirce's pragmatism was close to logical positivism (instrumentalism, translation terms). He argued, "Pragmatism solves no real problems. It only shows that supposed problems are not real problems."[j] And like the positivists, "almost every proposition of ontological metaphysics . . . is either meaningless gibberish . . . or else is downright absurd."[k] But, while he agreed that the experimental method was the best path to the truth, his definition of truth separates him from the positivists: truth is "the opinion which is fated to be ultimately agreed to by all who investigate" if belief "were to tend indefinitely toward absolute fixity."[l] Truth is the ongoing, open-ended conversation of a community.

Peirce's pragmatism was a part of his general project, which he described as a phenomenology (or **phaneroscopy**—admit that you just cringed) of thought and the uses of language. He developed a rich logic and vocabulary of sign behavior, which provided the ground for a "metaphysics" of predication or relations ("categories"). **Firstness** is quality, feeling, and possibility, and describes a single being existing by itself. **Secondness** is relation and actuality, and constitutes the relational reality of "facts"; it requires two terms. And **thirdness**, which requires three terms, is the realm of signs and symbols, of representation and mediation, of law and necessity, and of habits. Peirce was a metaphysical realist who believed in the existence of generalities or thirdness.[2]

This strangely mathematical metaphysics provided the basis for Peirce's reflections on logic or, more specifically, for his influential theory of **semiotics**, a general "logic" of sign behavior. He defined a **sign as tripartite**: A sign

---

2 He was a realist, as opposed to a nominalist; the latter only believes in the existence of the singular, the particular.

TABLE 19.1 Peirce's Logic of Signs

	Firstness	Secondness	Thirdness
Vehicle	Qualisign	Sinsign	Legisign
Referent	Icon	Index	Symbol
Interpretant	Rheme	Dicisign (dicent)	Argument

is anything that represents something in some way for someone.[m] A sign consists of three elements: a **vehicle** (the thing that represents), a **referent** (the thing represented), and an **interpretant** (the way it is represented for someone). Although his definition of a sign includes "for someone," Peirce actually said very little about this, the space where one might have expected him to discuss the subject. Each of the elements can be a first, second, or third, creating a complicated "architectonic" map of the different kinds of signs, as illustrated in table 19.1

   To illustrate one of the more familiar triads: an icon is a sign that "resembles" its object; an index is a sign of something because it is its effect (smoke is a sign of fire); and a symbol is a rule, norm, or habit that links the vehicle to its object through the necessity of interpretation. Peirce used these various triads to construct a table of the ten possible signs. Any particular sign is describable as a tripartite combination of three elements as given in the table: for example, smoke would be a sinsign-index-dicent. That there is a relation between Peirce's pragmatism and his semiotics is clear, albeit difficult to define.

JAMES

William James was born on January 11, 1842, in New York, into a wealthy family; his father was a well-known, independent Swedenborgian ("New Christian") theologian; his brother Henry was a leading US novelist, and his sister, Alice, was an eminent diarist. He suffered from a variety of physical and mental ailments and died on August 26, 1910, in New Hampshire. He studied medicine but never practiced. He taught a wide variety of subjects at Harvard between 1873 and 1907—including anatomy and physiology, psychology, epistemology, education, metaphysics, religion, and mysticism. His many influential books include *The Principles of Psychology* (2 volumes, 1890), *The Will to Believe* (1897), *Varieties of Religious Experience* (1902), *Pragmatism* (1907),

A Pluralistic Universe (1909), *The Meaning of Truth* (1909), and *Essays in Radical Empiricism* (1912). A cofounder of pragmatism, William James also taught the first university course on psychology in the United States and is credited with being the "father" of (functional) psychology. He was also a founder of the American Society for Psychical Research and a leading theorist of religious experience.

Peirce and James, despite their friendship, had very different understandings of pragmatism and very different styles of thinking. Peirce's work was scholarly and logical (even scientistic), while James's was deeply personal. James was a popular—public—intellectual, charismatic and generous, whose work addressed broad audiences. He acknowledged that his intellectual life was propelled by his own emotional crisis—a "sick soul"—which pushed him to find a way to justify free will and morality in the face of religious absolutism and scientific determinism.[n] He needed to legitimate the possibility of belief in the context of intellectual doubt.

For James, thought aimed to form ideas that could satisfy an individual's needs and interests. But ideas could not be divorced from action, from the practical demands of life. Belief is always a matter of practical decision-making; it cannot be separated from the question of action. For James, the value of ideas is a matter of how effectively and efficiently they allow us to move from "any one part of our experience to any other part, linking things satisfactorily, working securely, simplifying, saving labor."[o] The value of an idea, the truth of a belief, is in its efficacy, its ability to enable people to live the life they want, and to make such labors easier. Ideas are instruments for **taking reality into account**, to achieve and sustain satisfactory relations with the challenges of one's surrounding.

James was—and is still—attacked for presenting pragmatism in coarse and trivial ways in statements such as "'the true' is only the expedient in our way of thinking," and "our truths have only this quality in common, that they pay" (apparently equating truth with "cash value").[p] But keep in mind his audience and the historical context. What sounds like crass capitalism or the worship of efficiency is better understood as James's effort to use the language of ordinary people: something is good or true because it works in the situation, enabling you to make the situation better (according to your own needs), to get you from here to there.

James brought pragmatism into the realms of ethics and real-life choices, where truth means that the consequences of entertaining a belief are better than those of rejecting it. The truth of thinking is to know what definite difference it will make, in specific situations, to hold one belief ("world formula") or another. How does a difference of belief make a difference? For example, will your life be better if you do or do not believe in God, or if you do or do not believe in global warming?[3] But, in the end, this is not simply a matter of individual truths; it is about the relations among the truths and the actions they enable. As James wrote, "If theological ideas prove to have a value for concrete life, they will be true, for pragmatism. . . . For how much more they are true, will depend entirely on their relations to the other truths that also have to be acknowledged."[q]

In his later writings, James extended pragmatism into **radical empiricism**: "The only things that shall be debatable among philosophers shall be things definable in terms drawn from experience."[r] Experience is primary, and there is nothing outside of or behind experience. But James went beyond epistemology, claiming that reality is **pure experience**, and the world is a mosaic of multiple, diverse experiences.[s] Mind and nature are inseparable, constituting the **flux of experience** that is reality. The world is overfilled with experience, more than people can handle. James seemed to hold two different views of this flux. One was as an indeterminate mosaic of sensations, a "blooming, buzzing confusion."[t] The other was as a complex process that includes sensations and the referents or meanings that are assigned to them.[4] In either case, James assumed that the relations among things or sensations and meanings are as real as the things themselves. Foreshadowing Heidegger's claim that relations precede their relata, James argued that relations are themselves a moment of pure experience and that they are experienced as such.

But the flux of experience does not belong to or originate with a subject or consciousness, nor does it represent objective reality. Such things exist but only as they are produced by and exist within experience. Experience precedes subjectivity and objectivity. Think about supersaturated solutions— liquids containing more particulate than they can absorb. If you change the state of such a liquid, some of that particulate will "drop out" or be "sorted out," and that is experienced as subjects and objects. But there is no necessity here, so that what drops out as a consciousness in one context may just as likely fall out as an object in another.

---

3 Perhaps this was an attempt to bring rational thought to bear on Søren Kierkegaard's leap of faith and Blaise Pascal's wager over the belief in God.

4 The argument here—further enacted in the ontologies of Henri Bergson and Gilles Deleuze—hinges primarily on whether one understands sensations as an ontological rather than a psychological or epistemological category. Here I need to thank Bryan Behrenshausen for his help.

The relation between James's pragmatism and radical empiricism reproduces the question of the relation of epistemology and metaphysics, but in James, the relation is clear. Truth involves the attempt to live with and even manage the flux of experience.

DEWEY

If Peirce was drawn to science and logic, and James to ethics and religion, Dewey was driven by a commitment to community and democracy. He was the most influential of the three founding figures, and his achievements and importance were, in various contexts, compared to those of both Aristotle and Confucius.

John Dewey was born in Burlington Vermont, on October 20, 1859, and died in New York City on June 1, 1952. After a failed effort at K-12 teaching, he wrote a dissertation on Kant's psychology. He said that his discovery of the pragmatism of Peirce and James freed him from his neo-Hegelian commitments. He taught at the University of Michigan for a decade, and from 1894 to 1904 he served as the chair of the Department of Psychology, Philosophy, and Pedagogy at the newly founded University of Chicago (funded by the Rockefellers). From 1904 until his retirement in 1930, he taught at Columbia University in New York, although he spent two years in China. He was elected president of both the American Psychological Association and the American Philosophical Association.

He was a prolific author, publishing twenty-nine books and hundreds of essays during his lifetime. His collected works comprise thirty-seven volumes, not including his correspondence. His most important books include *Psychology* (1887), *The School and Society* (1899), *How We Think* (1910), *Studies in Logical Theory* (1913), *Democracy and Education* (1916), *Reconstruction in Philosophy* (1919), *Human Nature and Conduct* (1922), *Experience and Nature* (1925), *The Public and Its Problems* (1927), *Art as Experience* (1934), and *Knowing and the Known* (1949).

Dewey was also deeply involved in a variety of activities and institutions both inside and outside the academy. While in Chicago, he founded the Laboratory Schools as a venue to put his pedagogical theories—that education was about learning how to do things—into practice. With Jane Addams, he helped create Hull House, a settlement house for recent immigrants and a defining institution in the development of social work and community welfare. Dewey was also actively and visibly involved in a wide range of political issues, including labor struggles (e.g., he was a vocal supporter of the Pullman strike in 1894), antiracism (he was involved in the formation of the National Association for the Advancement of Colored People and served on its executive board), and democratic socialism (he served as president of the League for Industrial Democracy, part of which later became Students for a Democratic Society). He was a strong advocate for academic freedom (active in the campaign to support Bertrand Russell's appointment to the City University of New York, which was strongly opposed by the church because of his atheism). In 1915, with Arthur Lovejoy, he cofounded the American Association of University Professors. And, in 1937, he served as chair of the commission in Mexico that exonerated Leon Trotsky of the charges made against him by Joseph Stalin.

In the 1890s, Dewey helped connect an informal group of scholars, artists (e.g., the architects Louis Sullivan and Frank Lloyd Wright), and activists (Jane Addams), which came to be known as the Chicago school of social thought. It stood for many decades as the counterpoint to the increasingly scientific and functionalist work at Harvard and Columbia; it included figures such as Robert Park, W. I. Thomas, Herbert Blumer, and George Herbert Mead, and (at the University of Michigan) Charles Horton Cooley. The Chicago school helped establish urban sociology, reconfigured criminology, and developed symbolic interaction theory. Its work drew largely on pragmatism and qualitative research (e.g., ethnography). Its approach was described as "ecological" because of its emphasis on doing and context, and its arguments extended beyond the academy to highly contested questions of American identity, history, politics, and policy.

Dewey's pragmatism underlaid all his accomplishments and contributions. He described it as a theory of logic or inquiry, a method for thinking. He was most concerned with *intelligent* or **purposive action**, for that is what makes us human. Science—as "the experimental determination of future consequences"—provided the clearest model, but, unlike for Peirce, science was not the sole example of the general **conduct of inquiry**.[ii] Dewey studied the actual methods by which people successfully gain and warrant knowledge. He argued, like Peirce and James, that ideas are essentially instruments for the solution of problems rooted in a particular situation, defined by the purposes we bring into it.

As he put it, "Inquiry is the controlled or directed transformation of an indeterminate situation into one that is so determinate in its constituent distinctions and relations as to convert the elements of the original situation into a unified whole."[v] The situation is indeterminate in the face of a problem. Because you cannot make sense of it as a whole, it does not provide you with clear choices. Inquiry seeks or invents concepts or ideas that reconfigure the situation as a totality, offering a different sense of its possibilities. And the truth of the inquiry, of the ideas, is whether it succeeds in solving the problem. You are lost on campus and are going to be late for your class with that wonderful professor who is about to lecture on pragmatism. Truth is what gets you to class in time for what you know will be a wonderful time.

Thus, truth is contextual and genetic; every idea is an abstraction from some context of action. Truth does not involve an appeal to an external reality other than the situation as a problem. You can think something is true, but it ends up being false not because of some failure to represent the situation (as if you were a spectator standing outside of the situation) but because of its failure to remake the situation in such a way as to find a solution to your problems. Truth is problem-solving. Inquiry is "a reflective evaluation of existing conditions—of shortcomings and possibilities—with respect to operations intended to actualize certain potentialities of the situation so as to resolve what was doubtful."ʷ The "irritation of doubt" brings thought into existence. Thus, thinking only arises in contexts in which you have particular goals. The result is that knowledge is always value-laden. There is no value-free truth because the effort to solve a problem already inserts value into the situation.

Thinking is an active process, equivalent to the mind, which is itself an active process. Mind is a verb—minding. It is carried on in language as meaning in use, through the use of symbols, which are collapsed rules for action, predictions of possible actions and their outcomes: if I'm in a situation x, and I want to accomplish y, then I do z. Meaning and minding are social phenomena, part of both a nonsubjectivist psychology and an ongoing, collective engagement with the world. Language, then, is the sedimentation, the active memory of thinking; it is how people's experiences and knowledge are inscribed into a public and social domain. For Dewey, that collectivity or community is neither Peirce's narrowly defined scientific community nor James's individual facing a moral choice, but the larger community of inquiry, of thinking. The primary demand of this community is: do not block the road of inquiry.

Truth is mutable because of the transactional nature of the relation between the observer and the observed, the knower and the known, where the very act of observation itself inevitably affects the observed and, hence, the truth. More generally, Dewey argued that reality as experience was both continuous and processual, an ongoing **transaction** of "live creatures" and their situational—environmental—conditions. His naturalism, partly influenced by evolutionary theory, dictated that all experience belongs to the natural world. Dewey distinguished between the flow of experience and **an experience**; the latter results from interrupting the flow and congealing a unique unity or totality, most visible in art.

Dewey's naturalism also led him to what might be described as a theory of **sociogenetic parallelism**: the same natural processes emerge at higher levels of experience, in new configurations with new capabilities. Dewey once wrote, "Of all affairs, communication is the most wonderful."[x] *Communication*—language, symbols, inquiry—is the condition of possibility of social life. It is built on, recapitulates, and enhances two fundamental capacities, which, while they may exist in "lower" life-forms, are raised to new heights by language. **Empathy** is the ability to imagine another person's experience and to modify one's behavior accordingly. **Foresight** is the ability to see the likely consequences of one's action. Taken together, this is what symbols do, what communication is.

And insofar as people can develop a common language, they use the history of problem-solving stored in language to have the possibility of cooperation. If I can take the perspective of another, I can define common problems, goals, and solutions. In language, we can share these things and act together with foresight. Language gives us the foresight and empathy that enable community, and since community is the result of the very thing that makes us most human (language), it is, according to Dewey, the ideal form of human association. The community has another face, which defines the ideal form of political association, which Dewey called a **public**. A public is defined by having a shared set of interests and a sense of control over events (as a result of foresight and empathy). Democracy is the conversation within and among publics, and the ability to communicate is what keeps democracy alive and well.

Dewey (and his colleagues) shared a unique view of American history, which focused on the relations of communication and community.[y] Dewey challenged the dominant account of American exceptionalism, such as Frederick Jackson Turner's frontier thesis, which emphasized the heroic individuals who conquered the wild frontiers.[5] Instead, Dewey argued that the real American experience was defined by the people who followed and had to grow a community—inventing a new government, economy, and culture,

---

5 Most famously, Daniel Boone and Davy Crockett, who abandoned their families and communities.

starting with little or nothing in common. They had to invent their own language.[6] Such communities would be characterized by intimacy, cooperation, and homogeneity.

But Dewey believed the new communication technologies (railroads, telegraphy, and radio) were undermining foresight and empathy. Social organization was changing from community to complex, impersonal networks of association, over great distances, of alienated individuals incapable of controlling their own lives.[7] Communities could no longer predict the consequences of their actions and could no longer organize successful cooperative activities because distance had destroyed empathy. The "Great Society" was a society of damaged communities that were unable to cooperate. And this was a crisis of democracy as well.

At the same time, Dewey believed that the new technologies could be used to produce a new national organization of intelligence, a new common language, aimed at restoring the possibility of foresight and empathy, and thus of cooperation and the "Great Community." These technologies would have to bring the results of inquiry into the new, intricate national system of connections among communities, and between communities and the new, powerfully influential urban centers, so they could understand how the economy and politics were working,

Dewey moved to New York City, hoping to continue the battle for a pragmatic approach to social knowledge, and perhaps hoping to mobilize the media for inquiry, community, and democracy. But he soon realized that the capitalists who owned the media had little interest in building community, and the social sciences were only concerned with being scientific and, therefore, steadfastly apolitical (or, more accurately, they embraced the dominant forms of liberalism). In the end, he turned to Marxism for help.

Despite their differences, Peirce, James, and Dewey opened up new ways of thinking about human realities. Their focus on language defined another door, and their understanding of inquiry and mind as symbolic processes of problem-solving brought deep theory back to everyday life not as an abstraction but as an ongoing transactional relation between thinking and experiencing.

6 Admittedly, Dewey and his colleagues had a romantic vision of community and the small frontier towns.
7 This was a common theme in second modernity theories of social change, often described as mass society theory.

NOTES

a. F. Schiller, "William James and the Making of Pragmatism," 93.

b. Peirce, "How to Make Our Ideas Clear," in *Collected Papers*, 5:289.

c. James, *Pragmatism*, 97.

d. Gertrude Ezorsky, "Pragmatic Theory of Truth," in Edwards, *Encyclopedia of Philosophy*, 6:429.

e. Peirce, "Metaphysical Club."

f. Peirce, "Issues of Pragmaticism," 481.

g. Peirce, "How to Make Our Ideas Clear," in *Collected Papers*, 5:293.

h. Peirce, "Survey of Pragmaticism," in *Collected Papers*, 5:318.

i. Peirce, "Survey of Pragmaticism," in *Collected Papers*, 5:6.

j. Peirce, "Letter to William James," March 7, 1904, in *Collected Papers*, 8:189–90.

k. Peirce, "What Pragmatism Is," 171.

l. Peirce, "How to Make Our Ideas Clear," in *Collected Papers*, 5:300; Peirce, "What Pragmatism Is," 168.

m. Peirce, "Speculative Grammar," in *Collected Papers*, 2:127–269.

n. James, *Varieties of Religious Experience*.

o. James, *Pragmatism*, 34.

p. James, *Pragmatism*, 106, 104, 97.

q. James, *Pragmatism*, 40–41.

r. James, *Meaning of Truth*, 6.

s. James, *Essays in Radical Empiricism*.

t. James, *Principles of Psychology*, 488.

u. Dewey, "Development of American Pragmatism," in *Essential Dewey*, 9.

v. Dewey, *Logic*, 104–5.

w. H. S. Thayer, "Pragmatism," in Edwards, *Encyclopedia of Philosophy*, 6:434–35.

x. Dewey, *Experience and Nature*, 138.

y. Dewey, *Public and Its Problems*.

Wittgenstein

Ludwig Josef Johann Wittgenstein was born on April 26, 1889, in Vienna, and died on April 29, 1951, in Cambridge, England. Wittgenstein came from one of the wealthiest families in Europe—his father was an industrialist, primarily invested in steel. He also came from a very large family—he was the youngest of eight children. Although his family had a strong Jewish heritage, he was raised in the Catholic Church. His family home was a center of cultural life, especially in music.[1] The entire family was absorbed in the arts, and Ludwig, at various times, dabbled in music, sculpture, and architecture. In the last, he was influenced by the Austrian architect Alfred Loos, whose motto was "the meaning is the use."[a] Wittgenstein used his substantial family inheritance to support two Austrian poets, Rainer Maria Rilke and Georg Trakl, before giving the rest to his siblings.

---

[1] Regular visitors included Johannes Brahms, Richard Strauss, Gustav Mahler, Arnold Schoenberg, and Gustav Klimt. Maurice Ravel wrote the Piano Concerto for the Left Hand for Paul Wittgenstein, Ludwig's brother.

Wittgenstein's family also suffered from serious mental disabilities. A majority of his siblings were diagnosed with some form of insanity or clinical depression, and three of his brothers committed suicide. Ludwig himself suffered for much of his life from depression, suicidal thoughts, and debilitating anxieties. Although many of the leading intellectuals of the time described him as a genius, Wittgenstein consistently doubted his own abilities. This contributed to his history of intermittently leaving the academy, often retreating to a rather hermetic life in Norway, but also to teaching children in rural Austria (where he was once forced to flee a town for having hit a child), as well as serving as a gardener. He joined the Austrian army during the First World War (and worked in a hospital during the Second World War).

His life is commonly described as tortured, the result no doubt of his depression, his long-term economic insecurity, his uncertainty about the value of his philosophical labors, and his likely bisexuality. Wittgenstein was also a misanthrope: he viewed most people, including his academic colleagues, as inferior ("cursed" with having "half a talent" and being less than fully human). Against the abstractness of academic work, he valorized hard work and manual labor, which he found portrayed in the works of Leo Tolstoy. At the same time, there was a deep humanism to his outlook. As early as 1913, he wrote to Bertrand Russell: "How can I be a logician before I'm a human being?"[b] He had an enduring, deep sense of spirituality, despite his renunciation of Catholicism, which found expression in his deep admiration for Fyodor Dostoyevsky and German expressionist poetry.

He studied aeronautical engineering, designing a jet-powered propeller, but eventually discovered the philosophy of mathematics of Gottlob Frege and Bertrand Russell. In 1911, he showed up unannounced in Cambridge to work with Russell, convinced that mathematics was grounded in the tautologous nature of logic. During the First World War, he kept a philosophical notebook that eventually became the only book he published in his lifetime, *Tractatus Logico-Philosophicus* (1922). In it, he argued that all philosophical problems involved the logical relations between propositions and the world and defined the world as "everything that is the case" (i.e., the world is the set of logically true propositions).[2,c] Reality is a mirror of the logical structure of all true statements. Science and philosophy have only to put every claim to knowledge in its proper logical form.

2 In logic, every proposition can be put in the form "It is that case that . . ."

The members of the Vienna Circle read the *Tractatus* as logical positivism, but Wittgenstein resisted their efforts to appropriate him, and when he finally agreed to meet with them, he read from the mystical poetry of Rabindranath Tagore. When he defended the *Tractatus* in 1929 for his doctorate, he apparently told Russell and the eminent philosopher G. E. Moore that they would never fully understand his work. The *Tractatus* ends with Wittgenstein suggesting it was a ladder you climb to the top of the wall—language—that separates people from a reality that cannot be represented logically. The book revealed the limits of language (logic) so that you can see over the wall. Its final claim was "whereof one cannot speak, thereof one must be silent."[d] He was convinced that the *Tractatus* had accomplished all that philosophy could, and that the work of philosophy had come to an end. Whatever important questions remained could not be answered logically.

While Wittgenstein was teaching at Cambridge in the late 1920s and early 1930s, his work began turning from logic to everyday language use. It is uncertain whether this was a major break or simply the next step in his quest to understand the relation of language and reality.[3] From 1933 to 1935, he gave a series of lectures, copies of which were circulated as the *Blue and Brown Books*.

This turn in his work enabled him to address his paradoxical relation to academic work in general and philosophical work in particular. Since he devalued both in favor of manual labor, how did he justify a career in philosophy? He admitted he did not think that what he was doing was particularly meaningful or useful work, but he claimed he was "not fit for anything else," and, besides, he was "not harming anyone besides himself."[e] Allen Janik and Stephen Toulmin described his work as "intellectual sanitation," picking through the trash of language.[f] Soon after these lectures, Wittgenstein returned to Norway, where he began working on *Philosophical Investigations*, one of the most influential philosophical works of the twentieth century. It was published in 1953, the first of many works published posthumously. He retired in 1947, traveled in Ireland and the United States, and was diagnosed with cancer upon his return to England.

3 There are also many stories about what it was—and whether there was some event—that led Wittgenstein to rethink his position. My favorite, surely apocryphal, is that Wittgenstein, while on a train between Cambridge and London, saw a man "flip off" another.

Wittgenstein's later work argued that insofar as philosophers such as the positivists—but also the *Tractatus*—reduced the truth-functioning of language to logic, they created an ideal language, which did not and could not tell us anything about the world. We needed to get back to the world of actual, everyday language in use: "We have got on to slippery ice where there is no friction and so in a certain sense, the conditions are ideal, but just because of that, we are unable to walk. We have to walk, so we need friction. Back to the rough ground."[g] But this rough ground was not a back door into philosophy, as if everyday language use could provide answers to philosophical questions, for language always leads us into contradictions.

Language "bewitches" our thinking and intelligence. Philosophy can only cleanse language of its pretensions to truth, its claims of representation and universal knowledge. The point of philosophy is "to show the fly the way out of the fly bottle."[h] Language is a trap from which we must escape, and philosophy is a kind of linguistic "depth therapy" to help us untie a knot or massage a mental cramp that language itself had created. Philosophy does this by moving from the surface of language to a **language game** and its **depth grammar**.

In the later works, especially *Philosophical Investigations*, Wittgenstein did not present a continuous logical or conceptual narrative. There is little recognizable theorization. Instead, he thought through a series of anecdotes or **fables**: "Suppose a young child who has been playing outdoors runs into the house and grasps the kitchen tap, calling out as he does, 'Water, water'—this being a word he heard used for the first time only yesterday. And suppose someone now raises the question, 'Is the child telling us something, or showing that he has learned the meaning of this word, or asking for a drink? What are we then to do? Need there be any way of answering that question?'"[i]

This fable forces us to think about what someone is saying when they make a statement, and how we might know the answer. The most common answers attribute meaning to the utterance, whether ostensive (the child is pointing to an object) or intentional (the child has an idea in its head). But these are always incomplete. Is the child boasting? I know water when I see it! Or is it asking for water? Or is it stating that water comes from the tap? Wittgenstein challenged the question itself, which is always immediately translated into a different question: What is the meaning of those words? And you search for something called "the meaning," which produces a mental cramp. After all, meaning is a very strange kind of thing because it doesn't exist in any empirical sense: one can't hold it or know where it is (inside someone's head?); and without knowing what a meaning looks like (is it an object, an idea, a process?), how would you even recognize it if you ever found it? It is as if we assumed that language consisted of two parts, what we say and what it means.

LANGUAGE GAMES

The fable reveals two additional elements of Wittgenstein's efforts: first, the everyday use of language is flexible and variegated; and, second, the "meaning" of a word or expression can only be understood contextually, by its function within a context of rules and social activities. Wittgenstein did not deny that there are inner experiences, mental activities going on inside your head, whenever you use language. He just denied that they have any relevance to language use, to the ability to both speak and understand language meaningfully. The use of language does not involve mental—internal—pictures, ideas, or processes. Meanings are not things, possibly hidden, to be found; they are not derived from and do not refer to some inner experience inside your head. This is true for the full range of words we use to describe what we take to be the realm of inner or mental activities: meaning, intending, understanding, thinking, knowing, and so on. These terms do not imply that there is something else behind what is said or done. For example, if understanding were a mental process, when do you understand? And when the particular mental process is not present, do you still understand? Or do all the mental processes of all the things you understand have to be going on inside your head all the time? When someone says they know how to play chess, do you ask what's going on inside their head? Is knowing how to play chess something you know all the time, or just when you are playing it? What is the nature of understanding apart from its visible outcome?

Meanings are the functions an expression serves by following the rules of a language game. There are rules that govern the use of different expressions, and a particular set of rules constitute a depth grammar that defines a particular language game. The meaning of meaning is defined by the use of the rules of a particular language game. It is only the depth grammar that enables us to use words. Meaning, thinking, and understanding are all public and social activities. The use of these words is defined by rules of one or more depth grammars, and notice that this is plural; that is, each word may operate—differently—in multiple language games. The point is that to know chess means one knows how to play the game, how to follow the rules that define the language game of chess.

There are many language games, and many kinds of language games, from the simple to the complex. Among the examples Wittgenstein gave: "giving orders and obeying them/ describing the appearance of an object, or giving its measurements/ constructing an object from a description (a drawing)/ reporting an event/ speculating about an event/ forming and testing a hypothesis/ presenting the results of an experiment in tables and diagrams/ making up a story; and reading it, play-acting/ singing catches/ guessing riddles/ making a joke; telling it/ solving a problem in practical arithmetic/ translating from one language into another/ asking/ thanking/ cursing/ greeting/ and praying."[j] And one could go on: giving definitions, interpreting a text, teaching a class, and elaborating a philosophy of language games. Moreover, the multiplicity of language games is neither fixed nor given. Language games are continually coming into existence and becoming obsolete and forgotten. We are unaware of the multiplicities "because the clothing of our language makes everything alike."[k] Consequently, there is no universal—transcendental—language that all people have to understand before they can play the various language games. There is no such thing as (American) English that we all already understand apart from the language games. There is only the multiplicity of language games; the "'meaning of a word' is its use in the language"; and its functions are only defined by the depth grammars of the particular language games.[l] There are as many meanings of a word and as many different kinds of words as there are different language games. Language is a toolbox of rules, uses, and activities, and how it works—which tools are active—depends on the game being played.

As a result, there can be no general theory of language that describes a single, universal nature, function, or way of operating. You cannot describe the purpose of language as communication, representation, the construction of meaning, or expression. And there are no essential or universal criteria that establish an unquestioned commonality among the varied uses of a term or concept. There is nothing that unites all the uses of a term as if they were variations of a common thing. All there are are **family resemblances**. The only commonality that binds all language games together is that they consist of a set of rules that define the connections between language use and a set of nonlinguistic activities (constituting a form of life). But what such a set of rules might look like, and how such connections are forged, is never definable in general terms.

All language games are rule-governed, but rules are, again, multiple and varied. It is as difficult to define a rule, or how a rule functions, as it is to define a language game. Even the ways a rule may function can vary significantly:

> The rules may be an aid in teaching the game. The learner is told it and given practice in applying it.—Or it is an instrument of the game itself.—Or a rule is employed neither in the teaching nor in the game itself; nor is it set down in a list of rules. One learns the game by watching how others play. But we say that it is played according to such and such rules because an observer can read these rules off from the practice of the game—like a natural law governing the play.[m]

Consider a simple rule presented in figure 20.1. We can make statements in this language game. We can learn the game (the rule) by constantly referring to the figure, or by calling up images of the rule, or by having someone tell us the rule, or by watching someone else play and extrapolating the rule, or by playing the game over and over until we get it right, or by carrying out orders without ever having seen the rule.

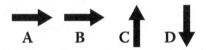

FIGURE 20.1

Rules can function in many ways, but again, there are a number of family resemblances. First, a rule is social and public, and this is only possible because the action defined by the rule has to be repeatable; it is not something one person can do, or something that can be done just once. You can't make up your own rule. Second, rules are arbitrary insofar as they are defined by the language game and not imagined to be in the service of some extralinguistic purpose. The aim of the rules is defined by the language game itself. In other words, we do not use language because it pays, but particular language games have been found to pay. We don't use language because it serves some abstract function, but we do play particular language games because they've been found to be useful.

Third, a rule is defined by the possibility of a mistake. A rule only exists if you can make a mistake, if you can say that something breaks the rule. It's not that anyone has to be able to know whether someone is making a mistake, nor that there has to be agreement about whether someone is making a mistake. Either you are or are not obeying the rule; it is an "objective"—that is, public and social—matter. In different language games, different sorts of mistakes are possible, and different ways of finding out whether someone has made a mistake are available. Consider: I am standing before my class, calmly telling the students that I am in agony, in excruciating pain, that I desperately need help, all the while behaving the same way I always behave while teaching. Can anyone say that I am not in pain? What would that mean? It certainly does not mean that someone knows what I am feeling. It means that I am not playing the language game of being in pain, and in that sense I am making a mistake. But maybe, in this case, I'm playing the language game of exemplifying Wittgenstein's philosophy. Much of what we might take to be mistakes are actually the result of not recognizing the language game being played. What looks like a mistake in one language game might be a legitimate move in a different one.

Consider (my oversimplification of) Wittgenstein's famous argument against the possibility of a **private language**. In *Philosophical Investigations*, this is a very specific argument with very specific conditions set for a private language: "The words of this language are to refer to what only the speaker can know—to his immediate private sensations. So, another person cannot understand the language."[n] Whether usefully or not, the argument is often generalized to argue against the notion that when we speak, we are referring to ideas "in our head." Let us assume that when I use the word *red*, I am referring to a patch in a drawer labeled "red" in my head. Now, I say red, and for me it means—refers to—that patch in the red drawer. I open the drawer, and sure enough, there it is. Then, sometime later, I say red again. What do I do? I open the drawer and look at it again, and sure enough, there it is. Do you see the problem? How do I know that I have opened the right drawer? Or how do I know that what is in the drawer is the same patch that was there minutes before? How could I ever know? What rules am I following? What would it mean to say I could make a mistake? I could not, because there is no possible criterion for establishing the possibility that I could be wrong, no possible way to compare what I think is red today with what I thought it was yesterday. There are no mistakes in a private language, and therefore, Wittgenstein argued, such a language is impossible or, if you prefer, it would not be a language. And if language cannot refer to something private inside our heads, the idea that somehow language involves taking a thought from inside one head and shipping it over to someone else and putting it in their head is senseless; there can be no mistake because there is no possible way of comparing the ideas.

A language game involves more than just a depth grammar. Any language game exists only in the context of particular human activities or **forms of life (*Lebensformen*)**. The forms of life define the conditions of possibility of specific language games, each defined by a depth grammar. There is always, speaking metaphorically (again), a story behind the language game, behind the rules of the depth grammar. It is the story that illuminates the rules; this story is the given, what has to be accepted. It describes a set of social activities. Language games taken together tell larger stories about the forms of life of an entire society. What lies behind language games as the practical activity of language in use is the history of forms of life.

Forms of life do not refer to some set of general facts behind language or to the opinions or the common sense of a people. They refer to the ways of living and acting of a people. They are the basic decisions that have constructed the specificity of any society and the story of human history, decisions about possible, allowable, and sometimes necessary forms of relationship to the world and to other people. They embody the **fundamental attitudes**, which are available only in the depth grammars.º Wittgenstein used the example of intersubjectivity: How do you or can you know that an other is a human being? And his answer was that "my attitude towards him [*sic*] is an attitude towards a soul. I am not of the opinion that he has a soul."ᴾ It is not that I believe or deduce that you are a person (based on some evidence?) and therefore could be wrong; I do not need proof that you are a person, and I am not even sure what such proof would look like. It is my fundamental attitude toward an other.

The availability of a language game and the applicability of a word, concept, or statement depend on previous human decisions that have become second nature. Language games express decisions to take a certain path and so to reaffirm, reject, embrace, or add a particular dimension to experience. These fundamental attitudes are embodied materially in the activities that make up a people's everyday lives. The forms of life describe the set of acceptable and even "essential" actions shared by people of a particular time and place. Language games can create new paths for action. From the heights of the soul, let's drop to the depths of dirt. Different societies embody forms of life that treat dirt and cleanliness in often radically different ways. They even live with and enact excretion in different ways and design toilets that express their decision. What constitutes a life of cleanliness embodies decisions that have been made (somewhere in the anonymous past) about our relations to our bodies. Thus, in the end, everything is grounded in the ways a people live a history of decisions about their relationship to the material world. Out of or alongside those activities, language games emerge as depth grammars, as configurations of rules and actions.

Wittgenstein saw philosophy as a practical affair. He argued that the history of forms of life—the stories of human history—is "a history of deep disquietudes; their roots are as deep in us as the forms of our language and their significance is as great as the importance of our languages."q He suggested that "the sickness of a time is cured by an alteration in the mode of life of human beings, and it was possible for the sickness of philosophical problems to get cured only through a changed mode of thought and of life."r In the end, Wittgenstein believed, despite his apparent disdain for philosophy, that philosophy, even as a language game, had a special and necessary place in the postwar world: "The philosopher is the man who has to cure himself of many sicknesses of the understanding before he can arrive at the notions of the sound human understanding. If in the midst of life we are in death, so in sanity we are surrounded by madness."s He proposed a different way of thinking in which the philosopher becomes the therapist—and all therapists must undergo therapy—who can lead society out of its madness (and away from death), to be able to see the crises in our forms of life.

NOTES

    a. Cited in Janik and Toulmin, *Wittgenstein's Vienna*, 207.

    b. Wittgenstein, "To B. Russell," Christmas 1913," in *Wittgenstein in Cambridge*, 63.

    c. Wittgenstein, *Tractatus Logico-Philosophicus*, 31.

    d. Wittgenstein, *Tractatus Logico-Philosophicus*, 189.

    e. Cited in Janik and Toulmin, *Wittgenstein's Vienna*, 206.

    f. Cited in Janik and Toulmin, *Wittgenstein's Vienna*, 206.

    g. Wittgenstein, *Philosophical Investigations*, 107.

    h. Wittgenstein, *Philosophical Investigations*, 309.

    i. Loosely cited in Janik and Toulmin, *Wittgenstein's Vienna*, 228.

    j. Wittgenstein, *Philosophical Investigations*, 23.

    k. Wittgenstein, *Philosophical Investigations*, 224.

    l. Wittgenstein, *Philosophical Investigations*, 43.

    m. Wittgenstein, *Philosophical Investigations*, 54

    n. Wittgenstein, *Philosophical Investigations*, 243.

    o. Wittgenstein, *On Certainty*, 238.

    p. Wittgenstein, *Philosophical Investigations*, 178.

    q. Wittgenstein, *Philosophical Investigations*, 47.

    r. Wittgenstein, *Remarks on the Foundations of Mathematics*, 57.

    s. Wittgenstein, *Remarks on the Foundations of Mathematics*, 157.

Structuralism

The concept of "*structure*" as the **organization of the parts of the whole** is everywhere. It has migrated from architecture (classical Greece) to grammar and anatomy (seventeenth- and eighteenth-century Europe) to literature and the human sciences (nineteenth-century Europe). The major "structuralist" of the late nineteenth century was Émile Durkheim (1858–1917), who in a number of works investigated symbolic culture (such as religion and classification systems) and argued that symbols or **collective representations** have a facticity of their own and that they operate as socially objective, normative structures that regulate and constrain behavior through systems of beliefs.

The concept of "structure" has proliferated wildly in the twentieth century, but here I am interested only in *French* structuralism, although neither its origins (located in such diverse thinkers as Durkheim, Vladimir Propp, the Swiss linguist Ferdinand de Saussure, the Danish linguist Louis Hjelmslev [1899–1965], and the Russian linguist Roman Jakobson [1896–1982]) nor its adoption was limited to France. It garnered serious attention and visibility in the 1950s, often embedded in analyses of particular sign systems such as kinship, myths, food, gender, literature, philosophy, and so on. Its first public appearance was when a young anthropologist, Claude Lévi-Strauss, scandalously attacked Jean-Paul Sartre, a revered national and intellectual hero. Sartre was a founder of existentialism, a phenomenology-based humanism emphasizing individual consciousness and freedom in a meaningless universe, who then, in *The Critique of Dialectical Reason*, had synthesized it with a Marxist theory of history. Lévi-Strauss, like those who followed him, rejected Sartre's humanism (subjectivity), his equation of historical (chronological) time with the "human order," and the resulting historical method.[1]

As I did with the three figures of the Enlightenment, I will break linear chronology by reversing the chronology of French structuralism's two most influential figures. After a general discussion of structuralism, I will discuss Lévi-Strauss (writing in the 1950s) followed by Ferdinand de Saussure (writing in the early twentieth century).

FRENCH STRUCTURALISM

French structuralists argue that the human subject is not the author of meaning or truth, not the source of its own experience, and certainly not in control of its own actions. They emphasize necessity and determination, which they find in the **deep structures** of language as sign or symbolic systems, over freedom; yet the deep structures are also the ground of innovation and creativity. They are largely uninterested in knowing the world beyond its determined meaningfulness and often, rather unreflectively, assume the objectivity, even scientificity, of their analyses. And, despite appearances, they are not interested in interpreting the content or meaning of some object or text. To avoid confusion (and following Saussure), the structuralists generally refer to the deep structures as systems of **value**, a second-order construct, rather than meaning.

They are concerned with how meaning itself is possible. How is the world made meaningful? How is the intelligibility of the world constituted? Meaning and intelligibility are not already present in the world, waiting to be reproduced in language. They are articulated onto the world by a set of unconscious (not in a psychoanalytic sense) structured relations—sometimes called the **structural unconscious**—which enable people to experience the world as meaningful, to live in an ordered, comprehensible reality. What people take

1 See the opening chapter ("Search for a Method") of Sartre's *Critique* and the last chapter of Lévi-Strauss's *Savage Mind*.

to be empirically given is already constituted by a structural system. But unlike the various hermeneutics of suspicion, this formal deep structure does not hide itself.[2]

The structuralists' **critique** sought the conditions of possibility of the intelligibility or meaningfulness of the world. The French phenomenologist Paul Ricoeur described structuralism as "Kantianism without a transcendental subject."[a] It is neither human beings nor a transcendental subject who makes the phenomenal world but the deep structure of language: the reality of humanity is inseparable from language, and language is inseparable from society. Roland Barthes (1915–80) argued that the deep structures fabricate or compose the world as a **simulacrum**, defined by a formal organization of elements into relations. And man himself—the human subject—is constructed in the simulacrum.[b] As Foucault put it, "It is not man we set in the place of God, but anonymous thinking, knowledge without a subject, theory without identity."[c]

According to Barthes, structuralism is the activity or technique of recomposing the world, of constructing a simulacrum of the simulacrum. The structuralist decomposes (dissects) and recomposes (articulates) experience (in language), making visible its constitutive, functional relations, an underlying, formal order of differences that constitutes the intelligibility of the world. Consider Foucault's famous example—despite his rejection of structuralism—challenging readers to question their own deep structure, to imagine what it would be like to live within a different system of intelligibility:

> This book first arose out of a passage in [Jorge Luis] Borges, out of the laughter that shattered, as I read the passage, all the familiar landmarks of my thought—*our* thought, the thought that bears the stamp of our age and our geography—breaking up all the ordered surfaces and all the planes with which we are accustomed to tame the wild profusion of existing things, and continuing long afterwards to disturb and threaten with collapse our age-old distinction between the Same and the Other. This passage quotes a "certain Chinese encyclopedia" in which it is written that "animals are divided into: (a) belonging to the Emperor, (b) embalmed, (c) tame, (d) sucking pigs, (e) sirens, (f) fabulous, (g) stray dogs, (h) included in the present classification, (i) frenzied, (j) innumerable,

---

2 The question then becomes whether such structures are universal or instead are culturally specific. And if different structures create different realities, are we back to Hegel sans telos? Is there a proper way to inhabit a particular simulacrum?

(k) drawn with a very fine camelhair brush, (l) *et cetera*, (m) having just broken the water pitcher, (n) that from a long way off look like flies." In the wonderment of this taxonomy, the thing we apprehend in one great leap, the thing that, by means of the fable, is demonstrated as the exotic charm of another system of thought, is the limitation of our own, the stark impossibility of thinking *that*.[d]

Every system of signs is organized along two axes, each defining a particular form of relation or association; each axis operates according to specific codes that define "normal" use, while violations of the codes are often the source of creativity. First, the codes of the **paradigmatic** axis define the possibilities for substitution, what elements can be substituted for another: for example, the flower is red, blue, yellow, white; the chair, the table, the wall is red; dog bites man but not clock bites man or chair bites man. The codes of the **syntagmatic** axis describe the allowable forms of association or connection, the possible sequences within the system: for example, "the chair is in the room" but not "room is chair in." Consider Noam Chomsky's famous example: "colorless green ideas sleep furiously."[e] This is a perfectly good sentence, syntagmatically, but paradigmatically unacceptable (hence, meaningless).

Echoing Georg Wilhelm Friedrich Hegel, the definition of any element within a system is given only by the totality of its relations to all the other elements in the system. No element or term has an intrinsic meaning, identity, or essence—or, more accurately, value—in and for itself. Further, structuralists argue that the relations within any system are defined only as **negation**, but not as logical or substantive contradiction. Rather, negation is a formal— often referred to as functional—relation of **difference**. The deep structure comprises only differences. Every term is merely an empty place in a system of immanent, contentless differences. In this **diacritical** theory of relations, no element within the system has an essential or guaranteed identity (a **positivity**) of its own; it is simply what everything else in the system is not; its value depends only on its place among all the other empty places.

For example—and not without controversy—there is no essential meaning of *woman* or *Black* or *working class*. These terms are defined only by their place in a system of differences. And in these (and many other) cases, the structuralists are commonly interested in codes of binary opposition. But not all differences are binary. Foucault's Chinese encyclopedia offers a radically different structure of differences, constituting a different organization of meaning and a different phenomenal world. Or consider the system of traffic lights, a system of three terms—*red*, *yellow*, and *green*. Perhaps you have noticed that the colors—the actual shades of the colors—can vary considerably from one place to another. In fact, sometimes, the red looks more orange and the green looks bluer. So, it's not the colors (the actual content) that matters; it's the difference between the three colors. As long as you can differentiate the three colors, it works. This is a paradigmatic code. Given the serious consequences of this symbolic system, the difference is also constituted syntagmatically, in a spatial arrangement that defines each color by its location on a vertical plane.

However, structuralism argues that such analyses only work if the system is closed, internally complete. It is bounded in space; there is no exteriority. Intelligibility does not depend on reference to something outside the structural system. It is not concerned with the empirical world except insofar as the surface level of sign behavior is empirical. The system is also bounded in time, temporally stable; it is a moment frozen in time, and therefore it cannot change; it has no history. Consequently, structuralism is not interested in how people actually use language.

LÉVI-STRAUSS

Claude Lévi-Strauss, the first public face of French structuralism, was born in Brussels on November 28, 1908, of French-Jewish parents, and died in Paris on October 30, 2009. He studied law and philosophy, but his first appointment was in sociology in Brazil (1935–39), while accompanying his anthropologist wife, who was studying Indigenous Amazonian peoples. When his wife fell ill, Lévi-Strauss continued and completed her fieldwork, his only foray into ethnography. After France's surrender in World War II, he immigrated to the United States and taught at the New School for Social Research in New York City. Between 1959 and 1982, he was a professor of social anthropology at the prestigious École pratique des hautes études. He published over twenty-five books, but his fame was almost instantaneous following the publication of *The Elementary Structures of Kinship* (1949), followed by *Tristes Tropique* and "The Structural Study of Myth" in 1955. Other important works include *Structural Anthropology* (1958), *Totemism* (1962), *The Savage Mind* (1966), and the four volumes of *Mythologiques: Introduction to a Science of Mythologies* (1964–71).

Lévi-Strauss was influenced by Durkheim, Propp, and Jakobson (with whom he worked at the New School). Durkheim enabled him to argue against the reduction of culture to its function or role in maintaining a social system, understood as an organic whole. Instead, Lévi-Strauss proposed that symbols are not for eating but for thinking with.[f] Propp had demonstrated that the multiplicity of Russian folktales could be explained by a small number of actor types and action types, organized by systematic rules of combination.[g] And Roman Jakobson and Morris Halle had developed the concept of "distinctive features" marked by differences in their studies of phonology.[h]

For Lévi-Strauss, structuralism was an alternative theory of ideology and, hence, an alternative to Marxism. While he recognized the cultural specificity of symbolic systems and their deep structures, he also claimed that aspects of the structural unconscious (including its very existence) were universal. This was perhaps his most famous and controversial claim: that the structures that determine the lives of "primitive" societies are no different from those that determine the lives of "civilized" ones. The fundamental codes of the structural unconscious were the same: binary differences (e.g., the raw and the cooked) in which the two terms are weighted differently (e.g., one positive, one negative).[i]

Let's consider some examples of Lévi-Strauss's contributions, beginning with the study of kinship.[j] While his objectification of women in functional terms has been and should be criticized, it is still a valuable example of structural analysis. He argued that kinship is not defined by biological identity and function, not by objective ties of descent or consanguinity, but by the cultural relations produced by arbitrary symbolic systems. Such systems define relations of exclusion and inclusion, with women being the symbolic carriers of (exchange) values connecting the various groups in specific ways. These systems provide an operational answer to the incest taboo, which dictates that a man must obtain a female from another man (for the sake of genetic diversity). Kinship is one manifestation of the structural logic, the communication function, of culture. That is, the key to understanding any cultural system is in the rules it creates for exchanging signs—in this case, women.

Lévi-Strauss identified the fundamental unit of any kinship system as a system of relations between two binaries: brother/sister and father/son. The different relations and their valuations constitute the specificity of a particular kinship system. This enabled him to "solve" another anthropological problem: the avunculate, where there is a special relation between an uncle (a parent's brother) and his sibling's child. For example, Lévi-Strauss summarized one instance of the structural law of the avunculate: the relation between the maternal uncle and his nephew is to the relation between brother and sister, as the relation between father and son is to that between husband and wife. The actual content of this law is less important for our purposes that the formal code of the structural unconscious: $a:b = c:d$.

More famous is his study of totemism, a phenomenon that had stumped anthropologists, most visible as the poles found in many Indigenous cultures around the globe.[k] They are, most commonly, a hierarchical set of stylized but recognizably different creatures, which are then used to name the different clans or subgroups of the tribe and to regulate kinship and marriage relations (for example, see figure 21.1). The obvious question is: What is the relation or correspondence between the animal and the clan? Anthropologists often searched for characteristics that bound the totem animal and the particular clan that bears its name.

In *The Savage Mind*, Lévi-Strauss argued that anthropologists were asking the wrong question. Since symbolic systems are used to think with, you have to understand their logic. The totemic relationship is not about meanings or objects. The totemic representation has nothing to do with what any animal is. The relation is not one of a literal correspondence between totem and society. Rather, the totem constructs a homology or analogy between two systems of difference: the order of nature and the order of society. The totem establishes a system of "natural" differences; each animal is clearly differentiable from the others. Then this code of differences is used to map—to differentiate and organize—its clan structure; one clan is as different from another clan as one totemic animal is different from another.

The totem creates a system of pure difference that makes the social world intelligible, operating according to a logic or practice of bricolage. **Bricolage** is an improvisational "science of the concrete"; it involves collecting and organizing items from the natural environment, without logic or rationality, and using them to create a symbolic system that organizes social reality. This is how the "primitive" mind, *le pensée sauvage*, works.[3]

The "civilized" mind of the West is not that different. It too constructs symbolic systems of difference that it uses to organize its social reality. But rather than bricolage, it works through "engineering." Instead of thinking with the immediate and concrete, the modern mind thinks with conceptual differences. It organizes its "clans" abstractly, as classes, quintiles, races, ethnicities, and so on. Both kinds of symbolic systems operate like a language, a means of communication by which we can think the world intelligibly.

Most famously, Lévi-Strauss studied myths. The traditional approach involved interpreting the content: each society has its own myths, mostly about its founding. Lévi-Strauss saw myths as a dehumanized way of thinking: it's not

3 In French, the phrase means both "the savage mind" and "the wild pansy."

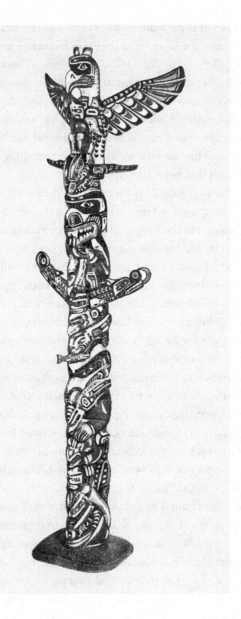

FIGURE 21.1

that people think in myths but that "myths think in men, unbeknown to them."[1]
Myths can only be understood by finding the code and then figuring out how it
resolves key, even universal, contradictions facing humanity. Myths are truth-
making structures that operate by a rigorous structural logic, which aims to
reconcile experience with the larger metaphysical dilemmas of humankind.

Lévi-Strauss defined a myth as the collection of all versions of a particular myth cycle and treated it as a language composed of particular elements or units—**mythemes**, each with its own unique properties defined by the relation linking a given subject to a given function or action (e.g., Oedipus kills). The assemblage of all the mythemes in all the versions is where you find the structural code, the real value of the myth. The significance of the myth has nothing to do with the surface narrative. Its truth lies in the deep structure, the code. What is it that the myth enables people to think?

Consider his best-known (and largely discredited) structuralist reading of the Oedipal cycle, which was greater than Sophocles's famous Theban trilogy (*Oedipus Rex*, *Oedipus at Colonus*, and *Antigone*).[m] Lévi-Strauss not only expanded the Greek myths included in this particular cycle but also claimed to have discovered versions and variations of the Oedipus cycle in many unconnected (primitive) societies. Consequently, the myths can't be about the founding of a specific tribe or society. Instead, while they had different names and actions, they all rehearsed the same social relations and dilemmas.

Lévi-Strauss identified and distributed the mythemes into four categories or columns. The following are only a few of the most recognizable examples, but he found many examples in many versions:

1 The overvaluation of kinship, even violating the law for the sake of kin: Cadmus rescues his sister Europa from Zeus; Oedipus marries his mother; Antigone buries her brother Polynices against King Creon's prohibition.
2 The undervaluation of kinship: Oedipus kills his father; Eteocles kills his brother Polynices.
3 The killing of monsters: Cadmus kills the sacred dragon of Ares; Oedipus defeats the Sphinx.
4 Difficulty in walking straight and upright (found mostly in names signaling deformities): The name Oedipus means swollen foot or clubfoot; Laius, his father's name, means left-sided (seen as a deformity by the Greeks); and Labdacus, his grandfather's name, means lame.

He further argued that the key to this symbolic structure was in the relation between columns 3 and 4, which were about the origin of man.[n] (Obviously, the answer was predetermined by Lévi-Strauss's identification of the mythemes.) The question is: Is man born of the earth, of one (e.g., God brings forth Adam, Dionysus is reborn from Zeus's thigh), or is man born of two, man and woman? In the myth, the third column denies that man is born of one, of the earth (autochthony) and affirms the necessary sociality of the individual; the fourth affirms autochthony as the special nature of humanity. While humanity arises from the earth (unable to walk), it emerges as human precisely by denying the monstrosity of its own origin. The problem is real because there is always the threat of autochthonous birth, that the infant is born of a single being (the mother). In more practical terms, while maternity is known, paternity is unknowable (until DNA testing). How does any society live with this contradiction?

Lévi-Strauss concluded that the truth of the myth is to provide a "logical tool" to relate this deep ontological contradiction to a more comprehensible and reconcilable contradiction. He proposed a structural code or mirror equation: $1:2 = 4:3$. Overvaluing kinship is to undervaluing kinship as the affirmation of autochthony is to its denial. The myth takes an irresolvable contradiction and resolves it in the possibility of a kinship system that neither over- nor undervalues kinship. The Oedipal myth is a structural message that founds and legitimates every kinship system. The myth presents kinship systems as a solution to a fundamental paradox at the heart of social life. Myths provide a logic for living with, for thinking through, the contradictions.

Lévi-Strauss proposed studying every aspect of social life with the methods and concepts employed in (structural) linguistics, suggesting that language and social life were isomorphic. But he went further, asking whether they are not all phenomena "whose inmost nature is the same as that of language."[10] He thought he was discovering the universal linguistic or communicative (for him they are the same) basis of all social life, which is describable in the differential, contrastive relations among the elements of the social codes.

SAUSSURE

The single most influential figure in structuralist theory, often identified as its founder, preceded it by fifty years. Ferdinand de Saussure was born on November 26, 1857, in Geneva, Switzerland, and died on February 22, 1913, in Vufflens-le-Château, Switzerland. He was a scholar of phonology (language sounds), especially in Sanskrit and Indo-European. In addition, he proposed a rather strange theory suggesting that the phonetics of Greek poetry were built on an anagrammatic deep structure. In 1907, he taught the first of three iterations of *Course in General Linguistics*. His students gathered, edited, and published his lectures in 1916, which provided the foundation for much of French structuralism.

The *Course* was meant to introduce students to a **science of linguistics**, which did not yet exist. Linguistics at the time consisted of philology (the study of historical texts and languages) and grammar (the study of phonology, morphology, and syntax). Saussure set out to invent the science he was supposed to teach; he started by claiming that a science had to have an object that was capable of being treated scientifically. Previous efforts to study language had failed to identify such an object. Fortunately, unlike English, which differentiates only language and speech, French differentiates *langue* (language as a system) and *parole* (language in use), and includes both in *langage*.

Saussure argued that for language to be capable of being treated objectively, it must exist as a closed, unchanging system. Parole varies across space (in dialects) and time (slang, neologisms, etc.), and these features are its essence. There can be no science of parole. Langue, on the other hand, underlies the variability of a common language (so that, despite regional variations, people could recognize that they were all speaking French); moreover, it can be treated ahistorically (**synchronically** as opposed to **diachronically**). Saussure did not deny that langue changes but assumed that because it changes at a significantly slower rate, you can freeze it in time without violating its nature. Consequently, linguistics is not concerned with the origin of language. It is only concerned with synchronic langue as its object. It does not matter whether it has a real existence or exists only as a methodological fiction. For Saussure, langue is the deep structure, the underlying objective system, the condition of possibility that enables all uses of language.

Saussure defined langue as a **social system of signs**. The sign, the fundamental unit of this deep structure, is too commonly thought of as parole, as a specific material or substantial entity—such as a particular sound, visual image, or graphic mark. Each sign is further assumed to refer to (signify, name) some other ontologically distinct entity—an independently existing thing or meaning/concept, which is assumed to be real and, often, universal. And since the sign exists apart from the external world, it can have more than one meaning or referent and, hence, will always be ambiguous.

Saussure, on the contrary, began by defining the sign as a union of two elements: a **signifier** and a **signified**. The line, both separating and relating them here, marks their union as a sign.

Sd (signified)
———
Sr (signifier)

But since the sign belongs to langue, the deep structure, it cannot be understood in particularistic and substantive terms. Saussure spoke of signs as psychological—but social rather than individual—entities, as formal, abstract **values**. The signifier is the form of a material image rather than concrete sounds or graphic scribbles; the signified is a formal concept rather than concrete objects or thoughts. The sign is the unity of a particular (abstract) signifier and a particular (abstract) signified, and thus it has its own identity. The sign is the only thing in Saussurean linguistics with a positive identity. As a result, a sign cannot be ambiguous; it cannot have more than one meaning. If it appears to, one is dealing with different signs: two different unions of a signifier and signified.

Signifiers and signifieds exist only as empty positions within diacritical systems of negation, arbitrary organizations of pure (functional) differences. Within each system, there are only differences with no positive terms, so that, to echo typical Saussurean statements: something is only what the others are not; something is only what it is because it isn't what everything else is; and, most succinctly, something is what it isn't. The systems of signifiers, and the systems of signifieds, are grids of empty spaces—pure forms, purely relational entities that exist only in their difference. They each can be represented as in figure 21.2.

The grid of signifiers consists of or, better, arbitrarily constitutes the differences that define the image-forms. When Saussure talked about sounds, he was not talking about the empirically real sounds but about abstract, acoustic images. They exist only within the deep structural system of differences defining the plane of signifiers—in this instance, of sounds. The grid is constructed by arbitrarily dividing the continuum of sounds into formal differences: within a particular deep structure, a long A is different from a short A, a hard P is different from a soft P.

The deep structure organizes the possibility of making and hearing acoustic differences. We don't hear some acoustic differences. Others might be heard but don't register as significant. Some sounds do not even exist within a particular langue. Some languages have a very hard guttural, almost phlegmatic ch. This sound has no place in English. Or consider that people all over the country say my name (Larry) differently, and yet, they are all the same signifier because they are not any other signifier. If one utters a sound outside the formal possibilities of difference, then one either is not speaking the language correctly or is speaking a different language.

Similarly, a grid arbitrarily differentiates every material continuum: this color is different from that, this written scribble is different from that. Consider

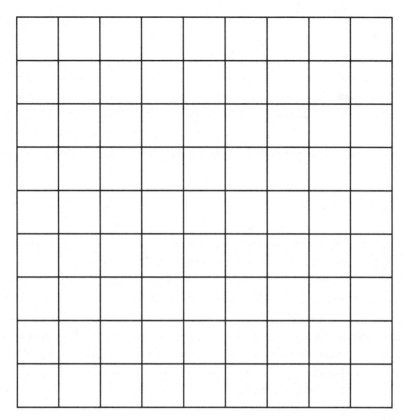

FIGURE 21.2

the game of chess. It does not matter what the different pieces are, as long as you can differentiate them. When I was young, we used bottle caps. The game depended solely on our ability to know the differences among the bottle caps. Or take train schedules, which rarely describe the actual times of trains. Rather, the times differentiate and therefore can be used to identify the trains.

The same arbitrariness of difference applies to the plane of the signified. Again, rather than actual meanings, the grid defines a system of formal or abstract values, pure—negative—differences. Imagine an undifferentiated plane of thought, a cloudlike, undivided conceptual universe. Now think of all the possible ways of dividing it up, changing an amorphous stratum into a structure. (Remember Foucault's Chinese encyclopedia.) Let me elaborate with some examples. People who live in the Arctic often do not have a single concept of snow but many different concepts that differentiate among snows. Similarly, nomadic desert dwellers may have many concepts of sand and camels. English distinguishes a stream from a river, largely (but not entirely) as a matter of size. If you come across a small, narrow river, you assume it must widen and deepen somewhere. French distinguishes a *fleuve* from a *rivière* based on flows: a *fleuve* flows into a *rivière*, a *rivière* flows into a sea. A *fleuve* can be a tributary of a *rivière*, but a *rivière* is never a tributary of a *fleuve*. The conceptual universe itself is arbitrarily divided up into systems of difference—in one, it's size, and in the other, it's flow.

In English, one raises sheep but eats lamb (or sometimes mutton), and someone would be put off if they were offered sheep for dinner. In French, on the other hand, they have one "value" for the entire field: *mutton*. One raises *mutton*, and one eats *mutton*. One more example: the French structuralist/ linguist Émile Benveniste (1902–76) studied the different systems of pronouns (Srs) and the different systems of subject positions (Sds).[p] These are perfect examples of value rather than meaning, since the referent or meaning of each pronoun in parole varies from one situation to the next, but the value remains the same. Furthermore, different langues organize the field of subject positions differently: many European languages distinguish between the formal and the informal addressee (*tu* versus *vous*), a distinction that does not exist in English.

There is no rationality to the different ways of organizing the two planes of values. Different langues have different but equally arbitrary differentiated systems of signifiers and signifieds. But the two planes are, within any langue, arbitrarily put into a relation. Imagine two sheets of paper, each inscribed with its own grid; langue places the two pieces of paper together, so that every empty space (difference) on one grid is made to correspond to one on the other. How they are aligned is not given by any principle. Langue emerges when two systems of difference are brought together, constituting a social system of signs. The relation between a particular signified and a particular signifier is an arbitrary—unintentional—product of history. There is no reason that this signifier and this signified belong together. Mark Twain's *Diaries of Adam and Eve* provides a nice metaphor. The diaries—Twain claimed to have discovered them on a train—describes Adam and Eve's walk through the Garden of Eden. Adam says, "There's a tree," while Eve, pointing to the same thing, says, "Oh, no, let's call that a tiger." Adam replies, "It's not a tiger, it's a tree." Adam believes things have their proper names, that signs have their proper composition: this signified necessarily belongs to that signifier. But Eve believes words mean just what she wants them to mean. There is nothing necessary and intrinsic that links word and thing, signifier and signified. Eve is a structuralist—the sign is arbitrary.

CODES

The deep structures of langue are largely constituted by **codes**, which have a determining influence on the larger patterns of meaning and experience. I have already identified codes of substitution (paradigmatic) and association (syntagmatic).[4] But there are other codes that operate, some generally and some only in specific genres or contexts. For example, many structuralists emphasize the importance of **binary codes**—simple structures of opposition, including male/female, black/white, and "good guys always wear white while bad guys always wear black." Other codes are more complicated. Roland Barthes described metalanguage and connotation as "second-order" codes.[q] In **metalinguistic codes**, a sign becomes the signified of another sign, as shown in figure 21.3. These codes constitute or govern the ways language is used to talk about language. This entire book is a metalinguistic exercise, for example. All criticism and possibly all reflective uses of language are metalinguistic.

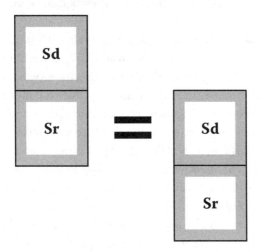

FIGURE 21.3

4 Roman Jakobson suggested that these corresponded to the literary figures of metaphor and metonymy, respectively.

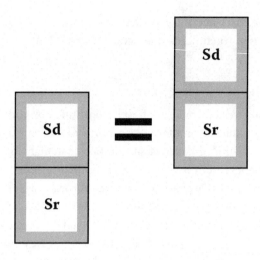

FIGURE 21.4

Connotative codes are the most common and powerful codes, governing the possible uses of language (in parole) to think and talk about things beyond the direct reference or "literal" meaning (the **denotation**). In a connotative code, the sign becomes a signifier for another sign, as shown in figure 21.4. Barthes also refers to such codes as mythic and even, sometimes, as ideological.

Consider the American flag. It's an arbitrary sign. It is the unity of a particular graphic signifier (which exists in an arbitrarily differentiated field of flag signifiers) with a particular signified, in this case, the geographic and political entity that is the United States of America. But that's not the end of the story. There are numerous metalinguistic codes that circulate around the sign of the flag itself, such as these sentences. But there are also connotative codes: the flag itself becomes a signifier of the sign of patriotism. Most people who wear a flag pin are not announcing that they belong in this country but are connoting their love for this country. If I do not wear the pin, or, even worse, if I burn the flag, I might be accused of being unpatriotic. The flag as patriotism can then become a signifier of the Second Amendment and the right to bear arms, and then it can go on forever. In a different but related connotative code, the flag and the country can become the signifier of certain political values—of freedom and justice, or of liberty and free markets, and then we end up with multiple "ideological" codes. Politics often involves struggles over such connotative codes.

Any sign can become the starting point for multiple codes, including both metalinguistic and connotative. The power of such codes does not lie with individuals: just as you enter a social system of signs, you live under the codes that order that system, and, consequently, you can get pulled into positions you never chose and would never choose. For example, at a certain moment, the sign "family values" entered a connotative code that took it from a relatively neutral politics to a starkly conservative set of ideological positions. This does not mean one cannot resist: there may be competing codes pulling in different directions, and the presence and power of particular codes may change, sometimes as a result of struggles. It does mean, in structuralist terms, that such codes are part of what defines the possibility and nature of experience.

Finally, although Saussure aimed for a science of linguistics, he also proposed a general science of **semiology** (or **semiotics**) that would study all sign systems. Linguistics would be a subfield, but semiology would "discover" laws that are applicable not only to linguistics but to all sign systems. Many scholars—structuralists and nonstructuralists alike—have taken up this challenge. Some have followed Saussure; others have followed Hjelmslev's theory of language as the union of a plane of expression and a plane of content, each of which has both form and substance (e.g., Christian Metz and Roland Barthes).[r] And still others have followed Peirce's triadic theory of the sign (e.g., Umberto Eco, as well as the "US school," including Ray Birdwhistell and Thomas Sebeok).[s]

While structuralism challenged many of the assumptions of humanism, it still had to face a challenge that humanism posed: the nature of subjectivity. So, how does structuralism answer the challenge? Come back soon for more on structuralism.

NOTES

a. Ricoeur, *Conflict of Interpretations*, 52.
b. Barthes, "Structuralist Activity," in *Critical Essays*, 213–20.
c. Quoted in Broekman, *Structuralism*, 2.
d. Foucault, *Order of Things*, xvi–xvii.
e. Chomsky, *Syntactic Structures*, 15.
f. Cited in Hall, *Cultural Studies 1983*, 60.
g. Propp, *Morphology of the Folktale*.
h. Jakobson and Halle, *Fundamentals of Language*.
i. Lévi-Strauss, *Structural Anthropology*, 31–54.
j. Lévi-Strauss, *Elementary Structures of Kinship*.
k. Lévi-Strauss, *Totemism*.
l. Quoted in Hawkes, *Structuralism and Semiotics*, 27.

m. Lévi-Strauss, "Structural Study of Myth," in *Structural Anthropology*, 206–31.

n. Lévi-Strauss, "Structural Study of Myth," 215.

o. Lévi-Strauss, *Structural Anthropology*, 62.

p. Benveniste, "Nature of Pronouns," in *Problems in General Linguistics*, 217–22.

q. Barthes, *Elements of Semiology*.

r. Hjelmslev, *Prolegomena to a Theory of Language*.

s. Peirce, "Speculative Grammar," in *Collected Papers*, 2:127–269.

Structuralism and Subjectivity

The structuralists argue that anonymous deep structures enable the world to be experienced as meaningful and intelligible, that is, as livable. But most structuralists have little to say about the *subject and subjectivity*, other than that they too are constructed by the structural system; they do not exist outside of, independently of, or prior to the deep structures. The very experience of *consciousness as interiority*, of being a subject, is produced by the diacritical system of differences.[1] But how?

---

1 Many key debates in contemporary politics concern how experience and subjectivity are treated and whether they are valorized as the final ground of truth. While few deny the existence of structures, for example, of racism, the question is where and how one measures and judges their effects—for example, in the experiences, whether individual or collective, of those who suffer from them, or in the very construction of the systems of relations and differences that enable such experiences.

A LINGUISTIC STRUCTURALISM: BENVENISTE

The French linguist Émile Benveniste attempted to answer this question. Benveniste was born in Aleppo, (Ottoman) Syria, in 1902; his parents were Sephardic Jews, and he first studied to become a rabbi but later turned to Saussurean linguistics. He taught for over three decades at the prestigious Collège de France and served as the first president of the International Association for Semiotic Studies, until his death in 1976.

Benveniste defined subjectivity as "the psychic unity that transcends the totality of the actual experiences it assembles and that makes the permanence of the consciousness."[a] It is the uniquely individualized position from which a person experiences the world, the site of the presumed origin of meaning, intention, and will. It is the active, unifying center, if not the author, of experience, an interiority of consciousness as the scene of thinking. It is also the place from which a person appears to "master" language, using it to capture, express, and share their thoughts and intentions. And, paradoxically, it is necessarily split since it is aware of itself, able to know itself.

Benveniste argued that subjectivity results from humanity's unique relation to language, which is embodied in the capacity of language to stage a dialogue and of any individual to posit themself as a speaker in it. This means that subjects do not communicate; communication constitutes subjects. The possibility of such dialogue depends on the diacritical system of pronominal differences. The fundamental pronoun positions are defined by the strict opposition between "I" and "you," which in turn provides the foundation for the third person (he-she-it). The first- and second-person pronouns are purely linguistic positions (signifiers) that are conditional on the instance of their utterance. In a sense, in this instance, langue is specified only in parole. "I" marks the one who is speaking, and "you" marks the symmetrical position of the one spoken to. The subject is the one who says "I" and thereby "*appropriate[s] to himself* an entire language" precisely as the subject in control of language.[b] In an episode of *Star Trek: The Next Generation*, the *Enterprise* captures a Borg drone—a member of a species that exists only as a collective mind. Picard teaches it to say "I" as opposed to "we," changing its relationship to itself and the rest of the collective.[c] No longer an anonymous part of the whole, it is now a subject, responsible for its experiences and utterances.[2]

2 Another langue may offer different pronouns, and other positions of subjectivity, which would not center the individual subject in a field of experience, or identify an individual as the speaker of language, or give the ownership of experience and language to the individual.

What about the relations of language, subjectivity, and power? Power can attempt to prevent people from entering into language as "I," leaving only the objective (third) position. It can attempt to deny people their own experiential validity. Fortunately, it is rarely fully successful. From the other side, the very production of individuated subjectivity may itself invoke relations of power. Such questions move structuralism toward a hermeneutics of suspicion in which a structuralist theory of subjectivity builds on new readings of Marxism and psychoanalysis. Discussing two key figures—Louis Althusser and Jacques Lacan—will "complete" my previous discussions of Marxism and psychoanalysis, respectively.

A STRUCTURALIST MARXISM: ALTHUSSER

In my earlier lecture on Marx, I identified three theories of ideology. The first sees ideology as epiphenomenal; it is an illusion, without reality or effect (other than distraction). The second sees ideology as false consciousness; it hides the truth by deluding, deceiving, duping people into thinking something else, something that is at best only partially true. The third sees ideology as a necessary, mediating system of meaning, a shared or consensual worldview, enabling people to navigate their way through existing social conditions. Any ideological struggle can be read into any of these theories. For example, consider the dominant consumerist ideology, which "tells" us that consumption is good, that it can solve our problems, and that our worth is measured by how and what we consume. If we just had the right "things," we would be better and more successful people; we would get the beautiful lovers, be more attractive, be better cooks, be better parents, be more creative, and so on. Is this a mere epiphenomenal distraction, a form of false consciousness, or a shared worldview? What difference would it make to how we understand consumerism or, just as important, how we might oppose it?

In that earlier lecture, I briefly suggested that there is a fourth—structuralist—theory of ideology associated with the French Marxist Louis Althusser. Althusser was born in Birmendreïs (Bir Mourad Raïs), in French Algeria, on October 16, 1918, and died in Paris on October 22, 1990.[3] He spent his entire academic career at the semiautonomous, elite École normal

---

3 The fact that many of the leading postwar French intellectuals—including Benveniste and Althusser and, as we shall see, Derrida and Foucault—were born or lived in colonized countries and a significant proportion were Jewish should make us think about what we mean when we describe this work as French.

supérieure. He was highly influential, offering lectures and seminars and workshops attended by many of the leading French thinkers of the time. He had a tumultuous relation to the French Communist Party, which rejected both his (structuralist) antihumanism and his staunch defense of the idea of the dictatorship of the proletariat. On the other hand, Althusser lamented the party's failure to realize a "science" of history. His major earlier books included *For Marx* (1965), *Reading Capital* (1965, with Étienne Balibar, Jacques Rancière, Roger Establet, and Pierre Macherey), *Lenin and Philosophy* (1969), and *Elements of Self-Criticism* (1974). In his later work (e.g., collected in *Philosophy of the Encounter*, 2019), Althusser turned to Spinoza, offering an aleatory Marxism. He suffered from bouts of severe depression and melancholia and, in 1980, murdered his wife and was committed to an institution for the criminally insane, where he died.

Althusser argued that structuralism allowed him to "return" to the "true" Marx.[d] He identified an **epistemological break**—a notion he took from French philosophers Gaston Bachelard (1884–1962) and Georges Canguilhem (1904–95)—in Marx's work. A **symptomatic** reading of Marx demonstrated that his project, as well as his understanding of both the economy and the social totality, changed radically. Marx was trying to formulate a structural Marxism before structuralism, but he did not have the (structuralist) tools to identify and fully accomplish the break. Following the break, Marx presented a new *problematic*, that is, a new fundamental question and new epistemic practices.[4] He was attempting to think "**the necessary complexity of the unity of a structure**."[e] Abandoning his earlier empiricism and humanism, Marx sought a theoretical antihumanism that could ground a scientific history in which knowledge was not defined by correspondences between thought and reality but was itself a particular kind of practice, defined outside of any social interests (and hence not part of the superstructure).[5] For Althusser, this theoretical antihumanism entailed seeing history as a "**process without a subject**."[f] He also viewed individuals as the supports or **bearers** of the determining structures of the social formation.

It may be useful to very briefly recall my earlier discussion of Althusser. A social formation is an ensemble of three levels or practices (economic, political, and ideological).[6] Each level has its own specificity and its own

4 Perhaps it was more of a transition than a break.
5 Many of Althusser's followers reject the notion of Marxism as a science.
6 I am ignoring the fourth level, science, by which he meant Marxism or historical materialism.

relative autonomy.[7] Every practice or event in the social formation is **over-determined**: theoretically, every practice determines every other practice, making it impossible to describe the immediate or direct relations of determination. Later, Althusser referred to this concept of determination as **structural causality**: the system in its totality determines every element in it.[g] The three levels of practices are held together through real effort, in "a (sometimes teeth-gritting) 'harmony.'"[h] They are organized hierarchically— as a **structure in dominance**—in terms of their respective power to define the totality.[i] Yet, it was always the economic that determined the dominant level and the hierarchical order, although it is determining only in the last instance, and the last instance never comes. So, you can never identify exactly how or where that determination is operating.

Althusser presented his structuralist theory of ideology in his essay "Ideology and Ideological State Apparatuses (Notes towards an Investigation)" (1970), known as the ISAS essay. The essay, one of the most important and influential in contemporary theory, opened up a fertile field of thinking necessitated by the coexistence of and struggles among competing ideologies.[8]

The essay consists of two parts. The first questioned the function of ideology in the social formation. Unfortunately, Althusser's answer was rather mechanistic and functionalist: ideology serves to reproduce labor power and the labor force that is necessary for an economy to operate. This is accomplished through the institutions of civil society; unlike many Marxists, Althusser located them within the space of the state, referring to them as **Ideological State Apparatuses**. Families produce and socialize children; schools, churches, the media, and so on all further the outcome, "convincing" people—"indoctrinating" them into the dominant ideology, which tells them that they need and want to work; that good people work; that the meaning of life is to be found in one's ability to earn a living and ultimately support a family; that those who don't work are lazy, criminals, welfare queens, or maybe socialists or communists, all conning and exploiting the goodwill of the people and the state. Further, the Ideological State Apparatuses socialize people into desiring and preparing for particular types of jobs. This is not a question of the intentions of families, teachers, ministers, cultural workers,

7 *Reading Capital* offered an analysis of the specificity of the economic; probably the best exposition of the specificity of the political is given in the works of Nicos Poulantzas, one of Althusser's students.
8 Althusser left little space for class struggle and competing ideologies. He later addressed these in Althusser, *Essays in Self-Criticism*.

and so on, since Althusser was not talking about people but the structural effects of the practices of the Ideological State Apparatuses. Failure to accomplish their task would result in the collapse of the social totality.

The more revolutionary second part of the essay asks how ideological practices work. For Althusser, ideologies are not ideas in people's heads or in some strange realm of abstractions but, rather, the material practices of discourse, broadly understood, always located within definite institutional forms. That is, they are the constitutive elements of the various Ideological State Apparatuses, present in every society throughout history and geography, which foster, create, and disseminate ideological discourses. While these institutions may appear to change over time, the structure and effects of ideology (and of the Ideological State Apparatuses) do not. Hence, "ideology has no history."[j]

While this argument is challenging, what followed really upset the proverbial apple cart. First, Althusser argued that ideologies are true, in the peculiar sense that they are **necessary misrepresentations**. Consider that in the first chapter of the first volume of *Das Kapital*, Marx suggested that the commodity is both the ideology and the truth of capitalism. That is, the commodity does describe (even as it constitutes) the reality of life in capitalist society, so it cannot be said to be false. Marx's critique of the commodity does not mitigate his acknowledgment that we live in a world of commodities, that our lives are ruled by commodities. The commodity is the necessary misrepresentation of the locus of value that enables people to live in capitalism.

Althusser defined **ideology** as "the systems of representation in which people live their imaginary relationship . . . to their real conditions of existence."[k] Starting with the assumption that there are real material conditions of life, like any good Kantian/structuralist, he assumed this reality was outside the realm of intelligibility. Marxists who assumed that they could distinguish between false and true consciousness, as if they could measure each against those "real" conditions, were simply misguided. In fact, the only realities we can know are the experiences constituted by the structural codes of difference. People experience the real conditions, but that is both ontologically and epistemologically different from knowing the truth of the real conditions. It is ideology that produces people's experience of the world, and that is all you can know. You live inside ideological discourses.[9]

9 Hence the need for a Marxist science of history.

The idea of **imaginary relations**, borrowed from Jacques Lacan, does not refer to something merely imagined but to a *"mirror recognition" structure*. In lived reality, individuals see the symbolic systems of ideology reflected back to them as reality, that is, experience. People see the world in the images of ideology, and ideology in the image of the world. We live in an ideological discourse that tells us everything is a commodity, and the world mirrors back the very reality of our discourse, so that everything is a commodity.

If ideology produces experience, there is no experience without ideology. And there is no authentic experience; the more innocent or less ideological an experience seems, the more ideological it is. The more certain you are about the *reality* of an experience, the more ideological it is. As Althusser put it, "Those who are in ideology believe themselves by definition outside ideology: one of the effects of ideology is the practical *denegation* of the ideological character of ideology by ideology: ideology never says, 'I am ideological.'"[l] The people who see communists, or liberal conspiracies, or capitalist plots, or racists everywhere are neither delusional nor "right." They live within an ideologically constructed world in which such experiences are entirely real: they do see communists everywhere, and so on. People who experience the world as a marketplace for commodities rightly perceive that the advocacy of health care or education as a nonmarketized public good is delusional and evil. Such proposals deny the very essence of reality and, if allowed to proceed, would tear everything apart, and anarchy would reign. They are speaking their truth; they live in the mirror image world that ideology creates for them.

Ideology does not simply tell them or show them the truth; it places them in the world of that truth. This doesn't mean that reality is subjective because ideological practices are not individual but social, or that knowledge is relative because that would require some autonomous relation to the world, outside of ideology, against which all such claims could be judged. There can be no appeal to experience—and, hence, no version of empiricism—to provide a foundation for truth, which calls into question the all-too-common strategy of "speaking truth to power." There cannot be a world without ideology because that would be a world in which no one experiences the world. The utopian vision of a society that transcends or escapes ideology is nonsensical.

Still, we might ask: How does ideology construct experience? Why is experience so authoritative? How does ideology place us into its reality? Althusser's answer is that there is "no ideology except by the subject and for subjects. . . . all ideology has the function (which defines it) of 'constituting' concrete individuals as subjects."[m] Ideology **interpellates** the individual as a subject, as *the* subject of *their* experience. Althusser said that it **hails** the individual, as when a police officer calls out, "Hey, you," as you walk down the street, feeling anonymous. Suddenly, you are called out, made into a subject, identifiable, locatable, and potentially held responsible for something.

Ideology inserts you into its discourse as the one speaking it; therefore, it inserts you into its experiential world as the one experiencing it. In ideology, the individual becomes the author of the ideological statement and, hence, of their own experience. Ideology makes you into both the subject and the source of your own experience. It places individuals in a structure in which they recognize themselves in the world, in which they see the world as existing for them, and in which their very experience of themselves as the responsible authors of their experience guarantees the truth of ideology. These are things that *you* experience, and you're certain about them, because they are *your* experiences, because you are the subject of those experiences. And just as your experience is apparently irrefutable, so your subjectivity is beyond doubt. Ideology is a system of discursive effects that guarantees the certainty of experience by producing the subject as the author of that experience. But the system of representation is a deep structure, a structural unconscious.

Even the problems with this theory have opened important arguments and developments. First, Althusser seemed to envision the existence of only one ideology—the dominant ideology. He did not recognize that multiple, even competing and contradictory, ideological discourses or systems of representation exist in every social formation. Consequently, he left little room for either failure or struggle, including class struggle.[10] Second, he did not recognize the multiple ways in which discourses may operate in the larger sphere of culture; as a result, he did not acknowledge that discourses might have effects other than ideological (e.g., of fantasy). Third, like all structuralists, he assumed that one could consider ideology apart from historical change. The fact that he saw history as a process without a subject results in a subject without a history. This becomes clearest in the concept of interpellation. Althusser assumed that all ideologies interpellate all individuals in the same way, into the same subject position, which is basically that of the enlightenment subject, which he then identified with the capitalist—laboring—subject. So, whatever the ideology, in whatever social formation, the subject remains constant, even universal. There is no time or place when the individual is not a subject;

10 Although Althusser does mention "different regional Ideologies" (*Essays in Self-Criticism*, 112), he assumes they are all united by the ruling ideology. He addressed this objection in *Essays in Self-Criticism*.

even before birth, one is always already implicated in, caught up in, ideological discourses, for example, of the family, childhood, or medicine.

A STRUCTURAL PSYCHOANALYSIS: LACAN

Just as Althusser thought that structuralism enabled him to find the true science of Marx, Jacques Lacan called for a "return to Freud" via a structuralist reading (although his thinking incorporated a good dose of Hegel as well).[n] Basically, Lacan argued that psychic reality is uniquely dependent on the intersubjective world of language, and that the relation between psychic and social realities follows the structuring processes of language.

Lacan was born on April 13, 1901, and died on September 9, 1981, having lived his entire life in Paris. He was involved with many of the avant-garde traditions of literature and the arts in the 1930s and 1940s and was aligned with the leftist insurrections of the 1960s. Besides having a long career as an analyst, beginning in 1951 Lacan offered yearly seminars that were attended by many of the leading French intellectuals, artists, and activists of his generation and the next. His early, important publications included "The Function and Field of Speech and Language in Psychoanalysis" (1953), *The Four Fundamental Concepts of Psycho-Analysis* (1964), and a volume of essays, *Écrits* (1966). Subsequently, his twenty-seven years' worth of seminars were published.

Lacan's heresies and his stinging criticisms of prevailing psychoanalytic theories and practices resulted in a tumultuous relation with the psychoanalytic establishment: he was expelled in 1954 from the Psychoanalytic Society of Paris, one year after he had been elected president, and he was expelled in 1963 from the French Society of Psychoanalysis, which he and his followers had founded. The next year, he created the École freudienne de Paris. The most visible "scandal" resulted from Lacan's rejection of the institutionally agreed-on length of a therapy session (fifty minutes). He argued that it was necessary to disrupt the sense of comfort that a preset duration gave the patient in order to arrive at a critical moment of insight. He allowed his sessions to vary in time, according to his own sense of how the session was going (most were between five and fifteen minutes). Yet patients were charged the same rates—and analysis is expensive—as for the traditional sessions.

The key to Lacan's rereading of Freud was his claim that **the Unconscious is "structured like a language."**[o] This enabled him to champion "the supremacy of the order of the Sr [the Symbolic, the discourse of the Other] over 'man' who makes his entry into it and finds himself subjected to it."[p] Lacan's accounts of this claim resulted in some of the densest theorization and difficult if not obscure writing (often including numerous quasi-mathematical diagrams). His elaborations took at least three different but interrelated paths. First, he addressed questions of the nature and aim of analysis as therapy, arguing that the point is not to build or strengthen a stable and secure self or ego but to enable the patient to name their desire, making it intelligible. Second, he reread Freud's developmental biography of the individual. Third, he offered a general theory of the active role of language in the constitution of subjectivity.

How one reads Lacan often depends on which project is given priority. For example, the initial uptake of Lacan in the English-speaking world, driven in large part by feminists and film theorists, was built on the second, developmental, presentation of his theories. However, it is the third, embodied in Lacan's identification of the three orders (or logics) that constitute psychic-social life (the real, the imaginary, and the symbolic), that has defined his greatest influence. For the moment, think of **the Real** as unity, **the Imaginary** as the binary relation of representation, and **the Symbolic** as the triadic relation of signification.[11] Yet, all three orders exist within discourse or language itself; each is a modification within the structuralist diacritical logic.

Let's begin with the development of the child. Lacan emphasized that the various stages through which the child grows, while having a certain temporality, do not have a predefined duration. Nor do they move as a simple linear progression from a beginning to an end, where one stage is simply replaced by the next; rather, each continues and remains active throughout the life of the individual, each a part of the permanent structure of subjectivity. They are interacting processes in the dialectic of language and subjectivity, a nonlinear but still temporal story from infancy to subjectivity, from polymorphous perversity to gendered identity.

The story starts with **infancy**. The infant has no sense of individuality, identity, or self. This moment or phase is characterized by the infant's sense, which cannot yet be described as experience, of unity with the world and with everything in that world.[12] There are no differences, no separations, no other. The unity may never be ontologically real (or it may be that the real is itself never real), but the infant has no sense of its own existence as a unique entity in the world. It has no position from which it can distinguish and sepa-

11 Not to be confused with Peirce's theory of the sign.
12 The infant, not yet fully inhabiting language, does not have experience in structuralist terms.

rate itself from its surroundings. It lives its oneness with the world. Everything in the world is a part of whatever it is. When the infant is hungry, food comes, just as its arm responds when it is supposed to.

The infant's life is ruled by the **ego drives** and, subsequently, the **libidinal or sexual drives**, which emerge by "leaning" on the former. The infant needs milk; as it instinctively sucks on the breast, its need is satisfied, but it also "experiences" additional pleasures (from the warm milk in its gullet, and from the pleasure of contact on the lips). The result is a complex economy of needs. This is where the traditional Freudian narrative of oral and anal stages occurs. For Lacan, this unity defines what will become an **originary lack**—the lack defined by the unity of the Real or, more accurately, the impossible unity of the infant and the world—as the infant moves into the mirror phase.

In the **mirror phase**, the child begins to see itself in the image of the other (person), usually the primary caregiver, whom both Freud and Lacan assumed to be the mother.q This begins a series of ego identifications (including the ego ideal). The other effectively operates as a mirror image, a specular, visual image; the infant comes to see itself as a body separated from the world by taking the image of the other to be its own image. Insofar as the image has an individuated existence, so the child becomes individuated. But it is a mistaken, alienated individuation. The child is alienated from itself as it sees itself in the other, as a necessary misrepresentation (the mirror image) of its own unity. The child objectifies itself through the objectified specular image. The child is further alienated from itself through a series of identifications with the body images it confronts; its own body image is presented as a unity that fractures its originary sense of unity, and the body image of its primary caregiver (the mother) poses the figure of omnipotence that both contradicts and affirms its own infantile sense of omnipotence, as it increasingly confronts its own isolation and limited capacities. In this stage, one often hears the child refer to itself in the third person. Here, the originary lack is transformed into a fantasy, the imagination of reconstituting a phantasmatic unity.

As the child moves into the **Oedipal stage**, it has to renounce its identification with the mother, and its fantasy of returning to a unity with the mother is transformed into a demand to be the object of the mother's desire, that which would fulfill the mother's desire.[13] Lacan called this object *the phallus* (or *l'objet petit a*).r In Freud's version, the father intercedes between the

---

13 While both Freud and Lacan tell a story of child development that is masculine, Lacan and members of the *École freudienne* published *Feminine Sexuality*.

child and the mother as the one who can satisfy the mother's desire, not as the object of that desire but as the one who possesses the object (the phallus as penis) that can fulfill that desire; but in Lacan's retelling, the phallus is not the biological penis but the figure of the power of the Symbol. The phallus, then, is a signifier, a third term inserted between desire and its satisfaction. It is a metonym of the **Other**—of the larger Symbolic system, of Language and, by extension, of the Social and the Law. It is the Law as the power of negation or prohibition carried only in Language. Hence, the phallus is the power of speech that the child lacks; consequently, it must appropriate the power of language as its own: not to be the object of desire but to possess the power over desire. The child can only do this by inserting itself into language. The child enters language to master it, but language masters the child. It names it "I," constituting the child as the speaker in and of language and, hence, as a subject (and a male). But it actually constitutes him as a signifier within language, in which the signifier "I" represents the subject for another signifier ("you").

To accept the position language offers the child, he must reject his own self-alienation; he must move beyond, although never leaving fully behind, the negation of his self in the mirror stage. Moreover, he must deny—even more, repress—the originary fantasy of being one with the mother, even of being the object of the mother's desire. Thus, the moment when subjectivity is produced is also the moment of a **primal act of repression**, when the Unconscious is produced alongside subjectivity. This primordial repression is a further alienation at the heart of subjectivity, which now begins an entire history of desire and repression. Lacan referred to this as the *Spaltung* (the **splitting**), a second alienation in which both the subject and the Unconscious are constituted. Just as the subject exists as a signifier within a system of signifiers without any signifieds, so what is repressed is itself a (cathected) signifier, which is not simply an empty position in a system of differences because, like the Subject, the Unconscious has a history.

Lacan transformed the structuralist system into a process, defined by the ongoing production of difference, the ongoing production of signifiers. The Unconscious exists as the continuous sliding of signifiers. The originary desire (lack) is deferred through the figurative possibilities of language itself (re-reading Freud's dreamwork). The self alienates itself in language, alienates its instinctual needs through the mirror identifications—creating demand and, through language, creating desire. Both the Subject and the Unconscious are only ever the surplus of the sliding of signifiers, which cannot be represented outside Language. Both exist within and as the discourse of the Other. The subject represses this history to affirm its own identity as Subject, that is, as self-consciousness. The Unconscious "thinks in a place where it is impossible to say 'I am.'"⁵ The Unconscious cannot name itself as a subject; consequently, the signifier of the Unconscious acts independently of its signification and without the subject being aware of it. As a result, psychoanalysis is a "structural analysis of the position of the subject," who always moves at "the intersection of the imaginary representation and symbolic speech."ᵗ

The story of the child's development through three stages is not equivalent to Lacan's description of the three discursive orders—the Real, the Imaginary, and the Symbolic—although they are somewhat parallel. The Real refers to that which is impossible to achieve, an undifferentiated totality lacking nothing. It is the principle of a singular unity outside language (although the Real has its effects in language) that resists all symbolization. It cannot be thought of in terms of existence (e.g., Kant's noumena), for it is the logic defining both the aim and the limit of language and thought. The Real carries with it the assumption of an impossible transparency of language, of an absolute unity between the signifier and the signified, between the child and the world.

The Imaginary order describes a specular field of images constituted as binary relations, in which each term finds its existence as an objectification provided by the other. It establishes an immediate opposition in which each term becomes its opposite and is lost in the play of reflections. This is an alienation in a system of identifications, a necessary misrepresentation of each term. The Symbolic order refers not to language (which always involves elements of the Real and the Imaginary) but to the logic of Structure, to the insertion of the signifier into the diacritical logic of radical alterity or pure difference (e.g., in which the "Other" is a system that operates as Law). The Symbolic is the site of subjectivity but also of meaning; or, more accurately, it is the logic of the impossibility of both.

Lacan transformed Freud's hermeneutic of suspicion into what I call a **hermeneutic of failure**. Freud argued that the existence of the unconscious meant that humans could not know themselves. There is always something hiding, always some displacement that means one can never grasp the truth in its totality. Lacan brought this all into discourse and, more specifically, into the diacritics of the signifier; he emphasized the impossibility of ever achieving the unity that is the primordial fantasy propping up almost every understanding of intersubjectivity, communication, and language, on the one hand, and of knowledge, on the other. Consequently, he argued that the most powerful desires defining both human existence and modern philosophy—the desire for a unified and transparent subject, the desire for a correspondence between signifier and signified, the desire for intersubjectivity as a union or communion between subjects, and the desire for a language that can successfully touch or at least represent reality—are all doomed to failure.

Only the Sr is left, which is always producing other Srs from which it can differentiate itself. The very nature of language makes humans unable to ever achieve the fantasy of a perfect relation, a perfect union of differences. Nevertheless, language enables us to live with and within the "failed unicity" of communication, referentiality, and subjectivity.[u] This impossible desire and the processes it inaugurates take us beyond structuralism into the beginning of "postmodern" thinking.

NOTES

a. Benveniste, *Problems in General Linguistics*, 224.
b. Benveniste, *Problems in General Linguistics*, 226.
c. Lederman, "I Borg," *Star Trek: The Next Generation*.
d. Althusser, *For Marx*.
e. Hall, *Cultural Studies 1983*, 68.
f. Althusser, *Essays in Self-Criticism*, 51 (emphasis added).
g. Althusser et al., *Reading Capital*.
h. Althusser, "Ideology and Ideological State Apparatuses," in *Lenin and Philosophy*, 101.
i. Althusser, *For Marx*.
j. Althusser, "Ideology," 107.
k. Althusser, "Ideology," 109.
l. Althusser, "Ideology," 118.
m. Althusser, "Ideology," 115, 118.
n. Lacan, *Écrits*, 126–60.
o. Lacan, *Seminar of Jacques Lacan*, 3:167.
p. Lemaire, *Jacques Lacan*, 53.
q. Lacan, *Écrits*, 1–8.
r. Lacan, "Signification of the Phallus," in *Écrits*, 311–22.
s. Lemaire, *Jacques Lacan*. 38.
t. Antoine Vergote, "Foreword," in Lemaire, *Jacques Lacan*, xx.
u. Laclau, *On Populist Reason*; Lundberg, *Lacan in Public*.

The Postmodern
(Third Interregnum)

If thought is grounded in and understandable as responses to significant sociohistorical and cultural changes, the emergence of "the modern" describes historical reality, experience (modernity), and expressive discourses such as art and theory (modernism). We have seen, although greatly oversimplified, two iterations or configurations of the modern. A third, often referred to as late modern or, more commonly, the **postmodern**, became an important and common concept in the mid-twentieth century, the result of many changes coming together; and because it claims to be the dominant experience in the contemporary West, I want to consider it in some detail.

THE EMERGENCE OF THE POSTMODERN
This third composition of the modern emerged as Western societies faced the profoundly disturbing consequences of fascisms, the Second World War, and colonial/anticolonial violence. Beyond the "ordinary" horrors of wars, three shock waves stared back at earlier modernities with contempt, the first of which was the genocidal violence of the Holocaust (Shoah). There had

been genocidal wars previously (as well as enslavements such as the Middle Passage and the "resettlement" of Indigenous people). The Holocaust was unique because of its rationality and industrialization. Nazism created a calculated, industrially efficient, and scientifically grounded death machine in which six million Jews and six million other noncombatants (including homosexuals, Roma, political and religious opponents, Russians and Poles, and various peoples of color) were conscripted into slave labor and slaughtered in concentration camps.

Just as frightening, many ordinary citizens of various countries, across class positions and educational levels, allowed and even cooperated with what was happening in front of them. When the full horror was finally revealed and acknowledged, the reverberations were profound, including the eventual establishment of Israel. In the United States, the Holocaust birthed a highly visible, theological-intellectual movement: "the death of God."[a] Maybe Friedrich Nietzsche was finally right: humanity had killed God.

The second shock wave originated from the atomic bombs dropped on Hiroshima and Nagasaki by the United States. Whatever the military value or ethical failure of the bombing of these Japanese cities, it cast a shadow over the world; for the first time in human history, human beings had the capacity to destroy themselves and the planet.[1] And this capacity was in

---

1 The images of nuclear holocaust—linking the two figures—were omnipresent in popular culture, particularly in the movies: images of the threat of nuclear destruction and sometimes its actualization, both serious and humorous (*Invasion USA*, *On the Beach*, *The Day the Earth Caught Fire*, *The Day the Earth Stood Still*, *Dr. Strangelove*, *Seven Days in May*, *Colossus*, *WarGames*, *Fail Safe*, etc.); and images of the unintended consequences of nuclear experimentation and fallout in an endless series of monster movies (*The Blob*, *Creature from the Black Lagoon*, *Them*). In the last, giant mutant ants trampled my home in Brooklyn.

And the threat of atomic war was felt to be very real and very immediate. Perhaps you have seen the "duck and cover" public service announcements. When I was in grade school, we had these cheap little wooden desks. Every month, in addition to fire drills, we had nuclear war drills. A bell would ring, and we would get under our desk, such as it was. For some years, we were also given cheap metal ID bracelets with our names badly engraved on them. We were told these were necessary because if the bomb was dropped on New York City, where I grew up, which was highly likely if there was a war, the bracelets would be needed to identify the bodies. Now, you don't have to be very smart to realize that if ID bracelets would be needed to identify the bodies, getting under a plywood desk in an open classroom in the heart of New York wasn't really going to do much good.

the hands of politicians who thought that détente built on mutually assured destruction, an obviously irrational strategy, was a reasonable way of ensuring peace.

A third shock wave arose from anticolonial struggles, which had begun before the war but gained new strength and visibility in the decades that followed. The colonies of Western European nations demanded liberation and independence in Africa, Asia, and the Pacific Islands. In many cases, these were long-term struggles, and in some cases they were extremely violent and forced the West to confront its long history of barbarism. They inspired and were joined by the emerging civil rights movement, which was itself built on a long history of Black struggles in the United States since the end of the Civil War.

World War II also reconfigured global geography as the world was divided into three parts: the liberal capitalist nations (the First World, the West), the communist nations (the Second World, the East), and the third world of mostly "nonaligned" nations.[2] The United States moved to the center as a new global power, both leading and speaking for the West. This new spatiality fueled a new global politics, the Cold War, both abroad (where the East and West competed for influence and resources) and in the United States (where political paranoia led to reactionary extremism and anticommunist paranoia [McCarthyism, the John Birch Society], as well as revivals of racism, anti-Semitism, and so on).

While the latent and manifest terrors of these changes were integrated into everyday lives,[3] they were countered, at least into the 1970s, by the production of a largely white middle class, with a presupposed consensus of normalcy. This assumed that the United States (with Europe following behind) was realizing the best of all possible worlds: an increase in homeownership,

---

2 Twenty-nine of them met at the Bandung Conference of 1955.
3 It all came together in the Cuban Missile Crisis in October 1962, a thirteen-day confrontation between the United States and Russia. The United States accused Russia of sending nuclear missiles to Cuba and "quarantined" the island nation to prevent additional missiles from being delivered. (Officially, a "blockade" would have been an act of war.) Russia threatened war if the United States stopped any Russian ships from entering or leaving Cuba. In New York, schools were closed. We sat in dark homes, glued to our tiny TV screens; most normal programming was canceled, and we watched for hours (we did not have 24/7 broadcasting then) waiting to see if the world was about to end, whether we were about to live through what would be the surprisingly brief war to end all wars, quite literally.

suburban development, and shopping malls; the expansion of (very limited and unequally distributed) social welfare benefits; the rapid increase of consumer goods emphasizing comfort, convenience, and pleasure; and an expanding universe of educational opportunities, on the one hand, and leisure activities, mass media, and popular culture, on the other. These changes were built on a negotiated compromise among capitalism, labor unions, and the state, which also served to hide the growing power of what Dwight Eisenhower, a Republican president, called "the military-industrial complex," as well as extractive energy and continuing imperialist exploitation. Such developments accelerated through the turn of the millennium, especially after the collapse of the Soviet Union in 1989: the extraordinary growth of corporate power and commercial culture and the reconfiguration of relations among capitalisms (with the rise of finance and technology); the explosion of digital and social media; the appearance of new global crises (climate change); and so on, all reinforcing the continuing sense of a break with previous iterations of the modern.

This dominant "American liberalism" was deeply, socially conservative, with a strong imperative to avoid "rocking the boat." Generations (including large numbers of immigrants) had lived through the Great Depression, fought against the fascists, and come home to live a peaceful and comfortable life. They worked hard—in a highly gendered and racially organized system of social relations—so they could move up the social ladder, and their children would have a better life.

Many marginalized groups and countries did not benefit from or share this new sense of normalcy. The postwar decades were rocked by protests, demonstrations, and revolutions, from both the left and the right, as well as from those who could not be so neatly located. Anticolonial struggles and the civil rights and Black Power movements helped inspire and coexisted with antiwar, antinuclear, and anticapitalist struggles; second-wave feminism; gay liberation; ecological awareness; immigrant and Latinx worker organizing; and a renewed class struggle (through the power of unions). These worldwide struggles often continued into the 1970s and 1980s.

In some ways, the emergence of youth cultures built largely around popular musics and generational conflicts, including the countercultural movements of the 1960s and 1970s, was most disturbing to the image of liberalism. These movements, largely urban and college-based, disrupted the new sense of normalcy because they largely involved white, middle-class kids rebelling against the middle-class lives of their parents. Ironically, just when mainstream society dedicated itself to youth, youth rejected it. Youth was celebrated by the liberal consensus as the salvation of the future, and across many social sectors, enormous investments were made to enhance the possibilities of the new generations.

For example, there were significant public investments in education, especially higher education, to meet the growing needs of returning military personnel and the increasing expectations of the middle classes and the needs of the baby boomers.[4] This changed the nature and influence of universities, as well as their relations to both governments and capital (industry). Research grants and tuition became major sources of funding for universities but also posed new demands on both administration and curriculum. But the expansion of education was, like most other advances, limited in scope and unevenly distributed, reinforcing existing economic, social, and political divisions. It also opened a space for "tenured radicals," who laid the ground for the rise of Theory, which exacerbated a growing divide between those who had attended college and those who had not, partly correlated with an urban/rural divide.

Most youth cultures condemned the dominant society and culture as being unethical, hypocritical, boring, cowardly, crazy, crudely materialist, and lacking real pleasure and imagination. Young people rejected their parents' values and social conventions, and dreamed of other worlds, other ways of living. In the 1960s, a "movement of movements" sought to shock and change the world.[5] Yet, those who participated in this movement continued to live a contradiction at the heart of the second modernity: a radical individualism of freedom and pleasure and a deep commitment to communalism.[6]

4 In many rural parts of the United States, soldiers returning from the Vietnam War were the only conduits of the new youth cultures.

5 Its effects—successes, failures, and transformations—have yet to be fully accounted. See my "We All Want to Change the World."

6 These were captured in various avant-gardes (e.g., minimalism, Pop Art) as well as the revival of antibourgeois and bohemian arts and lifestyles (e.g., the Beats). Novels such as *Catcher in the Rye*, *Catch-22*, and *Been Down So Long It Looks Like Up to Me* captured this spirit. The experiences of those who participated in this movement of movements were often enhanced by mystical insights and various meditative practices, mind-expanding drugs, and Indigenous understandings that were not possible or even imaginable in the world they were destined to inherit. These people, protesting a present they did not choose and a future they did not desire, eschewed the alienation of labor and the even greater alienation of technology for the delights of the natural, except when technology enhanced their lives (e.g., for music—in transistor radios, boom boxes, and all the technology that was required for the live performers of rock). It was a world that sought pleasure and wisdom everywhere, a world of sex—made possible

Even now, many people are still living in the shadow of these developments and the disruptions and challenges they produced, especially when you include the rise of a reconfigured conservatism (combining religion, nationalism, and capitalism, originally under the umbrella of anticommunism), even on college campuses.

From the 1950s on, the "structure of feeling" of US culture was partly defined by a changing balance and tension between an unearned optimism (both in the liberal mainstream and among protesters) and a pessimism defined by horrors, boredom, and uncertainty. The tension was often captured in the music of the times, nowhere as clearly as in the theatrical works of the Belgian performer Jacques Brel, whose lyrics tell us: "We would build a new world, if we only knew how. . . . In the dreams that we dream, we ask what have we done."[b]

MODERNISTS IN SEARCH OF THE POSTMODERN

People always try to make sense of their "present," even without the comfort of distance. They try to describe the water in which they swim or, better, the currents and tides that both enable and constrain their capacities and movements. Not everyone following the war agreed that humanity was living through a momentous historical transformation, akin to the enlightenments and the two previous modernities. And yet, more than in previous eras, no doubt partly as a result of mass and social media, people are aware of—sometimes in awe of and sometimes horrified by—the forces determining the present era and their consequences. But they do not agree about the postmodern: When did it begin? Is it a rupture, a shift in the tectonic plates, a reconfiguration of human reality? How are history, culture, experience, and thought interacting? What is new, old, or significantly altered? What is the character of this new epoch and its most important determinations? Perhaps what sets the postmodern apart is its self-awareness of the present as a construction, so that any attempt to capture it reenacts a hermeneutics of suspicion, but with an awareness that it is constructing what it is trying to describe. And yet, ironically, the very effort to tell the story of the postmodern seems to throw us back into a modernist project.

Three intellectuals offered influential elucidations of the postmodern: Jean-François Lyotard, Fredric Jameson, and Jean Baudrillard. Their stories

---

by perhaps the most consequential invention of the 1960s, the birth control pill—which "freed" both women and sex.

did not, in themselves, offer new deep theories—new ways of thinking—but instead observed the emergence of a new way of thinking within the historical culture itself. In 1979, the French philosopher Jean-François Lyotard (1924–98) published *The Postmodern Condition: A Report on Knowledge.*[7] Lyotard was commissioned by the Council of Universities of Quebec to study the future of higher education, especially concerning the sciences and the impact of technology. Rather than address these concerns, he contemplated the larger state of knowledge and culture in the Western world, describing a generalized skepticism about, even the collapse of public faith in, the values and promises of the enlightenments.

He described the end of the **metanarratives** that had sustained people's faith in progress, authority, and knowledge, whether framed in religious or secular terms, whether liberal or communist. The **grand narratives** of historical progress no longer held sway over popular—or even intellectual—sentiment. People no longer believed the world was getting better or that more knowledge would make it so. Many no longer believed that knowledge was possible; they no longer believed in "objective" and "neutral" representation—in either epistemic or political terms. Perhaps the only authoritative source left was people's own experience, but they no longer believed there was a common set of experiences that could bind people together as a nation. Ironically, Lyotard offered a grand narrative about the end of grand narratives.[8]

Beginning with his essay "Postmodernism, or, the Cultural Logic of Late Capitalism" (1984), Fredric Jameson (1934–), the leading Marxist literary theorist in the United States, has offered an account of both postwar postmodern culture as the new **cultural dominant** and its relation to broader socioeconomic developments.[c] This new culture is defined by a number of aesthetic or stylistic characteristics (although these characteristics also describe the

7 Lyotard offered his own philosophy—paralogy—a sort of postmodern take on Wittgenstein.

8 It is worth thinking about this description by Lyotard, written more than forty years ago, in light of the present moment; many people today seem to think the conditions they face (ranging from fake news to the loss of faith in government, to the attacks on education and knowledge, and so on) are new. But Lyotard observed these as the conditions of the postmodern. Even contemporary debates about social justice and identity politics, about political correctness and cultural appropriation, about the lack of a common vision and the increasing palpability of ideological polarization, while not simple reiterations of earlier moments, are clearly variations on the conditions Lyotard described. Yet, I also wonder how deep and widespread the "end" of grand narratives really is. It is hard, after all, to abandon the future.

nature of postmodern experience): the rejection of all forms of unity, including identity, totality, coherence, and closure, and of all forms of depth, including meaning, subjectivity, and origins. Instead, postmodernism embraces
fragmentation, hybridity, discontinuity, surfaces, heterogeneity, and chance.
Instead of claiming originality and truth, postmodernism parades its use of
pastiche, parody, and quotation.

Jameson identified four significant consequences of this cultural shift,
the first being the disappearance of history in favor of nostalgia (and entertainment). History becomes the occasion for fashion and sentimentality, and
popular culture increasingly presents a "sentimental parody" of history. (Think
of the many films and TV shows that rewrite history for the sake of profit.)

Second, the postmodern replaces the authentic, unified subject with a
fractured, even schizophrenic individual with no essential identity. In his
book *Mind, Self, and Society* (1934), the pragmatist George Herbert Mead
offered a social theory—symbolic interactionism—partially built on the distinction between the "I" (the authentic self) and the various "Me's" or social
roles one plays.[d] In the 1950s, the German psychologist Erik Erikson described an "identity crisis" in which (primarily) youths were unable to find
a true and stable identity.[e] Where is the "I" in the face of our many roles?
Over time, this "crisis" has been naturalized, celebrated, and commercial-
ized. The assumption of a real subjectivity behind my statements and actions
has simply become a matter of fashion and nostalgia. Shape-shifters like Ma-
donna and Lady Gaga become the icons of this fluid and fragmented subject.
If there is no true subject, however, then alienation as both an experience and
the foundation of a politics is no longer real. But some critics have argued
that if the subject was never as unified as we imagine, it is probably not as
fragmented as we assume. Besides, there has been a constant if not growing
demand for authenticity in response to this crisis.

Third, Jameson described a new "emotional ground tone," or **affect**, of
everyday life. Affect refers to the intensity and color of one's experiences,
including emotion and the quality of attention or investment. Postmodernity
is the **waning of affect**, resulting in an increasingly flat relation to the world.[f]
Again, some critics have argued, against this claim, that while postmodernism shows a growing indifference about *what* matters, it demands a growing
intensity in how one feels or cares about anything. Affective intensity becomes everything: if you care or feel strongly enough, you are right, and you
will succeed. Jameson did acknowledge moments of extreme intensity, but
only the negative emotion of anxiety and the positive emotion of euphoria.

Fourth, the absence of meaning and truth results in a crisis of **cognitive mapping**. People are no longer able to understand the big picture, to map the relations between their everyday lives (including culture) and the socioeconomic structures that determine them. The complexity of the world appears overwhelmingly chaotic, and culture reflects that incomprehensibility. We can no longer identify or understand our place in the world. For example, Jameson uses the Bonaventura Hotel in Los Angeles as iconic, a hotel designed to be so incoherent and confusing as to make it impossible to navigate.

Finally, Jameson argued that postmodern culture and experience are the **cultural logic of late capitalism**, which emerged after the Second World War. In particular, he observed that the increasing economization of culture means that the last remnants of culture's partial autonomy and its capacity to serve as a critique of commodification (a strong impulse in modernist culture) have been undermined. And he concluded that the crisis of cognitive mapping is the result of the increasing complexity, fragmentation, and globalization of capitalism. Does anyone, including capitalists, actually understand how finance economies (e.g., the derivative markets, the debt economy, arbitrage, monetary markets) work? Does anyone understand the relations among finance, manufacturing, service, extraction, logistics, agriculture, technology, and so on?

If both Lyotard and Jameson approached the postmodern as a discursive—epistemic and ideological—problem, Jean Baudrillard (1929–2007) subtly slid between questions of discourse, experience, and reality by presenting a history of **simulacra**. A simulacrum defines the relations between sign and reality and, in doing so, defines reality itself.

Baudrillard's (Eurocentric grand) narrative comprises five "orders" or logics of simulation.[g] The first four should be familiar: the first—**premodern**—sees the world as, or makes the world into, the expression of God, the signs of God's design.[9] To misunderstand or misspeak the word is to commit a sin, a violation of the Word of God. This simulacrum is embodied in various mystical and magical systems of thought that identify the word and the thing. To call the name is to call up the thing. (Hence, for example, one cannot say the name of God in Judaism.)

The second simulacrum, **representation**, is embodied in science and empiricism. It assumes there is an object in the world that can be accurately or

---

9 This is my reading. Baudrillard discussed three or four orders.

inaccurately captured in signs; statements are either true or false, objects are either real or counterfeit. And to represent the real falsely is to either make a mistake or tell a lie. In both the third and the fourth simulacra, the sign (word) is a **construction** of reality as experience; the world one lives in is created through language. The difference is whether it is the content of language (i.e., ideology) or the structure (i.e., structuralism) that is productive.

Nothing strange about any of these, but wait. Baudrillard argued that all previous simulacra—except perhaps the premodern—have at their core some concept of difference. Baudrillard claimed that the world—or at least the United States—was living in a new simulacrum, which he sometimes, unfortunately, called the **simulacrum (or hypersimulation)**. In this postmodern simulation, difference itself has disappeared or, at least, difference no longer makes a difference. It can no longer be the ground of one's theory because it no longer constitutes the real. The poles in any difference have collapsed, rendering difference ineffective and meaningless. All those differences that defined thought and experience are gone: the sign and the real, the word and the thing, the signifier and the signified, the map and the territory, use value and exchange value. The map has become the reality, and reality has become a map of itself. They are one and the same thing.

Baudrillard did not argue that the map is more real than the reality it purports to simulate, as if the map had colonized the real, although he sometimes wrote as if the real is only what can be simulated, such as when he describes the real as increasingly "satellized."[h] It is **indifference** of the word and the thing that defines the real, which is not the same as a demand that reality conform to the simulacrum.

Since any talk about meaning or the social exists only within differences, hypersimulation entails the implosion of meaning and of the social. But unlike Jameson, Baudrillard did not mourn the loss of the real; there is no nostalgia in his description. The previous orders of simulation—magic, representation, construction (both materialist and structuralist)—are no longer active. Everything is visible, nothing is hidden; nothing stands behind the word. The real is real precisely because it is no different than the sign, and vice versa. People live in a simulacrum in which reality becomes—is—for example, the code rather than merely needing to resemble the code.

Baudrillard often presented his argument in anecdotes (metonyms) about particular events or scenes. His most famous and controversial was about the first Iraq war (1990–91).[i] Even during the war, many commentators compared it (or its coverage?) to a video game. The "reality" of the video game's signs had been normalized by popular culture. But, according to Baudrillard, there was more at stake (which was, in part, that there were no stakes). The difference between the war and a video game no longer mattered. It was not that the war wasn't real, as if people did not die: "A war is not any less heinous for being a mere simulacrum—the flesh suffers just the same, and the dead ex-combatants count as much there as in other wars. . . . What no longer exists is the adversity of adversities, the reality of antagonistic causes, the ideological seriousness of war—also the reality of defeat or victory, war being a process whose triumph lies quite beyond these appearances."[j] The reality of the war and that of the video game were both hypersimulated.

The fact that we continue to speak of the real as if it were a secret waiting to be revealed is merely the "alibi" that allows us to live with the disappearance of difference. Consider: "Disneyland is there to conceal the fact that it is the 'real' country, all of 'real' America, which *is* Disneyland (just as prisons are there to conceal the fact that it is the social in its entirety, in its banal omnipresence, which is carceral). . . . It is no longer a question of a false representation of reality (ideology), but of concealing the fact that the real is no longer real and thus of saving the reality principle."[k] Americans live in a perpetual, universal Disneyland, and Disneyland functions to hide that reality by simulating a difference that is no difference. The prison is the "alibi" that allows people to go on living as if they were not already living in a prison. After all, they live under constant surveillance, anxious about the unpredictable future, afraid of punishment.

Baudrillard assumed the new simulacrum was largely the product of the new—digital—media and technologies, where the virtual and the actual no longer differ. The apparent autonomy of the actual only exists as an alibi, and people only exist as nodes in the digital network. Consequently, "the masses and the media are one single process," neither of which can be "represented."[l] This constitutes a "catastrophe of meaning," in which people are left only with a screen and a network through which information circulates.[m] The result is a new political crisis to which the only response is to refuse the demand for meaning and difference, to refuse the alibi of resistance and revolution, and, instead, to embrace indifference itself. People must enact a **hyperconformism** within the simulacrum, absorbing and neutralizing all meaning and, with it, all power.[n] They must adopt an attitude of fascination with the simulacrum, to perform the power of silence itself. As you can imagine, Baudrillard's quasi-ontological understanding of the postmodern has been hotly debated.

Lyotard, Jameson, and Baudrillard are modernists writing about the collapse of the enlightenments and the end of the modern. To a large extent, their responses to historical changes are framed within the terms and with the tools of modern thought. They each offered their own grand narrative to explain why there can be no grand narratives: Lyotard offered a quasi-scientific story of the collapse of the enlightenments; Jameson's story was that of a Marxist mourning the destruction of the very conditions of possibility of Marxist critique. Baudrillard mounts an all-encompassing grand narrative of the course of Western history as a history of semiotic ontology, of the relations between word and thing. None of them presents serious critiques of modern thought itself, except perhaps to say that it is not adequate to the historical challenges at hand.

THE SPACES OF THE POSTMODERN

We are still left with the question: What is "the postmodern"? Just like the modern, it is a complex and often contradictory assemblage of different practices, experimentations, and commitments. The appearance of the term does not quite mirror the history of "the modern." The latter was first a marker of historical periodization and experience, which was then extended, in the middle to late nineteenth century, to modernism (as a cultural-aesthetic label). In contrast, the term *postmodernism* was first used in the late nineteenth century (e.g., by the art critic John Watkins Chapman) to describe emerging aesthetic movements that opposed the dominant "modernist" styles. After the First World War, various historians, including Bernard Bell (1926) and Arnold Toynbee (1939), used it to describe what was then the current historical period.[o] But neither use gained significant traction. The term appeared again, beginning in the late 1940s and growing increasingly common in the 1950s and 1960s onward, to describe aesthetic movements—in the literary and visual arts but most prominently in architecture.

No doubt, some of the roots of this "postmodernism" lay in the various avant-gardes of the nineteenth and early twentieth centuries, although one might extend those roots even further back to the medieval Gothic and the early seventeenth-century to mid-eighteenth-century Baroque. Postmodernism in the arts covers a broad range of styles and movements, and the line between "transitional" figures and those who are properly part of postmodernism is blurry at best. Nevertheless, its early figures would include architects such as Michael Graves, Philip Johnson, and Robert Venturi (co-author of the highly influential book *Learning from Las Vegas*); writers such as Jorge Luis Borges, William Burroughs, Samuel Beckett, Ishmael Reed, Marguerite Duras, Octavia Butler, Kurt Vonnegut, Thomas Pynchon, Gabriel

García Márquez, and so on; and visual artists such as Jackson Pollock, Robert Rauschenberg, Jasper Johns, David Hockney, Andy Warhol, and Cindy Sherman. These artists' work was hotly contested, often seen as strange if not incomprehensible or unworthy. Venturi elevated kitsch to design; Graves created a hodgepodge aesthetic by incorporating different styles in his buildings; and Johnson built hotels that were almost impossible to navigate. Pollock made chaos by chance, Warhol copied popular icons (Campbell Soup cans, Marilyn Monroe) and sold them for a lot of money, then made more copies that he sold for a pittance, while Sherman took photographs of herself as other, famous, people. Beckett created stories going nowhere; García Márquez wrote magic realism; Vonnegut and Pynchon created convoluted, fractured mythologies, reducing art to the banal. Burroughs created cut-ups, while Butler redefined science fiction. Even in cinema, a generation of directors (e.g., Steven Spielberg) made movies with disarmingly simple plots composed almost entirely of quotations of shots from cinema history. (I had friends who took great pleasure in ruining my enjoyment of a film by constantly identifying the source of each shot.) With so many different and strange things happening in the worlds of culture, it is not surprising that it has been difficult to define the unity of postmodernism.

I have already suggested that part of what sets postmodernism apart is the specific way in which it recursively reflects on its own lack of identity, a hermeneutics of suspicion without a deep structure, caught in a kind of feedback loop. There is something else unique about the way it has been taken up. While being modern became part of a system of identification and differentiation, modernism itself rarely entered into popular discourses or popular culture; with a few exceptions, it remained in the realms of high culture. But postmodernism is everywhere in public discourse and popular culture. It may be, as numerous authors have suggested, that it is (just?) (high) modernism "in the streets," but it has nevertheless opened up new paths for thinking.

Too often, postmodernism is simply defined by its rejection of modern aesthetics and thought. The results can be represented as a series of binary oppositions: "if modernism . . . , then postmodernism . . ." Moreover, if we take postmodernism as a critique of modernism, the various particular oppositions are generally assumed to be equivalent, creating two largely homogeneous and consistent formations. Despite the serious shortcomings of creating a new binary opposition, I present it here as table 23.1.

Based on this table, one might assume that postmodernism sought to undermine modernism point for point, to reject all those assumptions and

TABLE 23.1 Defining the Postmodern against the Modern

If the Modern Values	Then the Postmodern Values
Harmony and homogeneity	Heterogeneity
Unity and identity	Fractures and differences, pluralities
Stability	Instability and fluidity
Planning	Chance
Purpose	Play
Coherence	Incoherence
Originality	Appropriation and quotation
Big ideas and grand narratives	The small and the local
Universality	Specificity
Causality, determinacy	Contingency, indeterminacy
The one (or the binary pair)	The many (multiplicity)
Order—hierarchical or centralized	Horizontal dispersal
Depth, foundations	Surface (superficiality)
Structure (completion)	Process
Presence	Absence
Transcendence	Immanence
Meaning (signified)	Signifier
Truth	Truths (relativism)
Declarative	Irony
Authenticity	Inauthenticity
Origins	Effects
Purity	Eclecticism, hybridity
Reason	Affect
Esoteric	Ordinary
Closure and totality	Uncertainty and incompleteness
Subjectivity, consciousness	Bodies, unconscious
Separation of science, art, politics, etc.	Negating and collapsing them
Art, esoteric	Popular, obvious

values that constituted modernism. It would be more accurate to say that the various postmodernisms were challenging basic assumptions passed down from various enlightenments and modern deep theories.

RETHINKING THOUGHT

Each era of thought I have discussed (enlightenments, first and second modernities) includes some thinkers who challenged the dominant developments. The enlightenments had the counter-enlightenments, including Jean-Jacques Rousseau and Giambattista Vico but also Baruch Spinoza, who implicitly and sometimes explicitly rejected their humanism. In the first modernity, hermeneutics of suspicion either limited or rejected the claims of humanism but also delivered major blows against universalism (especially Marx). The thought of the second modernity was largely structured by an argument between phenomenology's humanism and the various antihumanisms of the various deep theories grounded in language. The latter, to varying degrees, can be seen as contextualists challenging universalism.

In the aftermath of the Second World War, some thinkers saw the historical catastrophes and traumas as the realization of the human capacities of evil, which had always been there but were now unavoidably visible as they operated on a scale that no one had ever imagined possible—unless, of course, you had been on the receiving end of such violence for centuries. But others felt compelled to confront what can only be described as the failure, even the devastating cost, of enlightenment and modernity. They were forced to agree with the German Marxist—and sometimes mystical—philosopher Walter Benjamin (1892–1940), who, caught up in the horrors of the Holocaust, put it quite succinctly: "There is no document of civilization that is not also a document of barbarism."[p]

The crisis intellectuals faced was not the universality of evil but the recognition that this unimaginable barbarism did not merely accompany the enlightenment and modern projects; they were both the conditions of possibility and the result of this history of thought.[10] You don't have to deny the positive effects of this history to recognize that they were partly achieved

---

10 What came as something of a shocked self-realization to many intellectuals who were, as Pierre Bourdieu described them, a subordinate fraction of the dominant classes, was hardly news to scholars of color all around the world, to colonial and African-diasporic intellectuals, whose influence would begin to increase as the century moved on. Bourdieu, *Field of Cultural Production*.

through barbarism. How do you decide whether it was worth it, whether you can really call this progress? How can thought respond to this challenge? The French philosopher Michel Serres (1930–2019), in a moving passage, describes the experience of those European thinkers whose lives were marked by the barbarities of the mid-twentieth century:

> My generation lived through these early years very painfully. The preceding generation was twenty years old at the beginning of these events and, as adults, lived them in an active way, becoming involved in them. My generation could only follow them in the passivity of powerlessness—as child, adolescent—in any case, weak, and without any possibility of action. Violence, death, blood and tears, hunger, bombings, deportations, affected my age group and traumatized it, since these horrors took place during the time of our formation—physical and emotional. My youth goes from Guernica (I cannot bear to look at Picasso's famous painting) to Nagasaki, by way of Auschwitz. . . . My generation was formed, physically, in this atrocious environment and ever since has kept its distance from politics. For us power still means only cadavers and torture.[q]

These questions presented a real challenge, and a number of intellectuals further distanced themselves from key aspects of enlightenment and modern thought. They sought to question more deeply and radically the fundamental premises and ways of thinking that had resulted in the crisis of the contemporary world. Some of those assumptions and ways of thinking—whether humanism, subjectivity, individualism, or anthropocentrism, whether the choice between rationalism and empiricism, or the particular logic of identity and difference, or the privilege of epistemology over ontology—may have been wrong, but they are certainly inadequate to the current crises. As the Portuguese intellectual Boaventura de Sousa Santos argued, we are facing "modern problems for which there are no modern solutions."[r] These thinkers attempted to find a new beginning—admittedly a rather modernist gesture— or at least an alternative path, to think outside or beyond at least some of the determining constraints of modern deep theories, to inaugurate other ways of thinking, to think otherwise, to offer a new **figure or image of thought**. They might be appropriately described as postmodern or even antimodern philosophers rather than philosophers of the postmodern.[11]

---

11 There is an interesting geographic aspect of the postmodern. Almost all the modern philosophers I have discussed, from Kant through Heidegger at least, are German-

How should we think about the "break" between modern and postmodern thought? What exactly is the question? What sort of argument is it? It is not merely addressing substantive assertions about the world, the forms of reason, the nature of evidence, and the logics of argument. It is not merely a paradigm shift, offering different presuppositions and practices of knowledge, because the arguments addressed fundamental questions about thinking. Were they engaged with science, they would challenge the very possibility and desirability of science itself. Were they economists—either capitalist or anticapitalist—they would deny the existence of economies per se. There are different theories of value and markets—paradigm conflicts—but what if you threw it all out and, as a result, suggested there is no value and no markets? To do economics, must you enter into an entirely different realm of thought? Have you reimagined what it means to think?

The postmodern thinkers I will discuss are not trying to provide new answers to old questions, or new questions for old problems. Their first concern is not with making a historical argument about the emergence of a new epoch; they are reconstructing the very nature of thinking, living, and, sometimes, reality. Many of them reached back to some figure of past thinking, constructing a different history, what Gilles Deleuze called a **minor history**. Thus, my backstory takes an odd turn, doubling back on itself to find a different beginning so as to head off in another direction, into what may sometimes appear as a different universe: Martin Heidegger to the pre-Socratics, Deleuze to Spinoza, Jacques Derrida and Michel Foucault to Nietzsche, Stuart Hall to Karl Marx, almost always reading them against the grain.

In the remaining lectures, I will follow two routes out of modern thought, both attempting to found a **new empiricism**, both partly driven by the recognition of the costs of enlightenment and modern ways of thinking, especially their binary logics. As a result, some of these new empiricisms find themselves having to speak radically new languages, whether based in speculation or concrete analyses. They are all challenging the very recognizability and intelligibility of thought.

---

speaking or of Germanic roots. Despite the diversity of enlightenments, modern thought was largely dominated by Germanic traditions. On the other hand, the turn against enlightenment and modern thought, at least beginning with the structuralists in the 1950s and 1960s, was largely defined by French intellectuals. While Heidegger, especially in his later works, had a continuing influence, to a large extent the influence of these works, for complicated reasons (no doubt having to do in part with his Nazism), resonated most strongly in France. The axis of influence shifted after the Second World War.

The first, often described as the **ontological turn**—most commonly seen in the work of Heidegger, Derrida, and Deleuze—offers a speculative deep theory that attempts to grasp the nature of reality, agency, and discourse (and that often slips back into universalism as ontologies are wont to do). Immanuel Kant is the enemy: his practice of critique was predicated on the exclusion of metaphysics, on the assumption that human beings cannot touch or know a reality outside that which they have created, that is, that they cannot experience the world—whether sacred or profane—as it really is, independent of human thought. Hadn't people and reality always been affecting one another?

The second offers a **radical contextualism**,[12] visible in the work of Deleuze and Guattari, Foucault, and Hall.[13] Their break with enlightenment and modern thought is less severe and absolute, although all question humanism but have little interest in ontology. Instead, they start by rejecting all universalisms, bringing deep theory back to questions about the concrete contexts of thought and power.

If you have found the material covered so far to be difficult (and strange), get ready for the ride of your life; you are about to enter what may feel like the Twilight Zone or the Upside Down. You may at times think you have stepped into another universe, certainly not the one you live in. But that is the point: What if our ways of thinking, the concepts and languages we use to cut into reality, have actually hidden the truth of the world, the truth of how that reality is made? What if they have produced an unlivable reality that has led us to the contemporary crises?

But, then, maybe it isn't science fiction at all. Physics describes a universe very different from that which we are certain we live in. For the most part, we think and act as if we live in a Newtonian universe, a stable and predictable universe that is describable in a set of fixed, universal laws that we are capable of discovering. But that is not true, however convenient it may be and no matter how much it seems to fit our experience. Quite the opposite: we live in a fluid and highly indeterminate universe, a relativistic universe of quantum mechanics (even if physicists cannot unify the two), a universe of strange particles and even stranger quantum entanglements, perhaps one universe among many

12 This path is not always categorized as postmodern but certainly is part of the "post."
13 Foucault is often linked to Deleuze, and they certainly had a close relationship for many decades. Hall, a diasporic (Anglo-Jamaican) intellectual—my teacher and friend—may have been the most consistent contextualist of all: a contextual theorist of contexts, a theorist without a theory.

universes, perhaps even a hologram. Maybe Baudrillard was right, and we are living in Disneyland, at least in what used to be called Future World. It is time to step into the abyss.

NOTES

  a. Altizer and Hamilton, *Radical Theology and the Death of God.*

  b. Brel, "Alone" ("Seul"), in *La valse à mille temps.*

  c. Jameson, "Postmodernism," in *Postmodernism.*

  d. Mead, *Mind, Self, and Society.*

  e. Erikson, *Identity.*

  f. Jameson, "Postmodernism," in *Postmodernism*, 10.

  g. Baudrillard, *Simulations.*

  h. Baudrillard, *Simulations*, 64.

  i. Baudrillard, *Gulf War.*

  j. Baudrillard, *Simulations*, 70.

  k. Baudrillard, *Simulations*, 25.

  l. Baudrillard, *In the Shadow*, 44.

  m. Baudrillard, *In the Shadow*, 103.

  n. Baudrillard, *In the Shadow*, 107.

  o. Bell, *Postmodernism*; Toynbee, *Study of History.*

  p. Benjamin, "Theses on the Philosophy of History," in *Illuminations*, 256.

  q. Serres and Latour, *Conversations*, 2, 4.

  r. Santos, "Public Sphere," 46.

PART IV.

Routes

into the

Post

LECTURE | NO. 24

Heidegger Again

The later works of Martin Heidegger make a crucial pivot into postmodern ontologies. In his "Letter on Humanism" (1947), he announced a turn (**Kehre**) in his thought. *Kehre* is neither a right-angle turn nor a 180-degree reversal; it is a turn in skiing in which you gradually adjust your trajectory. But Heidegger had begun this effort even before the war, revisiting the *Seinsfrage*, the question of Being itself, relocating its erasure in the Socratic origins of Greek philosophy.[1] His lectures in the mid-1930s on the pre-Socratic philosophers (Anaximander, Heraclitus, and Parmenides) had already begun constructing another way to think Being, which he elaborated in his influential lectures "The Origin of the Work of Art" (1935–37) and "The Age of the World Picture" (1938).

In the decades that followed, Heidegger wrote an extraordinary number of important essays, including "The Thing" (1949), "Building Dwelling Thinking" (1951), ". . . Poetically Man Dwells . . ." (1951), "The Question concerning

1 He also drew heavily on the works of Georg Trakl and Friedrich Hölderlin.

Technology" (1953), "The Way to Language" (1959), and "The End of Philosophy and the Task of Thinking" (1964), and books, including *On the Way to Language* (1950–59), *What Is Called Thinking?* (1951–52), *Identity and Difference* (1955–57), and *On Time and Being* (1962–64).

In "Letter on Humanism," Heidegger argued against reading *Being and Time* as another humanism, as Jean-Paul Sartre had done. Heidegger argued that this approach misunderstood his argument to be a description of human nature, a phenomenological philosophical anthropology. As a result, Sartre and others assumed Heidegger was offering an ethical voluntarism that made Dasein (humans) capable of and responsible for the choice of whether to be authentic. The humanists could not grasp truth as *aletheia* (letting be), which assumes that truth reveals itself in the clearing. Again, the humanists made Dasein responsible for the clearing and, therefore, for making the Truth of Being possible. Such readings threw Heidegger back into the arms of Immanuel Kant and the metaphysical tradition he despised. The existentialist mantra that "existence precedes essence" was not, Heidegger insisted, his argument, for it is simply the negation of one metaphysical statement, which is itself a metaphysical statement.[a] I will leave unanswered the question hidden in this dispute: Does *Being and Time* offer itself as a humanism? Was Heidegger using the dispute to implicitly criticize his own limits or mistakes?

Being and Time was Heidegger's preamble to unconcealing the question of (the meaning of) Being by disclosing the ontology of beings who are concerned with their own Being, thus suggesting some pre-understanding of the question. It did not take him very far, but he realized that he could not simply reverse his analysis, studying the object rather than the subject, as if Being were simply hidden in the existence of the—any?—object. His antihumanism (and antisubjectivism) did not entail objectivism, since the very "opposition" between subject and object is only disclosed in the clearing of the enlightenments. In any case, universalizing this particular clearing would not disclose an ontologically grounded ethics of being-in-the-world, which, Heidegger admitted, was his real project, not unlike Spinoza's. One cannot interrogate Being by looking at a particular relationality, including Dasein's being-in-the-world, or by enumerating the possibilities of existence.

THE *KEHRE*

In the *Kehre*, Heidegger argued that the hermeneutic relation, a relation that precedes the terms of the relation, is what is real and primordial, not as a structure but an active process, a constant relating. The real question, then,

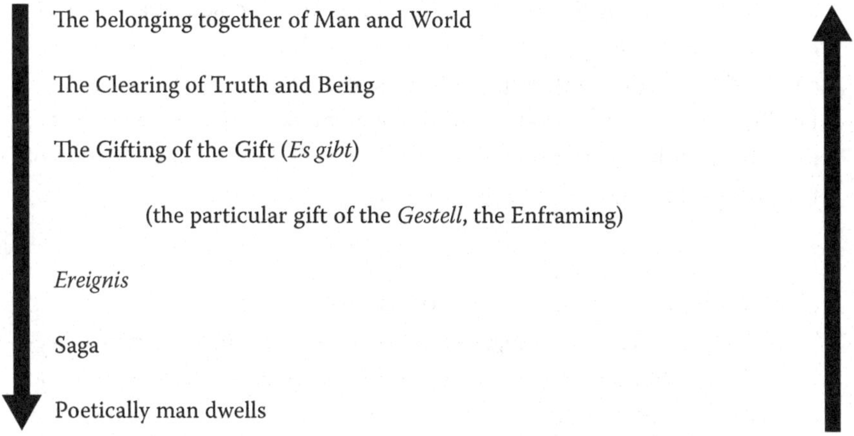

The belonging together of Man and World

The Clearing of Truth and Being

The Gifting of the Gift (*Es gibt*)

    (the particular gift of the *Gestell*, the Enframing)

Ereignis

Saga

Poetically man dwells

FIGURE 24.1

is what makes the primordial relation—the Being of beings, the **belonging together**, or the involvements of Being and beings—possible? How is the disclosure of Truth as relationality possible?

Heidegger's answer was original and perplexing, leaving enlightenment thought behind while allowing it its place. Let me provide a preview of the movement of Heidegger's thought. In *Being and Time*, Heidegger excavated Dasein's ontic being to unconceal ever more ontological truths. He unconcealed Being as a (historical) mode of appearing or presencing. Existence is appearing, and appearance is existence. A specific being is its mode of appearing. What exists—the Truth of Being—is what appears in the light of the clearing. And Dasein is always thrown into a clearing.

With the *Kehre*, Heidegger proposed, first, that the clearing is a *gift*, the space-time of a historical epoch. In the clearing, specific modes of relations, situatedness, or involvements exist as Being and Truth, which are themselves historical. Heidegger had moved from a universal to a historical ontology. Second, the clearing is the gift of a fundamental, universal, ontological process (*Ereignis*) that gathers or appropriates different positive elements—Heidegger called them *haecceities*, or "thisness"—into an ensemble of relations constituting a clearing.[2] Third, *Ereignis* is the expression of the *poiesis* of the universe, of the power of relating, the power to create, to bring

2 The term *haecceities* seems to have originated with the medieval philosopher and rhetorician Duns Scotus to refer to the particularity and singularity of any individuated thing, that is, whatever it is that makes it what it is, that makes it this rather than that. Heidegger wrote his habilitation on Duns Scotus.

something into being that did not exist before. Fourth, poiesis is an infinitely creative Language (*Saga*).[3] This is the condition of possibility, the deep ontology, of the historicality and linguisticality of both Dasein and Being itself. Finally, the ethical life is one in which one embraces the creativity of the universe: one dwells poetically. Figure 24.1 is a schematic representation of this increasingly ontological understanding.

CHANGING THE ONTOLOGICAL QUESTION

To explain the clearing of Being, I want to use another metaphor, remembering that metaphors are inadequate and even dangerous if taken literally or too far. Imagine a room with black lights. Much that you would normally see is simply gone, and some things that you had not seen before suddenly appear. Now let's expand the metaphor: a dark stage lit by a single spotlight. The only things that exist on the stage are those lit by the spotlight. Outside the spotlight, nothing exists. If the color of the spotlight changes, some things will disappear, and others will appear. What exists is what is unconcealed by the spotlight, and different colors might unconceal different realities; the very meaning of existence, and the resulting existents, will be determined by the mode of unconcealing (the light color). Truth is unconcealed by the light that lets Being be. And what is not in the light, what is not in the clearing, does not exist. "To exist" means to exist in the light. And as the light changes, existence and the very meaning of Being change. The Being of beings is what happens in the clearing, resulting in different **historical epochs of Being**.

The very question of ontology has changed. In *Being and Time*, Heidegger questioned the meaning of Being. But in the *Kehre*, the meaning of Being changes with the clearing, with the different epochs of Being. The *Seinsfrage* was forgotten because the gift of the historical clearing was concealed by metaphysical thinking, so that people thought there was only one Truth, one reality, which humans themselves had made. It was concealed by the hubris of humanism, which thinks that humanity creates meaning and its own reality. Both hid the "Beingness of beings" as well as "the subjectivity of the subjection."[b] And this has had momentous consequences, as we shall see.

So, how does humanity **dwell** in the clearing of truth? Humanity—as well as every other being—exists in specific kinds of relations. Humanity "stands" in and out (*ek-sistence*) of the clearing: "Thrown . . . the human being stands

3 Many translations use not *Saga* but "the Saying" (from German *Sage*).

'in' the openness of Being. 'World' is the clearing of Being into which the human being stands out on the basis of his thrown essence."[c] Humanity is claimed by Being as its neighbor, to live as the **shepherd of Being**. Humanity cares for Being in the clearing.

Here we can see the limits of my metaphor. Even if we give up the assumption that there's a reality beyond the appearance, we are likely to assume that things continue to exist outside the spotlight. We wonder where things "are" before they come into the light. And we wonder where the light comes from, who is in charge of it, and who gets to change the color. Perhaps we fall back into thinking humans are the light or in control of the light. Humanity does not create Being or author Truth; it does not even choose to let them be. Heidegger denied there is a subject (God), a magical source, a lighting engineer, shining a light—producing, overseeing, and changing the clearing that calls forth Being. Such efforts lead us into all sorts of paradoxes and back into metaphysics. We have to think otherwise.

Heidegger moved the question into a different, more ontological register to suggest that the clearing is a **gift** without a giver. "It is given." *Es gibt*. While this sounds like the passive voice, it is actually "the middle voice"; its most common use in English is the phrase "It's raining." It is the description of an event, an active happening. We are given the gift of rain (whatever its scientific causes), and we are given the gift of Truth and Being. But how does the gift itself happen? What makes it possible? The clearing is the gift of *Ereignis*, which is the event or eventing of appropriation. *Ereignis* is the primordial gathering together, creating relations out of pure and unrestrained multiplicities or differences, constructing the many possibilities of Being. Once again, let me offer a useful but inadequate metaphor: the quantum universe is the endless production of relations among the fundamental particles and forces. These are defined in positive terms by specific properties and potentialities—akin to the *haecceities*, differences, or "thisnesses" that *Ereignis* gathers. These relations—particular particles and forces in particular proportions—are the foundations of the universe as we know it. They are gifted to us; we are thrown into them. Is it possible that there could have been or even are other universes composed of different particles and forces, in different proportions and relations? Is it possible that there are other clearings, other modes of Being?

One more ontological move to go: the universe is essentially **poiesis**, the pure creativity of language, the endless creation of meaning, which for Heidegger is relationality, expressing itself as *Ereignis*. But how does this creative process of relationing happen? What is the giving of the gift? Heidegger's answer was that it happened in *Saga* (or *Sprache*) as the language in which the stories of the gods and creation are told, in which the gods tell their own stories of creation. It is the language of John 1:1, which reads, "In the beginning was the Word, and the Word was with God, and the Word was God."[d] Remember Baudrillard's premodern simulacrum. *Saga* is the power to create meaning and relationality, Truth and Being, which are all the same.[4]

The real question of ontology is not the "meaning" of Being but the becoming of Being (as meaning or relationality) in the poetics of *Saga*. *Saga* is the voice of the universe. Thus, Language (*Saga*) "is the house of Being. In its home human beings dwell."[e] *Saga* speaks the clearing and brings the gift of an epoch of Being. It discloses, gifts, a world before the speaking of any natural language. As poiesis, in its multiple ways of gathering together, it creates the various modes of the belonging together of Man and World. There is always a disclosure of Truth (existence) before humans speak. This primordial creation of meaning is the ground of the intelligibility of existence, the condition of possibility of all possible meanings of Being, of all possible Truths. To speak metaphorically again, it is as if Heidegger had ontologized culture or discourse.

The gift, however, is not only a clearing but the possibility of other clearings, of other ways of relationing, of being in the world. The result is an ontological deepening of the ethics of care (and possibly of authenticity) in *Being and Time*, which demands being open to the multiplicity of gifts. Heidegger captured this in the words of his favorite poet, Friedrich Hölderlin: "**poetically man dwells**."[f]

What does it mean to say that other clearings are possible? Consider some ontic anecdotes. There are Indigenous people in Peru who talk to the mountains.[g] My wife talks to her plants, and no one is bothered by it; it's not so unusual. But the mountains talk back to the Indigenous people. Undoubtedly, your first response is to assume that this supposed conversation is not real, only a superstition (as opposed to science). Mountains don't talk. But what if they do talk? What if these Indigenous people live in a clearing in which mountains do talk to people? What if this is a different gift?

Or consider the plight of a whale that happened to get separated from its pod and swam into an inlet on the northern Pacific coast of Canada.[h] The bay was inhabited by an Indigenous tribe being driven to extinction by modern development and extraction economies. Their land was being taken, and

---

4 Plato thought poetry had the power to call into being other realities, other kinds of possibilities, making it the enemy of Logos.

they were being killed off. They saw in the whale the spirit of the "founder" of the tribe, whose totem was a whale, returning to lead them in their struggles. Enter Greenpeace activists, who said that the whale would die if it were not returned to its pod. The local tribe said that the whale would not die because it had its people, but they would die if the whale were taken from them. What would you do? Do you follow Greenpeace or the Indigenous people? Heidegger would challenge us: your choice probably has its origins in a particular clearing, a particular mode of the revelation of Truth. Are you so certain that there cannot be other revelations?

Quantum mechanics can appear rather magical—after all, it's not as if anyone has seen a neutrino, a quark, or an antiproton. And many of its assumptions (e.g., quantum entanglements) are well beyond any fantasy. Physicists extrapolate from lines on a photometric plate or numbers in a mathematical dataset to relations that are, for the most part, consistent with a specific clearing. Some might call the faith in the fundamental particles superstition. And let's not even get started on vibrating strings. What if that whale really is, in some other reality, the spirit of that tribe? What if the mountains do talk because their listeners live in a different clearing?

TIME AND THE CRISIS OF BEING

Time figured prominently in Heidegger's thought. In *Being and Time*, he argued that Dasein was time, that it temporalized Being. In his reimagined ontology, Language as *Saga* is not just the happening of Being but also the happening of time; Heidegger ontologized temporality itself. Language is the temporalizing—what Heidegger called the **destiny**—of Being and Truth. The result is a paradox at the heart of Heidegger's ontology: the ontological universality of *poiesis* expresses itself always and only as both an ontological temporality and a historical ontology (a history of the epochs of Being).

Heidegger claimed that humanity was facing (is still facing?) an ontological crisis, which he called "**the oblivion of Being**."[i] He described the contemporary condition of humanity as a **homelessness**,[5] for it had lost sight of Being and Truth as gifts, and as a result, it had closed itself to the *poiesis* of *Saga* and the existence of other clearings, other ways of belonging together in and with the world. This is a crisis unlike any other because humanity no

---

5 Perhaps he thought he was also explaining the rise of fascism and in so doing, perhaps, explaining his own ethical failure.

longer understands that its Truth does not belong to it, that it is not the only one and is not universal. It has forgotten that it lives in the house of Being, as the shepherd of Being. It has lost the capacity to dwell "poetically." That is, people have forgotten that the real lesson of thinking is the possibility of being—and thinking—otherwise.

Heidegger offered a number of descriptions of the crisis and of the clearing in which this crisis had arisen. It is a crisis of both Being and Truth, since they are both realized only in the gift of the clearing. In a sense, it is as if modern thought (starting with the enlightenments) and the broader realities of modernization had come together, in the clearing, in a necessary but particularly disturbing way. The paradox of Heidegger's ethics is that humanity is thrown into a clearing; it is not responsible for the havoc that Truth and Being have wreaked because they speak and perform the truth of the modern clearing.

His earlier hermeneutic of Dasein included an interpretation of the worldhood of the world, which disclosed how the world was always already constitutive of the situatedness of Dasein as a being-in-the-world. He further concluded that the originary existence of this world is equipmentality, being ready to hand. The world presents itself to serve people's purposes and needs. The world is there as resources, to be used (and used up?). Only when it fails to do that, or when it breaks down, do we see the world as objects that exist apart from us, as present at hand.

But he also contrasted his own hermeneutic thinking with the representational nature of modern thought of modernity, which assumes its task is to represent reality, however it was created. The modern understands thinking as picturing the world, and the world as whatever can be successfully pictured. Heidegger said the "fundamental event of the modern age is the conquest of the world as picture."[j] We live in the age of the **world picture**. Modern thought has objectified, secularized, and disenchanted the world, giving itself over to science and reason.

One of the most visible manifestations of the crisis today is the ongoing degradations, partly at the hands of humanity, of the environment; but they are neither new nor only newly visible. Did people not realize for the past three hundred years that they were destroying the earth? Did no one stop to ask about the costs of modernity, and whether the benefits were worth it? There are many examples, spanning centuries and spread across the planet. In the late eighteenth century, the Thames, the major river that runs through London and is a vital source of water for much of England, was so polluted, the smell so bad, that Parliament, located on the river's bank, could not meet.

Did no one observe what industrialization was doing? Did no one notice that coal mining was destroying the mountains and polluting the waterways? Did no one think to question the effects of the various forms of power generation? Did no one consider the consequences of the industrialization of food production, or the technological overpowering of communication and culture? Has modern society ever seen a technology it did not like or was not willing to use, until it was too late?

While Marx would have blamed this mostly on capitalism, Heidegger argued that the crisis of modernity in its many expressions resulted from our ontological relation to the world and the coming together of representation and resource in the modern clearing. Questioning what humanity has been doing to the world would be meaningless, sheer imaginative fantasy, because such questions can only be asked from outside the reality into which we have been thrown.

In "The Question concerning Technology," Heidegger revisited his description of Dasein and, in particular, of the worldhood of the world. He acknowledged that the mode of being-in-the-world he investigated in *Being and Time* was only a single clearing, a single gift of *Ereignis*, a single **epoch of Being**. This clearing provided the ontological ground of the enlightenments and (Euro)modernity. In other words, he historicized both Dasein and the world. He did not dispute his earlier analysis but merely limited its claim to truth. Within the clearing of modernity, the world does exist as equipmentality, as a resource, and truth does operate representationally.

I have already talked about the emergence of modernity in previous lectures; more precisely, I have described some of the things that were happening, not quite at the same time or in the same places. Yet the fact that these things (and others) were happening does not explain how the modern—the various modernities—came about, how these developments came together in the ways and places they did or why they came together at all. Yet they did so in ways that provided very specific forms of mutual reinforcement and, lo and behold, modernity came into being. Heidegger rejected the two easiest accounts: contingency and humanism; the former assumes it was accidental, the latter that humanity was responsible.

For Heidegger, the condition of possibility of modernity, of not only these developments but also their ability to forge specific productive relations, was the clearing—the gift—of modernity itself. Enlightenment and modern thought "work" because they *are* describing reality, but it is the reality of a particular clearing, which is but one moment in the destiny of truth, one epoch in a historical ontology. Heidegger put it this way: "The unconcealment of the unconcealed has already come to pass whenever it calls man forth into the modes of revealing allotted to him. When man, in his way, from within unconcealment reveals that which presences, he merely responds to the call of unconcealment even when he contradicts it."[k]

Heidegger ontologized the modern clearing as **technology**; he began by linking technology to an ontological understanding of causality, in which cause is "that to which something is indebted."[l] Cause identifies those forces or beings that are responsible—again, notice a certain ethical resonance—for bringing something into existence. Technology is an event by which something comes into existence. It is a **bringing forth** or unconcealing of Truth. Following Aristotle, Heidegger identified four causes: material, formal, final, and efficient.[6] It is the gathering together of these causes (in and as poiesis) that brings something into the clearing of Being.

Heidegger described the clearing of technology having two demands working in consort: first, a **setting-upon** that gathers Man and World together, constituting Dasein; and second, a **setting-in-order** in which humanity takes responsibility for ordering the worldhood of the world as a **standing reserve** of resources. Humanity exists as the engineers of the world, and the world as equipment to be used. This is the disclosure of the particular way of revealing that is the essence of the modern clearing, which Heidegger calls the *Gestell*, or **Enframing**.

Returning to the environmental crises, the problem is not simply that we search for solutions in new technologies that use up other resources but that we encounter the world as technology. This is the paradox of our destiny, for the **Technological Frame**, a seemingly self-destructive mode of Being unable to sustain itself, precedes both humanity and the disenchanted world. It is the Truth into which we have been thrown and for which we are not responsible. This may sound rather pessimistic, because what we need is a different gift of a clearing, a new epoch of Being, another way of being in the world. But that is not something we can bring about, so are we supposed to just wait for it to come?

As if this were not bad enough, Heidegger thought the real threat of the *Gestell*, the real "danger as such," is that the *Gestell* conceals the giv-

6 In other essays, Heidegger talks about the constitution of any Being as a four-folding, which gathers together the four causes as expressions of the possibilities of the particular clearing: material cause = earth, formal cause = sky, final cause = divinities, and efficient cause = mortals. See Heidegger, "The Thing" and "Building Dwelling Thinking," in *Poetry, Language, Thought*, 163–86, 143–61, respectively.

ing of the gift—the unconcealing—of Being itself. Consequently, humanity can no longer encounter itself as spoken to in *Saga*, as dwelling poetically. Enframing drives out the possibility of other clearings: there can be no alternative. And by concealing the very *poiesis* that lets Being come forth into presencing, the *Gestell* conceals the gifting itself; it blocks the "shining-forth" and "holding-sway" of Truth. Humanity's "ownmost possibility of freedom" is possible only if we can open ourselves to see the *Gestell* as a gift. Thus, Heidegger concludes: "It is precisely in Enframing, which threatens to sweep man away into ordering as the supposed single way of revealing, and so thrust man into the danger of the surrender of his free essence—it is precisely in this extreme danger that the innermost indestructible belonging of man within granting may come to light, provided that we, for our part, begin to pay heed to the coming to presence of technology."[m]

ART AND DWELLING POETICALLY

Unless we re-cover (unconceal) our existence as poetic dwellers, we will not receive the possibility of other worlds. The universe may be offering us other gifts, other clearings, but we cannot hear them, do not have the possibility of hearing them, because we are caught inside the world picture of the *Gestell*. Yet Heidegger was not, in the last instance, a pessimist. There is always the possibility of recovering the knowledge of our own essence as "poetic dwelling," and of opening ourselves to *Saga*. In fact, it is more than a possibility; it is always and already a reality in our lives, even in the *Gestell*. One of the paradoxes of modernity is that alongside its worship of science and technology (and money), people continue to care deeply about creativity and art. What is the power of art? In "The Origin of the Work of Art," Heidegger argued that art is the happening of *poiesis* itself; the work of art both discloses another clearing and performs an opening to *Saga*, to dwelling poetically.[n] Referring to language as the house of Being, he had already declared, "Those who think and those who create with words are the guardians of the home."[o] But he did not limit himself to the arts of the word, painting, sculpture, architecture, and so on. Art, anywhere *poiesis* is given voice or made present, pushes us to question the certainty of the *Gestell*, and thus return us to "**the piety of thought**,"[p] which is the key to facing the "danger as such."

Heidegger began the "Origin" essay by **deconstructing** the various traditions of understanding the work of art: treating it as a thing with fixed qualities or essences, assuming it is a representation of reality, assigning its power to the genius of its creator, or making judgment into a relativistic matter of convention or a subjective matter of taste. The origin of the work of art is not in the object or the subject, or even in the relation between them; it is in the **work-being** of the work of art itself. Whether something is—or is not—art depends on what it does. What work does the work of art do? What is happening in the work of art? For Heidegger, the work of art opens up its own clearing—and in this clearing, the belonging together of Man and World is illuminated as a possibility. The work of art discloses its own truth, in which the very possibility of relationality, of a belonging together, is made present. Thus, "in the work, the happening of truth is at work."[9] The work of art is the clearing, disclosing Truth in another possibility of Being, and consequently, it discloses the horizon of the historical possibilities of Being. That is, the work of art opens humanity to the happening of Truth as poetically dwelling.

How does the work of art work? What is its work-being? Heidegger argued that art stages the strife between the **setting up of a world** and the **setting forth of the earth**. One might loosely, and I emphasize loosely, think of this as Heidegger's attempt to rethink—to ontologize—the modern, constitutive opposition between culture and nature. The setting up of a world refers to the history of the clearings, the modes of openness and Truth, in which humanity has stood, including the *Gestell*. It is the presencing of the different modes of Being as the ground of relationality and the intelligibility of meaning; it is the history of the ways Being becomes accessible (as meaningful) to Man in different epochs. It is the happening of meaning that precedes humanity, as what grants humanity access to Being and Truth. For example, Heidegger contemplated Vincent van Gogh's *A Pair of Shoes*, looking beyond its materiality to the way in which the shoes themselves open up the world to which they belong.

The setting forth of the earth is not about the earth as a cosmological, astronomical, agronomical, or technological object. Earth is the ground of the materiality of Being as it appears in every epoch. In the essay on technology, it is the "stuffness" (in Greek, *physis*) as that which "shelters" humanity, as that on which humanity dwells, allowing itself to become the site of the world. For example, Heidegger noted how the ancient Greek temple discloses the solidity and spatiality of the earth on which it rested in specific ways.

The work of art, in its very Being, is the performance or happening of the strife between these—between the "materiality" of the earth and the organization of the world, where the clearing of Truth is disclosed. And it is there—in the between—that humanity dwells. Thus, while a particular work of art may disclose a particular way of Being (a clearing), what truly shines forth in the work of art is the very possibility of openness, of dwelling poetically. And in this possibility, art offers us a way, perhaps the only way, of escaping the self-destructiveness of the *Gestell*.

Heidegger's path out of enlightenment and modern thought took him from the hermeneutic of Dasein to the historical ontology of Being to the *poiesis* of *Saga*. Through it all, he retained a phenomenological logic: he not only privileged meaning even as he desubjectified it but also maintained the fundamental status of the hermeneutic relation. His work offered the most sophisticated statement of a phenomenological ontology. For many intellectuals, especially in France, it had to be engaged: Did Heidegger successfully move beyond the transcendence implicit in modern thought? Did his increasingly ontological turn suffice to escape Kant's humanism? Did the hermeneutic relation escape the power of the negative? Many of the thinkers yet to be discussed found themselves, whether explicitly or implicitly, wrestling with Heidegger while, at the same time, having to come to terms with Heidegger's commitment to Nazism.

NOTES

a. Sartre, *Existentialism Is a Humanism*, 20.

b. Heidegger, "Letter on Humanism," in *Pathmarks*, 252.

c. Heidegger, "Letter," 266.

d. *The Bible: Authorized King James Version*.

e. Heidegger, "Letter," 239.

f. Heidegger, ". . . Poetically Man Dwells . . . ," in *Poetry, Language, Thought*, 211–29; taken from Hölderlin, "In Lovely Blue," in *Hymns and Fragments*, 247–53.

g. De la Cadena, *Earth Beings*.

h. Blaser, "Political Ontology."

i. Heidegger, "Letter," 250.

j. Heidegger, "Age of the World Picture," in *Question concerning Technology*, 134.

k. Heidegger, "The Question concerning Technology," in *Question concerning Technology*, 19.

l. Heidegger, "Question concerning Technology," 7.

m. Heidegger, "Question concerning Technology," 32.

n. Heidegger, "Origin of the Work of Art," in *Poetry, Language, Thought*, 15–87.

o. Heidegger, "Letter," 239.

p. Heidegger, "Question concerning Technology," 35.

q. Heidegger, "Origin of the Work of Art," 58.

Poststructuralism and Derrida

Alongside Martin Heidegger's antihumanist ontology, structuralism's anti-humanism was gaining visibility and power in the 1960s, yet it was also facing criticisms from within. In 1967, Jacques Derrida published *Speech and Phenomena* (on Edmund Husserl), *Writing and Difference*, and *Of Grammatology*; Roland Barthes published "The Death of the Author," followed in 1970 by *S/Z* and in 1973 by *The Pleasure of the Text*. In 1969, Julia Kristeva published *Desire in Language* and Hélène Cixous published *The Exile of James Joyce*. These disruptive feminist works were followed by Cixous's "The Laugh of the Medusa" (1975) and Luce Irigaray's *Speculum of the Other Woman* (1974) and *This Sex Which Is Not One* (1977). Such thinkers were described as "poststructuralists," although it was not a label they had used; rather, it was invented for them, largely by American and British academics, with strong support from publishers.

Generally speaking, the poststructuralists offer two fundamental challenges to structuralism, even while continuing to articulate a diacritical philosophy of relations. First, they embrace the **primacy of the signifier**, against the assumed existence and privilege of the "signified." Second, they understand diacritics to operate through the **sliding of the signifier**, against the assumed closure and stability of structuralist systems. They saw diacritical relations processually.

Recall that the signified is a position on a plane of difference understood as conceptual value. But this suggests the existence, prior to any organization, of an amorphous conceptual universe. Although structuralists rejected enlightenment humanism by desubjectifying this privileged realm, the poststructuralists argue that by assuming the ontological reality of consciousness, not as a social-historical fact but as a universal condition of possibility of language, their challenge to humanism failed. This cloudlike reality had to preexist any system of signs. If this transcendental assumption was unwarranted, then the signified could be understood as an effect of the signifiers. Consider the dictionary game: You pick a word to look up, and you are presented with a number of synonyms, each of which can be looked up in turn. While the degrees of separation may vary, you will inevitably be returned to the original word. You look up A, and the dictionary says B, and B leads you to C, which leads you to D, and you end up back at A. The "meaning" of a sign is always and only given by another sign or, more accurately, by another signifier. There is no other reality (a signified), only signifiers. Hence, the primacy of the signifier.[1]

Further, the poststructuralists argued that sign systems are open, changing, and unstable. For some, this meant worrying less about deep, transcendental structures and more about the ongoing processes of signs in use. But all agreed that langue—now undifferentiated from *langage*—is the constant movement or production of signifiers, and since each signifier is defined only by its difference from all others, those that precede it and those that follow it, it is difference that is constantly being produced. A sign system involves only a sliding of signifiers, a constant process of the production of signifiers as difference.

The signified is only the product of this movement. To use yet another inadequate metaphor: Imagine a game of musical chairs in which, instead of people, signifiers are moving in a circle to the music. When the music stops,

---

1 Charles Saunders Peirce had made a similar argument.

some signifiers sit, but some cannot. We might say that some signifiers slide under others; the "seated" signifiers play the role of signifieds. The signified is a signifier occupying a different kind of position in a diacritical system, located "under" an (imaginary) line separating the Sr and the Sd (now Sr/Sd rather than Sd/Sr). This line, often referred to as a **slash**, marks a difference of position that appears as a distinction between the signifier and the signified. There is no ontological realm of signifieds, no independent reality of meanings or consciousness.

The obvious next question is where the slash comes from. Or, carrying the metaphor to its logical conclusion, who stops the music? For the poststructuralists, the slash is the mark of the subject, which does not mean there is a subject outside the sliding of signifiers who stops the music and produces the difference between signifier and signified. Émile Benveniste, Louis Althusser, and Jacques Lacan were already arguing that subjectivity is an effect of the system of signs, with langue as its author; the individual is represented in the system as a signifier, which is the real existence of the subject. Similarly, the poststructuralists argue that the individual is interpellated into language as a Sr at the place of the slash, as the author of the difference between signifier and signified. The subject *is* the slash as a signifier. The production of the slash constitutes the subject as that which puts the signifier into the position of a signified, constituting the difference. There is no subject outside the sliding of signifiers.

Recall that in structuralism, the sign has a positive identity all its own that defines it as being exactly what it is. According to poststructuralists, this attribution of identity invokes a logic of **essentialism**, which assumes that something, some relation, has a necessary, guaranteed, and even possibly universal, seamless **unity (or "unicity")** and totality. Essentialism privileges identity over difference and multiplicity, necessity over contingency. Consider how common essentialism is in our everyday thinking: when we assume that there is some stable way of defining various identity categories, such as women, Black, person of color, working-class. But what is the essence of being a woman or Black? Is it a matter of genetics, physiology, behavior, culture, experience, history? What does it mean to be working-class? Is it a matter of employment, income, culture, politics? What do you have to be to be an "American"? Is it a matter of one's place of birth, heritage, beliefs and values, skin color, religion, patriotism, soil and blood? What are we doing when we neatly divide the political terrain into three relatively homogeneous camps: the right, the left, and the center? We are essentialists whenever we assume that there is an authentic way of being something—proper behavior, beliefs, values, tastes, politics—which, if not actualized, means either that one is in-authentic, colonized, living in false consciousness, or simply deceiving one-self. The poststructuralists conclude that the logic of essentialism is a key element of modern thought; one might ironically say that essentialism is an essential aspect of most modern deep theories, although it was present in many premodern modes of thinking (including religions) as well.

The poststructuralists propose instead a radical **antiessentialism**. The claims that something has its own essential identity, that any relation has an essential unity, that two elements have a guaranteed correspondence, that there are seamless totalities, that anything is universal and transparent are unsustainable. Such claims always come up against the difference that under-mines them, the incompleteness that challenges "the solace of closure." Every claim to identity or unity is illusory, at best a construction that is always temporary, fragile, waiting to be undone by its own logic.

Yet many poststructuralists recognize that you sometimes need to make reference to the signified or the subject. They may not be ontologically real, but we still live and think as if they are. They still operate as necessary formal functions within the logic of the reality we inhabit. Jacques Derrida, inspired by Heidegger, suggested putting such unreal but necessary concepts **under erasure** rather than negating them or flipping their privilege. In his writ-ings, Derrida literarily x's out the subject, the signified, and so on (e.g., Sd), graphically marking their status as only **traces** of the sliding of signifiers. But this may sound easier than it is, for in some ways we cannot do without these ascriptions of consciousness (but we cannot have that).

DIFFÉRANCE

Jacques Derrida was the leading and most visible figure associated with post-structuralism and its most articulate spokesperson. He was one of the most influential intellectuals of the late twentieth century. He also was one of the most controversial. It is not just that people disagreed with him on some points, but that they questioned the very legitimacy of his project. His ar-gument was a devastating blow against enlightenment and modern ways of thinking. Wherever one stands, Derrida cannot be ignored.

Derrida was born in El Biar, Algeria, on July 15, 1930, of Sephardic Jewish parents—once again blurring the meaning of "French," especially given that his adolescence was marked by the anti-Semitic laws of the Vichy regime. He moved to Paris in 1949 to attend university. His earliest research was on Husserl and phenomenology. After teaching briefly at the Sorbonne, he obtained a position at the prestigious École normale supérieure in 1964 and then at the École des hautes études en sciences sociales in 1984. In 1983, he cofounded the International College of Philosophy. Beginning in 1986, he also taught at the University of California, Irvine, starting a practice of joint appointments across continents at US universities. He was a prolific writer and lecturer, publishing over forty books and hundreds of essays and lectures. Among the most influential, besides those mentioned earlier, one might include *Dissemination* (1972), *Glas* (on Hegel, 1974), *Of Spirit* (on Heidegger, 1987), *Specters of Marx* (1993), and *The Politics of Friendship* (1994). And he was something of a national media star in France; strikingly mediagenic, he frequently appeared on French television. He died in Paris on October 9, 2004.

Derrida's theorizing is unlike any we have encountered thus far, although it shares some qualities with Friedrich Nietzsche's, whose influence he acknowledged in *Spurs*. He did not offer a system per se, and he did not attempt to answer the major philosophical questions that defined modern thought. Derrida's argument was both logical and tropological (figurative). Derrida identified a specific insoluble paradox—an *aporia*—or impasse at the heart of enlightenment and post-enlightenment thought, and ultimately at the heart of every modern argument or text. Without meaning to belittle his contribution and influence, one might say that Derrida was a one-trick pony. He had one absolutely brilliant, absolutely stunning, absolutely devastating argument to make, and he made it over and over and over again in a variety of contexts, for a variety of problems, texts, concepts, and so on. But in each context, for each problem or question he faced, his logic had to take on a different conceptual configuration. And in each case, he gave the figure of his argument a different name (*différance, deconstruction, textuality, arche-writing, pharmakon, supplement, dissemination, undecidability*, and so on).

As we'll see, each figure opens up some identity and/or difference to the alterity that is its very condition of possibility. The very fact that Derrida found it necessary to proliferate such terms is itself an effect and expression of the logic of his position: a refusal to claim any stable identity for his concepts, while at the same time insisting that each occurrence was not simply an instantiation of a single concept, such as différance; rather, they all might be described as expressions of différance differentiating itself. Don't worry—all will be explained but never to the point of satisfying the expectations of modern thought.

Let me use Derrida's early critique of Husserl to illustrate this logic.[a] Derrida starts by correctly identifying Husserl's premise: truth is predicated on the appearance—the presence—of the phenomenon in consciousness.

Husserl assumed that the phenomenon appears in consciousness as it is; its identity is given, transparent, guaranteed. But Derrida demonstrated that the phenomenon cannot be a simple thing already present, existing apart from all relations, outside any structure of difference that would make the phenomenon identifiable. The phenomenon has to have its own genesis; it has to have come from somewhere. And that origin, whatever it is, is not present to consciousness with or alongside the phenomenon. The existence of the phenomenon in consciousness depends on the existence of something else, which is its origin and therefore is different from it, and which is not present in consciousness. But whatever that is, it too must have an origin, which is different, which is not present in consciousness. And so on. To put it simply: Derrida demonstrated that the phenomenon cannot be a "presence," a unitary, self-identical event existing outside of any structure of difference. This **originary complication** or **complexity** constitutes any moment of identity.[b] In this case, the phenomenon only exists by virtue of its participation and location in this originary complexity, a system of differences, which Derrida later called **différance**, a neologism that combines *difference* and *deferral*. (Once, when Derrida was on French television explaining his philosophy, his mother called in to complain about her son's poor spelling.)

Différance is not simply a structure of differences; it is the process of the endless production of difference, the sliding of the signifiers.[c] Every time you try to stabilize it, to grab hold of a particular term or even the process itself, to make present the originary complexity, you can't; it is always deferred, pushed further along, just ahead of wherever you are. Whatever you focus on, whatever you grasp, will be nothing but a trace of the originary complexity, of différance. Rather than a simple negation of presence, it is the ongoing, unstable, and ever-changing process of differentiating that is always deferred.

Différance exists a priori, entailing that any difference is both inadequate and necessary. Derrida was not offering a metaphysics of absence. Différance is the difference in the heart of identity that undermines and destabilizes both presence and absence. Rather, each is granted only in the very difference; each is always already contaminated by the other. This is a differencing that precedes both identity and difference, an unpresentable and unrepresentable other, which can only be known through its traces. It dismantles the presence, the very difference between presence and absence, between identity and difference, yet one can never get hold of it. Hence, any truth, any identity, any stable unity, any totality—including the claim of a single, stable difference—is always out of reach. You think you have grabbed hold of something that has an identity or essence—the phenomenon, the hermeneutic relation, langue—but all you are holding is a trace, like Friday's footprints in *Robinson Crusoe.*

LOGOCENTRISM

Derrida argued that enlightenment and modern thought were built on the foundational assumption that truth and reality are to be found in that which exists in itself, that transparently gives itself as being exactly what it is, as an identity or essence. He called this *logocentrism*, or the **metaphysics of presence**.[d] *Logos*, a key term in classical Greek philosophy (and in rhetoric, where it is contrasted with Ethos, or credibility, and Pathos, or emotion), generally refers to reason, meaning, and logic. Logocentrism generally works by locating a term in a relation of difference while assuming that each term has an identity apart from that difference, and then privileging one term as that which is present. Thus, logocentrism refers to the privileging of identity as/and presence.

To get beyond logocentrism, it is not sufficient to make the present absent (negating the presence), or by affirming absence, or by reversing the roles, making the absent present (and dominant) and the present absent (or subordinate). These tactics would simply end up creating another presence: the object instead of the subject, the signifier instead of the signified, transgression instead of the law. Presence must be rethought beyond all essentialism, beyond all logocentrism.

We need to **deconstruct** the primacy of presence, that is, to destabilize any moment of presence by relocating it in its originary complexity, to show that presence itself is nothing more than an effect of différance. Deconstruction demonstrates that each term of the difference presupposes and requires the other, each refers to that which is not present in itself, to that which is only a trace of the other. Moreover, deconstruction demonstrates not only that identity is always different from itself but also that any claim to identity or unity always undermines and undoes itself. There is always an aporia, a gap, an absence, that is the very condition of possibility of the identity or unicity. That is, any term exists only by existing outside itself. And any claim to or experience of a coherent identity is only accomplished by excluding its own conditions of possibility, its own otherness to itself.

But I need to correct myself, for deconstruction is not something that we as subjects need to do, or will to do. Rather, language (texts) as différance is always and already deconstructing its own claims of identity and difference, presence and absence. It is the text that is the site and agency of deconstruction. This is why Derrida's arguments are usually offered in meticulous, close readings of a text. It is not Derrida deconstructing Husserl's phenomenology; it is Derrida allowing the text to show us that it (Husserl's phenomenology) deconstructs itself. Derrida's attentive reading takes us to that point—the aporia—at which the phenomenology undermines its own claim to presence, unicity, and so on.

That also explains my earlier characterization of the multiplicity of figures in which Derrida identifies the workings of logocentrism. The figure is chosen by the text and the specificity of the way in which it deconstructs itself. (The wand chooses the wizard.)

Logocentrism has two primary expressions. First, it is the presentation of any **transcendental signifier**, any term the identity of which is offered as some final and ultimate Truth, like class in Marx, or spirit in Hegel, or consciousness in Husserl, or even the concept of a transcendental signifier itself. A transcendental term claims to have a simple unity or indivisible totality that is indisputably present in and as itself. There are many such transcendentals in modern thought: the subject, signified, law, meaning, and so on. But such transcendentals are constituted by denying their place in a prior constitutive relation. They are lifted out of a **binary relation of opposition**.

This leads me to the second expression of logocentrism: in such binarisms, one of the terms is always privileged; it is taken to be present, and to present itself as given, complete, self-enclosed, and self-identical. The other term is treated as derivative, functionally absent, or defined only by its subordination to the first, privileged term. There are many examples of this privileging of presence: the subject (over the object), consciousness (over the body), experience (over abstraction), the event (over structure), interiority (over exteriority), the signified (over the signifier), performance (over script), man (over woman), white (over Black).

For example: Why do we think that face-to-face communication is better than so-called mediated communication, including writing? We tell millennials to put down their phones, to stop playing video games, or to get off social media, and instead to go out and interact with real people. (Of course, previous generations said the same thing to their children about, for example, early novels, comic books, or television.) Why are the interactions one has through mediated communication—emailing, texting, participating in multiplayer online games, or even reading a book—somehow less real, less authentic, less valuable? Face-to-face or interpersonal communication is somehow more valuable, more real, more ontologically robust than mediated communication, presumably because in speech, the subject, consciousness, identity, is present to us. Think of how we value live music over recorded music even though, increasingly, live performances have to do a lot of work to reproduce the sound of the recording itself.

Speech is seen as the site of a plenitude or fullness of meaning, as if the voice of the speaker was the presence of consciousness itself made transparent to its other, which is privileged over writing (or media, for that matter). And, more generally, meaning (the concept, the signified) claims to present itself to thought without the mediation of the signifier, which is treated as a mere veil ("mere rhetoric"), exterior to meaning, that has to be torn aside. In either case, if the signifier or the writing refuses to be ignored, then it becomes an alienating interruption of the presencing of meaning. This is most visible when confronting the transgressions of logocentrism: How do we respond to someone who prefers reading the sports scores to watching the event, or someone who prefers to watch the game on television rather than go to the game, or someone who reads the reviews instead of seeing the performance?

Most of Derrida's writings deconstruct particular instances or regions of the metaphysics of presence, which is both a relation of power and the formal condition of the possibility of relations of power. For example, we treat man as presence and woman as the absent other. We treat white as presence and Black as the absent other. We treat the middle class as presence and the working class as the absent other. Consider the relation of the terms *man* and *woman*. The essentialism of common sense, as well as a lot of theoretical and political life, assumes that each names the identity of a specific unity (e.g., the set of all men), which can be characterized by its own necessary and universal traits. But the structuralists had already demonstrated that the terms are defined only within a system of difference: man is not woman, and woman is not man. Each term serves as the constitutive other, the negation in a diacritical system. Derrida took this logic of difference further: If man is not woman, then woman is part of the constitutive existence of man and, so, man already includes woman; woman is already "inside" (the meaning of) man. But then man is part of the constituent existence of woman, because woman is not man so that man is already "inside" (the meaning of) woman. Thus, man is not woman, not man, not woman, not man, not woman, not man—and the sliding of signifiers, différance, continues. That is, rather than thinking constitutive otherness, Derrida argued for the more complex entanglement of differences, so that one cannot even separate or isolate a singular relation of difference.

We can deconstruct the male/female binarism, but what happens next? Some deconstructionists argue that if there is no essence, no singular identity of woman, then there cannot be a feminist movement. How can you have feminism if there's no universally shared identity to woman? But that's not Derrida's position, which Julia Kristeva articulated clearly.[e] She argued that the point of feminism is not to reverse the binary relationship, to put women in the dominant position of power; it is to undermine the difference itself, to see that the difference itself is part of the originary complexity. This doesn't mean you can do away with male and female, and it doesn't mean you can magically erase power struggles between men and women. It means that you start conceptualizing them outside the terms of logocentrism, of identity and difference. It's not that either there is woman or there is no woman; it is not a choice between A, not A, or not not A. The difference between man and woman—as well as their existence within a specific binary relation—is a construction, a consequence of the différance itself. You cannot deny the terms or the relation, but you can rethink them, embrace their multiplicities, relocate them in their originary complexities, and use them in new and creative—antiessentialist—ways.

A second example will demonstrate that any effort to embrace the full presence of some term or the unicity of a relation is always doomed to failure because there is always more, always something left out, always some excess. Consider: What is the identity of a text? Logocentrism assumes that a text has a fixed identity, a beginning and an end, bound between the covers, as it were. The text is a finite and usually linear string of signifiers, making it a material unity. But the text also has a meaning present within it, which is what truly gives the text its identity (e.g., often identified with the intention of the author or the authority of the critic). Derrida argued that the chains of signifiers are not confined to "the words on the page." A text always refers to and locates itself in chains that extend beyond its supposed boundaries; it always already includes other texts that have been or can be connected to it. Kristeva referred to this as **intertextuality**, an interweaving of signifiers and, ultimately, of differences.[f]

For Derrida, **supplementarity** describes the condition of any text, always reaching beyond itself, always defined by that excess that is not included in it. No one ever reads William Shakespeare's *Hamlet* without already being caught up in the play of signifiers and texts into which it is bound, including its many interpretations. No one ever reads *Hamlet* as if there were no other texts in the world. How you read it may depend on the particular intertextuality in which you locate it. There is no text of *Hamlet* that can be essentially identified and interpreted to find its true and only meaning; there is only the intertextuality, the supplementarity, that keeps it endlessly producing signifiers and, hence, appearing always to have a meaning. Further, Derrida argued, a text seeds itself (like Johnny Appleseed fertilizing the barren fields) into textualities outside its apparently proper place, in a process of **dissemination**. Meaning, which we know to be the sliding of signifiers, is always spreading itself, making it impossible to ever grasp it in some pure state of existence and identity. The processes of definition, identification, and interpretation can never be completed; hence, one is always left abandoned to a condition of **undecidability**.[g]

Let me offer a personal example: I used to write about rock and roll, but I never wrote about a particular song, album, or concert. In Derridean terms, in order to write about a single text, I would have to assume it was a presence, with an identity, an interiority of its own. But no one listens to a piece of music by itself; the identity, the meaning, the pleasure of particular music depends on intertextual connections—ultimately differences. And that supplementarity is partly defined by the ever-changing system of differences of the universe of popular musics. A particular musical text or performance is intertextually citing all sorts of other musics (as well as visual imagery, literary references, political challenges, etc.). It is part of larger fields of textuality or différance even as it is itself disseminated across the fields. Anything I would write would be an attempt to hold back the supplementarity and undecidability of meaning and experience by claiming a privileged subjectivity that corresponded to my identity as a critic. And that seemed disingenuous.

TEXTUALITY AND ONTOLOGY

This would all be rather interesting and possibly useful but not so earthshattering as to be described as a revolution that undermines the history of modern (if not Western) thought. But Derrida took one more step, going where no one—at last no other structuralist and possibly no other poststructuralist—had gone before. Derrida ontologized his theory of différance.[2] Rather than just a theory of sign systems or textuality, it is, in a way, a theory of everything, at least everything within human realms. Everything that is, is only possible as what it is by virtue of its existence as a trace of différance. "Reality" is only an economy of traces, of that differencing that is always deferred. Derrida famously claimed that "there is no outside-text," which suggests that there is nothing outside **textuality**.[h] This has often been

---

2 Both Heidegger and Derrida end up being suspicious of the term *ontology*.

mistakenly interpreted as saying that there is nothing outside of texts and language, a common enough claim among some less ironically totalizing poststructuralists. But Derrida argued that différance describes—as much as one can "describe"—the creativity of the universe and the production of reality. That is, rather than denying materiality, he refused to embrace the binary of language and materiality, or to make materiality into a new presence (or absence, for that matter; remember Heidegger's *physis* from lecture 24).

On this reading, Derrida's deep theory might be seen as a critical revision of Heidegger's ontological turn after the *Kehre*. For both, the relation/difference between identity and difference is itself produced. Heidegger described the creativity, the poiesis, of the universe as the *Saga* of *Ereignis*, an endless gathering together, the ongoing production of relations, which then becomes the gift of Being; these belongings-together are the primordial elements of Being in Heidegger, preceding the difference between terms. But for Derrida, the creativity of the universe is not a positive production of relations (unities) but a negative production of endless differences. Derrida argued that the positivity of the relation in Heidegger was itself an expression of the logocentric metaphysics of presence as the very negation of différance.[i] For that reason, Heidegger did not just fail to escape the logic of the enlightenments; he fell back into it. His desire to critique the legacy of the enlightenments led him to try to overcome it by becoming ever more ontological. But he ended up reproducing a logocentric metaphysics of presence.

On the other hand, Derrida's ontology was not simply a metaphysics of absence. If we take différance as either a fetishism of absence or the affirmation (making present) of difference, if we give it a substantive existence, or if we make it itself into the positivity of a "real" process that can be grasped and rendered somehow visible—rather than as something available only in its traces—then différance would become yet another iteration of a metaphysics of presence.

But, like Heidegger, Derrida also remained imprisoned by the enlightenments, within the space of Kant's thought. Both Heidegger and Derrida offered an ontology of phenomenal reality, which led each into a different way of defining and privileging Language, whether *Saga* as *poiesis* or textuality as différance. While Derrida accused Heidegger's *Saga* of simply replacing Kant's transcendental subject, and while Derrida may have thought of différance as being immanent to the existence of the phenomenon, it can too easily take on a quasi-transcendental status of its own. Derrida, of course, would then have had to deconstruct the very difference between immanence and transcendence, and then put transcendence under erasure. But the problem goes even deeper. Derrida cannot escape the very aporia he identified in logocentrism.

Consider what it means to escape from something: it assumes that there is an inside and an outside to that thing; it assumes a border separating the interiority and the exteriority—and poststructuralism is, in a sense, all about borders. An obvious opportunity for deconstruction! Interiority is a very powerful signifier of presence that is visible all over the place—subjectivity, home, nation. And what's not interior is somehow bad or other. The interiority is always safe and valuable. The outside is threatening and problematic. But interiority is defined by its difference from exteriority. The interior is not the exterior, which means that exteriority is already inhabiting—inside—interiority. Interiority is already contaminated by exteriority because it is defined as the not exterior. Now, the exterior is defined by its not being interior, which means that the exterior is contaminated by, inhabited by, the interior. The interior is contaminated by the exterior, which is contaminated by the interior, which is contaminated by the exterior, which is contaminated by the interior, and so on, which can only point to, only be a trace of, the originary complexity that can never be captured because it is not a factually existing process that can be stopped. The very desire or effort to escape the interiority into an exteriority is impossible and serves only to reinscribe the logocentrism that removes the interior from its originary complexity.

The very nature of logocentrism as a logic means that it is impossible to escape it, for the very effort to critique and escape it can only be framed and made comprehensible in logocentric terms. The very desire to get outside of the enlightenments throws Derrida back into the logocentric logic of the enlightenments. The very argument that undermines enlightenment ways of thinking thrusts him back into the very same space of thought of the enlightenments. The desire to create an anti-enlightenment deep theory that would locate thinking outside the enlightenments has already constructed a totality, an identity, an interiority—a presence. It (re)constructs a new binary of identity and difference, the very formal condition of thought (logic) that we are trying to escape.

That's the trick of Derridean philosophy. It's a brilliant critique of enlightenment thought, one that can be brought to bear on every category, identity, relation, totality, and so on, for any unity assumes its own presence. Derrida could follow its logic to its own deconstruction, and there the story ends. He could not—did not imagine it as a viable possibility—construct an alternative deep theory, except that of always following logic to its self-destruction, to the erasure of its own presence. But, in fact, Derrida's project was never to negate enlightenment and modern thought in favor of something else but to deconstruct it, thereby refusing to reject it or render it absent. It was the unconcealing, to use Heidegger's language, of différance as that which can never be unconcealed. By acknowledging this limit, his failure becomes the very proof of his critique of logocentrism. This is the aporia, the strangely unavoidable, self-perpetuating trap that Derrida identified. Logocentrism is the trap that catches us all. To use a line from the song "Hotel California" by the Eagles, "You can check out any time you like / But you can never leave."[j] Or, as Joshua the computer says at the end of *WarGames*, "The only winning move is not to play."[k]

If Lacan's thought arrived at a hermeneutics of failure (this is not a criticism but a limit), Derrida's ended in what I might call a deep theory of failure, albeit one that recognizes its own necessary failure (and the fact that this failure becomes necessary is itself a further iteration of that failure). Derrida's ontology is a deep theory of the impossible necessity of failure.

In fact, the condition of possibility of the efficacy of any notion of presence is its impossibility or failure. It is accomplished only by a necessary exclusion or concealing of the originary complexity. Consider that the very possibility of communicating meaning between subjects (which Derrida somewhat naively takes to be the definition of communication) is predicated on the inability to make present the absence or, better, the difference that makes meaning possible.[l] That is to say, for Derrida, the very possibility of communication is its necessary failure—the failure of the unicity of language and meaning. Its success depends on its ability to hide the difference that makes the appearance of presence appear. So, the very possibility of communication depends on the fact that we can't actually communicate. We can only communicate that which is the trace of the message.

And yet, despite the pessimism that one might expect to emerge from failure, from the fact that the only guarantee available is that of failure, Derrida offers an optimistic deep theory of the open-ended future. That the production of difference is open, ongoing, constant, and undecidable means that the future is always unknowable, still to be written, never guaranteed. And the unknowability of the future—this hope—is what Derrida sometimes called "communism" or "democracy to come."[m]

NOTES

    a. See Derrida, *Writing and Difference*; Derrida, *Speech and Phenomena*.

    b. Derrida, *Problem of Genesis*.

c. Derrida, *"Différance,"* in *Margins of Philosophy*, 1–27.

d. Derrida, *Of Grammatology*.

e. Kristeva, "Women's Time."

f. Kristeva, *Desire in Language*, 64–91.

g. Derrida, *Dissemination*.

h. Derrida, *Of Grammatology*, 158.

i. Derrida, *Of Spirit*.

j. Eagles, "Hotel California."

k. Badham, *WarGames*.

l. Derrida, *Margins of Philosophy*, 307–30.

m. Derrida, *Specters of Marx*.

Deleuze

Gilles Deleuze has been the most influential figure of the ontological turn, seeding a wide range of interpretations and followers. He offered an alternative ontology of reality, built out of his construction of a **minor history** of modern thought, while taking up imagery and concepts from contemporary science. But let me warn you up front: put aside everything you think, and get ready to enter a very strange universe, both conceptually and linguistically. I have been reading Deleuze for decades, and while I think I understand his way of thinking, I cannot claim to grasp everything he does with it.

He was born on January 18, 1925, in Paris, and committed suicide in Paris on November 4, 1995, as he faced the increasingly disabling effects of respiratory illnesses he had suffered since youth, no doubt exacerbated by his chain-smoking. He lived most of his life in Paris and rarely spoke of his private life partly because he claimed to believe in "secrecy" but also because, as he commented, "Arguments from one's own privileged experience are bad and reactionary arguments."[a] Still, by all accounts, he led a rather normal, middle-class life with one visible eccentricity: he had extremely long fingernails.[1]

Deleuze taught at several universities and institutions (including the Sorbonne, the Centre national de la recherche scientifique, and Lyon); in 1969, he was invited by Michel Foucault to teach at the experimental University of Paris VIII (Vincennes), where he remained until his retirement in 1987. He published twenty-four single-authored books (starting with *Empiricism and Subjectivity* in 1953): about philosophers, including the Stoics, Gottfried Wilhelm Leibniz, Baruch Spinoza, David Hume, Immanuel Kant, Friedrich Nietzsche, Henri Bergson, and Foucault; about artists, including Marcel Proust, Franz Kafka, and Francis Bacon, as well as two volumes on cinema; and about particular concepts that drew on an extraordinary range of philosophers, writers, and artists. He also cowrote seven books with Félix Guattari.

Deleuze often elaborated his thought through interpretations (or, to varying degrees, misinterpretations) of other thinkers. He admitted to "sodomizing" those he drew on, either ventriloquizing them as Deleuzean avant Deleuze or setting them up as antagonists against whom he could define himself. Often his misreadings focused on a single key Deleuzean concept or argument. Consequently, the field of modern thought became what he would call an **immanent field** from which he constructed his processual, relational, and naturalist ontology of immanence.

SPINOZA TRANSFORMED

It is difficult to describe or systematize Deleuze's ontology partly because his vocabularies and arguments changed with his conceptual focus and the author being discussed. Some argue that Deleuze never offered a systematic philosophy, just a set of useful concepts. I will take the middle path by considering key concepts—immanence, becoming, monism, multiplicity, difference, affect or capacity, and the exteriority of relations, elaborated largely through his (mis)readings of others.

Although Deleuze's first foray into ontology was *Empiricism and Subjectivity* (1953), a reading and critique of Hume, his breakthrough moment came in 1968, when he published two books on Spinoza: *Expressionism in Philosophy: Spinoza* and *Difference and Repetition*. Before I discuss Deleuze's read-

1 These were necessitated, he said, by the absence of protective whorls on his fingers.

ing of Spinoza, recall my previous account. Spinoza differed from most enlightenment thinkers in at least three important ways: he primarily sought to define the possibility of an ethical life; he began with metaphysics rather than epistemology, even as he remained committed to "reason"; and he offered—rationally—an immanent and monist metaphysics. That metaphysics was defined by a hierarchy of three levels: God (Substance, the One); the Attributes, which are the universal and infinite expressions of God (while humans, in their finitude, are only aware of thought and extension); and the modes (the multiplicity of actual existents), which are expressions of the Attributes. Each level defined its own mode of existence. Spinoza's epistemology and ethics each reproduced this three-part hierarchy. His metaphysics defined immanence through monism: everything that exists, exists only in God, and only God exists perfectly.

Deleuze had no interest in Spinoza's God; he described own critical practice as thinking as $N - 1$, that is, as **subtracting** (rather than deconstructing or putting under erasure) the One (any identity, unity, or totality, including God, the noumena, *Geist*, the transcendental consciousness, and *Ereignis*). Such a rejection of transcendence is common among critics of enlightenment thought. He was also not interested in the Attributes. He was only concerned with the infinite multiplicity of individual **modes or modulations**. Rather than seeing God as the immanent cause of the modes, responsible for the "composition of finite modes," Deleuze transformed Substance into a plane of immanence, "in which finite modes operate."[b] For Spinoza, the modes were the expressions of the expressions of God; for Deleuze, "Substance turns around the modes."[c] Instead of Spinoza's monism of the One, Deleuze proposed a **monism of multiplicities** existing on a **plane of immanence**.

Deleuze's theory of immanence refused any appeal to something outside of and especially above the plane of immanence. But it went further. Spinoza's immanence argued that everything exists on the same plane (God or Substance) as expressions of Substance, *but* God, the Attributes, and the modes exist in different ways. Immanence and monism are distinct, yet mutually implicated. Deleuze, on the other hand, while continuing to argue that everything exists on the same plane, used the work of the medieval rhetorician John Duns Scotus (ca. 1265–1308) to redefine **immanence as univocity**. For Scotus, immanence is a matter of predication; it is about how one speaks or attributes existence to any being. For Scotus—and for Deleuze—immanence means that Being or existence is said of all beings in the same way. All beings have the same way of being; they exist in the same way, which Scotus called *haecceities*, or "thisnesses," and Deleuze, following Spinoza, called **affect**.[d]

The result was that monism and immanence were equated. There is only one mode of existence—affects—and consequently, everything exists on the same plane of immanence: cause and effect, a condition and its transcendental conditions of possibility, part and whole, language and reality, the particular and the general, all exist on the same plane.

Deleuze parted ways with Scotus because univocity was no longer simply a matter of predication but of existence. Deleuze returned to Spinoza's naturalism, in particular, his description of the modes (bodies), where every mode is also itself a multiplicity, a composition. At the same time, he changed it significantly. Recall that Spinoza claimed that *Deus sive natura*: God is nature, Nature is God. Yet he held on to the distinction between *natura naturans* (nature naturing, nature as the creative process) and *natura naturata* (nature as modes). Deleuze's definition of immanence as univocity erased this difference. Deleuze embraced the ontological unity of nature as an infinitely creative process and as the always finite existence of the modes.

IMMANENCE AND BECOMING

Deleuze offered a new way of thinking, a new "image of thought," aimed against the **four (dominant) pillars of reason**: identity, opposition (or negation), analogy, and resemblance.[e] Like both Martin Heidegger and Jacques Derrida, Deleuze thought of reality as creative. Like them (and against Spinoza), he assumed change (rather than Being) was fundamental, making reality processual. But both Heidegger (with *Ereignis*) and Derrida (with *différance*) continued to hold on to a transcendental and, in Heidegger's case, a transcendent, reality. Deleuze's radical antihumanism (and anti-anthropocentrism) meant that reality is produced—as ongoing change—by the very processes that define its monism/immanence. Reality produces itself. Reality is always **becoming** different.

He started with a natural universe in which every thing (including both humanity and ideas) is a body, and every body is itself a composite of bodies; further, a body and its parts exist on the same plane, in the same way, alongside each other. But naturalism is not materialism, since there is no material substratum defining the stuff of nature. Nor do bodies invoke a spiritual reality beyond the natural. Each body is a **pure difference** (or a **differenciation** that precedes differentiation). Reality is the becoming of pure difference, understood as the endless production of **positivities**. Pure differences are unmediated, preindividual qualities, defined not by a "difference between" but by a "difference within" the different, a difference-in-itself. Deleuze's concept of difference is not about identity, or the negation of identity, or diacritics, or numerical difference. Difference is positive.

Consider my body; it is composed of multiple organs, which are themselves pure differences, each composed of multiple cells, also pure differences, each composed of multiple organic molecules, again pure differences, and we can keep going to elements, atoms, subatomic particles, and so on. Reality is multiplicity and difference all the way up and down. The universe is the becoming of difference as multiplicities, an immanence of pure differences. This is the joyful creativity that is reality itself.

For Deleuze, following Spinoza, a body is not defined by its immutable properties but by what it can do, its affects—the capacities to effect change and to be changed.[2] A body is its capacities to become otherwise and to make something else otherwise. A body is its constantly changing states as specific capacities become activated by the affects—and, hence, the changing states— of other bodies. But, according to Spinoza, "No one has yet determined what the Body can do."[f] That is, a body's capacities are never fully and finally realized; there is always a surplus of affect; hence, bodies are always changing, always becoming other. It is these affects and the capacities they actualize that are the positivities of the Deleuzean universe. Deleuze described affects as intensities, lines of force or becoming, pure potentialities to become otherwise, always nonconscious, prepersonal, and nonsubjective. Thus, pure difference or affect is always a "between," where bodies are what they are by virtue of being in motion; bodies are not bounded entities but kinetic and dynamic processes: "A body is defined by relations of motion and rest, of slowness and speed between particles. That is, it is not defined by a form or by functions. . . . [It is] a composition of speeds and slownesses on a plane of immanence. . . . One never commences; one never has a tabula rasa; one slips in, enters in the middle; one takes up or lays down rhythms."[g]

Everything is only becoming and never simply is. Reality is endlessly producing a universe of becomings rather than of beings. You might think of this in mathematical terms where difference can be understood as the differential, the gradient of intensities, the degree of force. Consider some examples: every body has capacities—artistic, athletic, spiritual, social, emotional, and so on—many of which we are unaware of because they remain unactivated;

2 Spinoza differentiates *affectus* (the continual becoming as variations of modulations of a body's state of affairs, of its capacities) and *affection* (a singular point of encounter that actualizes a particular capacity).

nothing has ever impacted them with enough force to make them become what they could become. My capacities to teach, to synthesize and explain complex ideas in clear and enjoyable ways, and to think abstractly have been activated by my teachers (and other bodies as well), and now they are activated by my encounters with students even as (I hope) my body may activate students' capacity to think abstractly and critically. They may not know they have the capacity and, as a result, may never have enjoyed such endeavors until it is activated in my class. If they had not taken my class, if my body had not affected their body, the capacity might remain dormant, merely potentiality, forever.

On the other hand, despite years of instruction, I cannot play the guitar. Not every body has every capacity. Perhaps I do have the capacity, but my teacher did not have the capacity to change my body in that way. Maybe my capacity was never impacted by another body that had the necessary (qualitative) force or intensity to bring about a new state of being of my body, that is, to enable me to be the rock star I always dreamt of being.

Or imagine meeting someone who makes you feel things emotionally and physically that you never knew you were capable of feeling. They have activated capacities that you had only hoped you had. Perhaps you thought you were incapable of such feelings. As one of my favorite bands puts it: "I've never known love, this is just my best guess."[h] Perhaps you know someone, not necessarily a bad person, who seems incapable of love, or a sociopath who does not have the capacity for empathy. They are not necessarily bad people, just people who lack certain capacities that are generally highly valued. Various recreational drugs (including nicotine and alcohol) enable you to do, feel, and perceive things differently, to realize capacities, but they may not work for everyone. And what does a good book do except open the reader up to new imaginations, new possibilities, new capacities?

Deleuze's notion of affect describes a body's **relational** encounters with other bodies with the capacity to modulate its state of being—its "relative speed or slowness." It is those modulations of the state of existence that actually constitute bodies and produce realities. Deleuze's ontology is relational, but relations do not mediate; they are not dialectical, intentional, hermeneutic, or diacritical. Unlike Kant, for whom the terms precede the relation, or Heidegger, for whom the relation precedes (and produces) the terms, or Hegel for whom the relation overcomes the terms, Deleuze claimed that relations are themselves pure differences, that is, affects. Hence, relations and their elements also exist on the same plane and in the same way: they are all affects or modulations. He described this as the **exteriority of relations**.[i]

A relation is ontologically both independent of and equivalent to its terms. Relations are positive terms that exist alongside, on the same plane, as the terms of the relations. The relation actualizes the capacities of other bodies by having its own capacity activated by the very bodies it is changing. A relation is the intensity or line of becoming that brings about a change in the state of affairs of other bodies even as it changes its own state of affairs. Like any body, a relation can do only certain things, although its capacities may not be activated in any moment. Like any body, relations exceed their actualized capacities, even as capacities always exceed the actual relations. Relations neither exhaust nor are exhausted by the capacities that are actualized. In other words, every specific relation is partial and contingent.

Recall Spinoza's concept of the conatus: every body seeks to persist and persevere in its own being and to increase its power (capacities), moving toward its perfection in God. Affects are the forces that act on a body, producing greater or lesser states of power and perfection. Those that increase power, that make the body more active, that increase capacities, are joyful passions; those that diminish power, that make the body more passive, that diminish capacities are sad passions. For Spinoza, the conatus is a seemingly innate force driving change according to a strange teleology in which every being seeks to become what it already is in God. But since Deleuze threw God out of his universe, he is left with the wild, arational becoming of reality producing itself.

Deleuze also intentionally misread Spinoza's theory of **expression**. Spinoza argued that everything is an expression of God (or the Attributes) and, hence, of its place (inherence) in God. For Deleuze, "the world does not exist outside of its expression."[j] Notice the subtle difference, from the world is the expression of God, to the world exists in its expressiveness. Every mode is an expression of a world that does not exist outside of its own expressivity. Expressivity is the joyous affirmation of the creativity of existence, the continual becoming of reality as capacities. It is the affirmation of existence as the power to bring difference into being on a plane of immanence.

Deleuze's reading of Spinoza had implications for his understanding of both knowledge and the ethical life. He ignored Spinoza's three levels of knowledge: imagination deals with sensations and bodies; reason with concepts, laws, and generalities; and intuition with essences and the perfection of God. Spinoza did not claim to have arrived at intuition because it is only possible as a collective endeavor. Any single mode can only arrive at its proper place in God when every mode does. Deleuze placed knowledge itself on the field of immanence and proposed knowledge as a transcendental empiricism: "Empiricism truly becomes transcendental . . . only when we apprehend directly in the sensible that which can only be sensed, the very being of the sensible: difference, potential difference and difference in intensity as the reason behind qualitative diversity. It is in difference that movement is produced as an 'effect,' that phenomena flash their meanings like signs. The intense world of difference, in which we find reason behind qualities and the being of the sensible, is precisely the object of a superior empiricism."[k] Enlightenment and modern thought assume that language exists on a different plane than the empirical. Deleuze argued that knowledge was engagement with the expressive universe, which could only be defined by imagination and experimentation, existing on the same plane of immanence and working within the flux of pure difference, as both the **sensible** or sensation and the **intelligible** (or conceptual).

Deleuze's vision of the ethical life—which he sometimes called an **ethology**—was similar to Spinoza's. Both sought to enhance the ability of life to flourish by embracing the joyful passions and abjuring the sad passions. But while Spinoza emphasized necessity and determination, since we are becoming what we already are, Deleuze argued that since one never knows what a body is capable of, ethology becomes "a long affair of experimentation, requiring lasting prudence, a Spinozan wisdom."[l] Further, Spinoza's ethical vision was a postindividual or collectivist one: only a collectivity can be ethical, and only together can the ethical life be achieved. Deleuze's vision was more individualized and perhaps even preindividual, as he envisioned a life existing on the plane of immanence.

NIETZSCHE AND BERGSON REDEEMED

We could consider any number of thinkers whom Deleuze ventriloquized to varying degrees. One of his first books, *Nietzsche and Philosophy* (1962), helped inaugurate a "new" interest in Nietzsche as profoundly anti-enlightenment and antimodern. Deleuze read him as a naturalist and a processualist, who rejected humanism, anthropocentrism, transcendence, teleology, and representation. Nietzsche de-deified nature as an eternally enduring substance, instead seeing reality as chaos, as the becoming of difference, the expression of the will to power. But the will to power is composed of only empirical singularities. Deleuze wrote: "We should not ask whether, in the final analysis, the will to power is unitary or multiple—this would show a general misunderstanding of Nietzsche's philosophy. The will to power is plastic, inseparable from each case in which it is determined; . . . the will to power is unitary, but unity which is affirmed of multiplicity."[m]

According to Deleuze, the will to power is a principle of difference, a monism of multiplicity that renders all reality as quantities of affirmative force. It is not determined by anything outside itself; it acts for itself, driven by its own existence, an expression of its own positivity. The will to power does not seek or desire power. Power is "the one that wills in the will. Power is the genetic and differential element in the will. This is why the will is essentially creative."[n] It is a continuous differenciation of intensive processes, rates of connectivity, and multiple mutations.

According to Deleuze, Nietzsche rejected the enlightenments' **dogmatic image of thought**, which assumed the possibility, even the necessity, of a harmonious correspondence between thinker, thinking, and thought.[o] Nietzsche both completed and subverted Kant's project by bringing critique to bear on truth itself through his genetic method. All human knowledge has been nothing but a reactive force that captures the will to power in language. Instead, Nietzsche demanded a new and creative "sense" or image of thought: thought is an affirmation "to release, to set free what lives."[p] The close relation between the will to power and life itself might suggest that Deleuze's Nietzsche is a vitalist for whom reality is the creativity of life itself.

Nietzsche postulated that thought "has an essential relation to time: it is always against its time. . . . The philosopher creates concepts that are neither eternal nor historical but untimely and not of the present. . . . And in the untimely there are truths that are more durable than all historical and eternal truths put together: truths of times to come."[q] In *Difference and Repetition*, Deleuze elaborated Nietzsche's reflections on time, structured through three actualizations of time as forms of repetition: first, a contiguity resulting from the **passive synthesis** of the past in the present, making time present as habit; second, continuities and discontinuities resulting from an **active synthesis** of what does and does not exist across temporal distances, making time present as memory; and third, **eternal return (or recurrence)** as a pure repetition that is always other, the return of that which differs from itself. The first two syntheses always serve a fixed identity, while eternal return, according to Deleuze, is the possibility of the disruption of both habit and memory. It is not the repetition of the same event but the creative production of empty time as pure difference, the affirmation of the endless individuation of becoming. Eternal recurrence is lived as **amor fati**, an expression of the drive to appropriate something and, in so doing, to transform it into a function of one's own becoming. Amor fati is opposed to the drive to submit to the other, to become the object of desire of the other, to become a function of the other. It is the joyful embracing of life, of the differential origin of any and all individuality. It is the immanence of temporality itself.

Deleuze also drew on Henri Bergson (1859–1941), who, before Deleuze, offered a deep theory of process that emphasized immediate experience, intuition, change, and creativity over abstraction and reason. Bergson was something of an international celebrity. He won a Nobel Prize for literature and every major prize the French government awarded cultural figures and then renounced them all to protest the anti-Semitism of the Vichy regime, despite being offered special dispensation. Supposedly, the earliest traffic jam in Times Square in New York City occurred when Bergson first came to the United States to lecture at Columbia University.

Bergson distinguished between the **virtual** and the **actual**. According to Deleuze, these two planes constitute Reality. The virtual is the plane of immanence, pure difference, affect.[r] Let me, once again, use the inadequate metaphor I have used before. Quantum mechanics sees the universe (and, for some theoretical physicists, all possible universes) as composed of funda-mental qualitative existences: whether fundamental particles, forces, quanta, strings, and so on, each defined only by its capacities and effects. For example, in string theory, every string vibrates with unique harmonics and frequencies that produce resonances in other strings. In fact, that is all it is: the effects that define its potential quantum relations. And in this sense, any string may have/be the capacity to reach out in a million different lines of becoming, sometimes across billions of miles, to produce changes in the state of affairs of the other strings. A string is defined by what it can do, but no one knows what it can do. The virtual is existence itself as the wild flux of strings—becomings, pure potentiality (as opposed to possibility), which Deleuze (and Guattari) later renamed the **plane of consistency**. The virtual is the reality of capacities as potentialities, anchored in the empirical flux. Possibility has no such anchor; not every possibility can be actualized, and therefore, the possible is not real.

This virtual flux is, however, always organized. Specific capacities are ac-tivated in particular relations. This is how reality produces and expresses itself. The virtual can be actualized in many different ways, each constituting its own **plane of organization**. Deleuze stood with those theoretical physi-cists who argue that there are infinite possible actualizations of the quantum universe. There may already be multiple actualized universes. We live in one actualization of the virtual quantum universe, an organization in which, for example, the speed of light is constant, or Newton's laws work, or mountains do not talk. In our universe, those who talk to mountains are not really doing so; they are living out their own superstitions. To those who speak to mountains, the existence of strings or quanta is our own quaint superstition. Yet both may be real; both may even be actual.

For Deleuze, since there is no transcendence, both the virtual and the actual exist on the same plane. The plane of consistency and the plane of organization are variations (modulations) of the same reality—the plane of immanence, constituting what is sometimes (misleadingly) described as a **flat** or **horizontal ontology**. I say somewhat misleadingly because it seems to suggest that whatever structures may inhabit the plane of organization are somehow not as real as the plane of consistency. It is perhaps more useful to think of the real as always having its own immanent topographies, in which the virtual stands as both a condition of possibility and an enigmatic core that cannot ever be grasped entirely precisely because, to do so, would be to declare its actuality.

Deleuze's ontology was yet another revolution in the history of thought, but it also set the stage for a different—contextualist—deep theory, for it posed a new question: What is the relation between the virtual and the actual, between the plane of consistency and the plane of organization? Or, perhaps more in keeping with Deleuze's thinking, how does the virtual become actual? This is the question that drove the collaboration between Deleuze and Félix Guattari.

NOTES

a. Deleuze, "Letter to a Harsh Critic," in *Negotiations*, 12.

b. Quoted in Martin Joughin, "Translator's Preface," in Deleuze, *Expressionism in Philosophy*, 11.

c. Deleuze, *Difference and Repetition*, 377.

d. Deleuze, *Expressionism in Philosophy*.

e. Deleuze, *Difference and Repetition*.

f. Spinoza, *Ethics*, in *Complete Works*, 495.

g. Deleuze, "Ethology," 626.

h. The Airborne Toxic Event, "Elizabeth."

i. Deleuze and Parnet, *Dialogues*, 55.

j. Deleuze, *The Fold*, 132.

k. Deleuze, *Difference and Repetition*, 68–69.

l. Deleuze, *Spinoza*, 125.

m. Deleuze, *Nietzsche and Philosophy*, 85–86.

n. Deleuze, *Nietzsche and Philosophy*, 85.

o. Deleuze, *Nietzsche and Philosophy*, 103.

p. Deleuze, *Nietzsche and Philosophy*, 185.

q. Deleuze, *Nietzsche and Philosophy*, 107.

r. Deleuze, *Bergsonism*.

PART V

Contextual

Humilities

Deleuze and Guattari

While at Vincennes, following the events of May 1968, Gilles Deleuze began a deep friendship and collaboration with Félix Guattari, who was born on April 30, 1930, in Villeneuve-les-Sablons, and died on August 29, 1992. Unlike Deleuze, Guattari grew up in the French working class. Deleuze was devoted to philosophy; Guattari, despite having a strong interest in theory and politics, was a practicing, radical psychoanalyst who, after training with Lacan, worked at La Borde, an experimental clinic that rejected the traditional therapist-patient relation in favor of group therapy. He was a leader of the antipsychiatry movement, which located psychoanalysis in larger structures of social power.

Deleuze, while supporting various political causes, remained relatively silent and apolitical for much of his life. Guattari was politically militant his entire life: a Trotskyite communist and a friend of autonomous Marxism, and a vocal and active supporter of the 1968 protests, anticolonial movements, and environmental struggles. Whereas Deleuze was uninterested in institution-building, Guattari helped build a number of radically interdisciplinary and experimental political-intellectual institutions, such as the

Fédération des groupes d'études et de recherches institutionelles; the Centre d'études, de recherche et de formation institutionelles, which oversaw the highly influential journal *Recherches*; and the Comité d'initiative pour de nouveaux espaces de liberté.

Guattari was an original and prolific thinker, concerned primarily with the politics of subjectivity—"How do we produce it, capture it, enrich it, and permanently reinvent it in a way that renders it compatible with Universes of mutant value?"—as well as with ecology (in what he called "ecosophy").[a] He published seven volumes during his lifetime—including *Psychoanalysis and Transversality* (1972), *The Molecular Revolution* (1977), *The Machinic Unconscious* (1979), *The Three Ecologies* (1989), and *Chaosmosis* (1992)—as well as three other collaborative volumes (e.g., *Communists Like Us*, with Toni Negri, 1985). Another seven volumes of his work were published posthumously.

But he is probably best known for his work with Deleuze. Together they published seven books, including the two-volume work *Capitalism and Schizophrenia* (*Anti-Oedipus* [1972] and *A Thousand Plateaus* [1980]), which have been among the most influential books in contemporary anti-enlightenment thought. Michel Foucault described *Anti-Oedipus*, a searing critique of both psychoanalysis and Marxism, as "an Introduction to the Non-Fascist Life."[b] Other books included *Kafka: Toward a Minor Literature* (1975), *Nomadology* (1986), and *What Is Philosophy?* (1991). While Deleuze's contributions to the collaborative works are evident, much of what is new and unique in them is taken from Guattari's thought, including concepts such as **schizoanalysis** and **semiotic regimes**. These collaborative works, while still highly theoretical, turned Deleuze's ontology toward developing more politically and contextually sensitive tools for a historical ontology of the present. The resulting deep theory offered a radically **contextualist** and **formalist empiricism**.

Deleuze's ontology primarily addressed questions of the virtual and the plane of consistency. Together, Deleuze and Guattari, especially in *Capitalism and Schizophrenia*, addressed the relations between the virtual and the actual: How does reality produce itself? How does the virtual become actual, and how does the actual become virtual? How does one describe different actualities? What are the politics of these relations? Their work addresses these questions by redefining empiricism as an experimentation that maps (and remakes) the world rather than representing it. Especially in the first volume, they think through critiques of Freud and Marx, both of whom offered only **tracings** of what they assumed to be necessary and universal (hence, transcendent) models of the actual, in the realms of the psyche and the social, respectively.

But I want to tread carefully here because there is an ongoing debate about whether there is a single and/or systematic philosophy either in Deleuze's work or in his collaboration with Guattari. What we do know is that both authors affirm that theory (philosophy) works by inventing concepts, which function as tools for **mapping** the real. And since, consequently, thinking is always, in some way, pragmatic, their concepts take on different meanings or, better, do different work (often using the same terms) at different moments. They change as they are deployed in response to different questions and contexts. Further, the relations among the different concepts change as well, even while they seem to be constantly inviting the reader to see equivalences among them. These are problems that plague any consistent project of contextualism.

A DETOUR INTO CONTEXTUALISM

Ontology as a response to the contradictions of enlightenment and modern thought often comes dangerously close to reproducing the claims of universality, even while dismantling the structures of humanism and subjectivity, and the distinction between experience and the real. Alternatively, a number of postmodern deep theorists started by rejecting the assumption of universality, which then provides the launching ground from which they can question any and all assumptions, including humanism. Contextualists argue that such positions emerge from, and their "truth" can be judged only within, a particular context. Like Marx, the pragmatists, and Wittgenstein, all of whom can be read as contextualists, postmodern—radical—contextualists argue that thinking is inextricably bound up with its context. Even the distinctions and relations between the conceptual and the empirical are similarly bound to a particular context. The postmodern contextualists generally eschew ontological questions and renounce the search for the *right* theory, instead seeking useful tools, deploying whatever concepts and logics work best in a particular context. Such thinkers tend to be theorists without a single, necessary theory; instead, they are often maddeningly eclectic. Their "theoretical" work is best understood as the analytic practice of a critical empiricism rather than a substantive set of theoretical claims; concepts are tools inseparable from the empirical, from concrete analyses.

Any contextualist deep theory faces a number of problems. First, is it possible to think about a particular context without appealing to some concepts that extend beyond the specific context? Probably not, but then what is the status of such abstractions or generalizations? Different contextual thinkers offer different solutions, including appeals to scale as spatial reach, to "the changing same" as temporal continuities and discontinuities, to levels measured by concreteness and abstraction, or to operant categories (e.g., when we talk about category mistakes).

Second, radical contextuality is often accused of relativism because of its claim that what works (theoretically, empirically, and politically) in one context might not work in another. But relativism only makes sense when it is contrasted with some general or absolute idea of Truth. Radical contextuality does deny that there is Truth (with a capital *T*) and generally refuses to reduce disagreements to a matter of perspective or paradigms. It need not deny that there are truths (with a small *t*) within a particular context, but they can only be "discovered" through rigorous and self-reflective work. Sometimes, radical contextualists even speak as if there were an "objective" truth, without assuming a position outside all contexts. Truth is always only the truth of the context or, more accurately, only a truth, always incomplete. That need not undermine its authority or utility, but it does mean that theoretical work has to keep moving as the contexts change and as we learn more, which may contradict or at least complexify what we thought we knew. You have to be willing to question any assumption in the face of the demands of concrete realities and people's lives. But that does not deny that there are truths to be sought, and that in the analysis of a context, there are better and worse analyses.

Finally, the German social theorist Karl Mannheim (1893–1947) suggested there is a contradiction or paradox in the very assertion of radical contextualism because it claims the truth of something that is not contextual, namely, that truth is contextual. A radical contextualist might acknowledge that their deep theory is itself a response to a particular set of contextual challenges rather than a universal epistemology. Contextualizing epistemology is a provisional response to certain contexts. It is possible to imagine a context in which radical contextualism might not be the most appropriate way of approaching its challenges. Alternatively, a radical contextualist might argue that their deep theory is a practical or tactical choice: it not only proves useful and works well but also enables us to avoid the failures of enlightenment and modern thought.

Contextuality, whether radical or not, is embedded in actual critical practice. Not surprisingly, there are significant differences among different theorists; perhaps the most important—and the most visible—is their empirical understanding of context. For Marx, the context was a historically specific social formation, although his work often moved between more epochal descriptions (e.g., of industrial capitalism, although he still located his discussion in England and, to a lesser extent, Germany) and descriptions of particular situations or events (e.g., his discussion in the *Eighteenth Brumaire* of the 1851 coup in which Louis-Napoleon Bonaparte assumed dictatorial power in France). The pragmatists, for the most part, conceived of a context as a specific situation defined by a problem or decision. Wittgenstein defined a context by the conjunction of a specific language game and a form of life.

In this and the following three chapters, I shall consider three postmodern, radical contextualists. The collaborative work of Deleuze and Guattari implicitly worked with contexts as configurations of capacities on specific **plateaus**. Michel Foucault understood contexts in epochal terms, although his epochs were neither ontological nor as extended as those of Heidegger's historical ontology. Foucault described the emergence and operation of long-term, sustained formations of knowledge/power. And Stuart Hall, accepting the multiplicity of contexts both on and across different levels of abstraction, focused on what he called the **conjuncture**.

A CONTEXTUALISM OF ACTUALITIES

I will present the broad terms of Deleuze and Guattari's historical ontology by identifying three central, overlapping, and interconnected concept-sets or discourses (although there may be others): lines, assemblages, and machines. Each enables them to think different dimensions of the processes by which reality produces itself, by which the virtual becomes actual and vice versa. And each may even suggest its own politics. While all three may be operating at any moment, generally one will dominate (both in the becoming actual of the real, and in their analysis). Each set defines forms of organization and disorganization, of composition and decomposition, or, in Deleuze and Guattari's terms, of **territorialization** and **deterritorialization**. The result is a "new formalism," a **formalist empiricism**.[c]

The three discourses—each quite complicated (so please be patient)—offer new languages as critical tools for thinking and engaging reality. Each is an expression of and the imposition of an organization of **desiring production**, the fundamental force that brings relations into existence, thus realizing capacities and transforming qualities (capacities) into actualities. Although they wrote mostly about the production of human existence, the same processes operate at every level or **plateau** (region?) of reality. Table 27.1 offers a forecast of what is to come.

TABLE 27.1 A Tracing of Deleuze and Guattari's Deep Theory

Lines (Molecularity)	Assemblages (Molarity)	Machines (Becoming)
Of synthesis		
Connective	Root	Abstract or stratifying
Disjunctive	Radicle	Collective assemblage of enunciation
Conjunctive	Rhizome	Machinic assemblage
Of flight		
Relative		Coding
Absolute		Territorializing

LINES

The first set of concepts, a **discourse of lines**, describes the basic "building blocks" of any becoming actual, the intensities that actualize capacities, operating at the **molecular** level.[d] They define the primary level of relations. There are lines of synthesis and lines of flight. **Lines of synthesis** produce three kinds of becoming-relations out of nonrelations: connective, disjunctive, and conjunctive. A **connective line** is the simplest embodiment of desiring production, connecting two singularities without reason or purpose. The child reaches out to the shoe. The novel reaches toward the military machine. It is pure, random, and contingent experimentation, without power, producing a minimal organization on the wild flux of desiring production.

Disjunctive lines create decision forks; they mark choices (neither conscious nor even necessarily human)—either B to C or B to D—about which relation is produced, which line is followed. Disjunctive relations build logics of either/or into reality. In human realities, disjunctive lines most commonly (unfortunately) operate in the negative, as an exclusionary relation and a primary site of power. The child is forbidden their relation to the shoe, and their desire is rechanneled toward the proper object of the mother's breast. The student is told that connecting the novel to the war machine is not a proper reading.

Conjunctive lines are additive: A, and B, and C, and so on. Conjunctive relations are expansive and inclusive, often producing complexity or collectivity. But such syntheses also produce an excess of affect that has yet to be captured by any specific relation; the excess circulates outside whatever organization has been additively produced. The conjunctive synthesis is the second way power enters into reality. The family—mommy, daddy, and me, and the Oedipal law that follows upon it—is such a synthesis, and subjectivity is its excess. The organization of labor power is another, and capital (value in circulation) is its surplus.

But there are also **lines of flight** or **escape**, deterritorializing lines that undo or flee from the structures produced by the lines of synthesis. **Relative lines of flight** deconstruct particular relations; **absolute lines of flight** escape all relations and structures, eluding the very possibility of synthesis itself, in favor of the wild flows of desiring production. Absolute deterritorializations reach toward the virtual, to pure difference, threatening the very reality of any actuality. Deleuze and Guattari described such absolute lines of flight as becoming—schizo, molecular, minor, intensity, imperceptible, woman, animal, and a body without organs. Becoming a body without organs makes visible the possible consequences of such absolute deterritorializations, for it is a body without structure, without any relation to an other. It comes dangerously close to death and real insanity. Consequently, Deleuze and Guattari often were ambivalent about the absolute line of flight, both advocating it and backing away from its implausible consequences.

ASSEMBLAGES

The second form of the organization (and, hence, production) of the actual is **molarities** *or* **assemblages (*agencement*)**, which assemble relations, producing relations among relations. Assemblages are heterogeneous "totalities" without any singular unity, compositions of multiple—both quantitively and qualitatively—relations. They can vary greatly in size and complexity. Deleuze and Guattari describe three forms of assemblages, although they acknowledge that there may be others: roots, radicles, and rhizomes.

Root (or arboreal) assemblages are the most common in human societies, and most clearly embody structures of power. They can be either vertical (hierarchical) or circular (a distribution around a center). I am sure you can think of numerous hierarchical structures; in circular assemblages, the center is the locus of power from which everything else emanates, and anything can be measured by its distance from and expression of the center. Often, Deleuze and Guattari used the figure of a tree with a central root/trunk structure as the structuring locus of power for both root assemblages.

Radicle assemblages are more difficult to describe: "The principal root has aborted or withers away toward its extremity; grafted onto it is an immediate indefinite multiplicity of elaborate secondary roots. . . . Unity is endlessly thwarted and impeded in the object while a new type of unity, . . . a higher unity . . . of ambivalence" takes hold.[e] We have already seen such a strange arrangement in the work of Jacques Derrida, where the unity of any arboreal assemblage is deconstructed, apparently depriving it of an origin and power. But the unity and origin do not disappear; instead, they are displaced into a constantly deferred future (différance). Think of a plant grafted onto another plant; now imagine that original plant disappears into its grafted supplements. In such a case, the unity still exists but operates only indirectly, in its apparent absence. The power, however much deferred or displaced, still haunts the assemblage.

The final form of assemblage is the **rhizome**. Think of crabgrass, the bane of lawn growers everywhere. It is a unique weed, without origin or center, without any arborescent root structure. It shoots stems everywhere, and wherever it stops, it plants new roots, from which it continues to shoot stems everywhere. You cannot actually destroy it because you can't pull out its roots; it's just the endless production of relations without any structure, rationale, meaning, or ideology. It appears chaotic, but it is not the absolute chaos, the absolute flux and indeterminacy, of the virtual because it still involves the production of relations; it is still an assemblage, but it is the assemblage that comes as close to the virtual as any actuality can. Deleuze and Guattari described a rhizome as an arational, acentered, nonhierarchical, and nonsignifying assemblage, the multiplication of connective relations without any imposition of identity, unity, or homogeneity. A rhizome has no privileged meaning and no privileged structure.

For example, in his groundbreaking book *S/Z*, Roland Barthes divided up a "realist" short story by Honoré de Balzac in a completely random way, disallowing any predefined units—whether structural (phrases, sentences, paragraphs, etc.) or signifying (containing a self-enclosed meaning); he then recomposed the story approaching a rhizome. Unlike the radicle in which the unity or identity is deconstructed, a rhizome has to be made by subtracting any and every unity or identity—whether that of a subject or an object—from the multiplicity, allowing the multiplicity to flourish. If roots and radicles embody power, then the undoing of power demands a new figure of thought as $N-1$.

These three assemblages are (some of) the ways an actuality is organized, and all three exist in any actuality. We rarely find them existing independently, in some pure form; they are always intertwined, interconnected, embedded within one another: "There exist tree or root structures in rhizomes; conversely, a tree branch or root division may begin to burgeon into a rhizome. The coordinates are determined not by theoretical analyses implying universals but by a pragmatics composing multiplicities."[f] An actuality is defined pragmatically, by how it is composed, how it mixes the assemblages to give form to a multiplicity. In the contemporary world, you need only think of the heterogeneous relations among different assemblages—the roots of authoritarianism, the radicles of corporate capital, the rhizomes of social media. However, assemblages do not have predefined political valences, especially in the messy realities that result from mixing them together: not all rhizomes are good, and not all arborescences are bad. They are *formal* categories for analyzing the production of the actual.

The **principle of cartography** distinguishes two ways such formalist concepts can be used: tracing and mapping. **Tracing** refers to analytic practices that apply structural or generative models, known in advance, to the multiplicity; they trace what is already known, competences already claimed, onto that which is not yet constructed. Tracing forces every actuality to repeat the predictable. **Mapping** produces the actual through an experimentation that is constantly producing relations, an activity that we cannot control.

Mapping is both deterritorializing and reterritorializing and opens up at least two political possibilities. First, a politics of the **minor** or the **minoritarian**, which refers not to a demographic minority but to a way of inhabiting an assemblage.[g] It is the expression of a particular kind of marginalized social position, in which you live in a "cramped" space, a space in which you cannot be comfortable but from which you cannot escape. It is a space in which you must—always unsuccessfully—hide yourself, unable to speak or avoid speaking the dominant language. The result is that it is always spoken imperfectly, with a stutter or accent, often disrupting it just enough to make other possibilities visible. It is a voice without a people but a voice of futurity, of a coming community. It gives rise to an existential sense of political urgency and immediacy, but it is not necessarily revolutionary or subversive. For example, Franz Kafka, the Jew having to speak German, wrote in a minor voice.

The second politics is more radical, even revolutionary (without violence). It entails a deterritorializing **becoming rhizomatic** or **molecular**, by subtracting all power, making $N - 1$ the absolute principle of politics. Deleuze and Guattari constantly called us to fight against—or to avoid—the fascist in each of us and, further, to recognize the many microfascisms at work in every actuality. Fascism is the presence of the One, the demand for and imposition of an identity or unity. This has been read as the rejection of any structure whatsoever, as demanding a horizontal politics of structurelessness, as advocating an ethicopolitics of becoming virtual or at least rhizomatic ("schizo").

I disagree. First, if the actual becomes only through the production of relations and structures, then any actuality requires structure. A politics in which everything dissolves into the unformed chaos of the virtual is one reaching for a reality without actuality. Second, all forms of structures are not equally fascist. (Are all structures necessarily fascist?) Do all organizations instantiate the power of the One? Are there differing degrees and forms of such power? Are there other ways of engaging the politics of becoming actual?

MACHINES

Time to take a breath because things are going to get really weird (and you thought we were already there). We have yet to understand how this mapping is accomplished. How do the lines and assemblages arise out of the virtual and into the becoming actual? How does reality produce itself? How do we avoid falling back into some form of humanism—privileging consciousness, practice, or language? Deleuze and Guattari proposed a third set of concepts, a vocabulary of **machinic production**, which is not the same as mechanical production. Mechanics—for example, as inscribed in Newtonian physics and thermodynamics—views reality through the lens of the object. Machinic production, on the other hand, emphasizes processes beyond the control of humanity. It offers a theory of agency without subjectivity.

Reality produces itself by producing machines. Deleuze and Guattari assured us that this discourse was not metaphoric, although they do not offer a compelling account of the existence of machinic processes in the space of becoming, between the virtual and the actual. Let me offer another inadequate metaphor. Consider LEGO. Growing up, my son had boxes of LEGO pieces. He was never very interested in following the instructions and building whatever it was we thought we were buying him—a LEGO *Millennium Falcon*, for example. The pieces are, metaphorically, akin to the multiplicity of affects that constitute the virtual; each piece is defined by its capacities. My son organized the pieces by their capacities to fulfill certain functions, by the different relations into which a piece might enter with other pieces and, in so doing, actualize capacities, construct lines and assemblages. Now imagine organizing some pieces into a fluid but structured composition, capable of reaching into the box of pieces to build other lines and assemblages and, in the process, remake itself. Finally, imagine that the pieces are organizing themselves, that the virtual is constantly projecting itself, by synthesizing relations and assembling molarities, as machines or machinic processes that will define the becoming actual of the virtual. Machines are the instruction manuals for becomings, the processes that configure the actual out of the ("empirical") intensities of the plane of consistency.

The primary, even primordial, machine of actualization is the **abstract or stratifying machine**. Think of it as an immanent cause, such as geometric causality. Every triangle has certain properties and fulfills certain mathematical functions. How? There is no first cause that produces every possible triangle in the proper way. Instead, there is a **diagram** that operates formally and ontologically, rather than empirically, to map every triangle. According to Deleuze and Guattari, "An abstract machine is neither an infrastructure that is determining in the last instance nor a transcendental Idea that is determining in the supreme instance. Rather, it plays a piloting role. . . . [It] constructs a real that is yet to come, a new type of reality."[h] It is a formal ontology (a map) of an actual reality.

Deleuze and Guattari offered the rather fantastical image of a lobster, whose two claws reach into and across the virtual (the plane of consistency), assembling in each claw a random collection of pure differences, intensities, or capacities. The two populations, set apart from the chaotic multiplicity of the virtual, are **stratified**, that is, distributed into a particular formal relation on the plane of organization. The only ontological difference between the two populations of capacities is the plane or **stratum** on which they are placed: either the **plane of content** or the **plane of expression**.[1] And it is the nature of and relation between these planes that constitute an actual reality on the plane of organization. But if everything exists on the plane of immanence, then the virtual (the plane of consistency) and the actual (the plane of organization) also exist on the same plane of immanence, as do the planes of content and expression.

The distinction between the two populations as expression and content is not intrinsic to the elements of the population. The processes of the abstract machine are arbitrary or accidental; there is no reason or goal defining what elements the lobster scoops up with its two claws, or to which plane (expression or content) it assigns each population. But this distribution and assignment determine which capacities of each population are activated and actualized: what a body (on that plane) can do. The abstract machine activates particular capacities in each population. The planes of expression and content might be loosely thought of as Deleuze and Guattari's attempt

1 This concept and its further elaboration draw heavily on the work of the Danish linguist Louis Hjelmslev and Guattari's own highly sophisticated theory of semiotic and asemiotic regimes.

to provide immanent, nonhumanistic, and nonsubjective theories of agency and materiality (or objectivity), respectively. We might crudely describe the two planes within human realities as the sayable and the seeable; they are functionally—but not materially or ontologically—equivalent to the discursive and the nondiscursive.[i]

On the plane of expression, a **collective assemblage of enunciation** constitutes agency as a set of operations or functions that both enables and constrains the possible conduct of every element of both expression and content. Every body in this population can affect not only the bodies on the plane of expression but also those on the plane of content. On the plane of content, a **machinic assemblage** constitutes what is given as self-evident; it is the plane of the sensible. But the elements within it are not passive; rather, their capacity to affect other bodies is limited to those on the same plane of content. The machinic assemblage refers "to a precise state of intermingling of bodies . . . , including all the attractions and repulsions, sympathies and antipathies, alterations, amalgamations, penetrations and expansions that affect bodies of all kinds in their relations to one another."[j]

Multiple abstract machines produce multiple actualities (**stratifications**) on multiple planes of organization or plateaus: from quantum, to atomic, to molecular, to crystalline, to geological, to organic, to sentient bodies, to intelligent life, to individuated life, to social realities. The enlightenments might then be understood as abstract machines that enabled human beings to affect each other and the nonhuman world in particular ways but prevented the nonhuman world from affecting humanity in similar ways (Heidegger's *Gestell*?). On the other hand, the Indigenous people of Peru live in a different stratification in which mountains exist on the plane of expression and have an agency not identical to but as real as that of humans.

Deleuze and Guattari identified many other sorts of machines or machinic processes as tools for thinking about the relations of becoming between the virtual and the actual. I offer some illustrations. Deleuze and Guattari described abstract machines as **double stratifications**. The first divides expression and content; the second divides both expression and content into form and substance (the stuff of which it is composed, not reducible to a vulgar physical materialism), each of which has its own organization. What we can call **coding machines** inscribe the formal structures of identity and difference. **Territorializing machines** (here I use the term in a different and specific sense) organize substance according to relations of proximity and distance, of propriety and alterity. Coding machines are related (in some unspecified way) to disjunctive lines of synthesis; territorializing machines are related (again, in some unspecified way) to conjunctive lines. These machines operate on but independently of the stratification of expression and content. The result is that the collective assemblage of enunciation exists as formalized (or functional) substance, while the machinic assemblage exists as formed matter.[2]

The **war machine** and the **machine (or apparatus) of capture** are also important for the becoming actual of the real. The former is responsible for the production of lines of flight, fluidly raiding and dismantling the operations of the abstract machine. Machines of capture do exactly what the name implies: the "despotic state," for example, captures land and people, while the "capitalist machine" captures (surplus) value.[3]

Reality is always an ongoing production, always changing and open to unseen and unforeseeable possibilities, resulting from the multiplicity of machinic processes; there are always multiple machines of each kind operating on the same plateau. There can be many different abstract machines operating, sometimes in conjunction with one another, sometimes against one another, and sometimes relatively independently of one another. There can be struggles among competing coding and territorializing machines. And for any particular instantiation of any machine, antimachines may also be at work: destratifying, decoding, and deterritorializing machines. The complexity and instability of every actuality also result from the fact that machines almost always fail; the attempt to compose or configure the actual is always left incomplete or fragmented, or it is actively undermined. Reality keeps having to produce itself.

Deleuze and Guattari offered tools for the analysis of the composition and recomposition of the actual. Their postmodern, antihumanist, historical ontology has three immediate and powerful implications. First, other actualities are always possible; reality can always be otherwise; and while humans are not in control, they are certainly participants in these processes. Second, concepts (thinking) have no validity beyond their ability to map the specificities of any specific actuality—or context, although for the most part, their

2 To reach ahead, for example, Deleuze used Foucault's analysis of the modern prison as an example of machinic production. In this case, the plane of contents involves the prisoners as substance, and the prison (a particular structure that Foucault calls the panopticon) as its form. The plane of expression involves the substance of delinquency (as a subject position) and penal law as its form.
3 Machines of capture work somewhat paradoxically because the appropriation of a surplus (from some totality or "stock") happens simultaneously with the constitution of the very totality from which the surplus is extracted and captured.

concepts often remain at a level comparable to Heidegger's epochs. Finally, they remind us that thinking beyond modernity does not necessarily mean abandoning everything modern. For example, despite the common assumption that their rejection of modern thought entails a rejection of thinking as critique, I offer the following quotation: "Philosophy is at its most positive as critique, as an enterprise of demystification. And we should not be too hasty in proclaiming philosophy's failure in this respect. Great as they are, stupidity and baseness would be still greater if there did not remain some philosophy which always prevents them from going as far as they would wish."[k] And so, the conversation continues.

NOTES

a. Guattari, *Chaosmosis*, 135.

b. Michel Foucault, "Preface," in Deleuze and Guattari, *Anti-Oedipus*, xi–xiv.

c. Deleuze, *Expressionism in Philosophy*, 321; see also Deleuze and Guattari, "Rhizome," in *Thousand Plateaus*.

d. Deleuze and Guattari, *Anti-Oedipus*.

e. Deleuze and Guattari, *Thousand Plateaus*, 52.

f. Deleuze and Guattari, *Thousand Plateaus*, 15.

g. Deleuze and Guattari, *Kafka*.

h. Deleuze and Guattari, *Thousand Plateaus*, 142.

i. Deleuze, *Foucault*.

j. Deleuze and Guattari, *Thousand Plateaus*, 90.

k. Deleuze, *Nietzsche and Philosophy*, 106

Foucault and Critique

Michel Foucault was the most influential theorist of power since Marx. He has been described as a phenomenologist, a structuralist, a poststructuralist, a Heideggerian, and a Deleuzean. I will present him as a radical contextualist operating at the intersection of historical epochs and political problematizations.

He was openly gay and celebrated the pleasures of the queer underground, fascinated, intellectually and aesthetically, by the relations of violence, pain, and sexuality. Following the Marquis de Sade, Antonin Artaud, and Georges Bataille, he saw them as transgressions of the Law operating on the threshold of the (un)acceptable, and as affirmations of the "abnormal."

Paul-Michel Foucault was born into an upper-middle-class family on October 15, 1926, in Poitiers, France, and died on June 25, 1984, in Paris, as a result of complications from AIDS. He was educated in philosophy (especially of science) and psychology (interested in both Freud and the phenomenological psychologist Ludwig Binswanger). He taught psychology—as inseparable from philosophy and history—at universities in France, Sweden, Poland, and West Germany. From 1966 to 1968, he taught in Tunisia during a tumultuous political period, where he claimed to have been politicized (in antiracist and anticolonial politics) before May 1968.

He continued his education under the mentorship of Jean Hyppolite (1907–68, a scholar of Hegel and Marx), Louis Althusser, and Georges Canguilhem (1904–95, a philosopher/historian of science). He was also influenced by Immanuel Kant, Karl Marx, Friedrich Nietzsche, Martin Heidegger, Gaston Bachelard, and Gilles Deleuze. Although Foucault rarely addressed Marx directly, he commented that Marx was on almost every page of his work, but he did not think the complexities of power in the late twentieth century could be limited to capitalism and bourgeois culture. And he acknowledged Heidegger's strong influence, although it is rarely commented upon.

In 1968, he was invited to lead the philosophy department at the newly formed, experimental University of Paris VIII at Vincennes and brought his then friend Deleuze into it. He found himself at the center of student protests and broad social demonstrations. While Foucault had always been politically conscious and active, even briefly joining the Communist Party, the late 1960s moved him away from Marxist party politics and propelled him to other publicly visible forms of activism around a range of issues, including prisons, antiracism, anticolonialism, human rights, and more. While Foucault's politics were largely left-wing, he was at times highly critical of some tendencies (e.g., anti-Semitism) of factions of the left and had an on-again, off-again relation to Marxist-Leninism, Maoism, and ultraleftism. He was even accused of having abandoned his progressivism by defending neoliberalism. In 1970, he left Vincennes to become a professor of "the history of systems of thought" at the prestigious Collège de France, where he was only required to give twelve lectures a year, freeing him to visit SUNY Buffalo, New York University, and the University of California at Berkeley.

Foucault published fourteen books, starting with *Mental Illness and Personality* (1954) and including *History of Madness* (1961, *Madness and Civilization* in English), *Birth of the Clinic* (1963), *Words and Things* (1966, *The Order of Things* in English), *The Archaeology of Knowledge* and *The Order of Discourse* (1969, 1971, published together in English), *Discipline and Punish* (1975), and four volumes of *The History of Sexuality* (1976, 1984, 2018). In addition, nine volumes of lectures and essays were published between 1980 and 1988, and twelve volumes of his lectures at the Collège de France were published after his death, despite his wishes.

Foucault's "histories" were originally more successful with popular and political audiences than with academics. His books are surprisingly readable, often written in a voice of realism, as if he were simply describing the world.

But he never claimed to represent its Truth. His work presented concrete—albeit idiosyncratic—histories but without the rigorously documented narratives of academic historiography. He gathered a number of unusual, minor, and ignored statements and events, linked them together and to other events, and spun them into his **genealogies**.

Alongside these concrete investigations, Foucault wrote theoretical reflections on his critical practice, although the correspondence was rarely obvious. As the "objects" of his narratives changed, so did his concepts and the questions he posed. His understanding of his project changed with them: "Do not ask me to remain the same: leave it to our bureaucrats and our police to see that our papers are in order."[a] Foucault embraced the impermanence of theoretical positions, declaring that theory is a toolbox, and concepts are to be used contextually and pragmatically.[b]

What was Foucault's project? I can start by saying what Foucault was not doing. He was not trying to grasp "a whole society in its living reality," or to describe how reality is experienced.[c] Foucault refused to privilege—although he did not ignore—the reality of experience (which, in his later works, gained greater importance). He was not describing what Max Weber called "an iron cage," as if our lives were fully controlled.[d] He distanced himself from the hermeneutics of suspicion and did not believe in (hidden) deep structures. He was not interested in texts or sign systems as meanings to be interpreted, representations to be judged, experiences to be analyzed, or structural codes to be deconstructed. There were already enough people doing such things—uncovering ideologies or analyzing systems of codes that define the social unconscious.

MODERNITY AND CRITIQUE

Consider Foucault's response (1983–84) to Kant's "What Is Enlightenment?," which he used to interrogate the modern.[e] He concluded that it is a way of seeing oneself, of reflecting on one's own being as **present**. The modern is a question about the present in history, a question spoken in the present about the present. Unlike previous understandings of such self-reflections—as periodization (Marx), rupture (Christianity), or transition (Hegel), Kant saw modernity as a mark of difference and a way out of the past. It was a challenge that could only be met by the assertion of the will to reason against the power of authority: dare to know (*sapere aude*).

But Kant's true revolution, according to Foucault, was equating modernity with a particular philosophical task (critique), as a reflection on "today" as a difference in history. Unfortunately, Kant tied this task to humanism and synecdochical universalism, which established a system of power built on a fundamental distinction between the normal and the abnormal. Foucault renounced Kant's humanism and universalism but embraced critique, rereading it from his present—postmodern—moment.

Modernity is an **attitude** toward the present that defines it as a task. You cannot transform the present by destroying or negating it, nor can you discover the truth of the present in the present alone. You have to grasp the present as what it is and then transform it. Modernity both privileges the present and recognizes that it always points beyond itself—toward an eternal or "heroic" element captured in the moment. Critique enacts this "will to 'heroize' the present," to make the present into something new.[f] Accordingly, "for the attitude of modernity, the high value of the present is indissociable from a desperate eagerness to imagine it, to imagine it otherwise than it is, and to transform it not by destroying it but by grasping it in what it is."[g] Instead of "dare to know," dare to imagine the actual world and make it otherwise.

Charles Baudelaire's (1821–67) **flaneur** is often taken as the figure of modernity. The flaneur is the disinterested spectator, wandering aimlessly, observing the city and its marvels. The flaneur is the poetic empiricist, detailing the uniqueness of the present. Foucault favored Baudelaire's **dandy**, who takes themselves as an object of transformation, a work of experimentation and art. The dandy celebrates the possibility of being otherwise, living on the frontier in a "**limit-attitude**," refusing any authentic or fixed identity, constantly remaking their self.[h] The dandy performs the attitude of modernity, taking the actuality of their world as given and transforming it.

Critique makes the present—our present reality—into a philosophical problem: The questions of today, the questions about the present, about what is our actuality, are: What is happening today? What is happening right now? And what is this *right now* we all are in which defines the moment at which I am writing?"[i] Modernity poses the question, because only then can we know "the present field of possible experience."[j] Only then can we "separate out, from the contingency that has made us what we are, the possibility of no longer being, doing, or thinking what we are, do or think."[k] Foucault advocated a permanent critique of ourselves and our historical era, while desubjectifying this "**ontology of ourselves, an ontology of the present**."[l] In critique, an "extreme attention to what is real is confronted with the practice of a liberty that simultaneously respects this reality and violates it."[m] Critique is the elaboration of the event of the present in its contextuality and futurity.

Critique—discovering the present as an object of knowledge and a demand to be otherwise—becomes an empirical, historical, concrete, and contextual practice. Rejecting any need for interpretation (as if something were hidden), Foucault assumed that everything—all the relations (**relations of a nonrelation**) constituting reality—were available on the surface.[n] But that did not mean that everything was visible or that everyone could see it. Things have to be made visible; the connections have to be drawn or inscribed—always on the surface. This **new empiricism** had to be simultaneously historical (**archaeology**) and political/ethical (**genealogy**); understanding the present required a knowledge of how it came to be and how we became what we are. Foucault's investigations aimed to make the actualities of the surface visible, thereby **fabricating** or **fictioning** the real but always putting "itself to the test of reality, of contemporary reality, both to grasp the points where change is possible and desirable, and to determine the precise form this change should take."[o]

Foucault was a theorist of the concrete. He reconstructed the **positivity of an event**, which assumes that it is exactly what it is, right here and now, within a **field of immanence** (a context) without transcendence. The positivity of an event is its **effectivity**: what effects it is capable of producing, and what is capable of affecting it. The positivity of an event is only given contextually, by its **exteriority**, that is, by its relations with the other events in its field of immanence. But this was not an ontological claim that everything has the same mode of being—that of the **event**—because that would make it a transcendent category. He had no interest in the virtual; instead, he was concerned with, and worked through, an event's contingent and contextual specificity. His genealogies of the actual elucidated the forms of power that produce relations and effects, without seeking hidden origins or interests. Foucault refused any appeal to abstractions and generalities, such as class, race, or gender, and the task of the modern from "tasks that claim to be global or radical."[p]

For example, in 1973, the Nobel Prize winner Aleksandr Solzhenitsyn published *The Gulag Archipelago*, an account of the Soviet forced labor camps under Joseph Stalin. It was a decisive blow against those who still held some faith in the Soviet Union as an outpost of communism. It revealed the "truth" of Stalin's absolute authoritarian and repressive regime, the horrific conditions and treatment of prisoners, and the extraordinary number of deaths, even surpassing those of the Holocaust. The Gulag was quickly assimilated to other past events: Nazi concentration camps, Japanese internment camps, and Native American "reservations." For Foucault, the issue was not whether such comparisons were accurate but rather that the concept of the camp, because it transcends the actuality of the Gulag, avoids the modernist attitude and critique. By making the Gulag into another example of the more abstract—transcontextual—concept of "the camp," we avoid confronting its actuality, avoid coming to terms with its specificity and positivity.[q]

But Foucault used many abstractions (concepts) and generalizations in his empirical researches. To make sense of this apparent contradiction, we have to examine his idea of contexts as epochs, periods of history often spanning centuries. But he identified or constructed contexts always in relation to specific problematics of power (e.g., differentiation, normalization, subjectivation, governmentalization). While these might seem abstract, they can only be understood as operating in specific epochs. Even his concepts describing his practice of critique, his deep theory, depend on a specific context—the historical context of (European) modernity.

This is clear in his debate with Jacques Derrida, who had accused Foucault's *Madness and Civilization* of misreading the place of madness in René Descartes's *Meditations*.[r] Foucault responded in a fiery essay.[s] Derrida argued that Descartes defined reason by differentiating it from various nonreasons, including dreams, illusions, hallucinations, and especially madness. Reason and madness were presented as mutually exclusive, but for Derrida they are mutually constituted in an originary complexity, in différance: reason is only definable by the negation of its others, which are then themselves constitutive of reason. Madness especially was excluded to enable reason to claim a presence that is present to itself, and this is the inescapable dilemma of modern thought. All modern thought remains a prisoner of this originary différance. Hence reason (logocentrism) can never write a history of its other, which is exactly what Foucault had claimed to do in *The History of Madness*. Descartes's effort to define reason is still a necessary if impossible ground of thinking, and so, Descartes remains crucial to contemporary thought.

Foucault countered that you could not understand Descartes's exclusion of madness outside of his context. Descartes had distinguished madness's relation to reason from that of the various forms of sensory mistakes, but he only allowed the latter to serve as reason's other; madness was kept apart from the constitution of reason. Why was such a distinction necessary? To make sense of Descartes's statement here, Foucault proposed treating madness as a singular, historical, discursive event, locating it in its contexts of relations. What was happening in the larger society? Foucault observed that in the seventeenth century, there was a profound change in the way people who would be called mad lived. Previously, while they behaved oddly, they existed as human beings living alongside other people in daily life. Sometimes they were assumed to have religious or magical powers. But in the seventeenth century, such people were taken off the streets and put into newly created insane asylums, away from other people. Again, why?

It was certainly not Descartes's intention to legitimate this new exclusion. Rather, Descartes's argument existed alongside the emergence of a new logic of power and exclusion, differentiating the normal and the abnormal, constructing categories of the human, the infrahuman, and the nonhuman (visible in the emergence of classes, races, new forms of gendered differences, colonized others, etc.). Foucault did not explain the origins of this new logic; that was not his question. Descartes's definition of reason was early evidence of this new mode of power. His separation of reason from madness was not an innocent philosophical argument to be deconstructed by a "little pedagogue" who reduces discourse (and thought) to mere texts to be read, thereby establishing his own subject position as the master of the text.[t]

Descartes's definition of reason went hand in hand with—implicitly making sense of and providing good reasons for—real historical events, affecting real lives and real material geographies. Actual material existences were being reorganized at the intersection of discourse, including Descartes's, and power. The exclusion of madness was one of the originary moments of violence at the origin and privilege of the (modern) subject. It was the silence of the mad that made the subject's speech possible (as the speech of reason).

Descartes wrote at a moment when new forms of knowledge accompanied new material reorganizations of social life, and new principles and practices of power. Therefore, since we are no longer in that moment, Descartes's definition is irrelevant to contemporary thinkers.

DISCOURSE AND DISCURSIVE FORMATIONS

While Foucault flirted with structuralism in some of his early works, he later renounced any connection: "The question posed by language analysis of some discursive fact or other is always: according to what rules has a particular statement been made, and consequently according to what rules could other similar statements be made? The description of the events of discourse poses a quite different question: how it is that one particular statement appeared rather than another?"[u]

In what is often taken to be his structuralist moment, especially *The Order of Things*, Foucault described four **epistemes**, discursive formations of knowledge or, more accurately, the forms and conditions of the production of historical truths of life, labor, and language, which is to say, the historical truths of man.ᵛ Each presumes a unique relation between words and things. He identified these as finding the right word (truth as correspondence), the table of relations (truth as categorization), temporal series (truth as development), and language as a thing (truth as structural codes). Foucault did not question the legitimacy of these different epistemes as different historical productions of truth; he did not think they were deep structures. A better understanding might see them in Heideggerian terms as the historical clearings in which truth appears.

The concept of **discourse** and its elaborations (e.g., discursive practices and formations) are central to Foucault. Most theorists and critics use the term *discourse* to refer to any systems of signs (or signifiers), in any medium or form, which are either signifying or representational. Foucault used it to describe the material existence of semiotic utterances or **statements**. So, whether he was writing about a particular proposition, a text, a way of speaking, a picture, or a building, discourse referred to the very fact of the existence of a particular statement, kind of statement, or set of statements.

The question of discourse is not a hermeneutic problem of meaning and interpretation; it's not a question of origins and intentions. Statements are not to be treated as documents. Instead, statements are **monuments** to be taken literally; that is, they mean just what they say. And, like monuments, statements are rare; they do not proliferate wildly beyond their contexts. They are repeatable and regularized. And they are substantive; their accumulation as a multiplicity within the context is what makes them effective.

Consider: I am standing in front of a class, and I look at one student and say, "You have cancer." Certainly, an insensitive remark, but the student does not burst into tears or start throwing out questions about treatments and prognoses. Change the scene: I am still standing in front of a group of people but now in a hospital, wearing a white jacket and stethoscope, making the same statement. The conditions of possibility and the effects of those two statements are different. The meaning is the same, but the discursive statement is different. "You have cancer" is only effective in a particular field of evidence, in a specific institution, spoken by someone endowed with the authority to make such a statement (e.g., it would not have the same effect if uttered by an orderly). Similarly, the statement "Prisoners should be rehabilitated" emerged at a particular moment, into particular spaces, with particular effects, marking a new epoch. The statement "Diversity should be considered in college admission" came into being at a particular moment of an epoch. It was not, could not have been, uttered decades earlier, or, at least, it would not have had the same effects. It is always a matter of statements in contexts.

Foucault's empiricism started with the facticity or positivity of the statement. But the positivity of the statement, of what is said, is not immediately perceptible. It must be "discovered, polished, fashioned or invented."[w] It can only be grasped if we understand its conditions of emergence, insertion, functioning, and acceptance, only if we can make visible how it came to have the effects or power it does. The statement, then, despite its positivity, is not accountable in its own terms, for itself. It is constituted by its exteriority as a field of forces and possibilities.

But individual statements rarely stand alone; they are gathered together and related in a **discursive formation** or **apparatus**. Such formations are always more than discourse or language. They are heterogeneous ensembles of practices, including both expressive and nonexpressive materialities. Foucault's investigations endeavored to offer a material description of an event's—a statement's or a discursive formation's—existence within its spatial and historical context. That context is, similarly, broader than discourse; it too includes both discursive and nondiscursive events. That is, both the discursive formation as a context in its own right, and the context in which the formation itself exists, include not only discursive elements but all sorts of material, nonlinguistic, nondiscursive elements—institutional, technological, and so on.

Critique describes how that statement or formation and no other came to exist exactly where it did, in a particular place, in a particular field of immanence, and no others. Foucault described its emergence into and dispersal across the surfaces of particular social fields. What conditions enabled its appearance, and what effects does its appearance have? Foucault defined the effectivity of a statement or discourse as an **enunciative function**, which produces objects, enunciative modalities or subject positions, concepts, and strategies.

It is not that discourse creates such "things" out of thin air; rather, discourse configures the air in such a way that a discourse comes to stand out as a specific sort of problem, constituted by its enunciative function. Foucault was concerned with how forms of knowledge and power change, and how the two are linked. He studied those moments when new relations of the "articulable" (sayable) and the "visible" (seeable) are established. We can think of Foucault's genealogies of knowledge/power as *a* **history of problematizations**, where "problematization . . . is the totality of discursive or nondiscursive practices that introduces something into the play of true and false and constitutes it as an object for thought (whether in the form of moral reflection, scientific knowledge, political analysis, etc.)."ˣ What is the history of such problems? How are they made to be problems, and how do they demand responses?

Foucault suggested that the true site of problematization was the ***dispositif*** or **diagram**, which constitutes the historical specificity of our actuality and its field of the possible.[1] The diagram is an articulation of two kinds of discursive formations—one primarily discursive (knowledge) and one primarily material (power). There have been numerous formations of knowledge—religion, science, economics, and so on—each constituting its own space of truth. And there have been numerous formations of power. The two formations are not necessarily related, but once they are conjoined in a diagram, both are changed, and the relation appears inevitable.

Returning to a previous example, if I say to someone, "You are guilty of a crime," it has little or no effect. But in a different context or field of immanence, when a judge (with the full regalia of their position) utters this statement, it functions within a historical diagram connecting a discursive formation of knowledge (the law) with a discursive formation of power—the institutional spaces of the prison system (penality)—and the statement has a real effect. Just as Foucault had described the emergence of a new diagram of madness and the asylum, he later described the emergence of a new diagram of criminality. Foucault asked: How is it possible that a system of penal power is enabled or upheld by a system of knowledge? Consider the judge who regularly sentences Black men more harshly than white men, but who insists that he is not a racist. His acts of power, whether he knows it or not, rest on a formation of statistical knowledge, which says that Black men commit more crimes proportionately than white men.

A diagram is always contingent and contextually specific. It cannot be understood in terms of causality or intentions, origins or reasons. Not surprisingly, Foucault was never concerned with the nature of the transitions from one diagram to another, only with their conditions of possibility and effectivities.

Foucault's practice of critique—the substance of his deep theory—is embedded in his particular genealogical studies. The substantive theories and

1 It is not surprising that Deleuze read Foucault's diagram as equivalent to his and Guattari's concept of the abstract machine; Foucault at times acknowledged this debt.

concepts he developed to "describe" various diagrams are not abstractions that can be simply moved beyond the contexts of his analyses. Unfortunately, too many people treat his concepts, especially his theories of power, as if they were generalizable. Perhaps that is the likely fate of a radical contextualist. In the next lecture, we shall see how this all played out in Foucault's genealogies of knowledge/power.

NOTES

a. Foucault, *Archaeology of Knowledge*, 17.

b. Foucault, "Powers and Strategies," in *Power, Truth, Strategy*, 49–58.

c. Foucault, "Questions of Method," in *Power, Truth, Strategy*, 233.

d. Weber, *Protestant Ethic*, 123.

e. Foucault, "What Is Enlightenment?," in *Politics of Truth*, 97–119; "What Is Revolution?," in *Politics of Truth*, 83–95.

f. Foucault, "What Is Enlightenment?," in *Politics of Truth*, 106.

g. Foucault, "What Is Enlightenment?," in *Politics of Truth*, 108.

h. On "limit-attitude," see Foucault, "What Is Enlightenment?," in *Politics of Truth*, 113.

i. Foucault, "What Is Revolution?," in *Politics of Truth*, 83–84.

j. Foucault, "What Is Revolution?," in *Politics of Truth*, 94–95.

k. Foucault, "What Is Enlightenment?," in *Politics of Truth*, 114.

l. Foucault, "What Is Revolution?," in *Politics of Truth*, 95.

m. Foucault, "What Is Revolution?," in *Politics of Truth*, 83–84.

n. For relations of a nonrelation, see Deleuze, *Foucault*.

o. Foucault, "What Is Enlightenment?," in *Politics of Truth*, 114.

p. Foucault, "What Is Enlightenment?," in *Politics of Truth*, 114.

q. Foucault, "Powers and Strategies," in *Power, Truth, Strategy*, 49–58.

r. Derrida, "Cogito and the History of Madness," in *Writing and Difference*, 36–76.

s. Foucault, "My Body, This Paper, This Fire," in *Aesthetics, Method, and Epistemology*, 393–417.

t. For "little pedagogue," see Foucault, "My Body, This Paper, This Fire," 412.

u. Foucault, *Archaeology of Knowledge*, 27.

v. White, "Foucault Decoded," 30. Hayden White, one of the first scholars to introduce Foucault in the United States, argued that such truths "are nothing but what the relationship presumed to exist between words and things permits them to appear to be in a given age."

w. Foucault, "Politics and the Study of Discourse," in Burchell, Gordon, and Miller, *Foucault Effect*, 15.

x. Foucault, "Concern for Truth," in *Politics, Philosophy, Culture*, 257.

Foucault and Knowledge/Power

The problematization of knowledge/power explores the actual articulations of historical productions of truth and organizations of power. In this project, as explained by Michel Foucault, "critique is the movement by which the subject gives himself the right to question truth on its effects of power and question power on its discourses of truth."[a] "The question is no longer through what error, illusion, oversight or illegitimacy has knowledge come to induce effects of domination," according to Foucault, but how the "indivisibility" of knowledge and power can create both the conditions that make certain fixed realities acceptable and "a field of possibles, of openings, indecisions, reversals, and possible dislocations which make them fragile, temporary."[b] The question is how particular diagrams come to exist at particular places, with what effects. How does a particular conjunction of truth and power work in its concreteness and contextuality?

The relation of truth and power is not a matter of legitimation or representation (ideology) but of **rationalization**. Discursive formations of knowledge produce "truth," which provides the rationalities of formations of power. Foucault's *"political history of the production of truth"* was not concerned with matters of epistemology, truth and error, or belief and ideology.[c] He distinguished between **being in-the-true** and having **truth effects**, the former being a necessary condition for the latter.[d] That a statement is **in-the-true** does not mean it is true (i.e., has truth effects), or even that people think it is true; rather, it means that it is considered "reasonable" enough to question whether it is true. For example, many people in the West would not locate voodoo or astrology in-the-true; hence, it is futile—unreasonable—to seek justification or evidence. Such statements may have effects, but they cannot have truth effects.

A statement can have truth effects only if it is located within a discursive formation of truth, a **regime** or **technology of veridiction**.[e] Such regimes comprise systems of procedures for the production, distribution, equation, circulation, and operation of statements seeking to have truth effects. They are, again, heterogeneous ensembles of practices, assemblages of the discursive (scientific, therapeutic, etc.) and the nondiscursive (buildings, technologies, etc.). They prescribe what is sayable (and knowable) and what is visible (seeable), within a particular regime of veridiction, always distributing and accumulating statements at particular locations in its specific context. Some statements can be in-the-true, and even have truth effects, even if they are not thought to be true by some epistemological standard. For example, Newtonian physics, which is not true in physics, still has truth effects because it works in some circumstances; we still build bridges, tunnels, and buildings using Newtonian physics. It would be very weird to build them using quantum mechanics or relativistic theory.

Foucault also distinguished, within the political history of truth, two kinds of narratives: archaeology and genealogy. At any moment, in any context, there are always multiple regimes of veridiction; they may be dominant, residual, or emergent, and they all compete to be included in-the-true and to have truth effects. In these struggles, some regimes dominate, and they exclude or erase the others, some of which may have previously been in-the-true, had truth effects, and even been dominant. An **archaeology** recovers and constructs a history of subjugated knowledges or regimes of veridiction (e.g., mysticism and magic, Indigenous knowledges, women's knowledges, subaltern or colonized knowledges, homeopathic medicine). Archaeology does not narrate a continuous history; it does not explain how or why particular knowledges appeared or disappeared. It is more like a series of vignettes, an archive of anecdotes, a dictionary of the forgotten. A **genealogy** reanimates these subjugated, silenced regimes of truth in the present. It poses them as a challenge to the dominant veridical formations and their powers of exclusion by bringing what had been made absent back in-the-true. For example, Foucault's criticism of science (at least, positivism) was not epistemological; he did not deny its truth effects but, rather, its exclusion of any nonscientific claim to truth.

POWER

Foucault also offered archaeologies and genealogies of discursive formations of power or **regimes of jurisdiction**.[f] He rejected many common assumptions about power: that it is property that can be possessed; that it always exists in the same way (homogeneity); that it is located and localized in specific places such as the state; that it has a point of origin; that it is built on top of, and subordinated to, other, already existing relations.

Power is generally assumed to be external to people and working through negation—as either prohibition or repression. As a result, we tend to think of resistance as a struggle for liberation from power itself. Alternatively, power is assumed to be internal to and constitutive of the relations among people. Power constructs the very social relations in which it is to be found; it is a circular, closed system from which there is no escape. You are always and already trapped in particular structures of power. The only way out is a revolution that overthrows the totality of existing social institutions and relationships.

Foucault thought of power differently. First, power is heterogeneous, operating in and through many mechanisms and registers, including coercion (both physical and psychological), brutalization, death, regulation, differentiation, distribution, exclusion, consensus, normalization, disciplinization, seduction, and so on. Second, wherever there is power, there is resistance, although the problem of agency haunted Foucault. Third, power operates at the microlevel or molecular level (as **capillary power** or a **microphysics of power**) as well at the more obvious macrosocial levels. Capillary power does not work from or through totalities (e.g., individual bodies or minds, the state, the society), and it is never centered in a single, privileged place.

Capillary power is the effect of one force on another. It is mobile, fragmented, and dispersed, always immanent in other relations; therefore, it is always local and defined by the particular points through which it passes. It is strategic, defined operationally or functionally by what it does rather than by some (moral) standard outside itself. Capillary power is "the point where power reaches into the very grain of individuals, touches their bodies and inserts itself into their actions and attitudes, their discourses, learning processes and everyday lives."[g] It is not mediated by consciousness, subjectivity, or intention; it describes "how the relations of power are able to pass materially into the very density of bodies without even having to be relayed by the representation of subjects."[h]

Regimes of jurisdiction organize and deploy capillary power, often reconstituting power at macrosocial levels. They are the programmings, the procedures and strategies that control or conduct the conduct of bodies, both individuals and populations, creating the conditions for what they can and cannot do, but they operate below the levels of consciousness, of individuality or group identity.

A particular programming of conduct is secured by its articulation to the truth effects of a particular rationality. For example, consider "race." There is no universal, objective definition of race, and no single practice of racism. There are only the different regimes of veridiction that have spoken "the truth" of race, telling us what we can see and say: religious, anatomical, phrenological, dermatologic, genetic, and cultural technologies of race. Different formations of knowledge have produced different truths of who is "colored," or Black, and so on over the course of history. These racialogical discourses are not understandable in enlightenment terms; they are not about truth in an epistemological, biological, or phenomenological sense. They exhibit what the British cultural theorist Paul Gilroy calls a **rational irrationalism**.[i] They are articulated to various regimes of jurisdiction, defining the material ways in which these "truths" can be enacted (e.g., chattel slavery, Jim Crow, segregation, discrimination, criminalization).

GOVERNMENTALITY

Foucault's genealogy of **governmentality**, or the art of governance, offered a history of the ways power has been exercised over life and the body—a history of **biopower**—in modernity.[j] He identified four diagrams—sovereignty, discipline, biopolitics, and neoliberalism—that emerged at particular moments in European contexts, although they did not replace or displace each other, nor did they disappear. Indeed, they all coexist in the present, although Foucault did not say much about how they might interact with and affect each other.

The different diagrams control how we behave not by oppression, subjugation, or violence (although Foucault did not deny that these continued to exist) but by producing particular subjects. Echoing Louis Althusser, Foucault said that subjectivity—and the freedom that it implies—is the result of the forms of governmentality. Different diagrams establish **different subjects** and different definitions and expectations of **freedom**. They accomplish this by **subjecting** people to norms, although the very nature of the norms changes. Each diagram constructs a different "normal," through different procedures (regimes of normalization), creating subjects who will behave "normally."

Sovereignty is the premodern, absolute power of kings over life and death. The sovereign can kill at will or decide not to kill. And that power was based on, rationalized by, Christian theology. Sovereignty demands an absolute distinction between ruler and ruled, with the sovereign constantly reminding their "subjects" of the sovereign's power; consequently, the power over life and death is constantly on display, in often horrific spectacles of death. Sovereignty has lived on in dictatorships, as well as in public and spectacular acts of brutalization. Those who perpetuate such power often confirm its rationality by appeals to religion.

As the dominance of sovereignty—both its truth and its power—was challenged and slowly crumbled, Foucault noted the appearance of various discourses on the art of governance, on the best way to govern people (e.g., Niccolò Machiavelli and Thomas Hobbes). These reflections understood that power existed beyond the state and began to recognize the full range of practices by which people are governed, by which the conduct of conduct is enacted. They not only destabilized the difference between the ruler and the ruled but demanded that the ruler become familiarized with the life of the people, reframing the very nature of the relation in more pastoral terms.

The first truly modern diagram of governmentality was **discipline** (or an ***anatomopolitics of the body***).[k] It located power in enclosed, institutional spaces like the prison, the factory, the teaching hospital, and so on, and operated through surveillance. Foucault first identified this diagram in *Discipline and Punish*, an archaeology of the modern prison, which, he argued, took the form of the **panopticon** (figure 29.1), a drawing created by the utilitarian Jeremy Bentham (1748–1832).

The idea is quite simple. Imagine two concentric circles. The outer circle is composed of a series of cells that house prisoners. The inner circle is the guard tower. From the tower, the guard (or, more accurately, the eyes of the guard) can see into the entirety of every cell. The prisoner (or, more accurately, the prisoner's body) cannot hide from the gaze of the guard, and the

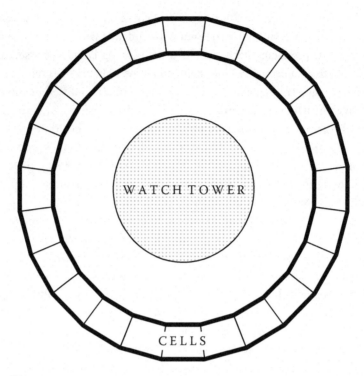

WATCH TOWER

CELLS

FIGURE 29.1

prisoner (or, more accurately, the prisoner's eyes) cannot see into the guard tower. The result is that the prisoners are under constant surveillance, or at least they must conduct themselves as if they were, even if they are not. The panopticon imposes—without the use of force—a form of conduct on the prisoner. It is normalization through the power of the gaze. The prisoner's body functionally internalizes the guard's eyes so that the prisoner is watching himself. The result is a **docile subject**, a subject who takes responsibility for governing himself by following the norms. This is modern citizenship: people act normally because they behave according to norms they have internalized as their own.

How did this come about? In the late eighteenth and early nineteenth centuries, various groups set about reforming the prison system, for different reasons and with different motives. What they ended up producing was the panopticon. Bentham's drawing did not enter into the discussions; no one consciously offered up the panopticon. The diagram was the result of the confluence of various forces in the historical context, the conjunction of particular regimes of veridiction and jurisdiction. The most important regime of veridiction for such disciplinary power was, according to Foucault, "pastoral" truth. Pastoralism refers to a transformation in the church, propelled partly by the Reformation and Counter-Reformation, which directed priests to focus less on preparing people for the next life and more on helping them live a good life in this world, less on theology and more on ministry. Just as the shepherd is meant to look after his flock, so the minister tends to his congregation, concerned with their well-being.

Discipline describes the operation of power in many modern institutions, including the modern classroom and its pedagogy: the teacher (the not so metaphoric guard) can see all the students all the time, and so they must act as if they are constantly under their scrutiny. That is why it is so funny (and a minor act of rebellion) when, in the movies, the teacher turns their back and all hell breaks loose, just until the very second when the teacher turns back to surveil the class. It is probably not coincidental that this pedagogical proxemics was first developed by the English in colonial India, to produce subjects who wanted to be English but were never quite good enough and could never succeed. Students are "normalized" to want to follow the norms of proper behavior.

While Foucault thought discipline could operate only in enclosed spaces, he did not foresee the contemporary omnipresence of surveillance. The result is that forms of docile subjectivity and self-responsibilization continue to have a strong influence on the conduct of our conduct, and our subjectivity.

In lectures he delivered in 1975–76, published as *Society Must Be Defended*, Foucault argued that a new diagram of governmentality—**biopolitics** or **securitization**—emerged in the mid-nineteenth century. Unlike discipline, it works on populations, especially as they are located in and move across space. It articulates a technology of veridiction based on the statistical calculation of probability, with a technology of jurisdiction that asserts control over all aspects of life, including life itself. Operating on the conditions of possibility, it seeks to "let things happen" or, more accurately, to strategically arrange the environment in ways that encourage or discourage certain ways in which life can flourish for certain populations (e.g., vaccinations). Biopolitical power manages the flows, circulations, and distributions of populations, resources, goods, and so on in terms of the probabilities of future risks.

In his 1979 lectures, published as *The Birth of Biopolitics*, Foucault suggested that a new diagram of governmentality had emerged in the twentieth century. **Neoliberalism** instantiated economics (particularly neoclassical economics) as the rationality for a regime of power in which everything was regulated according to economic calculations of value in markets. Unfortunately, the lectures focused almost entirely on economic theory as a regime of veridiction, with far too little attention to the forms of power themselves. And, somewhat confusingly, the lectures had little to offer in the way of an exploration of biopolitics itself.

TECHNOLOGIES OF THE SELF

Foucault's genealogy of governmentalities raised a question he had been dealing with his entire career: How is resistance possible? If subjectivity and freedom are produced within each diagram, how can a subject be capable of resisting the diagram? It is not sufficient to say—as he did—that where there is power, there is resistance, without specifying the **agency** through which resistance is manifested or expressed. It is not enough to say—as he did— that the fact that revolution happens is enough. It is not enough to invent a concept—as he did—of the **pleb** as the immediate principle and energy of popular resistance embodied in the masses.[l] Since he did not believe in the viability of revolution or the possibility of escape, Foucault concluded that political resistance is best aimed not at negating either the state or the diagram but at demanding that one be governed less or at least not in that particular way.

Foucault's solution to the question of the possibility of willed resistance rested on the existence of a third technology or regime, although it was never clear if and how **technologies of the self** were articulated to the diagram, or whether they existed as relatively independent apparatuses.[m] Foucault suggested that the project of modernity becomes possible only at the intersection of technologies of truth, power, and self. You will recall (I hope) that his icon of modernity was the dandy, who changes him- or herself—now we can say—by enacting a technology of the self against the effectivities of the diagrams of governmentality. It comes down to the possibility of using one diagram to counteract another, taking up the tools of one technology to resist the effects of other technologies, all of which attempt to produce the very subjectivity that is acting.

Foucault began to lay out a **pragmatics of the self**—exploring possible individualities/subjectivities—through a genealogy of "sex."[n] But "sex" here is something problematized and not an ontological or even biological reality to be assumed. If diagrams configure the actualities of people's lives, what is it they are configuring? If there are different regimes of "sex," what is the status of the concept of "sex" here? What are the different diagrams, diagrams of? Foucault refused the idea of an underlying, transcendental truth of all the different diagrams, existing "before" the operations of discourse and power. There is nothing that could be called "sex" existing as the raw material of the different diagrams. What "sex" is, is only what exists in a particular diagram. There are only the historical diagrams, existing in specific historical contexts.

The genealogy of sex and its relation to subjectivity was first announced in *The History of Sexuality, Volume 1: An Introduction,* which was then followed by *The History of Sexuality, Volume 1: The Will to Knowledge* (1976), *Volume 2: The Use of Pleasure* (1984), *Volume 3: The Care of the Self* (1984), and *Volume 4: Confessions of the Flesh* (2018). In the first volume, Foucault argued that the conduct of our "sex" lives has been the result, at least since the late nineteenth century, of the **regime of sexuality**, a diagram that produces "sexuality" as a problem, an object, and a separate sphere of life. The regime of sexuality is paradoxical because, on the one hand, it demands that sexuality be repressed and, on the other, it demands an endless production of discourses about sexuality. Its rationality derives from a regime of veridiction built on the concept and practice of confession. It is through confession that I reveal the truth of my innermost being, whether in church or therapy. Both are obsessed with people's sexual behavior, thoughts, fantasies, desires, and so on. The confession inscribes your sexuality as the key to, the truth of, your identity, even the very essence of your subjectivity. The result is that people themselves are constantly obsessing about sexuality, and sexuality is itself inscribed into almost every aspect of everyday life.

This "truth" of sexuality and self is linked to a regime of jurisdiction that defines very precise and inviolable norms of behavior and, in so doing, defines the realm of the sexual perversions, sexual deviance, unforgivable sins, and so on. This conduct of conduct normalizes heterosexual, procreative, missionary sexuality and dictates that the more you deviate from that, whether in the direction of homosexual practices, interspecies practices, anal intercourse, fetishes, or whatever, whether in your behavior or fantasies, the more society will judge and punish you.

But how does this get us any closer to the possibility of resistance and agency? Foucault sought out other diagrams in the past (from Greece and Rome), in other cultures, and in more transgressive sexual cultures. He identified at least two diagrams. The first is a **regime of *ars erotica,*** or the **erotics**

of sex, which foregrounds the production of pleasure as something other than an individual and subjective matter. While those who live in the regime of sexuality tend to think of, for example, the *Kama Sutra* as little more than a compendium of interesting and challenging sexual positions to increase one's own pleasure and, hopefully, that of one's partner, Foucault saw it as an expression of a diagram with different forms of truth, different understandings of pleasure, and different ways of conducting a sexual life.

The second diagram, the **care of the self**, from classical Greece, provided an answer to the question of agency and resistance. Such technologies operate by a **subjectification** that is distinct from the processes of **subjectivation**, the latter defining the ways subjects are constituted at the intersection of truth and power. The technologies of the care of the self enable subjects to act upon themselves, offering a kind of autointervention against the subjectivating diagrams of power/knowledge. Subjectification allows the subject to shape and deploy other possible individualities and subjectivities for itself.

Presumably, there is a link between the subject of the regime of sexuality and the various forms of the "liberal" subjects of governmentality, although Foucault clearly believed that this modern subject was being "washed away" by the tides of history. There is also, presumably, a link between the care of the self and the practice of critique. Both are, in some sense, politically neutral (which may help explain why Foucault's politics were so often challenged), but in the final analysis, Foucault argued that the intellectual (and the dandy) must choose where to stand in that context. As Woody Guthrie sang, "Which side are you on?"[10] In the end, modernity always poses an ethical challenge to both thinking and living.

I have described Foucault's contextualism as epochal. He offered a deep theory for identifying particular kinds of (discursive) forces, operating across centuries, particular diagrams of power/knowledge, and subjectification. But he refused to reduce reality, or power for that matter, to discourse. And he acknowledged that there are always other forces beyond such diagrams (such as capitalism, and colonialism), which, however bound to these diagrams, cannot be reduced to them. While the microphysics of power and critique reveal important understandings of modernity, they do not account for any particular instance of modernity. Such an account would have to examine the complex relations among the different forces, including those between the different diagrams. An even more radical contextualism would move from an understanding of contexts as epochs to one addressing a more concrete and overdetermined convergence of forces operating at multiple levels of abstraction. It would close the gap between deep theory and social analysis, allowing only the commitment to contextualism itself, in an effort to grasp the power relations of everyday life. It is to such a paradoxical deep theory that I now turn.

NOTES

a. Foucault, "What Is Critique?," in *Politics of Truth*, 47.

b. Foucault, "What Is Critique?," in *Politics of Truth*, 66.

c. Foucault, "Power and Sex," in *Politics, Philosophy, Culture*, 112.

d. Foucault, "Order of Discourse," in Young, *Untying the Text*, 48–78.

e. Foucault, "Questions of Method," in *Power, Truth, Strategy*, 223–38.

f. Foucault, "Questions of Method," in *Power, Truth, Strategy*, 223–38.

g. Foucault, "Prison Talk," in *Power/Knowledge*, 39.

h. Foucault, "Interview with Lucette Finas," in *Power, Truth, Strategy*, 69–70.

i. Gilroy, *Against Race*, 65.

j. Foucault, *Society Must Be Defended*; Foucault, *Security, Territory, Population*; Foucault, *Birth of Biopolitics*.

k. Foucault, *History of Sexuality*, 139.

l. Foucault, "Powers and Strategies," in *Power, Truth, Strategy*, 49–58.

m. Foucault, "Technologies of the Self," in *Ethics*, 223–51.

n. Foucault, *Government of Self and Others*, 5.

o. The Almanac Singers, "Which Side Are You On?"

Stuart Hall

The choice of a final chapter matters, if only because it offers the last word and the culmination of my backstory.[1] Stuart Hall was the most consistent radical contextualist, although he is rarely included in the pantheon of deep theory. He developed an eclectic set of concepts to make sense of the histories of **conjunctural** changes, and of lives marked by struggles, dislocations, and displacements. He constantly moved between and brought together the political and the intellectual, the academic and the popular, and often appeared on public media.

Hall was a Black, colonial subject, born in Kingston, Jamaica, on February 3, 1932. He immigrated to England in 1951 with prestigious scholarships to study literature, well before Jamaican independence in 1962, and remained until his death in London on February 10, 2014. His dark skin had made him

---

1 Full disclosure: My own thinking is deeply indebted to the work of Stuart Hall, who was my teacher, mentor, and friend and my son's godfather. I turned to Stuart whenever I could not find a way forward, a way to go on thinking.

an outsider within his own light-skinned, middle-class family, but his social position made it difficult for him to belong to the street cultures with which he felt more at home. His move to the United Kingdom was, at least in part, an attempt to escape his "unlivable conditions" in Jamaica.[a]

Part of the first generation of "West Indians," an identity created in England, who migrated from the periphery to the center of colonial power, Hall refused to present himself as a Jamaican or Caribbean intellectual. But he also refused to identify as an English intellectual. He was caught, thrice over, in **double consciousness**: first between his two positions in Jamaica; second, between the colonized and the colonizer, the periphery and the center, as a Black man in England; and third, between the colonial and the complex instabilities of the postcolonial.

The concept of double consciousness was introduced by the African American intellectual and activist W. E. B. Du Bois (1868–1963), one of the founders of the National Association for the Advancement of Colored People.[b] It names the experience of seeing oneself though another's eyes, of living between two worlds, belonging to neither, and it often results in a sense of existential and political urgency. While Du Bois thought of it primarily as an internal strife within marginalized or oppressed populations, it has become a powerful and often disruptive condition of possibility for new practices of critique.

Hall often described himself as a **diasporic** intellectual, homeless and constantly displaced by the routes (not the roots) of his life. His intellectual (literary) ambitions were unsettled by political events (e.g., the Soviet invasion of Hungary and the Israeli-British-French invasion of the Suez, both in 1956), leading him to join the Campaign for Nuclear Disarmament and to help form the New Left Club, a group of émigré thinkers who sought an alternative socialist analysis of and politics for the postwar conditions, partly by addressing the inadequacies of Marxism.[2]

2 To paraphrase his description of the major commitments defining the project of the New Left: (1) the need to reinvent a new conception of socialism (and an expanded understanding of politics) based on a new analysis of the political, economic, and social relations and dynamics of "our times"; (2) the need to take culture seriously; (3) the need to reject any and all binary choices between oversimplified options (e.g., the old and the new, the left and the right) in favor of seeking a third, more complex position defined neither by a simple compromise nor by a dialectical synthesis; for example, in political terms, he described the New Left's relation to state politics (and political parties) as a strategy of "one foot in, one foot out"; and (4) the need to inaugurate a popular

Hall was the founding editor of the *New Left Review*, one of the most influential "leftist" intellectual journals since the end of the Second World War. In 1964, he joined the newly created Centre for Contemporary Cultural Studies at the University of Birmingham, eventually becoming its director. In 1980, he moved to the Open University, a "distance-learning" experiment. Hall published hundreds of essays and interviews, a few of which were collected in his only solely authored book, *The Hard Road to Renewal* (1988). He coauthored and coedited many books, including *The Popular Arts* (1964), *Resistance through Rituals* (1976), and *Policing the Crisis* (1976), and numerous collections of his essays have been released posthumously. Given the difficulty of radical contextual thinking, it is not surprising that so much of Hall's work was done collaboratively, offering interventions into particular states of affairs and the arguments around them.

In the 1980s, Hall became deeply involved in the Black Arts Movement in the United Kingdom, mentoring numerous groups: two Black film collectives, Sankofa and the Black Audio Film Collective; Autograph ABP, an association for Black British photographers; and Iniva, the Institute of International Visual Arts. He devoted the last decades of his life to building Rivington Place, a visual arts space dedicated to cultural and geographic diversity.

THEORIZING WITHOUT THEORY

Hall's radical contextualism was enacted in his actual practice of critique as **cultural studies**, which he, more than anyone, shaped and made into a global intellectual force both inside and outside of the academy, no doubt partly due to his personal charisma and generosity. Cultural studies is a radically interdisciplinary effort to bring theory into conversation with concrete empirical research, in the service of better political possibilities. Understanding the politics of knowledge production, it embeds its theorizing in the complexities of the historical context.

Hall challenged the tendency to fetishize theory, to join the endless search for the *right* theory, one that would be impervious to criticism and provide answers to all the important questions. But since this never arrives, theoretical

---

politics that connects with people's lives and make questions of everyday life and agency central. It is not difficult to see in this description of the project of the New Left the essence of Stuart Hall's vision for cultural studies and the political arts. Hall, "The 'First' New Left," in *Selected Political Writings*, 117–41.

labor becomes little more than measuring and criticizing the inadequacies of other theories.

He thought the contemporary world demanded another way of thinking. Theory does not deliver truth; it merely provides the tools for the difficult work of constructing and mapping a concrete context. Hall treated every concept and theory as context-bound, with a rigor defined by the specifics of a concrete moment, and the need to keep moving "forward," toward a better but always imperfect understanding, and sometimes, by the need to stop theorizing: "I have a strategic relation to theory. I don't regard myself as a theorist in the sense that that is my work. I am interested always in going on theorising about the world, about the concrete, but I am not interested in the production of theory as an object in its own right. And therefore, I use theory in strategic ways. . . . It's because I think my object is to think the concreteness of the object in its many different relations."[c]

Hall was a theorist without a theory, an eclectic par excellence. His work drew from a wide range of thinkers without ever declaring fealty to any of them. He described working on the ground they set forth, "wrestling" with them.[d] For example, he wrote extensively about Marx but never claimed to be a Marxist. He did not "poach" concepts from others but identified those that might prove useful to his project. Acknowledging that they were tied (but not bound) to their original contexts, he said, "They have to be delicately dis-interred from their concrete and specific historical embeddedness and transplanted into new soil with considerable care and patience."[e] Thus, while Hall drew on a number of Gramscian concepts and tools, he was not particularly concerned with finding an exegetically correct reading of Gramsci.

For example, Hall argued that the logics of deconstruction, of dissemination, of différance, "must always be read in the context of colonisation, slavery and racialisation; they must not be read as an alternative to, but as part of their internal logic." Concepts often assumed to challenge or escape the stable binarisms of the asymmetrical structures of power—for example, hybridity, syncretism, third space, in between—are products of "the disjunctive logic which colonisation, slavery, and modernity introduced to the world."[f] So, Hall asked a different—contextual—question: Why do these binaries reappear?

Hall understood that the theoretical and the empirical, the epistemological and the political, were inseparable. He made no claims beyond the specific context. He was convinced, with all the passion of his political hopes, that changing the world, opening up the possibilities of people living together in a more humane world, demanded the best, most rigorous knowledge possible of the world you are trying to change. You need to know how and why all manners and forms of inhumanity and inhumaneness are continuously reproduced, albeit in different ways and forms. You need to understand how and why the world produces, albeit not necessarily through the same practices or in the same forms, the structures of inequality, injustice, violence, enslavement, subordination, and so on that have for so long constituted the limits of possibility of people's lives. Ideas matter, knowledge matters, and better knowledge matters even more. Such knowledge required something like Marx's detour through theory.[g] But its "adequacy" can only be judged by its utility in relation to the context, for the task of theorizing is always about "the grasping of real relations."[h]

He approached politics contextually as well. He rejected the self-confidence of political certainties: the assumption that you already know what is going on, what the stakes are, and what people should desire. Political change demanded that the intellectual meet people "where they are," and move (with) them, toward a better way of living. This meant that we have to stop blaming "the common people" and assuming that they are (cultural) dopes or always duped, always acting out of false consciousness, greed, or gullibility, and incapable of understanding what was happening.

Hall assumed that every context posed its own challenges and questions. Rather than assuming that it was always the same question, or that one could deliver the same answer over and over, he sought better ways of hearing and asking questions. Only then can you work on and through the discursive and material conditions and forces, the structures of social relations, and the organizations of practices that constitute a particular context. And you have to do this knowing that your accounts will be incomplete and open to legitimate criticisms, that they will need to be modified as both the context and the available conceptual and analytical tools change. Hall called this the **discipline of the conjuncture**.[i] To think otherwise was to indulge in the "solace of closure," to think that one knows how to wrap everything up in a neat, finished story. But the best knowledge is, ultimately, that which opens the context to change, that identifies points where power might be challenged and strategies might work to transform them. And that requires intellectuals to share what they have learned with others, with whoever will listen.

CONSTRUCTING CONTEXTS

Hall offered a contextual theory of contexts. He understood that contexts were not transparently given as a collection of observations. They had to be constructed by engaging with the empirical world through the affordances of specific concepts. Many contexts can be constructed from an empirical field, depending on the available concepts and, just as important, the (political) questions one chooses to hear.

The questions dictate an appropriate **level of abstraction**. Such levels do not define a continuum from the local to the universal but, rather, different spatial and temporal frames that identify the different reaches or pertinences of the forces organizing them as spaces of power and struggle and constructing populations and subjectivities. Consequently, while Hall rejected generalizations, he did not reject general concepts, that is, concepts that function on higher levels of abstraction.

Consider "commodification." It may help distinguish capitalism from feudalism, but only at a high level of abstraction, that is, the transition to a new epoch. But it may not help us understand the historical and geographic specificity of different configurations of capitalism, precisely what we need to understand if we hope to imagine new futures and new strategies for realizing them.

Or consider "race" and "racism." Hall refused any universal or even general definition of them, as if there were some unchanging "rational core." Of course, they involve differentiations, identifications, and distributions within a population, but that observation is not particularly useful at the levels at which political change is possible, where they demand more concrete, contextually specific definitions. While such efforts cannot ignore the effects of traces of previous historical contexts, they have to recognize that specific forms of race and racism are products of the present context. We bear witness to "the reworking of the tradition under the force of the present [context] . . . a reworking that precisely delivers the much more complex idea . . . of the **'changing same,'**" something akin perhaps to Ludwig Wittgenstein's notion of family resemblance—a relation with neither essence nor necessity.[j]

How did Hall understand this "reworking"? Like most modern and postmodern deep theorists, he began with the centrality of relations; any term (practice, event, discourse) is always constituted as what it is within a set of relations. But, unlike them, Hall's **"theory" of articulation** viewed historical reality as the ongoing configuration (relationing) of relations: the making, unmaking, and remaking of relations out of the field of existing relations. Hall argued that while relations are constructed, this did not mean they were not real. On the contrary, their reality is defined not by their origin but by their effects. They are real precisely because they have real effects. History is the ongoing effort (process) to articulate relations, thereby constructing differentiated unities or unities-in-difference.

The contingency of the world, the fact that it is continuously being made, means that the results of any relation are never guaranteed. The world was not destined to be what it is or to become what one fears (or hopes). Relations are never fixed once and for all, and their modifications are never given in advance. The demand for the rigorous study of historical specificity requires the elucidation of the actual relations; of how their strengths and weaknesses are accomplished, exploited, maintained, and struggled over; of their capacities; and of where they are most pertinent. Articulation theory embraces (rather than reduces or denies) the complexity, contingency, and ever-changing nature of social reality in order to intervene into it. This is what Hall meant by the possibility of "objective" truths.

And this entailed, according to Hall, the **refusal of reductionism** in its two forms: first, the claim that what is happening is the result of, all about, some one thing (e.g., the economy, or patriarchy, or racism). Articulation requires a logic of supplementarity or connectivity: an event is caused by or about many things: "and . . . and . . . and . . ." The second is the claim that everything is all about the same thing(s). In either case, knowing the answers in advance, you are unlikely to ever be surprised. Reductionism erases the complexity and multiplicity of determinations and relations. It does not reveal some hidden truth but denies the very reality it seeks to understand.

But the effort to construct and understand a context is even more complicated, for the refusal of reductionism also entails a refusal to treat any context as if it were all alone in the world. Every context is related to multiple contexts operating and interacting at both the same and different levels of abstraction, ranging from a specific moment, event, or situation (which is overdetermined beyond our ability to offer a critical account) to the epoch.

Finally, Hall saw resistance woven into the fabric of social power because of the complexity and contingency of power in any context. Agency is an empirical question: Who or what is constructed in the context to have agency, to have the ability to resist? In most social contexts, what people do has real effects; they have some agency despite its being constructed. Sometimes, people just try to do the best they can, to live the best life they can, in their circumstances. Hall described his position as a theoretical antihumanism and a political humanism. Subjectivities and agencies are constructed, but it you want to change the world, people have to believe in their own power to change it, and to act on that belief. The results may not be what they expected, but that is the nature of articulation: there are no guarantees.

The recognition of different levels of abstraction led Hall to identify the **conjuncture** as a particular level of abstraction, between the event and the epoch. The decision to work at this level was a response to his sense of the possibilities of intellectual rigor and political struggle in the context itself, which necessitated the ability to see intersecting political struggles and possibilities. A conjuncture is the level at which such work might be most effective in engaging with the complexities of the context. In different works, he cut into the conjuncture through specific forms of practices and relations, including subcultures, media, popular culture, identity and race, and the rise of a new conservative politics, although none of these ever became a defining object for him. In each, he foregrounded the importance of culture (discourse), asserting that it had become increasingly determining over the past century.

HEGEMONY

Perhaps his most famous intervention was his "theory" of **hegemony**, presented in his analysis of the rise of Thatcherism and subsequent conservative political formations.[k] Hall argued that any successful effort to oppose Thatcherism (as well as subsequent political developments) had to understand how its victory was being won: the processes and strategies by which it was undoing one set of relations and structures of power and redrawing the maps of power itself. Unfortunately, the British left did not get the message, but that is another story.

That work began in the collaborative research of *Policing the Crisis*, which started by questioning a single event—a mugging and the disproportionate sentencing of the young perpetrators—and followed it through a growing "moral panic" and a deeply racialized call for law and order. The analysis in this book concluded that important relations of social control and class experience were being "unbent" and "unsettled." And these struggles were themselves articulated to and by the disintegration of the postwar consensus and a growing sense of social anxiety in the apparent failure of that liberal consensus to realize itself. But while some relations were being—both actively and passively—disarticulated, new relations were being articulated out of the wreckage: "So we are concerned here with what it is in the social and material condition of subordinate classes which allows the dominant traditionalist ideologies to gain some real purchase, and to carry conviction, to win support. How is this traditional ideological 'unity' constructed out of disparate and contradictory class formations?"[l]

This rearticulation was constructing a new **common sense**, which describes the relatively disorganized and often contradictory collection of assumptions and beliefs that define how people make sense of the world. The increasingly visible success of these efforts led the authors to "predict" the rise of a new conservatism, ultimately embodied in the figure of Margaret Thatcher, that articulated a reconstructed (largely petit bourgeois) vision of traditional Englishness to the new neoliberal economic policies offered against their own construction of the failures of postwar Keynesian economics and the perception of what Hall described as the "managed dissensus" of the early 1970s.[m]

Hall theorized this struggle through the concept of **hegemony** as a contextually specific form of political struggle as opposed to seeing it as a necessary dimension of all "democratic" politics, opposed to the direct use of force (either as consensus or a frontier that sets "the people" against the dominant powers). He used the concept to describe a very specific confluence of conditions and struggles, which were in fact quite rare. In his conjuncture, the hegemonic struggle involved the rise of **authoritarian populism** (a transplanting of the Greek Marxist Nicos Poulantzas's "authoritarian statism").

Hall's theory of hegemony was not offered as a generalizable theory but as a contextually—conjuncturally—specific diagnosis. It was a response to a context that Hall described as "a highly transitional moment. . . . We are living in the moment of the post."[n] His conjuncturalism, then, was not a universal epistemology but the recognition of the need to historicize epistemology itself, that is, to embrace a "contextual epistemology" as a political and intellectual response to the conjuncture.

Let me briefly present the terms of Hall's intervention. First, hegemony is never an accomplishment; it is always on ongoing struggle through which a *ruling bloc* (an articulated unity of different interests and social positions) attempts to win the consent of the population to its **leadership**. You don't have to agree with their position or policies; you just have to believe they are the ones most capable of leading society out of its current crises. Second, a hegemonic struggle is only possible as a **war of positions** rather than a **war of maneuvers**. The latter imagines political struggle as a winner-take-all battle between two relatively homogeneous camps facing off across a single front; the former sees multiple struggles dispersed across the full range of social positions, relations, and institutions. This enables the ruling bloc to negotiate and even compromise with some constituencies in order to win their allegiance. A hegemonic struggle reorganizes the social formation as a distribution of power in concentric circles mapping out the proximity of various groups to the ruling bloc at the center. Different groups can move closer to and farther away from the ruling bloc and the structural agencies of power, while some are excluded from even belonging to "the people."

Third, a hegemonic struggle is largely carried out on the field of culture and **the popular**. People have to be won to (interpellated into) the new discourses; they have to be dislodged from one set of relations and moved into another (e.g., rearticulating working-class identifications into a different sense of class belonging and a different political identification). The popular refers to both common sense and the commonly shared languages and logics people use to calculate their decisions and actions, their moral compass, and their maps of what matters. These are embedded and struggled over in the discourses of everyday—popular—life, including but not limited to popular cultures.

Finally, hegemonic struggles commonly arise out of and demand an **organic crisis**, as an accumulation of multiple crises, a condensation of contradictions, a fusion of struggles, an articulation of differences. Within a hegemonic struggle, a conjuncture becomes "the complex historically specific terrain of a crisis which affects—but in uneven ways—a specific national-social formation as a whole."[o] An organic crisis constitutes a social formation as fractured and conflictual, along multiple axes, planes, and scales, constantly in search of a temporary settlement, a **balance in the field of forces**, a new structural stability.

But the organic crisis itself—its identity and even its very existence—has to be constructed and struggled over, whether as a major rupture or as a more "passive revolution," by fusing multiple, dispersed crises into an overarching crisis. An organic crisis problematizes the identity and unity of the social formation—however fractured and thin it may have been, as well as the forms of belonging by which "the people" are constructed as a unity-in-difference. The hegemonic bloc's success depends on whether the organic crisis it constructs is accepted as a diagnosis of what has gone wrong, and whether people believe it has a new, fundamental vision for responding to the crisis, promising a new unity and purpose. Hegemony is a struggle to remake the conjuncture, to create "a new reality."[p]

DIFFERENCE

Similarly, Hall's influential interventions into the politics of **difference**—particularly questions of race and racism—have to be understood conjuncturally. Although he is often read as having proposed a new theory of race, he repeatedly denied it: "I don't claim for my particular version of a non-essentialist notion of race correctness for all time. I can claim for it only a certain conjunctural specificity."[q] There is no single identity, no single or authentic way, no single determination, of being Black. Just as cultures are always reappropriations, any identity is always multiple and, in fact, any instance of identity is always hybrid, fractured, and contested. It embodies ways of belonging.

His understanding of identity *and* difference is not simply antiessentialist, but anti-antiessentialist, because identities are real (i.e., effective).[r] At times, the multiplicity of identities, the fragmented and dispersed instantiations of Blackness, might be articulated together, although he was suspicious of such efforts. In fact, Hall suggested that over three or four decades, "we have been passing through at least three, maybe more, differentiated ethnic identity moments," defined by new axes along which structures of racial difference have moved.[s]

Similarly, there have been many different, contextually specific racisms. Hall warned against "extrapolating a common and universal structure to racism. . . . It is only as the different racisms are historically specified—in their difference—that they can be properly understood as a product of historical relations and possess . . . full validity only for and within those relations."[t] Thus, he argued that understanding and combating racism posed empirical demands: "One must start, then, from the concrete historical 'work' which racism accomplishes under specific historical conditions—as a set of economic, political and ideological practices, of a distinctive kind, concretely articulated with other practices in a social formation. . . . The question is not whether men-in-general make perceptual distinctions between groups with different racial or ethnic characteristics, but rather, what are the specific conditions which make this form of distinction socially pertinent, historically active?"[u] Consequently, the strategies of antiracism will have to be contextually specific; they cannot be generalized across contexts: "It is perfectly possible that what is politically progressive and opens up new discursive opportunities in the 1970s and 1980s can become a form of closure—and have a repressive value—by the time it is installed as the dominant genre. . . . It will run out of steam; it will become a style; people will use it not because it opens up anything but because they are being spoken by it, and at that point, you need another shift."[v] Antiracist struggles are possible because the identities racism produces ("races") only exist at the intersection of identification and interpellation; social power seeks to define us, but it must always confront our own investments, desires, and needs.[w]

Hall refused to equate racism and colonialism, or to see one as a product and expression of the other. While racisms are historically changing ways of dividing and distributing populations, colonialism (and the modernity it helped create) constructed a very specific *disjunctive logic of roots*, in which people imagine a redemptive return to an unchanged origin as their authentic home. Their identity is unified, pure, homogeneous, and fixed, constituted in simple binary relations of colonizer and colonized. But this logic, this fantasy of return—whether in space or time—to a unity without differences, is a way to evade and repress the contingencies and displacements of the present.

Colonialism created a world that denied its own efforts and actually undermined the very logic of separable, self-sufficient cultures and economies, which fortified its power. Colonization had actually produced a world that was only describable through **figures of creolization, syncretism, hybridity, entanglement, translation**, and **articulation**, a world in which identity was always complex, impure, and contradictory. In colonialism, "the play of difference across identity" made every identity heterogeneous, processual, and incomplete, constituted in and by representations and identifications.[x] This was the distinctive form of dissemination-and-condensation which colonization set in play "to capture these different but related forms of relationship, interconnection and discontinuity."[y] It was colonialism itself that made identity into a political problem.

But colonialism was only the beginning of an ongoing reconfiguration of the field of relations. The emerging postcolonial reality is not an alternative formation but a continuing interrogation and disruption of the decentering and displacing of all simple figures of identity and power by colonialism. In this new conjuncture, defined increasingly by "lateral and transverse cross-relations . . . and displacements," the old experience of diaspora meets another diaspora—one defined by routes rather than roots, in which home has changed beyond all recognition.[z] The new mobility of identities means that experience is forward-looking rather than backward-glancing.

In the new **diaspora**, identity is constituted through **displacement** and **dislocation**. *Diaspora* is "the moment when the politics of class, race and gender came together, but in a new unstable, explosive articulation, displacing and at the same time complicating each other. It has transformed our understanding of the nature of social forces and of social movements. Accordingly, it does not provide us with ready-made answers or programmes but set us new questions, which proliferate across and disturb older frames of thought, social engagements and political practices: a new 'problem space' indeed."ªª Diasporas potentially make visible that which has been negated, repressed, hidden, and silenced, while offering no guaranteed consequences; but they can "maintain an open horizon towards the future. They are in that sense spaces of emergence." As Hall put it, "We grew up knowing the contingencies, the out-of-placeness, of history. . . . In a suitably paradoxical formulation, displacement moved to the centre of things."ᵇᵇ

For Hall, a life of displacements was articulated to questions of identity, identity is displaced into questions of belonging, belonging is displaced into questions of history, history is displaced into questions of power and resistance, and power and resistance are displaced into the intellectual project of cultural studies. In Hall's deep theory, deep theory itself disappears into the intellectual ground of social and political change.

NOTES

a. See Hall, *Familiar Stranger*.

b. Du Bois, "Strivings of the Negro People"; Du Bois, *Souls of Black Folk*.

c. Hall, "Politics, Contingency, Strategy," in *Essential Essays*, 2:250–51.

d. Hall, "Cultural Studies and Its Theoretical Legacies," in *Essential Essays*, 1:90.

e. Hall, "Gramsci's Relevance for the Study of Race and Ethnicity," in *Selected Writings on Race and Difference*, 297.

f. Hall, "Diasporas, or the Logics of Cultural Translation," 52.

g. Hall, "Marx's Notes on Method," in *Selected Writings on Marxism*, 19–61.

h. Marx, *Grundrisse*, 90.

i. Hall, "Gramsci and Us," in *Hard Road to Renewal*, 162.

j. Hall, "Subjects in History," in *Selected Writings on Race and Difference*, 333. The "changing same" comes from Gilroy, *Black Atlantic*, who transplanted it from Amiri Baraka.

k. See Hall, *Hard Road to Renewal*.

l. Hall et al., *Policing the Crisis*, 140.

m. Hall et al., *Policing the Crisis*, 238.

n. Terry, "'Not a Postmodern Nomad,'" 67.

o. Hall, "Popular-Democratic vs. Authoritarian Populism," in *Hard Road to Renewal*, 127.

p. Gramsci, *Further Selections*, 178.

q. Hall, "Politics, Contingency, Strategy," 258.

r. The term is from Gilroy, *Black Atlantic*.

s. Hall, "Aspirations and Attitude," 45.

t. Hall, "Race, Articulation and Societies Structured in Dominance," in *Selected Writings on Race and Difference*, 234.

u. Hall, "Race, Articulation and Societies Structured in Dominance," 236.

v. Bailey and Hall, "Vertigo of Displacement," 15.

w. Hall, "Who Needs Identity?"

x. Hall, "Ethnicity," 17.

y. Hall, "When Was 'the Post-colonial'?," in *Selected Writings on Marxism*, 306.

z. On lateral and transverse cross-relations, see Hall, "When Was 'the Post-colonial'?," 299.

aa. Hall, *Familiar Stranger*, 144.

bb. Hall, *Familiar Stranger*, 198, 62.

Postscript

Congratulations. You have reached the end. But backstories don't have endings. They have beginnings. We must go on thinking, but it is getting harder. May you continue the journey, thoughtfully and joyously.

Bibliography

Airborne Toxic Event, The. "Elizabeth." *Such Hot Blood.* Island Records, 2013.

Allison, David B., ed. *The New Nietzsche: Contemporary Styles of Interpretation.* Cambridge, MA: MIT Press, 1977.

Altizer, Thomas J. J., and William Hamilton. *Radical Theology and the Death of God.* Indianapolis, IN: Bobbs-Merrill, 1966.

Almanac Singers. "Which Side Are You On?" *Talking Union.* Keynote Recordings, 1941.

Althusser, Louis. *Essays in Self-Criticism.* Translated by Grahame Lock. London: Verso, 1976.

Althusser, Louis. *For Marx.* Translated by Ben Brewster. London: Verso. 1977.

Althusser, Louis. *Lenin and Philosophy and Other Essays.* Translated by Ben Brewster. New York: Monthly Review Press, 2001.

Althusser, Louis, Étienne Balibar, Jacques Rancière, Roger Establet, and Pierre Macherey. *Reading Capital.* Translated by Ben Brewster. London: Verso, 1977.

Anderson, Perry. *Considerations on Western Marxism.* London: Verso, 1976.

Aristotle. *The Works of Aristotle.* Vol. 2. Edited by W. D. Ross. Oxford: Clarendon Press, 1930.

Ayer, Alfred J. *Hume: A Very Short Introduction.* Oxford: Oxford University Press, 2000.

Ayer, Alfred J. "Logical Positivism and Its Legacy." In *Modern Philosophers.* Directed by T. Tyley. BBC Worldwide Learning. Season 1, episode 6, February 23, 1978.

Bacon, Francis. *The New Organon.* Edited by James Spedding, Robert Leslie Ellis, and Douglas Denon Heath. New York: Houghton Mifflin, 1875.

Badham, John, dir. *WarGames.* United Artists, 1983.

Bailey, David, and Stuart Hall. "The Vertigo of Displacement." *Ten 8* 2, no. 3 (1992): 15–23.

Barthes, Roland. *Critical Essays.* Evanston, IL: Northwestern University Press, 1972.

Barthes, Roland. *Elements of Semiology.* Translated by Annette Lavers and Colin Smith. New York: Hill and Wang, 1967.

Barthes, Roland. *S/Z.* Translated by Richard Miller. New York: Hill and Wang, 1974.

Baudrillard, Jean. *The Gulf War Did Not Take Place.* Translated by Paul Patton. Bloomington: Indiana University Press, 1995.

Baudrillard, Jean. *In the Shadow of the Silent Majorities . . . or the End of the Social, and Other Essays.* Translated by Paul Foss, John Johnston, and Paul Patton. New York: Semiotext(e), 1983.

Baudrillard, Jean. *Simulations.* Translated by Paul Foss and Paul Patton. New York: Semiotext(e), 1983.

Beck, Lewis W. *Early German Philosophy: Kant and His Predecessors*. Cambridge, MA: Belknap Press of Harvard University Press, 1969.

Bell, Bernard I. *Postmodernism and Other Essays*. Harrisburg, PA: Morehouse Publishing, 1926.

Benjamin, Walter. *Illuminations*. Edited by Hannah Arendt. New York: Schocken Books, 1968.

Benveniste, Émile. *Problems in General Linguistics*. Translated by Mary Elizabeth Meek. Miami: University of Miami Press, 1971.

Berkeley, George. *A Treatise concerning the Principles of Human Knowledge*. Edited by Jonathan Dancy. Oxford: Oxford University Press, 1998.

Berlin, Isaiah. *Against the Current: Essays in the History of Ideas*. 2nd ed. Edited by Henry Hardy. Princeton, NJ: Princeton University Press, 2013.

The Bible: Authorized King James Version. Edited by Robert Carroll and Stephen Prickett. Oxford: Oxford University Press, 2008.

Blake, William. *The Letters of William Blake*. 3rd ed. Edited by Geoffrey Keynes. Oxford: Oxford University Press, 1980.

Blaser, Mario. "Political Ontology: Cultural Studies without 'Cultures'?" *Cultural Studies* 23, no. 5–6 (2009): 873–96.

Bourdieu, Pierre. *The Field of Cultural Production*. Edited by Randal Johnson. New York: Columbia University Press, 1993.

Brel, Jacques. *La valse à mille temps*. 1959. Translation at https://genius.com/Jacques -brel-alone-seul-lyrics.

Broekman, Jan M. *Structuralism: Moscow—Prague—Paris*. Dordrecht: D. Reidel, 1974.

Burchell, Graham, Colin Gordon, and Peter Miller, eds. *The Foucault Effect: Studies in Governmentality*. Chicago: University of Chicago Press, 1991.

Carnap, Rudolph. *The Unity of Science*. Translated by Max Black. Bristol: Thoemmes Press, 1934.

Chisholm, Roderick M., ed. *Realism and the Background of Phenomenology*. New York: Free Press, 1960.

Chomsky, Noam. *Aspects of the Theory of Syntax*. Cambridge, MA: MIT Press, 1965.

Chomsky, Noam. *Syntactic Structures*. The Hague: Mouton, 1957.

Comte, Auguste. *The Positive Philosophy of Auguste Comte*. Translated by Harriet Martineau. Ithaca, NY: Cornell University Press, 1880.

Crane, Stephen. *The Works of Stephen Crane*. Vol. 10. Edited by Fredson Bowers. Charlottesville: University Press of Virginia, 1975.

Crawford, Claudia. *To Nietzsche: Dionysus, I Love You! Ariadne*. Albany: State University of New York Press, 1995.

De la Cadena, Marisol. *Earth Beings: Ecologies of Practice across Andean Worlds*. Durham, NC: Duke University Press, 2015.

Deleuze, Gilles. *Bergsonism*. Translated by Hugh Tomlinson and Barbara Habberjam. New York: Zone Books, 1988.

Deleuze, Gilles. *Difference and Repetition*. Translated by Paul Patton. New York: Continuum, 1994.

Deleuze, Gilles. "Ethology: Spinoza and Us." In *Incorporations*, edited by Jonathan Crary and Sanford Kwinter, 625–33. New York: Zone Books, 1992.

Deleuze, Gilles. *Expressionism in Philosophy: Spinoza.* Translated by Martin Joughin. New York: Zone Books, 1992.

Deleuze, Gilles. *The Fold: Leibniz and the Baroque.* Translated by Tom Conley. Minneapolis: University of Minnesota Press, 1993.

Deleuze, Gilles. *Foucault.* Translated by Sean Hand. New York: Continuum, 1988.

Deleuze, Gilles. *Negotiations, 1972–1990.* Translated by Martin Joughin. New York: Columbia University Press, 1995.

Deleuze, Gilles. *Nietzsche and Philosophy.* Translated by Hugh Tomlinson. New York: Columbia University Press, 1983.

Deleuze, Gilles. *Spinoza: Practical Philosophy.* Translated by Robert Hurley. Berkeley, CA: City Lights Books, 1988.

Deleuze, Gilles, and Félix Guattari. *Anti-Oedipus: Capitalism and Schizophrenia.* Translated by Robert Hurley, Mark Seem, and Helen R. Lane. London: Penguin Books, 1977.

Deleuze, Gilles, and Félix Guattari. *Kafka: Toward a Minor Literature.* Translated by Dana Polan. Minneapolis: University of Minnesota Press, 1986.

Deleuze, Gilles, and Félix Guattari. "Rhizome: Introduction." Translated by Paul Patton. *I and C* 8 (1981): 49–71.

Deleuze, Gilles, and Félix Guattari. *A Thousand Plateaus: Capitalism and Schizophrenia.* Translated by Brian Massumi. Minneapolis: University of Minnesota Press, 1987.

Deleuze, Gilles, and Félix Guattari. *What Is Philosophy?* Translated by Hugh Tomlinson and Graham Burchell. New York: Columbia University Press, 1994.

Deleuze, Gilles, and Clare Parnet. *Dialogues.* Translated by Hugh Tomlinson and Barbara Habberjam. New York: Columbia University Press, 1987.

Derrida, Jacques. *Dissemination.* Translated by Barbara Johnson. Chicago: University of Chicago Press, 1981.

Derrida, Jacques. *Margins of Philosophy.* Translated by Alan Bass. Chicago: University of Chicago Press, 1982.

Derrida, Jacques. *Of Grammatology.* Translated by Gayatri Chakravarty Spivak. Baltimore: Johns Hopkins University Press, 1976.

Derrida, Jacques. *Of Spirit: Heidegger and the Question.* Translated by Geoffrey Bennington and Rachel Bowlby. Chicago: University of Chicago Press, 1989.

Derrida, Jacques. *The Problem of Genesis in Husserl's Philosophy.* Translated by Marian Hobson. Chicago: University of Chicago Press, 1990.

Derrida, Jacques. *Specters of Marx.* Translated by Peggy Kamuf. London: Routledge, 1994.

Derrida, Jacques. *Speech and Phenomena: And Other Essays on Husserl's Theory of Signs.* Translated by David B. Allison. Evanston, IL: Northwestern University Press, 1973.

Derrida, Jacques. *Spurs: Nietzsche's Styles.* Translated by Barbara Harlow. Chicago: University of Chicago Press, 1978.

Derrida, Jacques. *Writing and Difference.* Translated by Alan Bass. London: Routledge, 1978.

Descartes, René. *The Philosophical Works of Descartes.* Vol. 1. Translated by Elizabeth Haklane and G. R. T. Ross. Garden City, NY: Dover, 1931.

Dewey, John. *Art as Experience*. New York: Milton, Balch and Company, 1934.

Dewey, John. *The Essential Dewey*. Vol. 1. Edited by Larry A. Hickman and Thomas M. Alexander. Bloomington: Indiana University Press, 1998.

Dewey, John. *Experience and Nature*. 2nd ed. Chicago: Open Court, 1929.

Dewey, John. *Logic: The Theory of Inquiry*. New York: Holt, Rinehart and Winston, 1938.

Dewey, John. *The Public and Its Problems*. New York: Henry Holt, 1927.

Diderot, Denis, and Jean le Rond d'Alembert. *The Encyclopedia of Diderot and d'Alembert Collaborative Translation Project*. Ann Arbor: Michigan Publishing, n.d. https://quod.lib.umich.edu/d/did/.

Docter, Pete, and Ronnie Del Carmen, dirs. *Inside Out*. Walt Disney Pictures/Pixar Animation Studios, 2015.

Douglas, Auriel, and Michael Strumpf, eds. *Webster's New World Dictionary of Quotations*. London: Macmillan General Reference, 1998.

Du Bois, William E. B. *The Souls of Black Folk*. Edited by Henry Louis Gates Jr. Oxford: Oxford University Press, 2007.

Du Bois, William E. B. "Strivings of the Negro People." *Atlantic Monthly*, 80 (1897): 194–98.

Durant, Will. *The Story of Philosophy*. New rev. ed. Garden City, NY: Garden City Publishing, 1933.

Eagles. "Hotel California." *Hotel California*. Asylum Records, 1976.

Edwards, Paul, ed. *The Encyclopedia of Philosophy*. Vols. 4, 5, and 6. London: Macmillan, 1967.

Erikson, Erik H. *Identity: Youth and Crisis*. New York: W. W. Norton, 1968.

Fichte, Johann Gottlieb. *Science of Knowledge*. Edited and translated by Peter Heath and John Lachs. Cambridge: Cambridge University Press, 1982.

Foucault, Michel. *Aesthetics, Method, and Epistemology*. Edited by James D. Faubion. Translated by Robert Hurley and others. New York: New Press, 1998.

Foucault, Michel. *The Archaeology of Knowledge and the Discourse on Language*. Translated by Alan Sheridan Smith. New York: Pantheon Books, 1972.

Foucault, Michel. *The Birth of Biopolitics: Lectures at the Collège de France, 1978–1979*. Edited by Michel Senellart. Translated by Graham Burchell. London: Picador, 2008.

Foucault, Michel. *The Care of the Self: The History of Sexuality*. Vol. 3. Translated by Robert Hurley. New York: Vintage Books, 1986.

Foucault, Michel. *Confessions of the Flesh: The History of Sexuality*. Vol. 4. Translated by Robert Hurley. New York: Pantheon Books, 2021.

Foucault, Michel. *Ethics: Subjectivity and Truth*. Edited by Paul Rabinow. New York: New Press, 1997.

Foucault, Michel. *The Government of Self and Others: Lectures at the Collège de France 1982–1983*. Edited by Frédéric Gros. Translated by Graham Burchell. London: Palgrave Macmillan, 2010.

Foucault, Michel. *History of Madness*. Edited by Jean Khalfa. Translated by Jean Khalfa and Jonathan Murphy. London: Routledge, 2006.

Foucault, Michel. *The History of Sexuality Volume I: An Introduction*. Translated by Robert Hurley. New York: Vintage Books, 1978.

Foucault, Michel. *The Order of Things: An Archaeology of the Human Sciences.* London: Routledge, 1970.

Foucault, Michel. *The Politics of Truth.* Edited by Sylvère Lotringer. New York: Semiotext(e), 1997.

Foucault, Michel. *Politics, Philosophy, Culture: Interviews and Other Writings, 1977–1984.* Edited by Lawrence D. Kritzman. Translated by Alan Sheridan. London: Routledge, 1988.

Foucault, Michel. *Power/Knowledge: Selected Interviews and Other Writings 1972–1977.* Edited by Colin Gordon. Translated by Colin Gordon, Leo Marshall, John Mepham, and Kate Soper. New York: Vintage Books, 1980.

Foucault, Michel. *Power, Truth, Strategy.* Edited by Meaghan Morris and Paul Patton. Sydney: Feral Publications, 1979.

Foucault, Michel. *Security, Territory, Population: Lectures at the Collège de France, 1977–1978.* Edited by Michel Senellart. Translated by Graham Burchell. London: Picador, 2007.

Foucault, Michel. *Society Must Be Defended: Lectures at the Collège de France, 1975–1976.* Edited by Mauro Bertano and Alessandro Fontana. Translated by David Macey. London: Picador, 2003.

Foucault, Michel. *The Use of Pleasure: The History of Sexuality.* Vol. 2. Translated by Robert Hurley. New York: Vintage Books, 1985.

Freud, Sigmund. *Civilization and Its Discontents.* Translated by James Strachey. New York: W. W. Norton, 1961.

Freud, Sigmund. *The Interpretation of Dreams.* Translated by James Strachey. London: Penguin Books, 1975.

Freud, Sigmund. *The Origins of Psycho-Analysis: Letters to Wilhelm Fliess, Drafts and Notes, 1887–1902.* Edited by Marie Bonaparte, Anna Freud, and Ernst Kris. Translated by Eric Mosbacher and James Strachey. New York: Basic Books, 1954.

Freud, Sigmund. *The Standard Edition of the Complete Psychological Works of Sigmund Freud.* Vol. 18, *1920–1922.* Translated and edited by James Strachey, in collaboration with Anna Freud, assisted by Alix Strachey and Alan Tyson. London: Hogarth Press/ Institute of Psycho-Analysis, 1994.

Freud, Sigmund. *The Standard Edition of the Complete Psychological Works of Sigmund Freud.* Vol. 19, *1923–1925.* Translated and edited by James Strachey, in collaboration with Anna Freud, assisted by Alix Strachey and Alan Tyson. London: Hogarth Press/ Institute of Psycho-Analysis, 1994.

Freud, Sigmund. *The Standard Edition of the Complete Psychological Works of Sigmund Freud.* Vol. 23, *1937–1939.* Translated and edited by James Strachey, in collaboration with Anna Freud, assisted by Alix Strachey and Alan Tyson. London: Hogarth Press/ Institute of Psycho-Analysis, 1994.

Freud, Sigmund. *Three Essays on the Theory of Sexuality.* Edited and translated by James Strachey. New York: Basic Books, 1977.

Freud, Sigmund, and Josef Breuer. *Studies on Hysteria.* Edited and translated by James Strachey. N.p.: Avon Books, 1966.

Gilroy, Paul. *Against Race: Imagining Political Culture beyond the Color Line.* Cambridge, MA: Belknap Press of Harvard University Press, 2000.

Gilroy, Paul. *The Black Atlantic: Modernity and Double Consciousness.* Cambridge, MA: Harvard University Press, 1993.

Goethe, Johann Wolfgang von. *Faust.* Translated by A. Hayward. London: Hutchinson, 1908.

Gramsci, Antonio. *Further Selections from the Prison Notebooks.* Edited and translated by Derek Boothman. Minneapolis: University of Minnesota Press, 1995.

Gramsci, Antonio. *Selections from the Prison Notebooks.* Edited and translated by Quinton Hoare and Geoffrey Nowell Smith. New York: International Publishers, 1971.

Grossberg, Lawrence. *Cultural Studies in the Future Tense.* Durham, NC: Duke University Press, 2010.

Grossberg, Lawrence. "We All Want to Change the World: The Paradox of the U.S. Left (A Polemic)." N.p: n.p., 2015. Accessed March 20, 2024. https://archive.wikiwix.com /cache/index2.php?url=http://www.lwbooks.co.uk/ebooks/we_all_want_to_change _the_world.pdf&redownload=1&selenium=0&iarefresh=1.

Guattari, Félix. *Chaosmosis: An Ethico-Aesthetic Paradigm.* Translated by Paul Bains and Julian Pefanis. Bloomington: Indiana University Press, 1995.

Hall, Stuart. "Aspirations and Attitude . . . Reflections on Black Britain in the Nineties." *New Formations*, no. 33 (1998): 38–46.

Hall, Stuart. *Cultural Studies 1983: A Theoretical History.* Durham, NC: Duke University Press, 2016.

Hall, Stuart. "Diasporas, or the Logics of Cultural Translation." *MATRIZES* 10, no. 3 (2016): 47–58.

Hall, Stuart. *Essential Essays.* Vol. 1, *Foundations of Cultural Studies.* Edited by David Morley. Durham, NC: Duke University Press, 2019.

Hall, Stuart. *Essential Essays.* Vol. 2, *Identity and Diaspora.* Edited by David Morley. Durham, NC: Duke University Press, 2019.

Hall, Stuart. "Ethnicity: Identity and Difference." *Radical America* 23, no. 4 (1989): 9–20.

Hall, Stuart. *Familiar Stranger: A Life between Two Islands.* Durham, NC: Duke University Press, 2018.

Hall, Stuart. *The Hard Road to Renewal: Thatcherism and the Crisis of the Left.* Edited by Martin Jacques. London: Verso, 1988.

Hall, Stuart. *Selected Political Writings: The Great Moving Right Show and Other Essays.* Edited by Sally Davison, David Featherstone, Michael Rustin, and Bill Schwarz. Durham, NC: Duke University Press, 2017.

Hall, Stuart. *Selected Writings on Marxism.* Edited by Gregor McLennan. Durham, NC: Duke University Press, 2021.

Hall, Stuart. *Selected Writings on Race and Difference.* Edited by Paul Gilroy and Ruth Gilmore. Durham, NC: Duke University Press, 2021.

Hall, Stuart. "Who Needs Identity?" In *Questions of Cultural Identity*, edited by Stuart Hall and Paul du Gay, 1–17. Thousand Oaks, CA: Sage, 1996.

Hall, Stuart, Chas Critcher, Tony Jefferson, John Clarke, and Brian Roberts. *Policing the Crisis: Mugging, the State, and Law and Order.* London: Macmillan, 1978.

Hamann, Johann Georg. *Hamann: Writings on Philosophy and Language.* Edited by Kenneth Haynes. Cambridge: Cambridge University Press, 2007.

Hawkes, Terrence. *Structuralism and Semiotics.* London: Routledge, 2003.

Hegel, Georg Wilhelm Friedrich. *Aesthetics: Lectures on Fine Art.* Vol. 2. Translated by T. M. Knox. Oxford: Clarendon Press, 1975.

Hegel, Georg Wilhelm Friedrich. *Hegel's Science of Logic.* Translated by A. V. Miller. London: Allen and Unwin, 1969.

Hegel, Georg Wilhelm Friedrich. *Lectures on the History of Philosophy.* 3 vols. Translated by E. S. Haldane and Frances H. Simson. Delhi: Lector House, 2020.

Hegel, Georg Wilhelm Friedrich. *Lectures on the Philosophy of World History.* Translated by Johannes Hoffmeister. Cambridge: Cambridge University Press, 1975.

Hegel, Georg Wilhelm Friedrich. *The Letters.* Translated by Clark Butler and Christiane Seller. Bloomington: Indiana University Press, 1984.

Hegel, Georg Wilhelm Friedrich. *Logic: Being Part One of the Encyclopaedia of the Philosophical Sciences.* Translated by William Wallace and A. V. Miller. Oxford: Clarendon Press, 1971.

Hegel, Georg Wilhelm Friedrich. *Phenomenology of Spirit.* Translated by A. V. Miller. Oxford: Oxford University Press, 1977.

Hegel, Georg Wilhelm Friedrich. *The Philosophy of History.* Translated by J. Sibree. Minneola, NY: Dover, 1956.

Heidegger, Martin. *Being and Time.* Translated by John Macquarrie and Edward Robinson. New York: Harper and Row, 1962.

Heidegger, Martin. *Nietzsche.* Vol. 1, *The Will to Power as Art.* Edited and translated by David F. Krell. New York: Harper and Row, 1991.

Heidegger, Martin. *On the Way to Language.* Translated by Peter D. Hertz. New York: Harper and Row, 1971.

Heidegger, Martin. *Pathmarks.* Edited by William McNeill. Cambridge: Cambridge University Press, 1998.

Heidegger, Martin. *Poetry, Language, Thought.* Translated by Alfred Hofstadter. New York: Harper and Row, 1971.

Heidegger, Martin. *The Question concerning Technology and Other Essays.* Translated by William Levitt. New York: Harper and Row, 1977.

Heidegger, Martin. *What Is Called Thinking?* Translated by J. Glenn Gray. New York: Harper Perennial, 1976.

Hjelmslev, Louis. *Prolegomena to a Theory of Language.* Rev. ed. Translated by Francis J. Whitfield. Madison: University of Wisconsin Press, 1961.

Hobbes, Thomas. *Elements of Philosophy: The First Section, concerning Body (De Corpore,* 1655). Translated by A. P. Martinich. New York: Abaris Books, 1981.

Hölderlin, Friedrich. *Hymns and Fragments.* Translated by Richard Sieburth. Princeton, NJ: Princeton University Press, 1984.

Hume, David. *An Enquiry concerning Human Understanding.* Edited by Tom Beauchamp. Oxford: Clarendon Press, 2001.

Hume, David. *Essays Moral, Political, and Literary.* Vol. 1. London: Longmans, Green, 1898.

Hume, David. *A Letter from a Gentleman to His Friend in Edinburgh*. Edited by
 Ernest C. Mossner and John V. Price. Edinburgh: Edinburgh University Press, 1967.
Hume, David. *The Letters of David Hume*. Vol. 1. Edited by J. Y. T. Greig. Oxford:
 Clarendon Press, 1932.
Hume, David. *A Treatise of Human Nature*. Edited by David Fate Norton and Mary J.
 Norton. Oxford: Clarendon Press, 2007.
Husserl, Edmund. *The Crisis of European Sciences and Transcendental Phenomenology:
 An Introduction to Phenomenological Philosophy*. Translated by David Carr.
 Evanston, IL: Northwestern University Press, 1970.
Husserl, Edmund. *Ideas: General Introduction to Pure Phenomenology*. 3 vols.
 Translated by W. R. Boyce Gibson. London: Macmillan, 1931.
Husserl, Edmund. *Logical Investigations*. 2 vols. Translated by J. N. Findlay. London:
 Routledge, 2001.
Husserl, Edmund. *Phenomenology and the Crisis of Philosophy*. Translated by Quentin
 Lauer. New York: Harper and Row, 1965.
Husserl, Edmund. *The Phenomenology of Internal Time-Consciousness*. Translated by
 James S. Churchill. Bloomington: Indiana University Press, 1964.
Husserl, Edmund. *Philosophy of Arithmetic: Psychological and Logical Investigations
 with Supplementary Texts from 1887–1901*. Translated by Dallas Willard. New York:
 Springer, 2003.
Hyppolite, Jean. *Genesis and Structure of Hegel's Phenomenology of Spirit*. Translated by
 Samuel Cherniak and John Heckman. Evanston, IL: Northwestern University Press,
 1974.
Jakobson, Roman, and Morris Halle. *Fundamentals of Language*. Ann Arbor: Michigan
 Slavic Studies, 1980.
James, William. *Essays in Radical Empiricism*. London: Longmans, Green, 1912.
James, William. *The Meaning of Truth*. Cambridge, MA: Harvard University Press, 1975.
James, William. *Pragmatism: A New Name for Some Old Ways of Thinking*. New York:
 Dover, 1995.
James, William. *The Principles of Psychology*. Vol. 1. Minneola, NY: Dover, 1950.
James, William. *The Varieties of Religious Experience*. Cambridge, MA: Harvard
 University Press, 1985.
Jameson, Fredric. *Postmodernism, or the Cultural Logic of Late Capitalism*. Durham,
 NC: Duke University Press, 1991.
Janik, Allen, and Stephen Toulmin. *Wittgenstein's Vienna*. New York: Simon and
 Schuster, 1973.
Jones, W. T. *A History of Western Philosophy*. Vol. 4, *Kant and the Nineteenth Century*.
 San Diego: Harcourt Brace Jovanovich, 1975.
Kant, Immanuel. *Anthropology from a Pragmatic Point of View*. Edited by Robert B.
 Louden and Manfred Kuehn. Cambridge: Cambridge University Press, 2006.
Kant, Immanuel. *Critique of Judgment*. Translated by James Creed Meredith. Oxford:
 Oxford University Press, 2009.
Kant, Immanuel. *Critique of Practical Reason*. Translated by Mary Gregor and Andrews
 Reath. Cambridge: Cambridge University Press, 2015.

Kant, Immanuel. *Critique of Pure Reason.* Translated by Norman Kemp Smith. London: Palgrave Macmillan, 2007.

Kant, Immanuel. *Foundations of the Metaphysics of Morals and What Is Enlightenment?* Translated by Lewis White Beck. London: Macmillan, 1959.

Kant, Immanuel. *Natural Science.* Edited by Eric Watkins. Cambridge: Cambridge University Press, 2015.

Kant, Immanuel. *Prolegomena to Any Future Metaphysic.* Translated by Gary Hatfield. Cambridge: Cambridge University Press, 2004.

Kant, Immanuel. *Universal Natural History and Theory of the Heavens.* Translated by Stanley L. Jaki. Edinburgh: Scottish Academic Press, 1981.

Kasher, Asa, and Shlomo Biderman. "Why Was Baruch de Spinoza Excommunicated?" In *Sceptics, Millenarians and Jews,* edited by David S. Katz and Jonathan I. Israel, 98–141. Leiden: Brill, 1990.

Kojève, Alexandre. *Introduction to the Reading of Hegel: Lectures on the "Phenomenology of Spirit."* Translated by James H. Nichols Jr. New York: Basic Books, 1969.

Körner, Stephen. *Kant.* New Haven, CT: Yale University Press, 1955.

Kristeva, Julia. *Desire in Language: A Semiotic Approach to Literature and Art.* Edited by L. S. Roudiez. New York: Columbia University Press, 1980.

Kristeva, Julia. "Women's Time." Translated by Alice Jardine and Harry Blake. *Signs* 7, no. 1 (1981): 13–35.

Kuhn, Thomas S. *The Essential Tension: Selected Studies in Scientific Tradition and Change.* Chicago: University of Chicago Press, 1977.

Kuhn, Thomas S. *The Structure of Scientific Revolutions.* 4th ed. Chicago: University of Chicago Press, 2012.

Lacan, Jacques. *Écrits: A Selection.* Translated by Alan Sheridan. London: Routledge, 1977.

Lacan, Jacques. *The Four Fundamental Concepts of Psycho-Analysis.* Translated by Alan Sheridan. New York: W. W. Norton, 1977.

Lacan, Jacques. *The Seminar of Jacques Lacan.* Book 3, *The Psychoses 1955–1956.* Translated by Russell Grigg. London: Routledge, 1993.

Laclau, Ernesto. *On Populist Reason.* London: Verso, 2005.

Lederman, R., dir. "I Borg." *Star Trek: The Next Generation.* Season 5, episode 23. May 11, 1992. Paramount Domestic Television.

Leibniz, Gottfried Wilhelm. *Philosophical Papers and Letters.* 2nd ed. Edited by Leroy E. Loemker. Dordrecht: Reidel, 1969.

Lemaire, Anika. *Jacques Lacan.* Translated by David Macey. London: Routledge, 1977.

Lévi-Strauss, Claude. *The Elementary Structures of Kinship.* Translated by James Harle Bell and John Richard von Sturmer. Boston: Beacon Press, 1969.

Lévi-Strauss, Claude. *The Raw and the Cooked: Introduction to a Science of Mythology.* Chicago: University of Chicago Press, 1969.

Lévi-Strauss, Claude. *The Savage Mind.* Chicago: University of Chicago Press, 1966.

Lévi-Strauss, Claude. *Structural Anthropology.* Translated by Claire Jacobson and Brooke Grundfest Schoepf. New York: Basic Books, 1963.

Lévi-Strauss, Claude. *Totemism*. Translated by Rodney Needham. Boston: Beacon Press, 1963.

Liebmann, Otto, and Bruno Baruch. *Kant und die Epigonen: Eine Kritische Abhandlung* [Kant and the epigones: A critique]. Berlin: Reuther and Reichard, 1912.

Locke, John. *An Essay concerning Human Understanding*. Oxford: Clarendon Press, 1975.

Lundberg, Christian. *Lacan in Public: Psychoanalysis and the Science of Rhetoric*. Tuscaloosa: University of Alabama Press, 2012.

Lyotard, Jean-François. *The Postmodern Condition: A Report on Knowledge*. Translated by George Bennington and Brian Massumi. Minneapolis: University of Minnesota Press, 1984.

Maimonides, Moses. *The Guide for the Perplexed*. Translated by Shlomo Pines. Chicago: University of Chicago Press, 1963.

Marx, Karl. *Capital: A Critique of Political Economy*. Vol. 1. Translated by Ben Fowkes and David Fernbach. New York: Vintage Books, 1976.

Marx, Karl. *A Contribution to the Critique of Political Economy*. Edited by Maurice Dobb. New York: International Publishers, 1970.

Marx, Karl. *Grundrisse: Foundations of the Critique of Political Economy*. Translated by Martin Nicolaus. New York: Vintage Books, 1973.

Marx, Karl, and Friedrich Engels. *Collected Works*. 40 vols. London: Lawrence and Wishart, 2010.

Mead, George Herbert. *Mind, Self, and Society: From the Standpoint of a Social Behaviorist*. Edited by Charles W. Morris. Chicago: University of Chicago Press, 1962.

Medina, Jose, and David Wood, eds. *Truth: Engagements across Philosophical Traditions*. Oxford: Blackwell, 2005.

Montaigne, Michel de. *Essays of Montaigne*. Vol. 2. Translated by Charles Cotton. New York: Edwin C. Hill, 1910.

Nadler, Stephen. *Spinoza: A Life*. 2nd ed. Cambridge: Cambridge University Press, 2018.

Newton, Isaac. *Newton's Principia: The Mathematical Principles of Natural Philosophy*. New York: Daniel Adee, 1846.

Nietzsche, Friedrich. *Basic Writings of Nietzsche*. Edited by Walter Kaufmann. New York: Viking Press, 1954.

Nietzsche, Friedrich. *Beyond Good and Evil: Prelude to a Philosophy of the Future*. Translated by R. J. Hollingdale. London: Penguin Books, 1973.

Nietzsche, Friedrich. *Human, All Too Human*. Translated by R. J. Hollingdale. Cambridge: Cambridge University Press, 1996.

Nietzsche, Friedrich. *The Portable Nietzsche*. Edited by Walter Kaufmann. New York: Viking Press, 1965.

Nietzsche, Friedrich. *The Will to Power*. Translated by Walter Kaufmann and R. J. Hollingdale. New York: Vintage Books, 1968.

Nolan, Lawrence, ed. *The Cambridge Descartes Lexicon*. Cambridge: Cambridge University Press, 2016.

Peirce, Charles Saunders. *Collected Papers of Charles Sanders Peirce*. 8 vols. Edited by C. Hartshorne, et al. Cambridge, MA: Harvard University Press.

Peirce, Charles Saunders. "The Metaphysical Club." *The Hound and Horn: A Harvard Miscellany* 2, no. 3 (April–June 1929).

Peirce, Charles Saunders. "The Issues of Pragmaticism." *The Monist* 15, no. 4 (1905): 481–99.

Peirce, Charles Saunders. "What Pragmatism Is." *The Monist*, 15, no. 2 (1905): 161–81.

Phelps, M. S. "Introductory Note to Spinoza: Oration by M. Ernest Renan, Delivered at the Hague, February 21, 1877." *New Englander* 37 (1878): 763.

Pinkard, Terry. *Hegel: A Biography*. Cambridge: Cambridge University Press, 2000.

Pippin, Robert. *Modernism as a Philosophical Problem*. Oxford: Blackwell, 1999.

Popper, Karl. *The Logic of Scientific Discovery*. London: Routledge, 2002.

Portmann, Adolf. *New Paths in Biology*. Translated by A. J. Pomerans. New York: Harper and Row, 1964.

Postone, Moshe. *Time, Labor, and Social Domination: A Reinterpretation of Marx's Critical Theory*. Cambridge: Cambridge University Press, 1993.

Propp, V. *Morphology of the Folktale*. Translated by Laurence Scott. Austin: University of Texas Press, 1968.

Ricoeur, Paul. *The Conflict of Interpretations: Essays in Hermeneutics*. Evanston, IL: Northwestern University Press, 1974.

Ricoeur, Paul. *Freud and Philosophy: An Essay on Interpretation*. Translated by Denis Savage. New Haven, CT: Yale University Press, 1970.

Rorty, Richard, ed. *The Linguistic Turn: Essays in Philosophical Method*. Chicago: University of Chicago Press, 1992.

Rousseau, Jean-Jacques. *Discourse on the Origin and the Foundations of Inequality among Men*. Translated by Helena Rosenblatt. Lambertville, MI: Bedford/ St. Martin's, 2010.

Rousseau, Jean-Jacques. *Discourse on the Sciences and the Arts*. Translated by Judith R. Bush. Hanover, NH: Dartmouth College Press, 1992.

Rousseau, Jean-Jacques. *Émile*. Translated by Barbara Foxley. Chicago: University of Chicago Press. 1911.

Rousseau, Jean-Jacques. *On the Social Contract: or Principles of Political Right*. CreateSpace Independent Publishing Platform, 2014.

Russell, Bertrand. "On Denoting." *Mind* 14, no. 4 (1905): 479–93.

Santos, Boaventura de Sousa. "Public Sphere and Epistemologies of the South." *Africa Development* 37, no. 1 (2012): 43–67.

Sartre, Jean-Paul. *The Critique of Dialectical Reason*. Vol. 1. Translated by Alan Sheridan-Smith. London: Verso, 2004.

Sartre, Jean-Paul. *Existentialism Is a Humanism*. Translated by Carol Macomber. New Haven, CT: Yale University Press, 2007.

Sartre, Jean-Paul. *Sketch for a Theory of the Emotions*. London: Routledge, 2001.

Saussure, Ferdinand de. *Course in General Linguistics*. Translated by Roy Harris. Chicago: Open Court, 1983.

Schiller, F. C. S. "William James and the Making of Pragmatism." In *Must Philosophers Disagree? And Other Essays in Popular Philosophy*, 93–105. London: Macmillan, 1934.

Schiller, Johann Christoff Friedrich von. *Schiller's Poems and Ballads.* Translated by
Edward Bulwer Lytton. London: Routledge and Sons, 1887.

Schopenhauer, Arthur. *The World as Will and Representation.* Translated by E. F. J.
Payne. Minneola, NY: Dover, 1958.

Scott, David. *Conscripts of Modernity: The Tragedy of Colonial Enlightenment.* Durham,
NC: Duke University Press, 2004.

Serres, Michel, and Bruno Latour. *Conversations on Science, Culture, and Time.*
Translated by Roxanne Lapidus. Ann Arbor: University of Michigan Press, 1995.

Smith, Adam. *The Wealth of Nations.* New York: Random House, 1994.

Spiegelberg, Herbert. *The Phenomenological Movement: A Historical Introduction.* The
Hague: Martinus Nijhoff, 1982,

Spinoza, Baruch. *Complete Works.* Translated by Samuel Shirley. Indianapolis: Hackett,
2002.

Spinoza, Baruch. *Ethics.* In *Complete Works,* 213–382.

Spinoza, Baruch. *Letters.* In *Complete Works,* 755–959.

Spinoza, Baruch. *Political Treatise.* In *Complete Works,* 676–754.

Spinoza, Baruch. *Principles of Cartesian Philosophy and Metaphysical Thoughts.* In
Complete Works, 108–212.

Spinoza, Baruch. *Theological-Political Treatise.* In *Complete Works,* 383–583.

Spinoza, Baruch. *Treatise on the Emendation of the Intellect.* In *Complete Works,* 1–30.

Stählin, Leonhard. *Kant, Lotze, and Ritschl: A Critical Examination.* Palala Press,
CreateSpace Independent Publishing Platform, 2016.

Strachey, Lytton. *Portraits in Miniature and Other Essays.* New York: Harcourt, Brace,
1931.

Strauss, Leo. *Natural Right and History.* Chicago: University of Chicago Press, 1953.

Taylor, Charles. *Hegel.* Cambridge: Cambridge University Press, 1975.

Terry, Les. "'Not a Postmodern Nomad': A Conversation with Stuart Hall on Race,
Ethnicity and Identity." *Arena Journal* 5 (1995): 51–70.

Toynbee, Arnold J. *A Study of History.* Vol. 5, *The Disintegration of Civilizations.*
Oxford: Oxford University Press, 1939.

Tronti, Mario. *Workers and Capitalism.* Translated by David Broder. London: Verso,
2019.

Trudell, John. "I'm Crazy?" Video of the US Social Forum (6–24–2010). YouTube video.
https://www.youtube.com/watch?v=ctUecTdPEOo.

Twain, Mark. *The Diaries of Adam and Eve.* Oxford: Oxford University Press, 1996.

Vico, Giambattista. *The New Science of Giambattista Vico.* Translated by Thomas
Goddard and Max Harold Fisch. Garden City, NY: Doubleday, 1961.

Vico, Giambattista. *On the Most Ancient Wisdom of the Italians: Unearthed from
the Origins of the Latin Language.* Translated by L. M. Palmer. Ithaca, NY: Cornell
University Press, 1988.

Viereck, George Sylvester. *Glimpses of the Great.* London: Henrietta Street London,
1930.

Weber, Max. *The Protestant Ethic and the Spirit of Capitalism.* Translated by Talcott
Parsons. London: Routledge, 1930.

White, Hayden. "Foucault Decoded: Notes from Underground." *History and Theory* 12, no. 1 (1973): 23–54.

Williams, Raymond. *Television: Technology and Cultural Form*. London: Routledge, 2003.

Wittgenstein, Ludwig. *On Certainty* . Translated by G. E. M. Anscombe and Georg Henrik von Wright. New York: Harper and Row, 1969.

Wittgenstein, Ludwig. *Philosophical Investigations*. Translated by G. E. M. Anscombe. London: Macmillan, 1953.

Wittgenstein, Ludwig. *Remarks on the Foundations of Mathematics*. Translated by G. E. M. Anscombe. Cambridge, MA: MIT Press, 1956.

Wittgenstein, Ludwig. *Tractatus Logico-Philosophicus*. Translated by Charles Kay Ogden. London: Routledge and Kegan Paul, 1922.

Wittgenstein, Ludwig. *Wittgenstein in Cambridge: Letters and Documents 1911–1951*. Edited by Brian McGuinness. Oxford: Blackwell, 2008.

Wordsworth, William. *The Complete Poetical Works of William Wordsworth*. London: Macmillan, 1890.

Young, Robert J. C., ed. *Untying the Text: A Post-structuralist Reader*. London: Routledge and Kegan Paul, 1981.

Index

Deleuze, Gilles, 98, 100, 280, 287, 353–54, 389–99, 403–4, 407–8, 413, 415–16, 418, 426–27; and Guattari, 114, 354, 403–5, 407, 409–16

democracy, 54, 64, 161, 221, 283, 288, 291–92, 386

Derrida, Jacques, 212, 325, 353–54, 373, 375–87, 392, 410, 422, 427

Descartes, René, 56, 70, 73–81, 86–87, 89–90, 97, 99–100, 103–4, 106, 126, 245, 247, 422–23. *See Also* Cartesian Geometry

Dewey, John, 280, 288

dialectical, 175, 182–83, 189, 194, 199, 394; idealism, 151, 177; materialism, 177, 179, 181, 183, 185, 187, 189, 191

dialectics, 23, 28, 145, 147–51, 153, 155–56, 162–63, 166–67, 182–84, 190, 201–2

différance, 376–79, 381–84, 386–87, 392, 410, 422, 444. *See Also* Derrida, Jacques

difference and repetition, 390, 397, 399

discourse, 66, 70–71, 74, 81, 269–70, 328–32, 334–35, 407–8, 423–25, 427, 429, 432–33, 437–38, 446, 448

discursive formations, 423, 425–26, 430–31

domination, 164, 191, 197–98, 208, 225, 429

double consciousness, 111, 114, 442

Durkheim, Émile, 21, 171, 305

economy, 19, 21, 32–33, 48, 181, 185–86, 191, 194, 198–200, 202–3, 291–92, 326–27, 447

effectivities, 421, 425–26, 436

ego, 228–30, 232, 236–37, 240, 254, 332–33. *See Also* Nietzsche, Friedrich

Einstein, Albert, 7–8, 11, 98

emergence, 26, 32, 36, 47, 50, 54, 171–72, 337, 340, 343, 423, 425–26

empirical world, 19, 128, 134, 189–90, 309, 445

empiricism, 60–61, 83–84, 90, 93–94, 102, 106, 119, 122, 127, 345, 352, 390, 395

empiricists, 78, 83–84, 86, 94, 122, 125, 187, 420

encyclopedia: of philosophy, 95, 192, 255, 293

Engels, Friedrich, 40, 176–77, 184, 192, 199, 205, 209

England, 3, 53, 84, 86, 89, 175–76, 295, 297, 366, 407, 441–42

Enlightenment: and modern thought, 352–54, 367, 371, 379, 386, 396, 405–6; thinkers, 55–57, 60, 63, 111, 147, 235, 391

epistemology, 22, 100–102, 105, 121, 129, 243, 246, 285, 287–88, 427, 430

Ereignis, 361–63, 367, 384, 391–92. *See Also* Heidegger, Martin

essentialism, 33, 375–76, 379, 381

ethics, 88–89, 99–102, 105–8, 114, 120–21, 123, 160, 283, 286, 288, 391

Europe, 32, 35, 45–47, 49, 65, 67–68, 84, 89, 158–59, 171, 176, 180, 222

exchange value, 205–6, 208, 346

existentialism, 211, 215, 243–44, 306, 371

Existenz, 268–69, 271–74. *See Also* Heidegger, Martin

expressionism, 114, 390, 399, 416

exteriority, 309, 380, 385, 390, 394, 421, 425

false consciousness, 196–97, 325, 376, 445

fascism, 36, 179, 259, 337, 365, 411

fascist, 340, 411–12

First World War, 170, 279, 296, 348

Foucault, Michel, 113, 280–81, 307–8, 321, 325, 353–54, 390, 404, 407, 416–27, 429–33, 435–39; and critique, 417, 419, 421, 423, 425, 427; and knowledge/power, 429, 431, 433, 435, 437, 439; and genealogies, 425, 432; and politics, 418, 438

foundationalism, 2

France, 4, 66, 73, 89, 167, 176–77, 179, 371, 377, 407, 417–18

French Revolution, 54, 64, 66, 146, 166

Freud, Sigmund, 113, 180, 208, 227–40, 331, 333, 335, 404, 417

Galileo, 56, 74–76, 81, 85

Geisteswissenschaften, 9, 21, 65, 69, 129

genealogy, 216, 218, 419, 421, 430–31, 436–37

general linguistics, 314, 322, 336

Germany, 3, 121, 179, 258, 407

Gestell, 362, 368–71, 414. *See Also* Heidegger, Martin

Gilroy, Paul, 439, 453

God, 44–45, 49–50, 76, 78–79, 100–104, 106–10, 121–22, 137–38, 153, 215, 221–23, 238, 263, 287, 345, 363–64, 391–92, 395

Goethe, Johann Wolfgang Von, 65–66, 70, 98, 220

Gramsci, Antonio, 40, 180, 195, 198, 444, 453

machinic assemblage, 408, 414–15

machinic production, 412, 415

manifold of perception, 133–36, 138, 140–42

Marx, Karl, 158, 175–88, 190–95, 197, 199,
202–9, 234–35, 239, 325–26, 328, 336, 351,
353, 404–6, 417–19; and Engels, 40, 176,
192, 209

Marxism, 177, 179–80, 187, 192, 195, 198–99,
280–81, 292, 310, 325–26, 453–54

Marxists, 9, 181, 184, 197, 205, 208, 327–28,
343, 444

materialism, 22, 60, 67, 175, 182, 184, 192,
282, 392

materialists, 61, 104, 182, 341, 346

materiality, 183, 187, 370, 384, 414

Mead, George Herbert, 10, 21, 280, 289

metaphysics, 3, 22, 100–102, 105, 120–21, 123,
137–38, 258, 280, 282, 284–85, 288, 391

Middle Ages, 35, 44, 46–47, 50, 56, 68, 159, 249

Mitsein, 266, 269–70. *See Also* Heidegger,
Martin

mode of being, 261–62, 264–66, 268, 363,
370, 421

mode of production, 178, 193–95, 198–200, 205

modernism, 32, 226, 337, 348–49

modernity, 29, 31–33, 35–39, 55–56, 337,
366–67, 369, 416, 419–20, 422, 432, 436, 438

monism, 60–61, 97, 100–102, 390–92, 397

Napoleon, 146, 166–67, 194, 220

natural philosophy, 48, 50, 56, 90, 107, 120

natural world, 9, 66, 90, 102–3, 140–41, 147, 155,
245, 291

Nazism, 3, 211, 213, 244, 259, 338, 353, 371

negation, 148–50, 154, 156, 164–67, 184, 188,
308, 334, 381, 384, 392–93

neo-Kantianism, 129

New Left, 37, 442–43

Newton, Isaac, 7–8, 65, 90, 95, 119, 122, 171, 354,
398, 412, 430

Newtonian science. *See* Newton, Isaac

New York City, 142, 285, 288–89, 292, 309,
338–39, 398

Nietzsche, Friedrich, 39, 63, 98, 114, 208,
211–26, 257–58, 338, 353, 390, 396–97; and
philosophy, 226, 396, 399

Nietzschean thought, 222–23

nihilism, 12, 35, 165, 172, 222, 224

noema, 250–53. *See Also* Husserl, Edmund

noesis, 250, 252–53. *See Also* Husserl, Edmund

noumenal worlds, 125–26, 133, 138, 244

objectification, 104, 122, 191, 206, 310, 335

objective materialism, 182–83, 194

objectivism, 246, 360

ontology, 269, 271, 352, 354, 360–62, 364–65,
367, 371, 373, 383–84, 389–90, 404–5, 407,
415, 420

order: of things, 321, 418, 423

otherness, 18, 148, 156, 379

parallelism, 101, 105, 108

Paris, 309, 325, 331, 376–77, 389, 417

Peirce, Charles Sanders, 280, 283–86, 288–90,
292–93, 322, 374

pessimism, 220, 224, 342, 386

phenomena, 7, 141, 244, 246–49, 252, 254–55,
259–62, 311, 314, 373, 377–78, 384, 386

phenomenal: world 125–26, 128–29, 132–38,
141, 147, 169, 181, 307–8

phenomenalism, 5, 249

phenomenologists, 243, 247–49, 253–55, 417

phenomenology, 162, 167, 172, 241, 243–46, 249,
253, 255, 257, 376, 380; and Husserl, 243, 245,
247, 249, 251, 253, 255

philosophy, 2–3, 21–22, 45–46, 48–50, 69,
74–76, 80–81, 94–95, 114, 146, 148–49, 156,
161–62, 244–45, 258–59, 296–98, 304–5, 399,
403–5, 416–17

phonology, 310, 314–15

plane: of consistency, 398–99, 404, 412–13;
of expression, 321, 413–15; of immanence,
391–93, 395–96, 398–99, 413

pleasure principle, 229, 236, 238–40

poiesis, 63, 122, 223, 361, 362, 368–69,
371, 384

political economy, 66, 89, 177–78, 180–81, 187,
204–5, 208–9

Popper, Karl, 5, 14

positivism, 2–3, 5, 7, 431

positivity, 160, 308, 384, 392–93, 397, 421–22,
425

postmodernism, 129, 337, 339, 341–45, 347–55,
405, 407, 415, 420, 446

poststructuralism, 212, 374, 376, 385; and Derrida, 373, 375, 377, 379, 381, 383, 385, 387

potentialities, 78, 150, 152, 290, 363, 394, 398
power, 38–39, 54, 57, 84–86, 108–10, 180–85,
  196, 216–26, 325, 334, 361, 369, 381–82,
  395–97, 408–12, 417–23, 425–27, 429–39,
  444–49, 452–53
pragmatism, 26, 279–91, 293
pragmatists, 279–82, 405, 407
privilege, 38, 122, 159, 215, 219, 270, 352, 374,
  376, 419–20, 423
pro-colonialism, 39
Prussia, 120, 146, 167, 175, 212
psychoanalysis, 227–29, 233, 239, 325, 331, 335,
  404; Freud, 227, 229, 231, 233, 235, 237, 239
psychology, 6, 10, 132, 143, 244, 246, 285–86,
  288, 293, 417
public, 288, 291, 293, 336
pure reason, 121, 130–31, 141, 143

racism, 8–9, 32, 39, 121, 146, 191, 323, 339,
  446–47, 450–52; identities, 451; single
  practice of, 191, 432
radical: contextualism, 354, 406, 438, 443;
  contextualists, 180, 406–7, 417, 427; empiricism, 280, 286–88, 293
radicles, 408–11. See also Deleuze, Gilles;
  Guattari, Félix; rhizomes; roots
rationalism: and Descartes, 73, 75, 77, 79, 81
rationalists, 83, 94, 100–101, 122, 125, 146
rationality, 58, 170, 311, 318, 338, 430, 433,
  436–37
realism, 49, 255, 418
relationality, 10, 26, 124–26, 130, 170, 249,
  257, 363–64, 370; and constructionism,
  10, 26
religion, 45–46, 64, 67, 84, 86, 89, 98–99, 101,
  120, 160–61, 186, 194, 196, 237–38, 375–76
Renaissance, 35, 43, 46–50, 57, 81
revolution, 44, 49–50, 64, 129, 167, 179, 182,
  340, 347, 431, 436
rhetoric, 12, 21, 50–51, 69, 161, 379, 381
rhizomes, 408–11, 416. See also Deleuze, Gilles;
  Guattari, Félix; radicles; roots
romanticism, 3, 65–66, 215, 245
roots, 12, 304, 348, 408–11, 442, 452. See also
  Deleuze, Gilles; Guattari, Félix; radicles;
  rhizomes
Rousseau, Jean-Jacques, 65–71, 146, 220, 351
Russell, Bertrand, 3–4, 296–97, 304

Sartre, Jean-Paul, 180, 250, 262, 306, 360, 371
Saussure, Ferdinand de, 305–6, 314–16, 321
Saussurean: linguistics, 316, 324
Schiller, F. C. S., 66, 70, 280, 293
Schlick, Moritz, 3, 5
scholasticism, 44–45, 48, 50, 79
Schopenhauer, Arthur, 27, 212, 217, 226
scientific psychology, 232, 238–39
scientism, 2, 6, 13
second modernity, 36, 38, 169–71, 279, 341, 351
Second World War, 2, 8, 36, 120, 251, 279, 337,
  339, 345, 351, 353
Seinsfrage, 262–64, 275, 359, 362. See also
  Heidegger, Martin
self-determination, 54, 63, 103, 108, 154, 162
semiotics, 284–85, 321
signifiers, 315–16, 318–20, 324, 334–36, 346,
  374–76, 378–83, 424
sign systems, 308, 321, 374–75, 383, 419, 424
simulations, 345–46, 355
singularities, 142, 361, 408
skepticism, 35, 50, 58, 87, 89, 93–94, 119, 131,
  165, 172, 245
Smith, Adam, 11, 48, 54, 89, 95, 178, 186, 192,
  204–5
social formation, 197–98, 200, 326–27, 330,
  407, 449–51
social realities, 31, 187–88, 190, 204, 208, 227,
  235, 311, 331, 414, 447
social relations, 54, 58, 169, 171, 181, 183, 185,
  190, 206–8, 442, 445
sociogenetic parallelism, 291
sociology, 2, 6–7, 21, 280, 309
Socrates, 49, 66, 162, 220, 262
Spinoza, Baruch, 70, 73, 97–111, 114, 145–47,
  152–53, 180, 182, 216, 237, 351, 353, 390–93,
  395–96, 399; and metaphysics, 101, 103, 105;
  and monism, 102, 391; and rationalism, 101
spirituality, 9, 63, 172, 296
structural anthropology, 309, 321–22
structuralism, 305–7, 309–11, 313, 315, 317, 319,
  321, 325–26, 331, 336, 374–75; and subjectivity, 323, 325, 327, 329, 331, 333, 335
structural Marxisms, 195, 200, 326
subjectivity, 61–62, 122, 136, 180–81, 227,
  229–30, 232, 253–54, 323–25, 329–36, 390,
  404–5, 432–33, 435–38, 446–47
subordination, 196, 380, 445